SKYWALKING

SKYWALKING

THE LIFE AND FILMS OF GEORGE LUCAS

DALE POLLOCK

HARMONY BOOKS/NEW YORK

Special acknowledgment is made to the following for permission to use previously
unpublished material: Early Drafts *American Graffiti* Screenplay,
Copyright © 1973 by Universal Pictures;
First Draft *Apocalypse Now* Screenplay,
Copyright © 1969 by American Zoetrope;
Star Wars Screenplay, Copyright © 1976 by Lucasfilm Ltd.;
The Empire Strikes Back Story Conference Transcript and Screenplay, Copyright © 1978
by Lucasfilm Ltd.; *Raiders of the Lost Ark* Story Conference Transcript and Screenplay,
Copyright © 1978 by Lucasfilm Ltd.; *Return of the Jedi* Story Conference
Transcript and Screenplay, Copyright © 1982 by Lucasfilm Ltd.; Interviews with
George Lucas by Carol Titelman, Copyright © 1977 by Lucasfilm Ltd.; Personal Correspondence
of George and Marcia Lucas, letter of June 23, 1967, Copyright ©
1967 by George Lucas; letter of October
28, 1975, Copyright © 1975 by George
Lucas; Personal Correspondence of
Francis and Eleanor Coppola, letter of April
1978, Copyright © 1978 by Francis Coppola.
Photographs courtesy of George Lucas,
Lucasfilm Ltd., and John Korty

Published by Harmony Books, a division of Crown Publishers, Inc.,
One Park Avenue, New York, New York 10016, and simultaneously in
Canada by General Publishing Company Limited.

HARMONY and colophon are trademarks of Crown Publishers, Inc.

Manufactured in the United States of America
Designed by Claudia Carlson
Library of Congress Cataloging in Publication Data

Pollock, Dale.
Skywalking: The Life and Films of George Lucas

1. Lucas, George.   2. Moving-picture producers
and directors—United States—Biography.   I. Title.
PN1998.A3L856   1983   791.43'0233'0924   [B]   82–21195
ISBN 0-517-54677-9

10   9   8   7   6   5   4   3   2   1

First Edition

To Susie—
Without you, I am less.

CONTENTS

Acknowledgments   ix

The Crash   xiii

1 It Wasn't My Fault   1

2 When Things Were Simpler   11

3 Reality Stops Here   41

4 Coping with Coppola   73

5 Rocking Around the Clock   99

6 The Vision of *Star Wars*   131

7 The Agony and the Ecstasy of *Star Wars*   159

8 How I Spent My Retirement   191

9 Ruling the Empire   231

10 A Time Not So Far Away   265

Filmography   279

Source Notes   291

Index   299

Photographs follow pages 80 and 208

ACKNOWLEDGMENTS

A biography of George Lucas, even an unauthorized one such as this, would have been impossible without the cooperation of George Lucas. Once granted, his cooperation was total, his access unlimited, and his interest unflagging.

Lucas's close associates matched his commitment to this project. Jane Bay and Sharon Appenzeller were tremendously helpful, as were Sidney Ganis and Susan Trembly, in supplying information and encouragement. Deborah Fine graciously made her research library available, and Miki Herman and Jim Bloom made life at Lucasland pleasant.

Marcia Lucas sacrificed much of her precious time with her husband for the interviews in this book. She was open and candid, as were Lucas's parents, George, Sr., and Dorothy Lucas, and Lucas's three sisters, Ann, Kate, and Wendy. Special thanks go to more than eighty other individuals who took the time and effort to discuss Lucas and his work.

The idea for *Skywalking* came from Bruce Harris of Crown Publishers, Inc. He and Peter Shriver, my editor, allowed me to write *my* book in *my* way; I am very grateful for that. My agent, Amanda Urban, was a model of support and encouragement, as were my lawyers, Bertram Fields and Ed Ezor. Special thanks go to Charles Champlin (for his faith), Connie Koenenn, Irv Letofsky, and Robert Epstein, my editors at the *Los Angeles Times,* for their forbearance and patience. My colleagues Peter Boyer, Lee Grant, and Deborah Caulfield deserve similar thanks.

This book would not have emerged in its present form without the editing, typing, and transcribing skills of Sharon Berryhill, Gwen Gunderson, Janet Ezor, and Diane Merryl. Doug Caryso of Newell Color Labs

ACKNOWLEDGMENTS

was helpful in reproducing the photographs. Essential support came from Henry Pollock and Jeffrey Pollock and is deeply appreciated. The kind of encouragement that sustains the author of a book written on weekends, evenings, and other snatches of time came from Jeff Jaffee, Charles and Harriet Schreger, Richard B. Nagler, Sheila Sosnow, Dan Polier, Jr., Gail Cippola, Maggie Wittenburg, and Donna Bass.

No one suffers through the writing of a book like the members of an author's family. They feel all the creative frustration and none of the creative satisfaction. My sons, Owen and Leo, are too young to read this, so they'll have to take my word for it that the book is finally done. If there is a single individual responsible for this volume, it is my wife Susan. She researched, typed, edited, criticized, encouraged, baited, exhorted, pleaded, and finally demanded *Skywalking* into existence. For that, she shares all credit for this book.

DALE POLLOCK

Los Angeles
October 3, 1982

Skywalker, Skywalker. And why do you come to walk my sky? All your life have you looked away. . . to the horizon, to the sky, to the future.[1]

—Yoda

THE CRASH

All the ding-a-lings get it sooner or later, maybe that's why they invented cars . . . to get rid of all the ding-a-lings. It's just tough when they take someone with them.[1]

—John Milner, *American Graffiti*

Tuesday, June 12, 1962, was one of those heat-drenched days in Modesto, when the San Joaquin Valley seemed like an oven with the door wired shut. Wendy Lucas sat out by the swimming pool, near where the walnut groves began their spidery extension into the horizon. It was just about the only cool place on the ranch property. There wasn't much else to do after high school except sun yourself, swim, and then sun yourself again.

A long summer lay ahead. School would be over on Friday, and Wendy's older brother, George, would be graduating—maybe. As usual, George had neglected his schoolwork. He had three term papers due Wednesday, not to mention his final exams. The exams were crucial: George had a D-plus grade average, and if he didn't make a good showing on his finals, he might not graduate with the Thomas Downey High School class of 1962.

Just then George, short and skinny as one of the ranch fence posts, came out of the house. He was going to the downtown library: Would Wendy come along? She sighed. She was often called upon to help her elder brother with his spelling, studying, and general survival. It was a role she had played since they were kids, and she had bloodied a few bullies' noses for picking on little Georgie.

"We argued about my going," recalls Wendy, now the wife of an evangelical minister in Orange County. "I said, 'No, I don't want to go,' so he said, 'All right, I'll go by myself.'" George turned on his heels and got into his Fiat Bianchina, a small, fast Italian import. He purposely peeled rubber as he drove off.

After just a few hours at the library, George was unable to concentrate. He started daydreaming about race cars and his planned trip to Europe that summer with his best friend, John Plummer. The trip was a graduation present from George's parents—if he graduated.

Deciding to go home, George drove east on Sylvan Road through Modesto's scraggly pastureland. He pushed the tiny Fiat's two-cylinder engine as fast as it would go, more than sixty miles an hour. The sun streamed in through what used to be the roof. George had flipped the car going around a curve and had installed a roll bar in place of the bashed-in roof.

Lucas loved to drive. He savored the thrill of taking a corner on two wheels. He would race the Fiat back and forth on acres of walnut trees. He had seen friends of his killed in car crashes—seven schoolmates died behind his house when their car, going one hundred miles an hour, ran into a tree. But it didn't slow him down.

As he neared the Lucas ranch, George began to make the left turn onto the short dirt road that led up to the house. It was around 5:00 P.M., and the sun was slowly sinking behind him. He shot a look at his rearview mirror, saw nothing, and turned.

At that moment, he heard the roar of an engine and a wildly honking horn. Frank Ferreira, seventeen, was barreling down the road in his Chevy Impala. The Fiat was directly in his path. Ferreira tried to go around it but instead hit the small car broadside, directly where George was sitting.

The impact was tremendous. The Fiat was flung sideways, and it flipped over quickly, four or five times, before wrapping itself around a sturdy walnut tree. On the third flip, Lucas was hurled out the open roof. His regulation racing seat belt—installed with a steel plate anchoring it to the car's floor—had miraculously snapped at its base and freed the driver from what would have been certain death.

George landed on his chest and stomach and was knocked unconscious. Blood poured from a gash on his forehead, and he began to turn blue as unoxygenated blood rushed to his damaged lungs. Shorty Coleman, who lived across the road, heard the cars and was at his front door just in time to see the accident. He called an ambulance and then hurried to check the condition of the Lucas boy. Ferreira sat in his Impala off the side of the road, dazed but not hurt.

Back at the ranch house, neither Wendy nor her mother heard the crash, which was just as well. Dorothy Lucas was not a healthy woman. She had just returned from the hospital, weighing only eighty pounds, after the latest in a series of illnesses that had continued through George's childhood. Dorothy and Wendy didn't learn of the accident until George Walton Lucas, Sr., arrived home from his downtown office and quietly broke the news that their only son was in critical condition at Modesto City Hospital.

When the ambulance arrived, the prognosis for George Lucas, Jr., looked grim. His heartbeat was barely discernible; he was in shock and was having difficulty breathing. As the ambulance sped the five miles to the local hospital, George began to cough and vomit bright red blood, a shocking contrast to the pale blue color of his lips and skin. Dr. Richard Treadwell, the Lucases' family physician, took one look at young George when he was wheeled into the small emergency room and yelled for the nurses to get Dr. Paul Carlsen, the hospital's best diagnostician.

"He was, first of all, scared to death," Dr. Carlsen recalls of George's condition. "He was in shock, his blood pressure was low, and he had a swollen left shoulder, with what felt like a fracture of his scapula, or shoulder blade. His belly was tender, and his chest wall was tender. And he had a big cut on his head, from which I presumed he had lost considerable blood."

Carlsen ordered an immediate blood transfusion and then began abdominocentesis by inserting four needles into the corners of the stomach area to determine the extent of internal bleeding. The test proved negative, so Carlsen proceeded to Lucas's chest; there he found large, spherical bruises scattered across both lungs, showing extreme hemorrhaging.

By this time, Dorothy Lucas had arrived at the hospital, Wendy in tow. She rushed into the emergency room and almost fainted at the sight. There were tubes in one of George's arms, pumping blood into his system, four needles in his stomach, and an oxygen tube up his nose. Lucas looked up at his mother, his eyes not quite focusing. Barely conscious, in a tremulous voice, he said, "Mom, did I do something wrong?" Dorothy began to weep, and Dr. Carlsen, hushing her, led her out of the room.

The next day the *Modesto Bee* ran a front-page article on the crash, including a picture of the Fiat, looking like a metal pretzel, welded onto the walnut tree. The tree had been moved a couple of feet by the force of the impact—a huge hole marked where the trunk had originally stood. The story also mentioned that Lucas was given a ticket for making an illegal left turn.

When George awoke that morning, he didn't know where he was or what had happened: "There was a nurse there, and she immediately said, 'You're okay. All your arms and legs are okay, and you'll be all right.' It was very reassuring to hear that, because I didn't know what parts of me were there or not. The fact that I was still alive was a miracle."

Resting in the hospital, George found his mind racing almost as fast as his Fiat once had. "I realized that I'd been living my life so close to the edge for so long. That's when I decided to go straight, to be a better student, to try to do something with myself."

George's accident was the classic 1950s' car crash, immortalized in such hit songs as "Teen Angel," "Detour," and "Tell Laura I Love Her." Coming at the crossroads of adolescence and adulthood, it had a profound effect on him. The perennial goof-off who never bothered to plan or think ahead suddenly realized he was living on borrowed time. "You can't have that kind of experience and not feel that there must be a reason why you're here," Lucas explains. "I realized I should be spending my time trying to figure out what that reason is and trying to fulfill it. The fact is, there is no way I could have survived that accident if I'd been wrapped around that tree. Actually, that seat belt never should have broken, under any circumstances. All that affected me seriously."

That kind of introspection is not unusual for a high school graduate, whose adulthood is suddenly thrust upon him. But his close brush with death had a deeper, more subliminal effect on Lucas. "He saw his own mortality," says his father. The accident transformed George from an aimless teenager who spent his time driving and dreaming about cars into a highly motivated young man filled with a sense of mission: "The accident made me more aware of myself and my feelings. I began to trust my instincts. I had the feeling that I should go to college, and I did. I had the same feeling later that I should go into film school, even though everybody thought I was nuts. I had the same feeling when I decided to make *Star Wars,* when even my friends told me I was crazy. These are just things that have to be done, and I feel as if I have to do them."

1
IT WASN'T MY FAULT

Your destiny lies on a different path. . . .
—Obi-Wan Kenobi to Luke Skywalker, *Star Wars*

George Lucas has accomplished more in his thirty-nine years than most people do in a lifetime. Hollywood is filled with people who would give anything for a fraction of his good fortune. Yet for all his success, his friends and colleagues agree that George Lucas is essentially the same person who woke up in a hospital bed in 1962 and decided to change his life. From a close encounter with death grew a fanatical commitment to hard work and artistic excellence. He is a natural born filmmaker with an instinctive grasp of what audiences want to see.

Lucas has directed only four films and produced four more, but he is credited with three and possibly four of the ten most successful movies ever made. *Star Wars* and *The Empire Strikes Back,* the first two of nine planned *Star Wars* films, have sold $888 million worth of tickets world-wide.[1] *American Graffiti,* Lucas's second film as a director, is the most profitable movie in Hollywood history in terms of cost ($750,000) over revenues ($117 million). *Raiders of the Lost Ark,* which Lucas conceived of and produced, has followed his *Star Wars* pictures on the list of all-time box office hits.

The staggering degree of this success obscures the memory of Lucas's commercial failures: *THX 1138,* his first feature film, and *More American Graffiti,* the 1978 sequel to the original 1972 hit. But *Return of the Jedi,* released in May 1983, may eclipse all of his previous accomplishments and become his greatest financial success.

1

Lucas estimates his personal net worth at $25 million. Lucasfilm Ltd., the private corporation he and his wife own, is worth about $35 million more in cash and other assets. These include Lucas's ownership of his films, his extensive land purchases, his oil and gas investments, and his long-term bond holdings. The merchandising bonanza from *Star Wars* has exceeded $1.5 billion in gross retail sales. What cannot be estimated is the value of the *Star Wars* saga itself, what the nine films and all they entail would bring on the open market. Trying to figure out what the *Star Wars* saga is worth is like guessing the value of the Mona Lisa—the sky is the limit.

Lucas has become a commercial art form by being himself: Everyman as moviemaker. "I'm so ordinary that a lot of people can relate to me, because it's the same kind of ordinary that they are," he explains. "I think it gives me an insight into the mass audience. I know what I liked as a kid, and I still like it."

But Lucas is determined to do more with his films than just entertain. He communicates a vision of an ideal world in which good ultimately triumphs over evil, and people learn to master their fate. His professional career is dedicated to preserving that vision on film—no one is allowed to tamper with or dilute it. Its success or failure hinges solely on the talent and ambition of George Lucas. This extreme self-reliance is a throwback to the gritty determination that brought his ancestors from Europe to Virginia to Arkansas and finally to California. George's career combines the legend of Horatio Alger with the technology of modern cinema.

Lucas and his films embody many of the complexities of the American character. He is a multimillionaire who dresses in faded blue jeans, work shirts, and sneakers. His political views remain liberal in general but are increasingly conservative on issues like crime and unemployment. An accomplished film artist with an enormous cultural impact around the world, he remains essentially anti-intellectual. He manages a multimillion-dollar company in the manner of a sophisticated business executive, yet its products derive from a basic American naïveté.

All this from a short man of slight build who likes to eat dinner in bed, watch television while mimicking its commercials, and is happiest when he's with his wife, baby, and dog. It's as if there are two George Lucases: the ruthless dictator on the movie set, who insists everything be done *his* way, and the bashful husband and father, who blushes easily and laughs softly. Both dimensions of Lucas incorporate his determination and tenacity: "I never have thought of myself as being very smart," Lucas says. "Once I commit myself to something, however, I'm really committed. I'll carry it through to the end. I'm basically a lazy person. The only secret to my success is the fact that I work harder than anybody else."

Lucas has made a lot of money, but he is by no means the richest man in Hollywood. Producers such as Norman Lear and Ray Stark, performers like Bob Hope and Cary Grant, have all amassed personal fortunes as great if not greater than Lucas's. But no one has done it so fast and so big. Lucas is the new American success story: the small-town boy who made good. It was never his intention to make $60 million, he insists. "It wasn't my fault" is a refrain that often accompanies his discussions about success. "It's a pain in the ass, actually," Lucas says with characteristic candor. "I mean, it's happened and there's not much I can do about it. And no matter how hard I fight it, it doesn't seem to make much difference. It's part of my fate. Win some, lose some."

Failure has a thousand explanations. Success doesn't need one.[2]
—Sir Alec Guinness

Success has provided Lucas with worldwide fame, a beautiful home atop a Marin County hillside, a $40,000 Mercedes Benz and a $35,000 BMW sedan, a private screening room, and the biggest toy box since Walt Disney unpacked Disneyland. George Lucas has become one of the most influential persons in the history of mass entertainment, occupying a special galaxy along with the Beatles and Elvis Presley. He has learned how to push all the buttons and whip the media into a frenzy upon the release of one of his films.

When Lucas makes a movie, it seems inevitable that it will be a hit. A toll-free number designed to give out information about the release of *The Empire Strikes Back* was short-circuited in one day when one hundred thirty thousand calls were registered. Fans send in more than two hundred thousand letters a year to Lucas and his leading actors. There are a mother and son who have seen *Star Wars* together at least four hundred times. Terri Hardin, a free-lance illustrator from Sun Valley, California, gained extensive press coverage when she waited two days in line for the premiere of *Empire*. She saw the film only 108 times; she saw *Star Wars* 181 times. Upon the release of *Return of the Jedi*, Lucasfilm made sure that a novelization, a record album, a film documentary, a book on the making of the film, and an entire new line of merchandising products would come out simultaneously.

Such extreme success can be dangerous. "When you're that successful and you've been proven right too many times, you don't give people an opportunity to argue with you, because they can't argue with success," cautions Willard Huyck, who cowrote *American Graffiti* with Lucas.

Marcia Lucas told her husband after the release of *Graffiti* that he had peaked too early. "Where are you going to go for the rest of your life?" she asked George. "You made the little seven-hundred-thousand-dollar movie that went out and made millions of dollars. How are you ever going to top that? What are you going to do for the rest of your life?" Then came *Star Wars*, followed by *Empire*, followed by *Raiders* and now *Jedi*. Marcia laughs. "Now I say, 'Okay, George, you can't go on peaking for the rest of your life. You've been peaking for seven years now.'"

Lucas calls himself the victim of his own success. "You're led to believe that when you're rich, everything is perfect. You have no problems. But the only difference between having the Toyota Marcia once had and the Mercedes she now has, is that every time it breaks down, it costs us ten times more to get it fixed. And it doesn't break down any less than the Toyota, so the inconvenience and frustration is much worse. I pay all this money, I shouldn't get a flat tire, right? It permeates a lot of things, because you sort of expect things to be done right."

Lucas surmounts the enviable problem of extreme wealth by behaving almost as frugally as he did when he had no money. When making a film, he still rigidly adheres to the budget. When he buys himself a sports car, he buys a used one. When he and Marcia eat out, it is at good, moderately priced restaurants, not expensive fancy ones. "People really *do* change," says Walter Murch, who insists that in the fifteen years he has known him, Lucas has not changed. "I think it just depends on how deep your roots are in some kind of bedrock, so when the tide comes up and washes over you, you don't get wiped out."

George Lucas believes that the tides of Hollywood are lethal. Normal, upstanding, and productive people inevitably get caught in a frenzy that subverts their morals and destroys their principles. Lucas sees Hollywood through the eyes of a Calvinist—moviemakers operate under the shadow of original sin. What protects Lucas from the temptations of Hollywood is his deep-seated belief that if people get too greedy, their greed will prove their undoing. With Lucas, the American ethic of honesty and fairness is alive and well in Marin County. "I always felt that if anyone had to make millions of dollars, George is the best person to do it," says accountant Lucy Wilson, one of the first people Lucas hired for his company, Lucasfilm Ltd. "Because he shares it, he's fair with it, he didn't turn into a monster egomaniac, and he's got real good ideals. He's really a good person."

Lucas has never lost the attitude of a simple small-town boy from

Modesto who is distrustful of big-city hucksters. He thinks the Academy Awards are a farce, for instance, a hyped-up way to sell films under the guise of art. Hollywood has returned his disdain. *Star Wars, Empire,* and *Raiders* have all won Academy Awards in the technical and crafts fields, but Lucas has never won an Oscar for writing, directing, or producing. Hollywood won't recognize Lucas as anything but a technobrat because the industry feels he has ridiculed them. Lucas has always prided himself on making his films outside of Hollywood, where people make movies, not deals.

"I think some of the people in the movie business are sleazy and unscrupulous, and I would say probably the majority are that bad. There are also some people down there who I think are very honorable, good people," Lucas says. George believes he has had the misfortune to work most often with the bad ones—his first two movies were taken away from him by the studios involved and reedited. "You look at how George was treated, and basically he was treated horribly," says director Michael Ritchie, another friend. "When these things happen, you tend to be a little sore at the system."

Lucas, always one to hold a grudge, set up his own system rather than complain about the existing one. Lucasfilm is a true alternative, not just a mirror reflection of Hollywood simply transplanted to San Francisco. Instead of just making movies, Lucasfilm is experimenting with the way children learn, using computerized programs as an educational supplement. Although Parker Brothers has sold $20 million worth of *Star Wars* video games, Lucasfilm is also developing bold new interactive games that challenge as well as entertain. Skywalker Ranch, the biggest of Lucasfilm's projects, will function as a think tank for tomorrow's movies and their makers. Lucas is building a monument to the spirit of creative independence with Lucasfilm, not just a tribute to himself.

"I don't know how long this whole thing will continue," Lucas says of Lucasfilm. "But I'm trying to cement my world as hard as I can before it all falls apart. The whole thing we're trying to do is get into the position where I don't *have* to make films in order to keep funding all this stuff. If it wasn't for the ranch, I wouldn't have made any more films. But once I decided that I could bring my vision into reality, then I realized I had to work in order to earn enough dollars to pay for it."

Making a film is like putting out a fire with a sieve. There are so many elements, and it gets so complicated.

—George Lucas on the set of *Return of the Jedi*

"George has been looking forward to making this movie for two years," says director Richard Marquand, four weeks into the making of *Jedi*.[3] But as the cold, damp English wind cuts through his fur-lined jacket, Lucas does not seem like a man looking toward anything other than the next scene, as he scurries across the Elstree lot outside London. Lucas nimbly steps around rain puddles as he winds his way through the studio. His wavy black hair is flecked with gray, as is his beard, which straggles down to his Adam's apple. His horn-rimmed glasses give him the look of an aging high school student. He arrives at Stage 7 and pulls open the heavy metal fire door with a grunt. He enters a different universe, one of grass huts and overhanging vines, towering redwood trees painted on canvas scrims, and a bewildering array of steel girders and pipes that support a set located forty feet up in the air. This is the Ewok village, inhabited by teddy-bearlike creatures played by dwarfs and midgets in cumbersome little costumes.

Lucas joins a second-unit crew filming background footage of the Ewoks. Although he stands well behind the camera, there is no question as to who is in charge. Before filming resumes, an assistant director says, "Hold it a minute and let George take a look." Lucas removes his glasses, looking surprisingly young without them, and peers through the camera's eyepiece. Judgment is passed quickly: "Great," one of the phrases he routinely uses, along with "Okay" and "Terrific." Lucas seems to know instinctively where everyone and everything should be. After answering a few questions, he is on to the next set.

Director Marquand is on Stage 4 shooting a complicated scene involving Jabba the Hutt, who is mentioned but never seen in *Star Wars*. Jabba is an immense sluglike creature, perhaps fifteen feet long and almost as tall. Made out of soft green and yellow latex plastic, Jabba dominates the low-ceilinged set that duplicates a palatial cavern with arching, vaultlike walls. Five men operate the spongy beast: one on each of his froglike hands, one for each huge blinking eye, and a dwarf positioned in the tail. Around the somnolent Jabba sit his slimy minions, both puppets and costumed actors, comprising a futuristic bestiary. Across the latticed floor under the arches, Jabba's court followers lounge on pillows. They are a motley crew: half-naked belly dancers, pig guards, a camel-faced monster, and assorted aliens.

"Hi, George, how are you doing?" Marquand says. The Welsh-born director has made only two theatrical features, neither of which was successful at the box office. But Lucas admired Marquand's craftsmanship in *Eye of the Needle* and chose him from a long list of potential directors.

Now, he and Lucas confer about the upcoming scene, which involves the entrance of Luke Skywalker, played by Mark Hamill, into Jabba's domain. Lucas checks the position of the main, or A, camera, and then looks through the eyepiece of the secondary B camera. He walks up to the Jabba model, whose giant brown eyes moistly roll about like oversize billiard balls. Lucas peers at Jabba's nose, from which a steady stream of green snot issues. A different shade of goo dribbles out of the creature's slobbering mouth. The stuff looks perfectly disgusting, and it's one poor assistant director's job to do nothing but mix and apply Jabba's effluence.

"Is that the goo for his mouth, or the goo for his nose?" Lucas asks, carefully wiping a bit of brown slime off Jabba's cheek with his finger. "No, the nose goo is green," replies Marquand, and Lucas nods with satisfaction. He suggests a little visual humor that can be easily inserted into the scene and then snickers aloud when a rehearsal proves his instincts right. Nearby, a crew member equipped with a holstered hair dryer (minus its heating element in order to cool the faces of mask-wearing actors) shakes his head in amazement. "This guy is *never* wrong," he says, gesturing at Lucas.

The members of the largely British crew do not seem in awe of their executive producer; they are also not particularly friendly. Lucas carefully avoids contact with most of them. When he speaks, it's usually in a detached professional manner, always polite but never warm or inviting. He sits on a stool next to the camera while Marquand sets up and conducts a second rehearsal of the scene. "Shut up!" bellows assistant director David Tomblin to the 150 people milling around the smoke-filled set. Lucas watches the scene and after a moment, moves the B camera a few feet to the left. He then asks Richard which angle he prefers. "Let's not waste time," says Marquand, who goes along with Lucas's camera placement. But Lucas is careful never to touch the main A camera—he does not want to give the impression that he is directing *Jedi*.

This uneasy collaboration leads to tension on the set during the first few weeks of filming. Lucas, nominally executive producer, is an active participant, at times confusing the cast and crew. Director Marquand once asked Carrie Fisher to stand up straight in a scene, like a guard at the Tower of London. When Lucas came on the set and spotted Fisher, he said, "You're standing like a guard at Buckingham Palace! Who told you to do that?' When informed that it was Marquand, Lucas immediately backed off. After three or four weeks, the relationship sorts itself out. "If there was a disagreement, I let Richard have his way," Lucas says.

Marquand professes to not be concerned by George's presence on the set: "I can turn to him and say, 'I've got a real problem with that monster over there, can you deal with that?' It's fabulous, because I've got the man himself, who goes and does it. He loves to do it, he's not involved in the boring details like directing intimate dialogue with actors, because he trusts me to do that."

Luke's entrance is filmed eight times in succession, even though it will last all of one or two minutes on screen. Still to be incorporated are the special effects that will not be "married" to the film for months. But Lucas seems pleased as he leaves the stage and heads off to the editing rooms.

George Lucas has spent much of his eighteen years as a filmmaker in small, dank cubicles such as the one at Elstree Studios, where he is huddled over a KEM editing table with Sean Barton, the British editor of *Jedi*. They review several scenes of the Ewoks, filmed without sound. All that is heard is the squeal of the film as it is advanced, rewound, and advanced again. Lucas periodically mutters "Neat" or "Right." A vision he has nurtured for twelve years is finally coming to life, albeit in rough form. He shows little excitement—instead, he seems resigned to seeing his vision compromised by the realities of movie making.

"How it comes out is all that counts," Lucas says, leaving the editing room. "It doesn't make any difference how you struggle to get there. It's what you finally produce in the end that means anything, and that's something we're not going to know for another year and a half. That's the unfortunate and terrifying part."

Lucas is interrupted by several deep, hacking chest coughs. He admits to feeling ill—he came down with the flu while on a weekend trip to Paris with Marcia and their six-month-old daughter, Amanda. He looks awful, with blotchy skin and an apparent fever. That night, his fever skyrockets and Lucas spends the next three days in his bed at Claridge's Hotel.

Filming continues during Lucas's absence, but his presence is subconsciously missed by the cast and crew. "He has ideas about every detail of this film," says Lawrence Kasdan, the film's cowriter. "Every tiny aspect of making *Jedi* stimulates clear responses in him, so clearly has he imagined this environment. He can bring to it this enormous backlog of feelings about how things should be. What you're talking about is a wonderfully resourceful, rich, imaginative life."

Lucas returns to Elstree by week's end, weak but eager to get back to work. In a screening room, watching two hours of silent daily footage filmed while he was gone, Lucas hardly speaks, shifting in his seat periodically. He takes no notes, but when the lights come on, he leans back and lists for his editor the specific shots that bothered him, particularly one featuring Luke.

After a discussion of the scene with Marquand, Lucas decides to reshoot it. A set that was meant to be torn down over the weekend will now have to be saved. Production designer Norman Reynolds is frantic to get new sets built. Refilming the scene also means losing a day on the shooting schedule and several days of construction time. Lucas determines that he can make do with a closeup of Hamill if he has just the set's ceiling as background. Grabbing a notepad and pencil, he sketches what he needs (apologizing for the sloppiness of the drawing) and tells producer Howard Kazanjian to discuss the situation with Marquand. "Let him worry about what to strike and what to keep," says Lucas. This time he's glad he's not directing.

Lucas walks away, still upset that an important scene was not filmed correctly the first time. "Now is the time to find out that the shot doesn't work, rather than six months from now," he says. "The problem is there are eight or nine people around that camera, and they all think they're the boss." But on a George Lucas film, there is only one boss: George Lucas.

2
WHEN THINGS WERE SIMPLER

I was just sort of letting the world float around me.

—George Lucas

When college friends at the University of Southern California asked where George Lucas came from, the shy young man invariably answered, "Northern California." Pressed further, he admitted, "south of San Francisco." Finally pinned down for an answer, Lucas mumbled, "Modesto."

His reluctance to acknowledge Modesto as his birthplace did not stem from embarrassment, but from resignation—hardly anyone had heard of it. Modesto was an unknown city, distinguished only for its heat (an average 110 degrees Fahrenheit during the summer), the Gallo winery on its outskirts, and its broad expanses of flat roads, ideal for car racing.[1] After that, Modesto doesn't do much to inspire loyalty. Although the city now has one hundred twenty thousand residents, eight times its population in 1944 when George Walton Lucas, Jr., was born, the area has changed little. It still has a small-town mentality with few big-city problems or pressures.

Modesto has always been, well, sort of *modest*. It wasn't much more than a group of flimsy wooden shacks until the 1850s, when the discovery of gold in Northern California brought hordes of eager prospectors into the nearby Mother Lode country.

Civic pride grew faster than the town. In 1912, a magnificent wrought-iron arch was built over the entranceway to the city, proudly proclaiming Modesto's virtues: "Water   Wealth   Contentment   Health." The slogan was accurate. There was enough rainfall, along with deep local artesian wells, to guarantee a plentiful supply of water. Fruit and grain middlemen became wealthy from agricultural transactions that dominated Modesto business and helped make the small city the Stanislaus County seat. Contentment and health? Why, just look around—where else could such healthy, contented folks be found?

These thoughts ran through the mind of George Walton Lucas, Sr., when he arrived in Modesto in 1929.[2] At age sixteen, he was already the breadwinner for a family struggling to get by *before* the Depression hit with full force. Since Lucas's great grandfather moved from Arkansas to central California in the 1890s, the family had never really prospered.

The son of Walton, an oil field roughneck, and Maud Lucas, George Walton Lucas was a tall, dark-haired, slim young man, as straight-backed as an oak kitchen chair. Born in 1913 in Layton, California, he was the only son in a family dominated by women. When he was fifteen, his father died suddenly from complications of diabetes. George became head of the family, and the early responsibility deprived him of his adolescence. Lucas went to four different high schools in four different years, as his family searched for better times, finally ending up in Modesto.

The first day at school, the brash sixteen-year-old caught sight of an extraordinarily beautiful girl in his history class. He went home that day for lunch and told his mother, "I saw this girl at school, and I'm going to marry her." Maud, no longer surprised by her son's directness, asked who the young lady was. "I don't know," replied George, "but I'm going to find out!"

Her name was Dorothy Bomberger, and without realizing it, young Lucas had made an excellent choice. The Bombergers were one of Modesto and the Central Valley's most prominent families, whose American roots went back to 1700, when the Bombergers arrived from Germany. Dorothy's father had settled in Modesto in 1913 and accumulated his wealth through careful real estate purchases after World War II.

A courtship began between serious-minded George Lucas and willowy Dorothy Bomberger, and less than four years later, in 1933, the young couple were married. George was about to turn twenty, and Dorothy was two years younger. Their honeymoon took place in the midst of the Depression.

Dorothy offered to go to work, but George absolutely refused to hear of it. This was an early indication of his iron will and traditional values. The newlyweds first settled in Fresno, some sixty miles from Modesto. There George got a good-paying job ($75 a month) in a local stationery store.

But his wife was homesick for her family and friends in Modesto; she wanted to have children and to be near her mother. George was finding out that Dorothy could be strong-willed, too.

Back to Modesto they went. George applied for work to a stationer who had begun his own business in 1904 in the heart of downtown Modesto. L. M. Morris was old enough to be Lucas's father, but he had no son and George had no father. Lucas had experience in the stationery business, was willing to work hard, and was hired. "I told him I wanted a store of my own, or at least part of one, by the time I was twenty-five," Lucas recalls. "Morris said that was admirable." Morris and Lucas got along well, and one day the elder partner came down the stairs from the second-floor office and asked Lucas if they could have a serious talk.

"George, do you like me?" asked Morris. Lucas nodded affirmatively. Morris then made him a surprising proposition: At the end of the next year, he would give Lucas 10 percent of the business and take him in as a partner. If Lucas agreed to continue working hard, eventually he would own 50 percent of L. M. Morris, Stationers. Lucas had no money to invest, but Morris said that wasn't important. "You can make this business go," he told the young man. "But a partnership is more difficult than a marriage. A lot of marital troubles are settled in bed, but we can't do that." Lucas says of the resulting partnership, "Never did we go home with an unsettled argument." The relationship lasted for fifteen years, until Morris finally sold out to Lucas and died three days later.

George Walton Lucas was now a successful businessman. L. M. Morris began carrying office equipment, typewriters, even toys and knickknacks. Lucas was devoted to his business, working long hours six days a week, then coming home and doing the bookkeeping himself, with Dorothy's help.

Dorothy was fulfilling her end of the bargain. The couple had been living in a repossessed apartment taken over by Dorothy's father. With the birth of their first daughter, Ann, in 1934, more room was needed, so Lucas purchased a house. Two years later in 1936, Katherine was born, and the upwardly mobile Lucas bought a lot on the edge of town on a quiet street named Ramona, with a down payment of $500. He built a single-story frame house for $5,000.

Things were going well for the Lucas family, but there were concerns, too. Dorothy's health began to fail shortly after their marriage. Although doctors could never determine exactly what the problem was, pancreatitis was suspected, and later a large tumor was excised from her stomach. But her frequent hospitalizations and recovery periods presented Lucas with a burden that would continue for twenty years. George himself was never sick and never missed a day of work.

Her doctors advised Dorothy not to have more children, and indeed, she had two miscarriages following the birth of Katy. World War II came and of course Lucas volunteered, but he was turned down because of his slender build and married status. George stayed at home, helping with the war bond drives and watching L. M. Morris prosper, putting him into the upper reaches of Modesto's middle class.

Unexpectedly, Dorothy became pregnant again in late 1943.[3] Early in the morning of Sunday, May 14, 1944, she began to feel her labor pains coming closer together. Lucas got his wife to the hospital just in time. Dr. Ralph Maxwell barely concluded his initial examination of Dorothy when her water broke and a baby's tiny head appeared at 5:30 A.M. "They laid him on my stomach, and I was laughing so, to think that he was a boy," Dorothy says. "At first I said, 'You've got to be kidding,' because I wanted one so badly. He was jiggling around and I said, 'Don't let him fall off, this is the only son I've got!'"

They named him George Walton Lucas, Jr. (rejecting the name Jeffrey), because he looked like his father: black hair, dark eyes, pointed chin, a well-shaped head, and protuberant ears. One ear was floppy, and that bothered, George, Sr. He talked to Dr. Maxwell about the possibility of plastic surgery but settled for having the errant ear taped up, much as people do with Doberman pinschers. "It became a good ear," George, Sr., says with satisfaction. The distinctive Lucas ears are a family trademark. All three sisters have them to varying degrees, but only George's stick out at the same angle as his father's. (In *THX 1138,* there is a closeup of a youngster with the same protuberant ears.)

The newborn boy seemed otherwise healthy, weighing in at five pounds, fourteen ounces, and twenty inches long. Dorothy breathed a sigh of relief—she thought this might be her last baby, and she knew how much George, Sr., had wanted an heir for the family business. Accordingly, young George did not want for care. Along with two adoring sisters, aged eight and ten, a doting mother and a proud father, the infant was cared for by a housekeeper named Mildred Shelley, whom the children and everyone else called Till. She came when little Georgie (one of his nicknames to distinguish him from his father) was just eight months old.

Till became a second mother to George and then to Wendy, when she was born almost three years later. With Dorothy in and out of the hospital and then confined to her bed for weeks upon her return, the Ramona Avenue house was ruled by Till. She was from Missouri and loved children. She could amuse them for hours with homespun tales in her odd southern dialect and yet wasn't afraid to discipline them. "I have very warm feelings about that time," says George, who is not alone in being a famous personage strongly influenced by a substitute mother—Winston Churchill and most other English dignitaries were raised by their nannies, not their parents.

Lucas enjoyed an idyllic American childhood—it was like Beaver Cleaver growing up in Modesto. He and his contemporaries look back on their upbringing as a hazy, golden, barely remembered paradise, a magical decade between the end of the war and the mid-1950s, when middle-class affluence was achieved and the silent generation was happy to be quiet.

George's favorite story as a toddler was "Goldilocks and the Three Bears," and he was fascinated by music. He would dance for hours when a record was played, particularly if it was a John Philip Sousa march.

Not all was sweetness and light for young George Lucas, however. "I was very much aware that growing up wasn't pleasant, it was just . . . frightening. I remember that I was unhappy a lot of the time. Not really unhappy—I enjoyed my childhood. But I guess all kids, from their point of view, feel depressed and intimidated. Although I had a great time, my strongest impression was that I was always on the lookout for the evil monster that lurked around the corner."

These contradictory emotions of security and anxiety, elation and depression, happiness and fear are common to all children. They find vibrant expression in the dual themes of good and evil in *Star Wars*. The evil monster becomes Darth Vader, whose malignant power is dispelled only by the benign influence of the Force.

A film record exists of these early years to substantiate Lucas's oral recollections. Grandfather Bomberger had a 16-millimeter movie camera, a rarity in those days, and he filmed elaborate home movies during the 1940s and '50s. Most of the footage depicts the weekly Lucas picnics in the backyard of the Ramona Avenue house, where George, Sr., barbecued chicken, and family and friends gathered for some food and company. Little George stared blankly at the camera, his small body dwarfed by his older sisters.

"He was quite small," Dorothy says, "really a peanut then." The puny youngster was frequently picked on by bigger acquaintances. At age six, George still weighed only thirty-five pounds and was forty-three inches tall.

Like many small children Lucas showed remarkable initiative. A favorite family story is of the time when the Ramona Avenue house was being remodeled. George, a two-and-a-half-year-old toddler, watched workmen ripping down an old wall to build a back addition on the house. Without anyone seeing him, he went in and got a hammer and chisel from his mother's toolbox. George proceeded to do exactly what the workmen were doing, only he picked a perfectly good wall in which to pound holes. To George's parents, the incident was an early indication that they had a child who was as strong-willed as they were. "He was going to do it his way," George's father says, rather proudly.

In the 1940s, Ramona Avenue looked much the same as it does now: two facing rows of small, one-story California bungalows, neatly tended with trees lining each parkway. The street has a midwestern feel to it, perhaps because so many Modestoans came from the midwestern states, importing their values and traditions intact.

Although Lucas was a self-reliant child, he had several close friends and was virtually inseparable from his sister Wendy. John Plummer and George Frankenstein were two of his earliest and closest companions. The best times together for the group came at the backyard carnivals that George organized. The boys devised little rides and games, a funhouse, even a zoo featuring neighborhood pets. Their crowning achievement was a roller coaster that rolled down an incline, rotated on a turntable (an old telephone-wire reel), and then rolled down again to the ground. "It seemed like it was fifty feet high, although it must have only been six feet," remembers Plummer. "How we didn't kill people, I don't know." Lucas was the driving force behind the thrill rides, but he resists the idea that he was already a showman at the age of eight.

The years between the end of the war and the 1950s were good ones. The economy was booming, consumer goods were readily available, and television was just around the corner. The elder Lucas refused to buy one of the early TV sets, preferring to wait until improved models came along. But that didn't stop George. John Plummer's father got the first television set in Modesto in 1949, and George became a fixture around the Plummer house. Plummer's father built bleachers in the garage, so the men in the neighborhood could watch the boxing matches on a tiny Champion set.

"George was over all the time to watch cartoons," Plummer remembers. The boys sat with their "Winky Dink" pieces of plastic, carefully placing them on the TV screen and then coloring just as the host of the show instructed them. They had spent the first five years of their lives listening to the radio. Now, suddenly, they were in the company of a magical box that not only talked and showed pictures, but *involved* them in its activities, too.

After 1954, when George, Sr., finally agreed to buy a TV set, the Lucases in effect lost their son to the flickering black-and-white images. George's favorite show was "Adventure Theater," broadcast nightly at six o'clock from KRON-TV in San Francisco, the lone channel available to Modesto. The adventures were movie serials from the 1930s and '40s, films with exotic titles such as *Flash Gordon Conquers the Universe, Don Winslow of the Coast Guard,* and others featuring Lash La Rue, Tailspin Tommy, the Spy Smasher, and the Masked Marvel.

The Lucases' TV set was on a revolving stand, enabling George to watch it at the dinner table and then turn it around and watch it in the living room. He and Wendy would bring their blankets and pillows and watch cartoons. George also devoured "Perry Mason" each Saturday evening and watched Westerns like "Have Gun Will Travel," "Gunsmoke," and "Maverick." There were also old movies on TV, hundreds of them, licensed to television by the film studios in a vain effort to dominate the new medium.

The endless parade of cliff-hanging endings on "Adventure Theater" eventually found its way into the *Star Wars* films and *Raiders*. They made such a strong impression that when Lucas decided to do a high-adventure children's film, he went back and looked at the original serials like "Flash Gordon." "I was appalled at how I could have been so enthralled with something so bad," he recalls. "And I said, 'Holy smokes, if I got this excited about this stuff, it's going to be easy for me to get kids excited about the same thing, only better.'"

Television had a lot of influence on Lucas's work: his attention to graphic design stems from years of watching TV commercials; so does his reliance on fast pace, action peaks, and visual excitement rather than content. Also imprinted permanently in Lucas's memory is the impatience he felt to get on with the show. If there wasn't enough fast action, he'd begin to feel restless, and pretty soon he'd change the channel.

What I enjoy most about Uncle Scrooge is that he is so American in his attitude.[4]

—George Lucas in *Uncle Scrooge McDuck* by Carl Barks

Before television, there were comic books: hundreds and hundreds of brightly inked, intellectually vapid comic books.

Lucas loved comics, and Scrooge McDuck was one of his favorites. "That kind of greed attracts all young kids, because you want to have all this stuff! Having it in a safe place and protecting it—that's real kid stuff." As it turns out, Scrooge McDuck isn't a bad metaphor for George Lucas and *his* money bin, Skywalker Ranch. But Lucas was also enthralled by Batman and Robin, Superman, *Amazing Stories, Unexpected Tales*—the list goes on and on.

John Plummer's father was friendly with the man who owned the local Modesto newsstand and was able to obtain unsold comics with their covers torn off. George would trundle over on a Sunday, and while John went through the ritualized Sunday family dinner, George sat on the front porch, "quiet as hell, reading all the time," according to Plummer.

To Lucas, comic books were an education as well as a pleasure. "I wasn't a reader when I was young. I was more picture-oriented. There were always a lot of facts in comics—strange facts—I learned what a *scone* was. I was never ashamed that I read a lot of comic books." Wendy remembers pooling allowances with George and buying ten comics. "We had so many that eventually my dad built a big shed in the back, and there was one room strictly devoted to comics, floor to ceiling. We'd take these big quilts and sit out there and read them." Lucas remembers storing at least five hundred comics in their hideaway.

Comic books had an immediate effect on George. They sparked his interest in drawing, for which he had already displayed a talent. He would spend hours sketching landscapes, always being sure to put people in them. Encouraged in school, he made elaborate personalized greeting cards and small whimsical pieces of sculpture for his friends and relatives.

Most important, comic books were just the kind of worthless activity that paid off for Lucas, much as cruising resulted in *American Graffiti*. The attractive graphics and simple messages made an indelible impression on him and percolated in his imagination for the next two decades until they leaped, seemingly fully formed, out of his imagination and onto the movie screen as *Star Wars*.

His parents thought George's reticence and his advanced motor skills were closely linked. George was always doing something with his hands, putting things together and then taking them apart again. He finished what he started, a trait remarked upon by his kindergarten teacher in an early report card. "He wouldn't talk about anything until he was done with it—he'd go to the very end," Dorothy says.

The reliance on solitary pursuits helped isolate George from his family. Lucas says his closest childhood companion was Wendy, but his sister now admits that she never really felt she knew him: "I never knew what he was thinking." She wasn't the only one kept in the dark. George Frankenstein, asked about his memories of Lucas, hemmed and hawed and finally acknowledged, "He was a nonentity. He just didn't make that big of an impression."

But George was popular. His friends liked the abundance of toys that came right off the display shelves of the L. M. Morris Company. "He had all the goodies, and he was very willing to share," Frankenstein recalls. Lucas owned the best train set in his neighborhood, a three-engine Lionel Santa Fe model with all the required passenger cars and hundreds of pieces of track. Friends brought over their own trains, and the tracks wound in and around the Ramona Avenue house, driving Dorothy to distraction.

George, John Plummer, and their other friends also created what Lucas calls "elaborate little environments." They gathered weeds and transplanted them into rows for farms. Berries from nearby bushes would be gathered, put on toy trucks, and hauled away. One friend's father worked at a lumberyard, and the youngsters had access to cement, which they poured into carefully constructed forms. Then they inserted bolts, drilled holes, and built small buildings and cities. The boys also played the usual war games, especially in the patriotic afterglow of the victory on both World War II fronts.

"I loved the war," says Lucas. "It was a big deal when I was growing up. It was on all the coffee tables in the form of books, and on TV with things like 'Victory at Sea.' I was inundated with these war things." Little wonder that *Star Wars* is punctuated by frequent if bloodless conflict. The Korean War brought home another side of combat to young George. Ann, his oldest sister, lost her fiancé in Korea. George had known the young man for years and thought of him as a surrogate big brother. It was a painful loss for a lonely nine-year-old who desperately sought out big-brother figures, role models more sympathetic than his hardworking, success-driven father.

It was also Lucas's first brush with death, a concept that had been sketchily explained to him in religious terms. Young children don't often sort out their feelings about God and religion until forced to, but George was an exception. At age six, he had a mystical experience whose effect still lingers with him: "It centered around God, what is God, but more than that, what is reality? What is this? It's as if you reach a point and suddenly you say, 'Wait a second, what is the world? What are we? What am I? How do I function in this, and what's going on here?' It was very profound to me at the time." Lucas was thus made aware of the mysteries of life.

George's formal exposure to religion was less effective. His parents were Methodists, but George loathed the religion's self-serving piety and especially resented Sunday School, which was worse than regular school in his eyes. Housekeeper Till was a German Lutheran, however, and occasionally took George and Wendy to her church services, complete with male parishioners in broad hats and beards, and women in bonnets, both speaking in deep, guttural accents. George looked forward to the outings; they were interesting, different, and they involved elaborate ritual, to which George found himself very attracted: "A kid imagines church to be a real strict, organized, serious kind of thing, and that's what this was, although it was friendly, too. I think church is a much better experience than Sunday School because it gets into what religion is all about; the ceremony provides something essential for people."

The strict discipline of the Lutherans was duplicated in the Lucas household. George, Sr., was a forceful taskmaster, though he was seldom home because of his work. The children were all started on allowances at age four: four cents a week, with annual increases as they got older. In later years they had to buy their own clothes with that money. To earn their allowances, they had to perform various chores. George and Dorothy had grown up during the Depression, and they were not about to let their children forget that "money doesn't grow on trees." "Every generation should have to go through a depression," George, Sr., says to this day. After all, he survived. He knew the score.

Young George puzzled his father, however. The boy was so scrawny and was as stubborn as his mother. At age eleven, George had to mow the lawn by hand each week to earn his allowance. The assignment wasn't arbitrary; it was a clear example of the work/reward principle. George didn't mind doing the work, it was just that he wasn't big enough to do it well. "The frustrating thing was that it was tough grass to mow, and I was a little kid," he remembers. To get the work done and still satisfy his demanding father, he saved his allowance every week for four months until he had accumulated $35. Then he borrowed another $25 from his mother (also repaid from his allowance) and bought his own $60 power mower. George, Sr., was furious at his son's boldness and impressed at the same time. He had been defied but in such an ingenious fashion that he couldn't really punish his son. George, Jr., learned a valuable lesson about using his head to triumph in a seemingly no-win situation.

Other than the occasional run-in over chores, George got along well with his parents. They pushed him into taking music and dance lessons which he detested, and tried him out on a variety of instruments, from piano to accordion, all with the same sorry results. George loved to listen to music and would sit in front of the big Magnavox hi-fi console for hours listening to his parents' collection of 78s. As he grew older, records and radio became more and more important, and eventually provided the framework for *American Graffiti*.

Some of the best times in Lucas's childhood took place away from home. The high point of George's youth, awaited with longing and expectation, was the annual trip to Disneyland in faraway Anaheim. Los Angeles was like a foreign country but Anaheim had the same kind of dry heat and scorched fruit orchards as Modesto. At Disneyland, George's fantasies came to life: Tomorrowland, Frontierland, the Monorail, and the steam locomotive—thrill rides and kid rides, junk food galore, and the freedom of being let loose in a safe, antiseptic, tightly controlled environment. Disneyland is a movie that invites its audience right into the screen, combining mass appeal with mechanical ingenuity.

Lucas was there from the start. He was eleven in 1956, when Walt Disney opened the gates of his Magic Kingdom and George and his friends were among the first in line. "I loved Disneyland," George recalls. "I wandered around, I'd go on the rides and the bumper cars, the steamboats, the shooting galleries, the jungle rides. I was in heaven." The Lucas family didn't just visit Disneyland for the day—they went for a *week,* staying in the Disneyland Hotel adjacent to the park and riding the Monorail into a world unlike anything to be found in Modesto.

The sense of thrill engendered by Disneyland has never deserted Lucas. It stayed buried deep inside him, emerging later on film. Disneyland was a fixture of his youth; as he grew older and became interested in cars, the winding model-car ride Autopia became his favorite. As a teenager, he would go to Anaheim to hear rock bands and chase girls. There was more fun in a week at Disneyland than in a year of hanging around home.

Not that Modesto was such a terrible place. There were parks for kite flying and tag football, and George went through the initiation rites common to youngsters growing up in the 1950s in America. He joined the Cub Scouts and played in Little League games, even though he couldn't hit or field very well.

Fourth of July parades down 10th Street in Modesto were held each summer—George decorated his bike with crepe paper and playing cards in the wheel spokes. He and his friends pedaled past the reviewing stand in front of the county courthouse, and prizes were given out for the best-decorated bicycle in front of the Strand Theater. After that, adults and children headed over to a nearby park for three-legged races, sack races, and a big community picnic.

Amid this peaceful, idyllic existence, George Lucas, Jr., blended right into the background. He was never the leader or the center of attention. But he found himself able to get along with every "group," the cliques inevitably formed by youngsters to exclude outsiders as much as to include each other. "I could hang out with anyone," Lucas now says with pride. But he never was committed to any one group. Instead, he kept his real self hidden, listened to what everyone else was saying, and waited for the time when his imagination could soar.

Reticence didn't make George the best of students. He recalls the terror of going to kindergarten by himself for the first time, "a feeling of total panic." As expected, he was shy at first, keeping to himself. But he quickly adjusted to the new routine and became an active participant in school activities and games. By the first grade at John Muir School, George was learning how to read, and the next year he was described as "very good" in science, art, reading, and numbers.

Lucas's first encounter with the theater came in third grade, when he appeared in a play called *The Message of the Hearts*. He received last billing—not an auspicious debut for a show-business giant. George sang in the school choir, was on the safety patrol, and appeared in other school plays, always in minor roles. He never distinguished himself as a student, and his grades rarely rose above the C level. "I was never very good in school, so I was never very enthusiastic about it," remembers Lucas. "One of the big problems I had, more than anything else, was that I always wanted to learn something other than what I was being taught. I was *bored.*"

He stayed bored through three years at Roosevelt Junior High School, and by the time he reached Thomas Downey High, he was daydreaming through his classes. "I wanted to *enjoy* school in the worst way and I never could," Lucas says. He woke up only when films or educational television programs were shown. He disliked reading, hated spelling—he remains a horrible speller to this day and is unable to write more than a sentence or two without a spelling error—and was terrible at math.

"I would have been much better off if I could have skipped that stuff," Lucas says. "I would have learned how to read eventually—the same with writing. You pick that stuff up because you have to. I think it's a waste of time to spend a lot of energy trying to beat education into somebody's head. They're never going to get it unless they want to get it." What

Lucas calls his "subversive" views on education had begun to form. Now they dominate his future plans for a new educational order, based on interactive video games that schoolchildren can program themselves.

When George was fifteen, his family left the house at 530 Ramona and moved out to a ranch-style house set on thirteen acres of walnut trees. The ranch was a considerable distance from the residential neighborhood where George grew up, out in the boondocks even for a small town like Modesto. "I was very upset to leave Ramona," George recalls. "I was very attached to that house." He threatened to run away, but eventually he and Wendy grew to enjoy the seclusion of the ranch. Pheasants scurried underneath their windows and inspiring sunrises glinted on the snow-capped High Sierras.

To ease the transition to their new home, George, Sr., built his son a unique shelter for his homemade "environments." The box had a wooden floor, sides, and back and a glass top and front. George spent hours carefully constructing papier-mâché hills, tiny towns, and earthworks— little microcosms of imaginary civilizations.

Lucas became even more withdrawn after the move to the ranch. The distance from Modesto was too far for his friends to bicycle, and they were not yet old enough to drive. "It got really bad," says John Plummer. "He was a total recluse. He'd stay in his room all the time." Plummer's memory is accurate. Lucas got home from school around 3:00 P.M. and headed right for his room. He got out his collection of 45s and 78s (everything from Elvis Presley's "Hound Dog" to Chuck Berry's "Roll Over Beethoven") and played them, one after the other, for hours on end. Sitting on his bed, he read comic books, ate Hershey bars, and drank Cokes.

Soon music eclipsed his other hobbies. Lucas has always immersed himself in a particular pursuit, often to the exclusion of all else in his life. Music dominated his early teens, and one of the highlights of that period was a journey to San Francisco to see Elvis Presley on his first northern California tour, right after the famous "Ed Sullivan Show" where Elvis was shown only from the waist up. In his room, George kept an autographed picture of Elvis, wearing his blue suede shoes and caught in midgyration.

Photography became another obsession. His father gave him a 35-millimeter camera and helped him convert a spare bathroom into a darkroom. George and Dorothy remember their son running for his camera whenever the drone of crop planes could be heard; sometimes the planes flew so low that he got shots of the pilots. Most often George took pictures of his nieces and nephews or trick shots of his cat jumping up to get pieces of meat, which Wendy held off-camera. When George got his little Fiat, he insisted on a trick photograph of him standing next to the car. Dorothy took the picture lying on the ground so that George seemed to tower over the car, clearly the fantasy of a short person. Later, he oil-tinted his photographs using Q-tips.

In school, George's grades continued to slide. He did well in art and music, but in his first year at Downey High School, he got Ds in science and English. He actually failed spelling and arithmetic in eighth grade and had to repeat them during the summer.

George changed after moving out to the ranch. He let his hair grow long and put gobs of Vaseline in it so he could slick it back into exotic hairdos like the Bop, the Detroit, or a plain ducktail. He wore Levis all the time and refused to wash them. He insisted on putting taps on his long, pointed-toe black shoes. All indications were that Lucas was turning into a juvenile delinquent, a "JD." The explanation for this was simple. George had discovered a new obsession, one that almost killed him. He began to live, dream, eat, and sleep cars.

Sixteen long years of being a short loser...[5]
　　　　—The description of Terry the Toad in *American Graffiti*

For a short kid who weighed less than a sack of cement, there had to be *something* to do in a flat small town like Modesto. Two choices were available: racing horses and cars. Rural as Modesto was, horses were not common. That left cars. The Modesto landscape is *made* for car racing.

George Lucas got his first car at age fifteen, even before he got his driver's license. He was like a slave being liberated: "I had my own life once I had my car. Along with the sense of power and freedom came the competitiveness to see who was the fastest, who was the craziest, and who was the bravest." When Lucas finally went to take the driving test for his license, he failed because he was sloppy about the rules. He eventually passed the test, but he still ignored the rules.

George, Sr., forced to recognize his son's infatuation with cars, played it safe. He bought him a Fiat Bianchina with a two-cylinder engine, the smallest car Fiat imported. It had what George called a "sewing machine motor in it. It was a dumb little car. What could I do with that? It was practically a motor scooter." The first day he drove it, he raced to the walnut orchard and spun out, bashing in the tail end. But he made an important discovery: the soil in Modesto was claylike and as hard as asphalt, the perfect driving surface. All George had to do was modify the Fiat to give it power and speed, and he was in business.

Lucas loved the thrill of racing. It was something that didn't require him to be strong. His small size and light weight were advantages when racing, as was his small car. George spent every day after school at the aptly named Foreign Car Service, altering the Fiat's suspension and beefing up its engine. One day, coming home from the shop and hitting seventy miles an hour, he went into a skid and rolled the car, although it quickly landed upright. Lucas wasn't even fazed. He cut off the bashed-in roof, put on a windscreen and a roll bar, and transformed the Fiat into a racy little sports car. John Plummer had rescued an old MG from the junkyard and restored it while George fiddled with the Fiat. There was an old go-cart track behind the Foreign Car garage where the two friends raced. "We'd just be going like a bat outta hell," Plummer says. "George could drive 'em. He was really good at that."

Racing marked the first time people could *see* that George was good at something. He especially loved driving around corners, not to the point where the car was out of his control, but at enough of an angle to get a thrilling sensation that quickly became addictive. Lucas still has intense feelings on the subject. "The engine, the noise, being able to peel rubber through all four gears with three shifts, the speed. It was the thrill of doing something really well. When you drift through a corner and come up at just the right time, and shift down—there's something special about it. It's like running a very good race. You're all there, and everything is working."

George's dream was to drive a formula race car. He fantasized being the Modesto equivalent to the silent lone gunslinger, coming into town and instead of beating the sheriff to the draw, whipping the Factory team with his own car. (The fantasy was articulated in *More American Graffiti,* in which John Milner embarrasses the Factory racing team.) By state law, Lucas couldn't officially drive in races until he was twenty-one, so he went to auto crosses held in parking lots and fairgrounds, where little red cones were placed around curves. George found his Fiat could easily negotiate the tightest of turns. Corvettes and other high-performance cars lumbered into one cone after another.

George was excited when he won his first racing trophy. He soon accumulated more from tracks across the center and south of the state: Stockton, Goleta, Willow Springs, Cotati, and Laguna Seca, all within one hundred miles of Modesto. It was at Laguna Seca that George met Alan Grant, the champion auto cross racer of California who won every single auto cross he had entered. Grant primarily drove modified sports cars. When he became twenty-one, he started Class C track racing and became George's hero.

Alan Grant recalls, "George was the type of guy who was not necessarily outgoing, but once you got to know him, he was always jabbering and telling a story. He was always in a make-believe world." Not everyone reacted to Lucas with such equanimity. Grant and Lucas once stayed in Santa Monica for a race, and at their boardinghouse George started telling a particularly vivid story. One of the other racers finally had enough. "George, can't you shut up?" he bellowed. Lucas, properly chastened, said not a word the rest of the evening.

George had few other vices. His parents enjoy telling the story of how he and Alan celebrated Grant's victory in a major race. A car dealer, sponsor of the winning car, threw a press party in a local hotel's presidential suite. "He had everything in the way of wine, women, and song," Grant remembers. While the booze flowed, a craps game started in front of the TV set. The clean-cut boys from Modesto walked in, said hello, and then went up to their rooms to bed. "We had a big race the next day," Grant says seriously. "That group was as straight as they could be," George, Sr., says approvingly.

George wasn't *that* straight. He was often ticketed for speeding by the Modesto police, who kept a careful eye out for back-road racers. So many tickets accumulated that George, Sr., had to accompany his errant son before the local traffic judge. George had his hair shorn to a crewcut and was dressed in an ill-fitting black suit. It is a picture taken at this time that appears in Lucas's high school yearbook, where he does indeed look, in the words of George Frankenstein, like a "nonentity." But owning a sports car in Modesto in the early 1960s could make a nobody into a somebody very quickly.

The car gave Lucas a new sense of belonging. He became an active member of the Ecurie AWOL Sports Car Competition Club, a local hotbed of racing enthusiasts. He was editor of *B.S.*, the club's official newsletter, and he doubled as secretary of the organization. The newsletter reflected Lucas's whimsical sense of humor ("As we stand here in the grease pit of eternity..." is how one editorial began) and featured his drawings of sports cars, which were becoming professional enough for Lucas to sell on the side. Alan Grant possesses a series of the watercolors and ink drawings, all marked by a distinctive Lucas signature. It is the signature of a would-be artist, already thinking about how his autograph will look.

The artist was well disguised as a hell-raiser, however. Lucas admits that by junior high school, he was at his rowdiest. "That was my period when I hung out with the real bad element," he says, a touch of pride in his voice. The car crowd *was* a rough group, and George fit right in: greased-back hair; filthy jeans; and a devotion to cars, girls, and rock 'n' roll. While John Plummer played football in high school, George Lucas hung around with what Plummer called "the undesirables and low-riders of town."

For George, who still weighed only one hundred pounds when he was graduated from high school, self-preservation was one good reason for his choice of companions. "The only way to keep from getting the shit pounded out of you was to hang out with some really tough guys who happened to be your friends," Lucas explains. He joined his greaser buddies at a hamburger joint called the Round Table, across the street from Downey High. Also a fixture at the Round Table were the Faros, the black-leather-jacketed hoods who exemplified the paranoid fantasies of every middle-class parent of that era. George wasn't really a Faro (he was unwilling to go that far), but he served as a useful stooge for the gang. "They'd send me in and wait until somebody would try to pick a fight with me. Then they would come in and pound 'em." Lucas laughs. "I was the bait. I was always afraid I was gonna get pounded myself."

George, Sr., was distressed by the changes in his son. Although he lectured him frequently, it seemed to do little good. Dorothy was ill again, and the business needed more and more of his time. As for the double life his son seemed to be leading, "We didn't know anything about it," George, Sr., now says. Wendy agrees with her father about George. "He never said anything. He just disappeared in the evenings. We didn't ask questions—he just went out. He would never say anything about what he was doing."

George was out cruising, and he wasn't about to tell his parents that. To Modesto teenagers in 1962, cruising was a way of life, best described in the story treatment for *American Graffiti* written by Lucas in 1971: "The dancing is created by cars performing a fifties ritual called Cruising. An endless parade of kids bombing around in dagoed, moondisked, flamed, chopped, tuck-and-rolled machines rumbling through a seemingly adult-less, heat-drugged little town. . . . The passing chrome-flashing cars become a visual choreography."

Lucas spent almost every night for four years driving up and down Modesto's streets from three o'clock in the afternoon until one o'clock in the morning. On Saturdays and Sundays he would do it all day long. He and his friends also cruised other areas in addition to the principal loop that went up 10th Street and down 11th Street. Lucas felt like a bad dude in a clean machine, checking out the girls, the cars, and the scene.

The routine was addictive, Lucas remembers. "Racing cars, screwing around, having fun, the endless search for girls." The social structure in high school was so rigid that it wasn't easy for someone like George to meet people. He was stereotyped as part of an unsavory clique and his social contacts began and ended there. On the streets, it was everyone for himself. Cars became a way of restructuring the social order. Out on the strip, slouching low in the seat, putting on sunglasses (who cared that it was nighttime?), and turning on the radio full blast—that made anyone feel cool.

Modesto was a major cruising town, drawing teenagers from as far away as Stockton. They gathered in droves for the big weekends on wheels. Gas was cheap, as little as seventeen cents a gallon. Time was limitless—TV was for kids, movies were for squares, the endless nights were for the young. Cars, music, and sex were what counted.

If the loop between 10th and 11th streets was the wheel of the cruising machine, and the spokes were the kids in their cars, then the hub was the drive-in hamburger joint, immortalized as Mel's Drive-In in *American Graffiti*. "It was like a big fraternity," remembers George Frankenstein. "We just parked and went into somebody else's car. It was all clean-cut fun."

Well, not all the time. Lucas remembers one Halloween night when his Faro friends decided to make Modesto a hot town for cruising. They poured gasoline on a four-lane street and lit it, resulting in a huge fire barrier right down the yellow line in the middle of the road.

Cruising also introduced Lucas to sex. Painfully shy with girls, he found anonymity in his car. "Nobody knew who I was. I'd say, 'Hi, I'm George,' but after that night I'd never see the girls again. It wasn't like in school, where you'd have to sit with them." Downey High was on the good side of town; Modesto High, on the lower-class side of the Southern Pacific tracks, had an abundance of the gum-chewing girls with bubble hairdos who weren't afraid to have a good time. Modesto High was where George headed on a Friday night and where he lost his virginity in one of the most important adolescent initiations: "The eternal search for a little nookey, a little action," as the treatment for *American Graffiti* put it.

Other than his midnight forays, Lucas never dated. He thought it was "dumb." Plummer remembers his friend being obsessed with blondes, however. "Yes, there were a lot of Debbie-type girls," George acknowledges, likening his female companions to the bleached blonde Candy

Clark played in *Graffiti*. "It's interesting that I never really had any high school kind of girlfriends or anything. I was always going around picking up girls and hoping for the best." What Lucas couldn't realize at the time was that his high school experiences were soon to make him a millionaire several times over.

To be renewed is everything. What more could one ask for than to have one's youth back again?

—George Lucas

The great wonder of movies is that they stop time and become a shared experience, a joint arrival at a place and time captured on screen. In *American Graffiti*, the place is Modesto, the time is 1962, and the experience is George Lucas's transition from adolescent to adult. "I was trying to re-create something that had been a huge thing in my life, and I did it exactly ten years later," Lucas says of the film's release in 1972. His experience resonated through the post-World War II baby boom generation, which had also changed in the intervening decade. Lucas stopped time in *Graffiti* at a point people wanted to remember, crystallizing, in 110 minutes, emotions shared by millions in their own lives, and shared again watching the movie.

A plot description of *American Graffiti* sounds as simple as the B movies after which it was patterned. Four buddies aged seventeen to twenty, who have grown up and goofed off together, reach a crossroad in their lives. Two of the boys are leaving their small California town to attend college. Steve has doubts and stays; Curt has doubts and leaves. The lives of the other two friends revolve around cars: Milner tries to maintain his superiority as king of the road, and Toad tries desperately to get drunk and laid in the car that Steve has entrusted to him. The action all takes place in one long, hot summer night of cruising.

Not the most original idea in the world, but fleshed out by details from Lucas's own life, *American Graffiti* becomes a personal statement with broad implications. Cruising, Lucas says, is more than a quaint practice of adolescent Americans. "It's a significant event in the maturation of American youth. It's a rite of passage, a mating ritual. It's so American: the cars, the machines, the cruising for girls, and the whole society that develops around it." The secret of the success of *Graffiti* is that it works on two levels, as a "kid's goofing-off movie" and as an anthropological statement about American culture and mores.

American Graffiti embraces California culture wholeheartedly, although not every small town has a teen-aged populace equipped with a fleet of cars. But what happens in the film seems indelibly real because it *was* real. George's life was broken into pieces and reassembled with the help of coscreenwriters Willard Huyck and Gloria Katz, a cast of talented actors and a dedicated film crew. This studious re-creation of a bygone era works by compressing four years into one night, and setting all the dramatic action between sunset and sunrise.

Lucas planned his film as a tribute to a cruising tradition relegated to the nostalgia heap by the 1970s. But *"American Graffiti* Night" is now a tradition of its own in Modesto. Teenagers come from all over the central valley—in customized pickup trucks now, rather than tuck-and-rolled T-birds. They roar up and down McHenry Avenue, paying homage not to a twenty-year-old custom, but to the movie that immortalized it. *Graffiti* is part of a large body of work that examines rites-of-passage ceremonies in primitive and contemporary society. College, manhood, sexual initiation—all these thresholds are crossed in *Graffiti,* and in later homages such as *Diner.*

By exploring his own adolescence on film, Lucas touched a basic nerve in his audience. After the film's release, he received letters like this one from an eighteen-year-old moviegoer: "I didn't know what being a teenager was, and now I do." Another fan wrote, "I'm sixteen and stoned all the time and I didn't realize you could have so much fun being a kid." Lucas realized he was on to something. Things that were meaningful to him as a teenager—having your own car or having girls giggle at you in the hallway—were important to other people who didn't grow up with or near him. Lucas had discovered a microcosm for an entire generation.

Willard Huyck and Gloria Katz, who cowrote *Graffiti,* are still amazed by the response. "The incredible thing about the movie is that it's very American, and yet it's also universal," says Katz. "It's not quite as naïve as it seems. We stylized it in a way that gave it a mythic quality, and then we were free to have fun with the characters." The most endearing aspect of *Graffiti* is its characters. Milner, the gunfighter past his prime, refuses to accept that he is older and can't keep drag racing forever. Curt, the intellectual, unsteadily embraces change and goes to college, come what may. Steve, the all-American boy, is unable to escape his past and start a new life. He'll stay in the small town and become an insurance agent. Terry the Toad makes the simplest and most complex changes as he gets a car and a girl, the twin poles of California adolescence.

These are types, to be sure. Steve is the class president, blond and athletic; Curt is the brain, quoting poetry and making jokes; Milner is the greaser, hair in a ducktail and cigarettes tucked in his rolled-up shirt sleeve; Toad is the nerd, the butt of everyone's jokes, the shame-faced possessor of "cooties."

"It's about every kid you ever went to school with, it's about everything that ever happened or didn't happen to you, or that you fantasize or remember as having happened to you," says Universal Pictures president Ned Tanen, the only studio executive willing to take a chance on making *Graffiti,* and the man who also almost prevented the film from being released.

The well-roundedness of the *Graffiti* characters is astounding, since they are seen almost exclusively on the street, in cars, and at the burger palace. The establishing shot and recurring image of *Graffiti* is Mel's Drive-In, the teenage equivalent of a gas station where the drivers, not their cars, get replenished with food, music, and girls.

The emphasis on girls is ever-present. The female characters in *Graffiti* are reflected through the adolescent consciousness of their male creator. They are either "good" girls or "bad" girls. Laurie, Steve's girlfriend and Curt's sister, is a good girl. She refuses to give him something to remember her by (a high school euphemism for sex) before he goes off to college, and partially because of that, Steve never goes. Debbie, on the other hand, is more than willing to put out for a little booze, which Toad agonizingly tries to buy.

Two more female types are conjured up in *Graffiti.* Carol is the young tomboy just discovering her femininity. She flirts with Milner, but has to be home by ten o'clock, still too young to date. The nameless blond driver of the white T-bird (Suzanne Somers in her first film role) is the sex goddess Lucas mooned over throughout his own adolescence. She represents the illusion of beauty that can't be found in a real person. Curt never connects with her, and she remains a disembodied voice on the telephone.

It is a tribute to Cindy Williams, Candy Clark, and Mackenzie Phillips, who play Laurie, Debbie, and Carol respectively, and co-screenwriter Gloria Katz, that the girls in *Graffiti* have a point of view at all. Lucas sees it differently. "The women in the film are as strong as they are because I wanted them to be," he says. Lucas admits that he's always had problems developing women in his movies—he can make them strong and independent but seems to have no idea of what they're thinking or feeling (witness Princess Leia in *Star Wars*). In a school bathroom scene, set during a dance at the local gym, the girls have only two topics of conversation: the way they look and boys.

If there is eroticism in *Graffiti,* it is lavished on the costars of the movie:

the cars. Lucas makes love to his cars, tracking them as they cruise up and down the boulevard. The dialogue reflects this affection. When Steve entrusts his car to Toad, he promises to "love and protect it until death do us part." The machine, he rhapsodizes, "is even better than Daryl Starbird's superflecked moonbird." Audiences may not understand the description, but it's poetry of the road.

The nighttime setting also idealizes *Graffiti*, giving it an aspect of madness that seems fitting for the longest and last night of adolescence. Humming with electricity, pierced by an endless stream of headlights, *Graffiti* presents a world peopled primarily by adolescents. The only adults in the film are either buffoons, such as the policemen whose patrol car is separated from its chassis in an elaborate prank, or cartoon figures, like the Moose lodge members who give Curt a parting lecture on the virtues of hard work. Lucas even includes a poignant fantasy: Curt strides down the empty halls of the building where he spent four crucial years of his life and walks up to his old locker. The combination has been *changed*. If that doesn't tell you his childhood is over, what does?

There is one adult whose presence is crucial to *Graffiti:* Wolfman Jack. The legendary disc jockey came to fame in the late 1950s over XERB, a 250,000-watt Mexican radio station whose signal was powerful enough to travel from New York to Los Angeles. The Wolfman was a delightful enigma to his listeners; they couldn't tell if he was black or white, thirty or seventy, human or animal. It didn't matter that his name really was Bob Smith and that he came from Brooklyn. He was the outlaw of the airwaves, the secret friend of a million anonymous listeners. In *Graffiti,* the Wolfman actually howls in the background, screaming, "Gonna make all your dreams come true, baby!" When Curt meets him near the film's end, the youngster is taken aback: "Gee, I've known you all my life, but you're not at all what I expected." The Wolfman stares at him, deep-set eyes behind a pompadoured head and goateed chin. "You'll find that applies to a lot of people," he replies evenly.

The Wolfman is there because the music is there. *American Graffiti* is a musical in its least traditional definition. People don't stop to sing or dance, but the evocative score of early rock 'n' roll hits begins before the opening credits and ends only when the final title fades. The music holds the film together.

In the opening shot described in the original screenplay of *Graffiti*, amber light and an electric humming fill the screen, gradually giving way to a giant number 11. Static is heard and then a large vertical band of red hovers across the screen, moving back and forth over more numbers.

Voices, snatches of song, more static commingle, until we realize that we're watching a car radio. The radio envelops *American Graffiti,* becoming the metaphor for the characters meeting and touching each other's lives, coming together and then drifting away. "Radio creates a fantasy that doesn't exist at all except in your own mind,"[6] Lucas told *Seventeen* magazine at the time of the film's release; he knew he was speaking to the right audience. The opening strains of "Rock Around the Clock" immediately jolt the viewers into remembering emotions they associate with the song. The music parallels and counterpoints the action on the screen, summing up a host of memories from the filmgoer's life.

The *Graffiti* soundtrack also captures the shift into a new phase of rock music, as the surfing sounds of the Beach Boys supplanted Buddy Holly. "Rock 'n' roll's been going downhill ever since Buddy Holly died," Milner complains to Carol, who doesn't even know who rock pioneer Holly was. "We're going to rock 'n' roll ourselves to death, baby!" howls the Wolfman—a musical era dies on screen, too.

The unifying force in the film is the 1950s, the glue of nostalgia holding an entire generation together. Although the 1950s craze took off after the release of *American Graffiti* (especially on TV with "Happy Days," "Laverne and Shirley," and other spin-off series), Lucas tapped into something deeper than just nostalgia. "Why can't things stay the way they are?" he jotted down in his preliminary notes for *Graffiti.* Teenagers are particularly unequipped for change—their lives are a torrent of conflicting desires and emotions. By introducing a quartet of symbols to illustrate the different reactions adolescents have to growing up, Lucas makes a general statement about a specific situation, one night in which everything and anything is possible. Steve fails to change, Curt accepts change, Milner refuses it, and Terry fakes it. What other alternatives are there? The film's approach seems simpleminded, but the agony of the decision is very real to a sixteen-year-old. Lucas remembered his own angst, and he was able to project it onto a larger canvas.

References to Modesto abound in *American Graffiti,* right down to the Ramona Avenue address where Carol lives and where Lucas grew up. The cruising loop, Mel's Drive-In, the Pharaohs (the spelling was changed to protect the guilty), Burger City, the radio station—all have real-life antecedents in the crowded nighttime streets of Modesto in the late 1950s and early '60s.

Lucas, like most writers, bases his characters on people he has known, including himself. Walter Murch has said that the four major male characters in *Graffiti* are derived from different aspects of George's personality—it is as if he took a hammer and hit his own self-image, breaking it into four clearly defined pieces. Lucas demurs at such a literal interpretation. "I was really only Toad and Curt. I was the shy guy in high school, and once I got into junior college I sort of became like Curt." Lucas longed to be Milner when he was in high school; the character is based on Alan Grant (although the name refers to John Milius).

The character Lucas had the most difficulty writing was Steve, the class president/star athlete/good student, who had no basis at all in George's personality. "Bill and Gloria really pulled him out of the fire," Lucas says. Otherwise, the film is a faithful re-creation of Modesto, right down to the dialogue: "Grind me a pound" for a driver grinding gears during shifting; "Take your cooties off me," the typical exchange between a good girl and a bad boy; "slipping a little pressed ham," a way of "shooting the moon." The final section of *Graffiti* closely parallels Lucas's own life. The movie climaxes with a fiery drag-race crash, one that almost kills Milner's rival Bob Falfa (played by Harrison Ford) and his passenger, Laurie. Shakily, the teenagers stumble away from the crash scene, just before Falfa's car explodes with a gasoline-soaked fury—and just as in 1962 when Lucas was in his car crash, everyone is thankful that no one gets killed.

Dad, you know you're going to do this morning exactly what you did yesterday morning. And tomorrow you'll do exactly what you did this morning. I only want to do something once.

—George Lucas

George stayed in the hospital for two weeks after his accident. He was then ordered to recuperate at home for the rest of the summer, except for daily visits to the hospital for physical therapy. His trip with John Plummer to Europe was canceled, and his Fiat was hauled to a junkyard. Lucas's high school diploma was delivered to his hospital room three days after the accident. George joked that the only reason he graduated was that his teachers felt sorry for him.

The accident put an end to the dream of a racing career George had cherished. The only option open to him now was junior college, since his grades were not good enough for a four-year school. That meant Modesto Junior College, the local campus that had a good academic reputation. Lucas was determined to make it in college—for the first time in his adult life, he began to study. He fell asleep over his books, but gradually the work became easier because he was learning what he wanted to learn: sociology, anthropology, literature, even creative writing. "These were things I was really interested in, and that sparked me. It was very hard, and I didn't have the background I needed—I couldn't even spell."

Lucas also began to read: Aldous Huxley's *Brave New World,* George Orwell's *1984,* and adventure books by Jules Verne that he had ignored as a child. He spent hours poring over anthropological studies, trying to understand how a culture works. "If I had been learning sociology in sixth grade, I would have been much happier," Lucas now says. His grades reflected his renewed interest: A's in astronomy, B's in speech, sociology, and art history. Most of his grades were C's, but that was a big improvement over high school D's. On June 9, 1964, Lucas was awarded his associate in arts degree—the worthless kid had become a junior college graduate.

Lucas had formed other interests following the accident. Instead of racing cars, he filmed them with a small 8-millimeter camera his father bought him. He had been shooting still photographs of the races since high school, and movie making was a natural extension. As he became more interested in movies (they corresponded to his fascination with art and painting), he became aware of film as a medium of expression. He saw art films in Berkeley and studied film books.

John Plummer was then attending the University of Southern California in Los Angeles, one of the most respected private schools in the country. Plummer told Lucas that USC was not as hard to get into as the school's reputation indicated and suggested the cinema school as a particularly easy means of access. Lucas had planned to go on to a four-year college, and he felt it would be easier to go to a state school, where he could study English and sociology. He applied and was accepted into San Francisco State for his junior year, starting in the fall of 1964, but he never got there.

Through Alan Grant, Lucas had become acquainted with Haskell Wexler, a prominent Hollywood cameraman and racing aficionado. Wexler took a liking to the weird skinny kid whose head was bursting with ideas. He went so far as to telephone some friends of his on USC's film school faculty and advised them to watch out for Lucas. "For God's sake, keep an eye on the kid," Wexler told one faculty member. "He's got the calling." But Wexler did not get Lucas into USC, as legend had it. Lucas had applied to the film school prior to meeting Wexler, and to George's and his father's amazement, he was accepted.

The decision to go to USC was not without its problems. "I wasn't very happy to see him wanting to get into the movie business," says George, Sr., with typical understatement. The acceptance to a school was fine, he reasoned, but why one with all those egghead liberal teachers? And why, for God's sake, study film, which was no better than studying art? That was no occupation for a career-minded young man. How could studying movies help train George to be a businessman? The argument over college capped an increasingly tense relationship between the elder and younger Lucases, one that simmered for almost twenty years.

He is his own man, he is not a son anymore, he is an equal.[7]
—George Lucas describing Luke Skywalker after his duel with
Darth Vader in *The Empire Strikes Back*

It is not unusual for the only son in a family dominated by women to have a strained relationship with his father.[8] Expectations are high, and reality can often prove disappointing, especially when the father is a strong-willed, self-made man. Lucas remembers his father as being very stern. "He was the boss; he was the one you feared," he recalls. But he also perceived an underlying fairness behind the strictures, with discipline that was tough but never dictatorial.

The elder Lucas was and is a popular man around Modesto, known for his sense of humor and his business acumen. George Frankenstein, who worked for Lucas's office supply firm when he was in high school, recalls George, Sr.: "He was *tough*. Boy, I tell you, if you were fifteen minutes late or a bill was wrong, he'd hang you out to dry. I mean, he screamed and yelled a good part of his day at L. M. Morris to keep everybody's heels clicking." When he went home, Lucas expected the same kind of obedience. George, Sr., always had the feeling that his son was going behind his father's back to get what he wanted from his mother. George, Sr., would go out of his way to deny things to his son. "I thought he shouldn't get everything he asked for just because he asked for it." He would tell "Georgie" stories about the hard times in the oil fields where he grew up, and the even harder times of the Depression. There was a moral there, and he wanted George to learn it.

The domineering presence of his father left young George with an overriding goal: "To be able to do something on my own, and have it be the way I envision it. I've always had a basic dislike of authority figures, a fear and resentment of grown-ups." The most prominent authority figure for any child is usually the father—George remembers feeling "incredibly angry" with his father at times during his childhood.

George, Sr., didn't help matters by making a point of shaving young George's hair off every summer. The annual ritual was a yearly humiliation for George, and it gave him the nickname Butch. John Plummer did everything in his power to avoid George, Sr.—he was scared to death of him. "Every time Mr. Lucas came around, you just kind of hid," recalls Plummer.

But the children enjoyed the other side of George, Sr.'s personality: his bizarre sense of humor. He spoke in rhymes and double-talk and made jokes about ice-cream cones carved out of wood. "He was a very funny, practical-joker type," Frankenstein recalls. Just the opposite of his son, whom no one can remember laughing as a child.

In a small-town, conservative milieu, George, Sr., was ultraright wing in his political beliefs and remains so to this day. "He is a conservative, self-made kind of man, with a lot of prejudices which were extremely annoying," says Lucas. "I learned very early on not to discuss politics with my father." Even now, when complimented on his son being invited to the White House to meet President Carter, George, Sr., growls, "If it had been anybody but Carter, we would have been a helluva lot prouder."

It's too easy to liken George's love/hate relationship with his father to Darth Vader and Luke Skywalker. Despite his obsession with conformity, George, Sr., gave his children great leeway and independence as long as they were willing to accept responsibility for their actions. George, Sr., realized early that his son was going to do things his own way, and nothing he could say would make a difference.

The two Lucas men were never really close, and the resulting void bothered George. He filled it by befriending big brother types such as Alan Grant, to whom he went for encouragement, support, and knowledge. "That's one of the ways of learning," Lucas explains. "You attach yourself to somebody older and wiser than you, learn everything they have to teach, and move on to your own accomplishments." That pattern repeated itself in a later apprenticeship Lucas served under director Francis Coppola and in Luke's devotion to Yoda, the Jedi Master.

The conflicts between father and son accelerated as George became old enough to work at L. M. Morris. His job as a summer delivery boy required him to lug around reams of heavy paper in the one hundred-plus degree heat of Modesto, then come back to the store to clean the toilets, sweep, and lock up. After two weeks, George was fed up and vowed never to do this for a living. George, Sr., was furious at his son. He called George Frankenstein and offered him the job, saying, "The damn kid won't even work for me, after I've built this business up for him."

George knew his father thought he would never amount to anything. Before the accident, when he told his father he was thinking of going to the

Art Center in Los Angeles, a tremendous row had ensued. "My father thought I was going to turn into a beatnik. He was still hoping I'd take over the business," Lucas recalls. "It was one of the few times I can remember really yelling at my father, screaming at him, telling him that no matter what he said, I wasn't going into the business." George remembers George, Sr., looking at him and saying, "Well, you'll be back in a few years." Standing toe-to-toe with his taller father, young George looked up at him and shouted, "I'll never be back; and as a matter of fact, I'm going to be a millionaire before I'm thirty." Even now, Lucas doesn't know where the vow came from. "It was one of those things that at the time I was shocked I had said. It sort of came out of left field. But it actually came true." A gauntlet had been hurled down, and Lucas had twelve years in which to make good his promise. He succeeded, as George, Sr., testifies:

"When I was young, we got things out of the Sears catalog. I'd tell George this, and he'd just listen and grin. I told him that the thing I really wanted was a steam engine. Nobody ever wanted anything as badly as I wanted that steam engine, and I was sure I'd get it somehow, someday. Well, I never got it. About ten years ago, we had the big family deal at Christmas and one of the children brought me this box, and in it was the steam engine. I had tears in my eyes, but that George never said a damn word, just grinned across the room at me, like a skunk on a garbage wagon. He said to me with his look, 'You didn't think I was listening, did you?'"

Although George eventually dropped the Jr. designation from his name, his father looks on his son's success as a joint achievement. "He's so proud, he just raves about George. You'd never dream they had ever had a questionable word," says Wendy. In some ways, the credit should be shared. The small-town conservative and old-fashioned entrepreneur passed on his values to his son, who has grafted them onto a billion-dollar business. "The way my father brought me up gave me a lot of the common sense I use to get me through the business world," Lucas acknowledges. He was also bequeathed a sturdy set of morals and principles, and an insistence on honesty and fairness.

"Have you met George's father?" asked Tom Pollock, Lucas's Hollywood attorney since 1972. "I did not understand him until I met his father and spent some time talking to him about his son. That's when you realize that George *is* his father, as most of us are." Pollock is referring to a long-standing Lucas fear of big-city hustlers: bankers, lawyers, intellectuals, deviants. The elder Lucas still refers to Hollywood as "Sin City."

Many of today's young movie directors had repressed or difficult childhoods. Martin Scorsese and John Milius suffered from severe asthma. Francis Coppola was stricken by polio, which kept him bedridden for two years. Steven Spielberg and Lucas were slight of build and scrawny. Often a child with physical limitations channels his unused energy into a particularly vivid fantasy life. Lucas sees nothing wrong with that. "I had a good life when I was a kid, a normal, tough, repressed childhood filled with fear and trepidation all over the place. But generally, I enjoyed it; it was good."

Like many people who succeed in the entertainment business, and particularly the movie business, Lucas retains a wide-eyed sense of wonder about his childhood. "When you meet George, he seems interested in very simple things," says Carroll Ballard, the director of *The Black Stallion* and a friend of Lucas's for more than ten years. "He's still living in his childhood in a certain way. He's able to reach back there and remember it vividly and share it. He can make sense of those things and sell them. But he's also a man of the world, a guy who really knows about money, is very calculating and business-oriented. He's a very interesting combination of both."

Both qualities emerged in Lucas while he was growing up in Modesto. What he labels, not at all sarcastically, his "Norman Rockwell upbringing," also contains his formula for success. In *Graffiti* he drew upon his adolescence; in *Star Wars*, he saw his childhood fantasies come to life. Even *THX* reflected the next part of his life to come, the escape from Modesto. But Modesto has never left George Lucas; it is permanently enshrined, both on celluloid and in his imagination. Bruno Bettelheim, in an essay about the power of movies on today's society, discusses the importance of Yoda in *The Empire Strikes Back* as a reincarnation of the teddy bear of infancy we turn to for solace. "Any vision about the future," Bettelheim writes, "is really based on visions of the past, because that is all we can know for certain."[9]

The astonishing thing about George Lucas is that no one had faith in his future. "George is a great inspiration for parents," says his sister Kate. "Nobody would have believed he was going to do anything. He was a total loss. He's a great example for parents not to lose their cool. I'm just amazed that a person that was so untogether could turn out to be so together."

3
REALITY STOPS HERE

Movie making is like sex. You start doing it, and then you get interested in getting better at it.[1]

—Norman Mailer

Arriving at the University of Southern California was a milestone in George Lucas's life—he had finally made it to a real college. Lucas set a goal for himself at USC that seemed impossible to attain: he wanted to become a professional filmmaker, whatever that meant.

His decision was greeted with skepticism from family and friends: "All my friends laughed at me and warned, 'You're crazy, you're going to become a ticket-taker at Disneyland. You'll never make it.'" It wasn't that George wanted to become the next John Ford or Orson Welles—he didn't even know who they were. He was just following his instincts, listening to the inner voice he had heard since his accident two years earlier. "I have found it's best to try to do what in your heart you feel is right," he says.

Lucas had to convince his father to help him with the costs of USC. The elder Lucas had ambivalent feelings about higher education. It was a goal that many men in his generation had failed to achieve, and it became paramount for their offspring to go to college. But there lingered a small-town distrust of the academic world, an inherent prejudice about the liberals and Communist sympathizers polluting the minds of innocent young men and women. Film school, in the eyes of George, Sr., was an even more perverted institution. "I fought him. I didn't want him to go into that damn movie business," Lucas, Sr., says. But he told George that if he applied the work ethic that had been drilled into him since childhood, he should do all right, and then he made an interesting proposal: he would *hire* George to go to college, paying him a salary (tuition) and $200 a month in expense money. School was to be considered a job, and George was expected to work at it. If he didn't do well at USC, L. M. Morris awaited him.

Lucas entered USC as a junior, following his two years at Modesto Junior College. Privately, George had doubts about his academic ability. He thought his IQ rating was in the nineties and feared he didn't have the intelligence to make it. "I was a little awed by the whole thing," Lucas recalls. "When I finally got there, everything seemed way over my head." It was the twenty-year-old's first extended stay away from home, other than his trips to Disneyland and car racetracks.

Lucas realized he was going to have to work his butt off to stay on top. He hated studying and writing term papers. "If it hadn't been for the self-discipline that made me chain myself to my desk and do it, my work would never have gotten done. I felt there were a lot of kids that never figured that out, and they just sort of whiled away their lives and woke up one day to find out they were thirty-five years old and hadn't amounted to much." This is Lucas's version of Darwinism, the survival of those who work the hardest. The summer before entering USC, sitting on a Malibu beach daydreaming about his future, Lucas read a pamphlet, *The Dynamics of Change*, put out by the Kaiser Aluminum Company. It contained a chart listing the accomplishments of famous young people, from Alexander the Great to Thomas Alva Edison. Lucas recalls, "I was very taken by that, realizing that a lot of the really significant things that have happened in history have come from people under the age of thirty." Asking himself, "So what have you done lately?" Lucas decided to make something of himself. He had ten years in which to do it.

His timing was right. "A bit of history opened up like a seam, and as many of us who could crammed in. Then it drifted back closed again," Lucas says. The system of entering the movie industry had crumbled in the 1950s, with the advent of television and the deterioration of the major film studios. In the 1930s and '40s, sons had often followed fathers into the industry craft unions, learning their trade at the same studios. As movie production in Hollywood ground to a halt and moved to Europe in the late 1950s, the studios laid off hundreds of workers, usually the younger ones. By the mid-1960s, the average age in the Hollywood labor force was fifty-five, and there was no one trained to replace them.

The idea of film school graduates taking over Hollywood was anathema to most faculty members at the three leading film programs: USC, the

University of California at Los Angeles, and New York University. Students were trained to make documentary and educational films, not Hollywood movies.

USC's film program was the oldest and largest in the country. It even *looked* the oldest—classes were held in rickety wooden barracks constructed from surplus World War I army lumber, emblazoned with the slogan "Reality Stops Here." For all its disdain of Hollywood, USC relied upon the movie industry to provide the structure for its film program. It was the first school to establish separate courses in writing, directing, camera, lighting, sound, and editing. Each discipline mirrored a studio department. The culmination of this training was the opportunity to make a fifteen-minute film using a student crew and university-supplied equipment and film. USC has graduated more than five thousand cinema and TV students since 1929, and 80 percent of them have gone on to professional work in the industry, although most of them have had only lowly jobs. In many ways, going to USCinema (as it is popularly abbreviated) constitutes a four-year apprenticeship in the movie industry.

Lucas arrived at USC after spending the summer in Los Angeles searching for a job: "I hit every two-bit movie company on Ventura Boulevard, a thousand of them, going door to door. Every one I went into, I said I was looking for a job and I'd do anything. No luck." How must these small-time production companies have felt just eight years later when they realized that the skinny kid whom they had given the quick brushoff had made a movie, *American Graffiti*, that sold $117 million worth of tickets? They could have had him for $75 a week. Lucas may not have found work, but he did enter USC a little more seasoned than some of his fellow students. He knew how tough it was out there.

The concept of the young, hot cinema student did not exist in 1964. The fifty or so full-time cinema students at USC were treated as the *Animal House* outcasts of the campus, scorned by the co-eds and dismissed as artistic weirdos by the rest of the student body. Inside the film department (television wasn't added to the curriculum and the school's title until 1977, typical of USC's traditional approach), there were other barriers to overcome. The rigid curriculum included film history, theory, and technical courses. The model used was the filmmaker as artist, not as Hollywood director. "The instructors would walk in and say, 'Good morning, this is editing, and although we're here to teach you the fundamentals of editing, you'll never use them because you'll never get into the upper echelons of the industry,'" recalls Howard Kazanjian, another USC alumnus.

A student was expected to move from writing to production planning to directing to sound recording and editing and finally to criticism, until he was capable of making his own short film. "Very few films are made by one guy," USC sound instructor Ken Mura says, summarizing the film school's philosophy. The final step in the process was the 480 Workshop, a graduate-level course that required student crews to make two fifteen-minute movies in the course of a semester. One film was to be taken to the stage of a rough answer print (the final stage a film reaches before it is reproduced in a film lab), and the other had to be a completed work. There were strict rules limiting the films' cost, scope, and ambitiousness. Most students found it a relief to blame the rules for their failures. Not Lucas.

"The department [instructors] never taught us much, other than the basics," he explains. "They opened the door, but we had to go inside and find out for ourselves. We students were learning things infinitely faster than the classes were teaching us. You had to in order to keep up with what was going on." Lucas believed the rules were there to be broken. "I broke them all—all of us did. Whenever I broke the rules, I made a good film, so there wasn't much the faculty could do about it. They were caught between the facts that it was the best film in the class and that I had broken all the rules. They had to relent."

Lucas did not make an immediate impression in his first year at USC. "Basically, George was a person you really didn't notice," says Ken Mura, who has taught at USC for more than twenty-five years. "He didn't stand out in a crowd, okay?" Lucas tried to blend into the background, as he had throughout his earlier school career. Matthew Robbins, who came to USC as a graduate student from Johns Hopkins University in Baltimore, remembers Lucas's terror of East Coast intellectualism: "He had a deeply rooted suspicion and fear of erudite refugees from the Ivy League." Hal Barwood, who became Robbins's filmmaking partner, recalls Lucas as "this little kid who weighed about a hundred thirty pounds in an oversize sports jacket with shoulders about four inches too wide and little silver threads running down through it. He looked like Buddy Holly or something."

Lucas had to cram two years of undergraduate film courses into his junior year at USC if he wanted to work on a senior film project the following year. Lucas never cared for dorm life and quickly found a three-story wood frame house for rent on Portola Drive, in the hills above Beverly Hills. He now had his own pad, even if it was a beat-up old house that cost only $80 a month. His father grumbled about the extra expense, but Lucas said he'd rather do without food than give up the place. At first, he lived alone, occupying the top-story living room, bedroom, and bathroom. The kitchen, along with another bedroom and bathroom, was on the second floor, with a garage underneath. There were no stairs; the only access between floors was an industrial ladder. Lucas turned the wet bar into a projection room and made the extra bedroom his office. Lack of money eventually forced him to take in a roommate, and Randal Kleiser, fresh from Rosemont, Pennsylvania, moved in. They could not have been more dissimilar. Kleiser was modeling for Pepsi-Cola at the time, and his face was smiling down from half the billboards in Los Angeles.

Lucas made the long drive to the USC campus in a silver Camaro he had bought after junior college. He hadn't abandoned his passion for fast wheels, although the accident had slowed him down, and he no longer had the racer's fearlessness. Lucas remained a car freak, but he finally began to grow up at USC. He developed a quality he had lacked: self-confidence. "George got along with people when he was in film school better than he ever did before," remembers John Plummer, who stayed close to Lucas at USC, where he was a business major. "That came from his confidence in what he was doing. It was the first time he became a leader." Lucas calls his years at USC one of the happiest periods of his life, "a time when I really blossomed. When I went in there, I didn't know anything. The school helped me focus on film, and I loved doing that. They helped me become what I am today."

Making movies is an apprenticeship for life.

—Robert Watts

A lot of college students in the 1960s got high on drugs. Lucas got high on films: "Suddenly my whole life was film—every waking hour. It was all new, neat, and exciting." Always drawn to popular arts like television and comic books, Lucas had found a new medium through which he could express his imagination. Making movies, he realized, "is like being able to cement dreams in concrete and then dig them up again a hundred years later and say, 'Oh, this is what they were dreaming about in those days.'" Lucas's film interest began in junior college when he and Plummer journeyed to the avant-garde North Beach section of San Francisco. They spent endless hours devouring the work of European directors like Fellini and Bergman, and underground filmmakers such as Jonas Mekas. "I was equally interested in all kinds of films and all kinds of filmmakers," Lucas says. But it wasn't until he reached USC that he realized film making was also a business and a means of making a living. He said to himself, "Well, this is great. I can always get a job directing commercials."

A sense of mystery and reverence was attached to film study at USC in the 1960s. Movies were magic. "You could wander into a room and they'd be showing a movie, and you'd see something that would just blow you away, that would just change your life," John Milius recalls. Lucas designed sound tracks on his student films that immediately attracted attention: "Whenever you played a movie in the main screening room, you could hear it all through the department. When there was a really interesting-sounding film, the whole department would come rushing in to see what it was. I tried to make films that sounded good as you walked from class to class."

Lucas quickly became a believer in the director as the major creative force behind a film: "It is a director's medium, there's no getting around that. The writer provides a very important element, but the final product is ultimately left in the hands of the director." Lucas admired certain directors for their vision, an individual style that dominated the contributions made by the writer, cast, editor, and technical crew. His years at USC coincided with the advent of the French *auteur* theory, which credits the director with the ultimate authorship of a film. Auteurism came out of the French New Wave in the early 1960s, led by critics-turned-movie-directors François Truffaut and Jean-Luc Godard. Their highly personal films paid homage to directors like John Ford, Howard Hawks, and Alfred Hitchcock. At USC, American films were often dismissed as mere popular entertainment. But a director like Godard was a cinematic hero. "I *loved* the style of Godard's films," Lucas recalls. "The graphics, his sense of humor, the way he portrayed the world—he was very cinematic."

Stanley Kubrick (*Dr. Strangelove*), Orson Welles (*Citizen Kane*), and Richard Lester were other directors whose work influenced Lucas during his formative years at USC. Lester's two movies starring the Beatles, *A Hard Day's Night* and *Help!*, amazed him with their virtuoso editing: images ran into one another, were speeded up and slowed down—Lester turned cinematic continuity into a shambles. Lucas saw there were no limits to what could be done with film. Introduced to the films of director Akira Kurosawa (*The Seven Samurai*), Lucas admired the formal Japanese sense of composition and texture and eventually incorporated it in his own films, especially in the final victory celebration in *Star Wars*. Lucas became so obsessed with film that accompanying him to the movies became an arduous experience. John Plummer recalls, "George started pointing out all this technical stuff, every mistake that a director or cameraman made. It got to the point where he would ruin the movie for me."

Like a fat man who couldn't stop eating, Lucas gorged himself on movies. He and his friends saw as many as five films on a weekend. Lucas's favorite films remained the shorts made by the National Film Board of Canada, particularly *2187,* an abstract film made up of news footage with image and sound juxtaposed out of context. Halfway through the film, a man wakes up and says, "You're 2187, aren't you?" and smiles, the only dialogue in the film. Lucas loved it: "I said, *'That's* the kind of movie I want to make—a very off-the-wall, abstract kind of film.' It was really where I was at, and I think that's one reason I started calling most of my [college] movies by numbers. I saw that film twenty or thirty times."

Lucas found his calling at film school. Suddenly it was clear to him what he was going to do, and the change was dramatic. George became a workaholic who insisted on doing everything himself. "He became very independent and came up with the slogan 'If you want to do it, *do it,'*" Plummer remembers. "This was a guy who never had any direction before, and now suddenly he had asserted himself and became totally devoted to one thing, film."

Lucas drove himself so hard that near the end of his first year at USC, he contracted mononucleosis, a result of staying up all night to edit film and subsisting on a diet of Hershey bars, chocolate-chip cookies, and Cokes from the DKA cinema fraternity snack bar. Close friends like Matthew Robbins think Lucas's determination to succeed at USC came from unspoken pressure from his father. Lucas claims that he was just having a good time. Even drugs, omnipresent on college campuses in the mid-1960s, failed to deter him. "I had all that young enthusiasm, and I was too busy to get into drugs," he explains. "After a while I could see it was a bad idea anyway. I have a lot of friends who take drugs, and I see what it does to people. It makes me very sad."

Lucas was motivated instead by the knowledge that he could create anything he wanted to on film. "He understood that film school was his only chance to explore his ideas his way and fail, if necessary," says Dave Johnson. "Most of the other kids played it safe. But George was willing to explore all the aspects of film."

God, my life is like a Jacqueline Susann novel sometimes—all these characters come out to Hollywood and become stars.

—Randal Kleiser

Lucas was not alone in his desire to consume movies. By happy coincidence or predetermination, a group of filmmakers emerged from the film schools in the mid-1960s that is the cinematic equivalent of the Paris writers' group in the 1920s. Instead of F. Scott Fitzgerald, Ernest Hemingway, and Gertrude Stein, the USC filmmakers consisted of people like George Lucas, John Milius, and Randal Kleiser. South of Los Angeles, at Long Beach State, Steven Spielberg invented his own film program and made a twenty-minute short that landed him a job at Universal Studios. Across town in Los Angeles, Francis Coppola, Carroll Ballard, and B. W. Norton, Jr., were beginning their careers at UCLA. Coppola became a hero in the student film world when *You're a Big Boy Now*, ostensibly his Master's thesis at UCLA, was turned into a studio feature. Across the country, Brian De Palma was making documentary films at Columbia University, and Martin Scorsese was amazing his professors at New York University's film school with his angst-ridden student films.

But nowhere was the renaissance of young moviemakers dawning faster than at USC. Between 1965 and 1970, the following students were graduated from and formed the nucleus of the USC "mafia" and a new Hollywood: Lucas, writer-producer Hal Barwood and writer-director Matthew Robbins *(Dragonslayer)*, director Randal Kleiser *(Grease)*, writer-director John Milius *(Conan the Barbarian)*, cinematographer-director Caleb Deschanel *(Escape Artist)*, editor Walter Murch *(Apocalypse Now)*, producer Howard Kazanjian *(Return of the Jedi)*, producer Bill Coutourie *(Twice Upon a Time)*, director Robert Dalva *(Return of the Black Stallion)*, producer Chuck Braverman (numerous TV specials and documentaries), writer-producer Bob Gale and writer-director Bob Zemeckis *(Used Cars)*, John Carpenter *(Halloween)*, writer-director Willard Huyck *(French Postcards)*, writer Dan O'Bannon *(Alien)*, composer Basil Poledouris *(Blue Lagoon)*, and writer David S. Ward *(The Sting)*.

"It was a miracle group," said the late Verna Fields, who gave Lucas his first job as an editor and later cut *American Graffiti* for him. "I've never seen so many people with so much talent in one place at the same time." Some of the participants think the "miracle class" description goes a bit too far. John Milius says, "It's mostly a myth. But there was a definite . . . *thing* going on there."

Lucas has always felt that his life has coincided with key periods of American cultural history: being a teenager in the 1950s, a college student in the 1960s, a hot young filmmaker in the 1970s. As someone dependent on his inner life for his inspiration, Lucas sees society growing up with him. He feels fortunate to have been at USC during all the excitement.

The members of the USC "mafia" even today refer to themselves as the Dirty Dozen, a reference to Robert Aldrich's movie about a group of convicts turned into commandos. "We really felt like we were part of a certain select group going in to make movies," says Caleb Deschanel. The only criterion for membership was to pass the critical test imposed by the other students. "If you went and saw a student film and said, 'Gee, this is kind of a boring film,' you just didn't ever associate with that guy," Walter Murch explains. "But if you went and saw an exciting film, you became friends with this guy. That was the way we all got together." The boys (there was not a female among them) who in their youth had dreamed of making their own movies and TV programs now had the opportunity. Graphics, pacing, and movement, rather than ideas and content, were part of their creative makeup by the time they arrived at USC—the legacy of a TV childhood.

Despite the common background and interests of the group, a healthy sense of competition flourished. Lucas remembers, "The unique thing about being at film school then as opposed to now was that it didn't lead anywhere. You concentrated more on what you were doing and on the people you were with, rather than thinking, 'Gee, if I make this kind of film, somebody will see it and I can get a job.' That was such a remote possibility that you didn't structure your life around it. The focus was on the films people made." Everyone brought up ideas for movies, and no one was concerned if someone used one, as long as the resulting film was good. Lucas is known as an excellent collaborator because of the enjoyment he experienced in sharing ideas at USC. "One of the biggest problems young filmmakers have is that they think everything is monumental," Lucas says. "It was understood in the department that ideas are cheap, and it kept everything from becoming too sanctified. We had a lot of fun."

The "480 class" was the initiation rite at USCinema. Five students made up a crew: the writer-director, cameraman, editor, sound man, and production manager, ranked in descending order of prestige. Lucas, like everyone else with half a brain and any ambition, wanted to be the director. Unlike most students, he invariably was. Crew loyalty was fierce—members of the group worked interchangeably on each other's productions, but when they worked on rival crews, friendship no longer counted. "We would go to extreme lengths to keep equipment out of the hands of other crews," Robbins remembers. "We'd keep the camera out and falsify records of when we had it so we could get more time." The best way to get extra time was to work at night—students climbed over a shed to get into the cinema compound and cleared out before anyone arrived in the morning. Night editing was essential because the school only permitted students two hours a day on the Moviolas, which stood in close proximity to each other, all blaring away. If a student didn't discover how to make movies on the sly, he didn't survive for long. "You went off and became something else," says Deschanel, "but not a filmmaker."

There was a great sense of male bonding among members of the group. They once took a zoom lens onto the patio of the cinema compound to watch the girls in the nearby dorm performing their nightly toilette. It was the closest they got to the USC co-eds. Lucas enjoyed being a campus outcast; he was fond of his image as a rebel against the academic empire. "I look back on it as being in some kind of battle," says Hal Barwood. "Everybody hopped in the trenches, and they blew a little bugle and you jumped out and ran toward the enemy lines. There's all this smoke and dust, and eventually you look around and a few of you are still left, and you say to each other, 'Jesus, hi, you made it! Fantastic!'"

Lucas got to know his friends by getting to know their movies. As different as the films were, the friends were mostly the same: male, white, from middle-class backgrounds, and roughly the same age. "George made a few friends at USC and decided that's about all he needed for the rest of his life," observes Willard Huyck, one of those friends. Indeed, Lucas has hardly added any new friends at all since his days in college.

George's USC friendships are long-standing, but they're not necessarily deep. Marcia Lucas feels her husband's film school bonds were more professional than personal, an opinion that may be influenced by her possessive attitude toward George: "George's relationship with his friends was more about making films. They were all struggling young kids. I never felt George had a very close, intimate, buddy-buddy kind of relationship with those guys." Lucas never was the one to down a couple of pitchers of beer with the boys, but there is a reason he has remained fond of the members of the USC group: "I have a tendency to be overly loyal to people. It takes an awful lot to make me give up." Miki Herman, who now works for Lucas as an associate producer, remembers the sound-mixing sessions for *Star Wars* in early 1977. "George would sit there for hours and all his friends would drop by. It was like a men's club—he would really confide in them and they had great fun. They're all like a bunch of little boys."

Lucas did not become the center of attention on the strength of his personality. His friends realized his instinctive understanding of film. Lucas also used his special ability to fit into almost any social group. He became friends with Walter Murch, Matthew Robbins, and Caleb Deschanel, all of whom had gone to Johns Hopkins, while being close to John Milius, who was suspended for punching a teacher in the nose. (The other members of the group went on strike until Milius was reinstated in the film program.) Even Randal Kleiser, the sometime model who wanted to act in and direct beach-party movies, was attracted to Lucas's enthusiasm and expertise. Lucas got along with just about everyone except for incompetents. He had no use for them and openly resented their presence: "I was really incensed at the democratic process of film making, where we helped the student who couldn't quite make it. I was into making it a competition, who can get it done first and best. If they couldn't cut the mustard, they shouldn't have been there."

Lucas was the opposite of incompetent, earning a reputation for surmounting any and all obstacles USC put in his way. "George fit right in and took over," explains Hal Barwood. "He sort of bore the standard, grabbed the little flag, and ran to the top of the building." Milius, ever the one for military analogies, compares Lucas to General George Marshall, the wartime diplomat with a benevolent heart. "George has a view that will help determine the shape of the world," says Milius. "The rest of us will only determine the shape of individual battles. He's five-star material." Walter Murch remembers the first time he met Lucas, in the darkroom at USC where Murch was working on a photography class assignment. Lucas had already been in the program for a year and didn't hesitate to suggest that Murch was developing his film the wrong way. "Who's this creep? Get out of here! What do you know?" Murch recalls saying. It was the beginning of a long friendship.

The shy, slight young man in sneakers and heavy glasses, quickly acquiring a reputation as a young genius filmmaker, was best at fitting together various aspects of technology. Nobody else could come close to his skill with graphic images. Lucas is more modest about his God-given gifts: "Common sense is the best way to put it, I guess. Marcia calls it being very centered. In a given situation, I seem to have the right answer that eludes everyone else." When it came time for him to be admitted to the cinema fraternity Delta Kappa Alpha, the resentment other students felt for Lucas surfaced. Fraternity president Howard Kazanjian nominated Lucas but other members thought he was a showboat who was not really serious about film—he seemed to enjoy himself too much. Kazanjian threatened to resign if Lucas was not permitted to join, a ploy that worked. Kazanjian had no way of knowing that his friendship would be rewarded more than a decade later when Lucas hired him as producer of *More American Graffiti*.

The DKA members were correct, in a sense—Lucas was not the serious type. "He was a zany guy," remembers Matthew Robbins. "He was very wacky, with a goofball sense of humor." George Lucas a goofball? It seems the least likely adjective to apply to a serious young man on a mission. Lucas may have been more easygoing in those days, but "goofball" is not the word that comes to Randal Kleiser when asked to describe his roommate: " 'Come on,' I used to say. 'Get excited about *something!* ' "

Lucas's friends at USC also included Christopher Lewis, actress Loretta Young's son. Lewis's father was a producer-director for a religious film company called Father Peyton's Family Theater, and the two students made frequent use of the editing equipment at the company's Hollywood studio. Lucas and Lewis even started their own production company, Sunrise Productions, in their senior year, but nothing came of it. Through Lewis, Lucas was introduced to the lifestyle Kleiser hungered for: dinner parties, limousines, and Hollywood stars. But Lucas's foray into Hollywood Babylon did not distract him. Robbins remembers Lucas saying, "I'll either be the biggest success or the biggest failure in Hollywood," a remark that surprised him "because it struck me that by being so involved in Hollywood, George was way ahead of me. Feature-film making was just starting to percolate in my mind as something that might actually be interesting. And here George was already trying to make feature films."

Try not—*do*. Do or do not. There is no try.
—Yoda in *The Empire Strikes Back*

George Lucas wanted to do only one thing while studying film at USC, and that was make movies. Film students are rarely able to finish a project, but Lucas never had that problem. He would close himself in a little room and come out a few hours later with a cut film. Lucas couldn't figure out why everyone else complained about not having enough film, or time, or a big enough crew. "I just started making movies," he says. "If I got sixteen feet of film, I made a sixteen-foot-long movie. Nothing could stop me."

The philosophy at USC was to learn the rules before breaking them, advice Lucas chose to ignore in favor of his own conviction that experimenting with rules was what movies were all about. Fred Roos, who cast *American Graffiti* for Lucas and produced *Apocalypse Now* for Francis Coppola, says the impact of this generation of filmmakers "stems from a basic thing back in film school of not liking the way the system ran. The key was having your own setup, not being answerable. That's what it comes down to." For all his rebellion, Lucas was admired by his instructors for his discipline and prodigious output. "We thought, here was a kid who might not zoom to the top, but he'll make himself known in documentaries or something," says Dave Johnson.

Lucas was surprised at the ease with which he dominated his classes. He had learned well from the example set by George, Sr. "Talent without hard work doesn't get you very far," he now lectures, a refrain that would make his father proud. "I think the most important thing is to work very hard, and if you have the talent, it will show. You *can* do something by working hard—that's discipline. If you keep at it long enough, sooner or later you get lucky and get your break." Lucas felt that he wasn't the best writer (that was Milius) or the best animator (that was Barwood). But he believed his talent was a mixture of ability and instinct, and he was reluctant to question it further because it came so naturally. "But I had to work hard at acquiring the skills for film making—they're all learned. After that, I had every bit of confidence when I was in film school that I was going to make it."

Equipped with a natural sense of film composition, Lucas's strength was in making the little he had to work with in his student films look like a lot on screen. "He understood very well the use of the camera and sound because he had a sense of structure and visual continuity," Dave Johnson recalls. But for all his apparent skills, there were drawbacks to George's approach to directing, according to Johnson. "His forte was designing and constructing film stories, but his attitude was 'Let someone else work with the people.' Look at his student films—they're all about things and facts. People are just objects."

Realizing his weakness when it came to characters, Lucas used pacing to disguise it. "Don't dwell on a shot that becomes boring. Keep things defined and interesting, with the emphasis on action and dialogue. Keep it moving, keep the pace going," is how Lucas's editing assistant Duwayne Dunham describes George's philosophy. Movement, action, simple dialogue, and relentless pace are qualities found in comic books and movie serials. Explains Dunham, "It's nothing that's written out on a piece of paper. I believe a scene is already cut in his mind when he talks about it— you can almost see it going around in his head." In movies, pace is created by editing. A character can run through a film for two hours, but without closeups on his body or intercutting to show his progress, the illusion of movement does not exist. It is the editor, Lucas learned, who determines ultimately what the filmgoer sees.

Lucas loved editing—he sat for hours running long lengths of celluloid through his white-gloved hands, marking his cuts with a grease pencil, the scent of splicing glue dominating the small cubicle where he worked. To

Lucas, writing or shooting a film didn't control the final product—editing did. It offered a way to manipulate the perceptions of the audience. "I'm a good editor because I have a sense of what people like," Lucas asserts. With half the editing time, Lucas could do twice as much as other students. "George has an internal time clock that he cuts to," says Dunham. "As soon as a shot becomes boring, bingo! You're out of there!"

When Steven Spielberg first saw Lucas's student films, he was awed by their editing. "George makes his visuals come to life with montage," Spielberg says. "That makes him unique in our generation, since most of us do it instead with composition and camera placement." By projecting the movie inside his head and knowing how many frames each sequence needs to be, Lucas the editor makes Lucas the director look good. Editing also gives George immediate feedback. The relationship between Lucas and his editing machine (he has since graduated from the old-fashioned Moviolas to the high-technology KEM tables) is symbiotic to this day. "He is more at home and aware of who he is behind an editing machine than any other place," says executive assistant Jane Bay. "He's like a master pianist sitting down at a piano, a person totally comfortable with his medium."

Lucas's sophisticated visual sense further enhances his editing skills. Lucas and the Industrial Light & Magic staff often run special effects footage in a screening room. The ILM staff are trained professionals who can spot minute flaws in a segment of film ten seconds long, and yet Lucas invariably sees a piece of "garbage" footage that the others miss. "It's almost a physiological talent," says Tom Smith, manager of ILM; "his eyes are so sensitive. This capability is something that film editors develop. But George goes even further—he can see something wrong with a shot, and he'll know whether or not we can get away with it."

Not surprisingly, Walt Disney had the same ability. In his book about Disney, *Life with Walt,* Charles Snow recalls the time Disney's associates tried to trick him by inserting a single frame of a stark-naked woman in a cartoon reel.[2] Film speeds by the naked eye at the rate of twenty-four frames per second, but halfway through the screening Disney yelled for the projectionist to stop. He demanded to know what the hell a picture of a naked woman was doing in the middle of a *Mickey Mouse* cartoon.

Lucas honed his editing skills because he was so weak at writing. He concentrated on visual films, abstract exercises, documentaries, and cinematic tone poems that could be constructed in the editing room, rather than on a typewriter. "My feeling at that time was that scripts were for the birds," Lucas recalls. "I disdained story and character; I didn't want anything to do with them." Lucas still has difficulty recognizing his storytelling skills. "I'm not convinced I'm real good at it," he says with characteristic modesty. But Lucas often complains about his strengths rather than his weaknesses. "When he complains about a weakness in an area, it's from a great satisfaction and strength in it," Steven Spielberg says. "When George *is* weak in an area, he doesn't talk about it at all."

Lucas's insistence on keeping his films simple in terms of plot and character has limited his work, however. Colleagues like Irvin Kershner, director of *The Empire Strikes Back,* admire Lucas's instinctive feel for drama and his skills as an editor, but they feel he doesn't trust the audience enough. "He's afraid they'll get bored, so he'll cut a little too fast," says Kershner. Lucas is fond of saying that the only parts of a movie that really count are the first five minutes and the last twenty minutes; everything in between is filler. If there is enough action, he believes that no one will notice that characters aren't as fully rounded and deep as they might be.

I wanted to make abstract films that are emotional, and I still do.

—George Lucas

Student films are to a feature-film director what college-literary-magazine works are to a writer.[3] They provide some clues and portents, but they're often not very interesting. The early films of George Lucas are an exception, not only showing where he was headed as a filmmaker, but offering a preview of the themes and style of his feature-length movies. The virtuosity of Lucas's student films acted as a beacon, shedding light on his talents and attracting widespread attention.

There were two kinds of film assignments at USC: short black-and-white exercises that students were given five weeks to complete and which had to be filmed within three blocks of the campus, and longer, ten-week projects. Few students were able to complete the five-week project, and it was a struggle to deliver anything resembling a finished film in ten weeks. Lucas raced through the five-week assignment and still found time to make a trailer of coming attractions from the longer film. He worked like a maniac, helping to write the scripts, editing the sound and music, photographing the films, and completing the answer print in time for the departmental screenings. When Matthew Robbins arrived at USC, Lucas was already a legend, even though he had been there only a year. "His films were just the most electrifying things you had ever seen," Robbins recalls.

Lucas took graphics and animation courses at USC because the idea of creating emotions through background design appealed tremendously to him. His first formal film was made in 1965 in an animation class taught by Herb Kossower—the assignment was to use still photographs to convey the illusion of movement and feeling. Traditionally students filmed a series of still pictures, but Lucas tried something different. He leafed through back issues of *Life* magazine, picking out an equal number of violent and peaceful images. He then developed a sound track for the film, which no one had previously attempted for such a minor assignment. *Look at Life* is one minute long and combines a montage of antiwar pictures with a score of jazzy calypso music and snatches of news broadcasts.

"It had quite a dramatic effect on the department at the time," Lucas recalls. "Nobody there, including all the teachers, had ever seen anything like it." Lucas established his movie-making style from the outset: a fast pace (a new photograph appeared every five frames, or each eighth of a second), a reliance on sound to convey emotion, and a spontaneous style with considerable dramatic impact. *Look at Life* won several prizes at the student film festivals that were springing up all over the country. Lucas felt proud: "It made my mark in the department. That was when I suddenly developed a lot more friendships, and the instructors said, 'Oh, we've got a live one here.' When I did that film, I realized I was able to run circles around everybody else. That's when I realized these crazy ideas I had might actually work. It was the melding of my San Francisco exposure to avant-garde shorts and my film school experience."

Lucas's second film, made with fellow student Paul Golding, was *Herbie,* a series of light reflections on a buffed and polished car that mirrors the headlights approaching then passing it on a busy city street. The title comes from a jazz composition by tenor saxophonist Herbie Hancock. The film's abstract graphics are impressive and made Lucas's star within the department shine even brighter. Although showing signs of becoming an accomplished filmmaker, Lucas didn't take his first formal classes in editing, camera, and sound recording until 1965, his second year. He picked a political subject for his senior film—*Freiheit*—the German word for freedom. "I was angry at the time, getting involved in all the causes," admits Lucas. "The draft was hanging over all of us, and we were bearded, freako prehippies."

Freiheit starred Randal Kleiser as a student escaping across the border from East to West Germany; for the first time the theme of escape, which dominates all of Lucas's work, is articulated. The film was photographed in the hills above the beachfront colony of Malibu and shows Kleiser running through the underbrush while gunfire and battle sounds are heard in the distance. Bullets rip into Kleiser and an announcer's voice intones, "Freedom is worth dying for." A gun-bearing soldier, played by Christopher Lewis, stands over Kleiser's motionless body as the film ends with the ominous warning "Without freedom, we're dead." Crude as it is, *Freiheit* introduces the philosophy behind Lucas's movies: we must escape a life of stifling routine, accepting responsibility for our actions as well as their consequences. That is as true for the young German student as it is for THX 1138 and Luke Skywalker.

Kleiser remembers that Lucas disliked USC students who felt it was necessary to die for one's country to defend democracy. "George wanted to make a statement about how easy it is to say that but how in reality people were getting killed," says Kleiser. Mel Sloan, who taught the class for which Lucas made *Freiheit*, said the Vietnam conflict had a strong impact on the entire USC group: "They had to grow up in a different way than other students had before, because this was the first time we were involved in an unpopular war. I think it influenced the kinds of films that they did and the seriousness with which they approached what they were doing."

As his graduation drew near, Lucas geared up for what he feared would be his last student film, a subject still close to his heart, auto racing. He wrote the screenplay, directed, and edited *1:42:08*, which was subtitled *a man and his car*. The short film was startling for its singlemindedness. It consists of a sleek yellow race car being timed in its laps around a racetrack. The only sound is the incessant revving of the car's engine, but the film's strength derives from the effectiveness of its editing. "There is graphic beauty inherent in a car going at full speed," Lucas wrote at the time, and the film bears him out. Lucas decided to make *1:42:08* (the title comes from the length of the race) in color, a technique strictly forbidden at USC. He also planned to shoot it at the Willow Springs Raceway, north of Los Angeles, an open breach of the regulation requiring student films be shot near campus. While shooting, Lucas met the cast and crew of a similarly themed film, *Grand Prix*, which starred James Garner. The student director was amazed by the contrast between his 14-man crew, unusually large for a USC production, and the 120-member Hollywood contingent. The studio cast and crew retired to portable dressing trailers at the end of a day's shooting, while Lucas and company headed for their portable sleeping bags.

1:42:08 did not have the impact of Lucas's earlier films, but he was still pleased. "It was interesting to me because I was interested in cars and the visual impact of a person going against the clock," he says of the production, which was criticized for being poorly structured. Shooting *1:42:08* also gave Lucas his first taste of directing a crew; to his surprise, he enjoyed it.

Lucas directed two other films when he returned to USC in 1967 as a graduate student. *Anyone Lived in a Pretty How Town* was made with Paul Golding, based on E. E. Cummings's poem. The film was in color and in a wide-screen format, another USC first. Lucas was determined to make *Anyone* in five weeks, not ten. Even his friends said it was impossible—it took ten days just to get color film processed in an outside lab. The haste with which Lucas and Golding made *Anyone* is apparent; it is the least likable and least impressive of George's student films. The story concerns a photographer who takes pictures of a young couple, turning them into black-and-white still photographs in the process. At the five-week screening, George showed a finished answer print; none of the other crews even had a rough cut completed. Lucas demonstrated that he could make a film under the pressure of a deadline and bring it in on schedule and on budget (his total out-of-pocket cost was around $40).

Lucas's most interesting USC film was a ten-week project called *The Emperor.* The twenty-minute documentary foreshadowed *American Graffiti* with an opening title card announcing "Radio is a fantasy." The film's star was Bob Hudson, a disc jockey for Burbank radio station KBLA in the mid-1960s. An egotistical, heavyset, middle-aged man, Hudson broadcast a nonstop sarcastic and scatalogical monologue. Intercut in *The Emperor* (the nickname Hudson bestowed upon himself) are sexy closeups of beautiful girls making suggestive remarks to the deejay; helicopter and ground-level shots of traffic jams on Southern California freeways; slow-motion footage of long-haired hippies frolicking at a San Francisco love-in; street interviews with radio listeners about Hudson; and commercials extolling the virtues of smoking bananas and offering a used rhinoceros for sale. Surprisingly, the mixture of styles and techniques works: *The Emperor* is entertaining, funny, and sometimes touching.

Lucas remembers, "I had always been interested in the phenomenon of radio and originally wanted to do the film about Wolfman Jack, but I didn't know where he was. I was amused by the fact that people have a relationship with a deejay whom they've never seen but to whom they feel very close because they're with him every day. For a lot of kids, he's the only friend they've got." The same theme is explored in *American Graffiti* with the real Wolfman Jack, but Lucas had a freewheeling freedom with *The Emperor* that he never enjoyed again. "George was using *Emperor* for what the experience ought to be," agreed USC's Mel Sloan. "He was trying something here that he'd never be able to try out professionally."

Wendy Lucas saw some of George's films at the USC screenings, which were open to the public, but she wasn't impressed. "They were too abstract for me," she sniffs. The final arbiter passed judgment favorably, however. George, Sr., and Dorothy came to Los Angeles for one screening and were "surrounded by long-haired hippie kids," the elder Lucas recalls. "Every time one of George's films would come on, the kids would whisper, 'Watch this one, it's George's film,' and our ears pricked up. We went out to the car and all over the campus all they were talking about was Lucas's films! Now I had been against this thing of his going to the cinema school from day one, but we guessed he had finally found his niche. As we drove home, I said to Dorothy, 'I think we put our money on the right horse.'"

Just think what kind of animals they'll be when they come back![4]
—Comment on the departure of the
Screaming Eagle paratroopers to Vietnam in the
first screenplay of *Apocalypse Now* by John Milius

After receiving his bachelor of arts degree in Cinema from USC on August 6, 1966, Lucas contemplated an uneasy future. The Vietnam War clouded his plans; if he was lucky enough to get a job in the movie business, the draft could quickly deposit him in Southeast Asia. Lucas considered himself politically active in the 1960s: he supported civil rights, was against the war in Vietnam and Lyndon Johnson, and in favor of all the right liberal causes. USC had a large military population on campus. Navy, air force, and army officers were taught basic documentary techniques in the film school. Several air force students told Lucas that with his skills and a college degree, he easily could become an officer in the service's photography unit. Lucas figured that he might as well look into enlisting in the air force, indicating there wasn't much behind his commitment to antiwar politics. At least it would be something to write and make movies about later on, he thought.

When Lucas tried to join the air force, however, he was rejected—not for health reasons but because he had a police record. All those racing tickets returned to haunt him. It wasn't a criminal record so Lucas could still enlist, but he was excluded from becoming an officer in the photographic unit. Faced with the likelihood of four years of combat duty, Lucas walked out of the recruiter's office. "I wasn't really that enthusiastic about going in the first place," he says. "I was just doing it out of desperation."

In his single-minded obsession with film, Lucas considered fleeing to Canada with friends like Matthew Robbins—after all, they were big fans of the National Film Board of Canada. But after talking to some USC students who had gone there to avoid the draft and were already homesick, Lucas rejected the option. Finally, the draft caught up with him. Resigning himself to the inevitable, Lucas went to downtown Los Angeles for his induction physical. To his astonishment, he failed—he had diabetes. He was relieved that he wasn't going into the army because he hated the thought of the government "lining us up for the butcher block." He was now a free man at twenty-two but burdened with an incurable disease for the rest of his life. "I remember when he found out that he had diabetes," says John Plummer. "He was very shook up. It scared him. He thought he'd passed through this once with his accident, and here it was again."

Lucas felt lost, without a purpose in life: "My whole life had been planned around the fact that I was going to spend two years somewhere slogging around in the mud, hoping to get assigned to something reasonable, and using the experience to write about in later years. Now what was I going to do?" He drove to Modesto where his sister Kate's husband, Roland Nyegaard, was a practicing physician. Roland repeated the tests the air force had done and sure enough, George had the classic diabetic curve on the glucose-tolerance test. Roland prescribed Orinase, a new wonder drug that had replaced insulin in the management of mild diabetes. If George used the medication regularly, avoided sugar and starches (including alcohol), and took good care of himself, he probably would not have to begin insulin injections until age forty, when diabetes can become a more serious problem.

The worst prescription for Lucas was having to abstain from chocolate, an addiction he had developed in childhood from devouring Till's chocolate-chip cookies, Hershey bars by the truckload, and gallons of chocolate milk shakes. Lucas sometimes cheats on his diet, but the disease enhances his squeaky-clean image: he doesn't smoke, drink, take drugs, or eat sweets. To his friends, Lucas seems almost without vices.

It was now too late to start graduate school in the fall of 1966, so George knocked on doors, looking for a job in the movie business. Armed with a USC cinema degree and an impressive portfolio of student films, Lucas quickly found work as an assistant grip (a crew member who carries objects and equipment) on a documentary for the United States Information Agency, which was then pouring millions of dollars into educational/propaganda films. Several USC students were hired to log footage on other USIA documentaries. Robert Dalva, one of Lucas's friends from the cinema department, was working on a film about President Johnson's trip to the Far East. Veteran film editor Verna Fields, a rare woman in a male-dominated business, needed additional help, and Dalva recommended Lucas.

Fields hired Lucas in early 1967, just as he was returning to graduate school at USC. Although he hated to do it, George had to ask his parents to support him for a little while longer. To his surprise, his father readily assented. Much as Obi-Wan Kenobi would later assist Luke in his time of greatest need, George, Sr., continued as benefactor to his once-errant son. He remembered the praise he had heard heaped on his son at the student film screenings and was honest enough to admit his earlier error in judgment. He sensed that George was on a path now from which he should not be deflected. If paying some more bills would help his son continue, George, Sr., was more than happy to oblige.

Feeling guilty about his dependence on his family, Lucas became a teaching assistant to a class of navy film students at USC. He taught evenings and worked during the day on the USIA project. Fields often found Lucas asleep at a Moviola in the living room of her suburban home—he had worked all night on his navy class project and had passed out during the day from exhaustion.

Lucas quickly demonstrated his skills as an editor, but he bristled at the restrictions the government agency placed on his work. Editors had to discard footage of President Johnson's bald spot and the First Lady's prominent profile. Politically, the footage had to be consistent with American foreign policy, and Lucas was criticized for the way he edited Johnson's visit to South Korea. "They objected to it on political grounds. They said I made the South Koreans look a little too fascist." Lucas was angry enough to abandon a possible career as an editor: "I realized that I didn't want other people telling me how to cut a film. *I* wanted to decide. I really wanted to be responsible for what was being said in a movie." The only way to have that final say was to make the film himself. The idea of becoming an independent filmmaker—writing, shooting, and editing his movies alone—began to look very attractive.

Fields did considerable business with Hollywood film libraries and hired an assistant editor named Marcia Griffin from Sandler Films to help with the overflow of USIA footage. Thrown together in a small editing room, Lucas and Griffin eyed each other warily, each intimidated by the other but unwilling to reveal it. "Marcia had a lot of disdain for the rest of us," George remembers, "because we were all film students. She was the only real pro there." For her part, Marcia felt intellectually inferior; she had gone to evening college classes while working but had never graduated. Eventually, George asked the cute, pert brunette to a screening of a friend's film at the American Film Institute headquarters in Beverly Hills. "It wasn't really a date," George says. "But that was the first time we were ever alone together."

Behind every successful man there stands an astonished woman.[5]

—Frank Capra

At first, they were an unlikely couple. She was a street-smart, industry-wise career woman who had emerged from a tough single-parent childhood determined to obtain financial success on her own. He was a shy, somewhat awkward student, lost in a private world of movie making. About the only things George Lucas and Marcia Griffin had in common were their shared birthplace of Modesto and a love of film. Although they worked in the same room of Verna Fields's sprawling tract house in the San Fernando Valley, it was months before they had a serious conversation and weeks after that before Lucas asked her for a date. The date in itself was unusual. "Once I got into film school, I stopped a lot of my living," explains Lucas. "I didn't have time to deal with the social graces because I hardly had contact with anyone—I was always working."

Lucas had never had steady girlfriends in college, contenting himself with occasional one-night stands. Even after taking Marcia out, he didn't fall in love with her. "It wasn't that I saw her in the editing room and said, 'I'm going to get that girl.' It was more like 'This is another girl and we'll have fun and what the heck.' I certainly never expected I would marry Marcia." Lucas never had found a woman he felt comfortable with; his relationships usually lasted for a few dates and a couple of sessions in bed and then petered out. "I think my relationship with women is not very complex," Lucas admits. "Up until I met Marcia, it was a very animalistic attraction."

The casual atmosphere at Fields's house was conducive to the growth of friendships. Marcia and George worked together because he was the least experienced editor and she was the most experienced assistant. Marcia knew more than George about editing technique, but her job was to help him. Often she looked over his shoulder and was impressed by what she saw: "He was so quiet and he said very little, but he seemed to be really talented and really centered, a very together person. I had come out of this hectic commercial production world and here was this relaxed guy who threaded the Moviola very slowly and cautiously. He handled the film with such *reverence*."

Marcia enjoyed being with George. He seemed so happy, humming and tapping his foot to the ever-present radio music in the editing room. When one of the other female editors asked her what she thought of the shy young student, she had a ready answer: "I think George is so cute. If only he weren't so small." Marcia thought she outweighed George, who was as thin as he was short (actually he is taller by a few inches). She loved his nose, set on a handsome face with good features. But Lucas was hard as hell to draw out in conversation. He might discuss the films he was working on but rarely did he bring up personal matters.

Their dates were usually at the movies—two on a Saturday, one in the afternoon and the other following dinner. Most of the other girls Lucas took out were not in the film business, and inevitably they wanted to do what he thought were "a lot of dumb things." The Hollywood social scene turned off both George and Marcia, who spent their time hanging out in their respective apartments arguing about the movie industry. George was the idealistic rebel filmmaker ready to abandon the Hollywood system, while Marcia was committed to working her way up the tortuous union seniority ladder until she became a full-fledged editor.

But Lucas and Griffin did eventually find themselves attracted to each other. Perhaps it was the pull of opposite personalities, outgoing Marcia and reserved George, although presumably the "animal attraction" had something to do with it, too. "Marcia and I got along real well," Lucas says, still sounding surprised. "We were both feisty and neither one of us would take any shit from the other. I sort of liked that. I didn't like someone who could be run over." Lucas also respected Marcia as an editor, the part of movie making that was still closest to his heart. "It really becomes your life, and it was Marcia's life, too. That's one of the reasons our relationship works—we both love the same thing."

The love match was surprising given their divergent backgrounds. Marcia grew up on the lower cusp of the middle class, in the suburbs of North Hollywood in Los Angeles's San Fernando Valley. She was an air force brat, born in Modesto only because it had the hospital nearest to Stockton Air Force Base where her father was stationed during the war. Griffin, a career military man, had an off-and-on marriage with Marcia's mother, eventually divorcing her by the time Marcia was two. Mae Griffin took her two daughters to North Hollywood where they all lived with her parents. After Marcia's grandfather died, the Griffins had to move into a small apartment in the neighborhood, and Mae worked as a clerk for a local insurance agency. Financial aid was not forthcoming from Marcia's father, who had remarried and was stationed in Florida; Marcia never knew him while she was growing up. She remembers that time as "a hard life": two new dresses a year, one at Easter and one at Christmas—the rest of her clothes were hand-me-downs from her cousins. "It wasn't a sad, bad time," Marcia remembers. "We had a lot of love and a very supportive family. But economically it was real hard on my mother."

When in her early teens, Marcia went to Florida to live with her father and his new family. The arrangement lasted for two years but never really worked out. She always had been keenly aware of her lack of wealth in a neighborhood where most kids had nice homes and swimming pools, not cramped apartments. Marcia compensated for her material shortcomings by improving herself: "I developed a nice personality and I was fun to be around." She returned to North Hollywood to finish high school and then hoped to go on to college.

Marcia felt a responsibility to help her mother financially and began working days and going to school at night. She got a job at a downtown Los Angeles mortgage banking firm and took chemistry courses at Los Angeles City College. A boyfriend who worked for a Hollywood museum wanted to hire Marcia to catalog donated movie memorabilia. But the only way to get the job was to apply at the California State Employment office for work as a librarian. Instead of the museum job, Marcia was sent to Sandler Film Library, which was looking for an apprentice film librarian, no experience necessary. The job paid less than she was making at the bank, only $50 a week, but she took it. "That's how I started working in film. I just walked in off the street," she says.

It was hard work. Marcia took orders for film footage that producers required, such as shots of a 1940s Ford turning left on a country road at night. If the material fit the scene, she ordered the required negative prints, a highly technical job that Marcia immediately grasped. She also found herself drawn to the instant gratification of editing.

It wasn't easy for an ambitious woman to break into the movie business in the mid-1960s. The more prestigious the editing job, the more likely a man would get it. Marcia worked her way up to assistant editor by the time she was twenty, but a long struggle lay ahead. She never lost sight of the fact that a commercial editor could make $400 a week. She knew her apprenticeship would last at least eight years, and she was ready to tough it out. To improve her skills, she edited trailers and promotional films. "I would have cut film for free because I enjoyed it so much," says Marcia. But advancement was slow. Marcia was told that girls couldn't lift the cans containing ten thousand feet of film and that editors used foul language that wasn't proper for a young lady to hear. "I thought I was a tough cookie, but I didn't realize what I was up against," she says in retrospect.

The job Verna Fields hired Marcia for seemed much the same, although

at a more relaxed pace. As her relationship with George Lucas began to
blossom, Marcia had to question her own goals. George wanted to go to
San Francisco and make avant-garde films. "I'm going to make movies,
and we'll work something out together," he told Marcia. "We'll make
them together and sell them there. It's probably going to be very hard."
Marcia was willing to take the risk because she had already learned
something about George: "Everything was a means to an end. George has
always planned things very far in advance. He always works out in his
head what may happen in a year or two and figures out what all the
possibilities are so that he can handle whatever situation pops up. He's
very good at capitalizing on all the options."

George kept silent about his new relationship, telling his parents only
that he had met a girl who was willing to make him dinner almost every
night. When the Lucases came down for the student-film screening, they
finally met Marcia. "The minute I saw them together, I knew that was it,"
Dorothy Lucas says. That Thanksgiving George took Marcia back to
Modesto for the formal introduction to his family. "He was very, very
open when he was with his family," recalls Marcia. "It was the most open
I had ever seen him. He was open with me, but as soon as it got beyond
just the two of us and our intimacy, he was again very quiet." Marcia was
particularly touched by a comment she overheard George make to his
brother-in-law Roland: "You know, Marcia is the only person I've ever
known who can make me raise my voice," George said. Roland looked at
him and grinned. "That's great, kid. Congratulations—you must be in
love." Marcia had passed the most crucial test of acceptance by George—
she was now part of his family. "I think family is a very important aspect
of the social fabric, it's very basic," says Lucas. There were now two
people who could make George Lucas angry: his father and his wife-to-be.

George's friends were stunned when they first met Marcia. "She was a
knock-out," remembers John Milius. "We all wondered how little George
got this great-looking girl. And smart, too, obsessed with films. And she
was a better editor than he was." John Plummer found Marcia "cute as
hell," but also strong-willed and domineering; he couldn't quite figure out
what someone as reserved as George was doing with such a little dynamo.
Marcia understood what kept her relationship with George in balance:
"We want to complete ourselves, so we look for someone who is strong
where we're weak." George concurs, noting, "Marcia and I are very
different and also very much alike. I say black, she says white. But we
have similar tastes, backgrounds, feelings about things, and philosophies."

To this day, only Marcia is brave enough to take Lucas on in a head-to-head dispute and occasionally emerge victorious. She is acutely aware of the varied roles she plays with her strong-willed, creative, and sometimes repressed husband: "I don't think George is real close and intimate with anyone but me. I've always felt that when you're married, you have to be wife, mother, confidante, and lover, and that I've been all those things to George. I'm the only person he talks to about certain things." If Marcia is sometimes the target of his misplaced anger, she also sees a dimension of Lucas's personality that is almost never publicly displayed: "He's so cute and funny and silly, and I'm the only person who has ever seen that side of him. I wish more people could, but he doesn't want anyone to see it."

Marcia says shyness is the only manifestation of Lucas's insecurity. "He's totally confident and he's totally in control," she marvels. "I'm capable of envy and jealousy—I've felt those emotions throughout my life, and I think they're normal emotions. But they are emotions George doesn't feel. I honestly have never seen George envious or jealous of anyone." Not that Lucas is a saint—Marcia, he says, is more aware than most people of his Machiavellian nature. "I have to admit that I do manage to get things done my way—sometimes when everybody else is dead set against it," Lucas says.

George and Marcia also share a moral sense of right and wrong. Friends call them decent, level-headed, and honest, not adjectives usually heard about successful people in the movie business. Their shared beliefs kept them together through the 1960s and '70s, two of the roughest decades for young married couples. "George's devotion to Marcia is unequaled in any other couple I've seen," says Miki Herman. She remembers working on *Star Wars* and seeing Lucas's eyes fasten devotedly on a picture of Marcia that he kept on the inside cover of his briefcase.

"I always felt I was an optimist because I'm extroverted," Marcia says. "And I always thought that George was more introverted, quiet, and pessimistic." Marcia and George balance each other out—she supplies the aggressiveness he lacks, and his gentleness tempers her abrasiveness.

George is the kind of phenomenon that happens once in a lifetime. I'm convinced he's a genius because he went forward so quickly. He *understands* film, and it's been borne out by what I've seen since he left here.

—Dave Johnson

Lucas had one more goal to meet before he abandoned Los Angeles and headed north with Marcia.[6] He had never made a solo workshop film, one in which he could use all his impressive talents. At a party at Herb Kossower's house in fall 1966, he mentioned an idea he had come up with for a student film, one that Matthew Robbins and Walter Murch might be able to use. "The idea had been boiling around in my mind for a long time," George says. "It was based on the concept that we live in the future and that you could make a futuristic film using existing stuff." Murch and Lucas wrote a one-and-a-quarter-page script about someone escaping from an underground civilization and emerging from a manhole cover at the end, but Robbins and Murch lost their enthusiasm. Lucas wanted to see the movie, so he decided to make it himself. Gene Peters, his old camera instructor, thought there was a way to do that.

Since the 1940s, USC had sponsored a training program for navy filmmakers. The trainees were usually career enlisted men to whom college was a good excuse to ogle girls and drink beer. The USC faculty and students disliked the navy men because of their unimaginative approach to movie making. Peterson's solution was to have Lucas direct his film, using the navy class members as his cast and crew. Lucas liked the idea. He knew that the navy gave its students unlimited color film, plus the lab processing for it. George had access to all the equipment he needed.

The navy students weren't happy to see a scrawny kid with a goatee and bookish glasses introduce himself as their instructor for the coming spring semester. There was outright antagonism from half the sailors, who were twice as old and twice as large as Lucas. George divided the class into two groups. He took one group to make his film, and the ranking navy officer took the remaining students for a different project. "I wanted to make it into something they could understand, which was a contest," Lucas explains.

Although the class ostensibly was about lighting films, Lucas set the tone for his group by telling them that they didn't have to light scenes at all—he would show them how to make a movie using only natural light sources. As George predicted, the contest became a serious macho competition with the navy crew committed to making the short script into a great fifteen-minute movie. "Within a week, those tough navy guys were licking George's boots," marvels Dave Johnson. "I don't understand how a low-profile guy like George can do those things! But they were following him around like puppy dogs." Lucas was allowed navy access to locations that otherwise would have been denied to him: the USC computer science department, an underground parking lot at UCLA, and the Los Angeles International and Van Nuys airports.

The pace was exhausting—Lucas worked weekdays at Verna Fields's house editing President Johnson footage, and each night and every weekend he directed *THX 1138:4EB*, the ultimate homage to his favorite film, *2187*. The story essentially was the same one he and Murch had concocted: an individual's escape from a futuristic society constructed from the reality of 1967. Lucas mixed video images and distorted audio signals and added the title character's search for an ideal mate. The film contains a startling innovation for a student work: computer graphics and numbers running across the bottom of the screen, ticking off the electronic minutes until THX makes good his escape. Lucas offers a mechanistic view of the future (and the present), symbolized by a powerful scene of THX's mind being electronically jammed, like an airplane's radar system.

Lucas edited the film on Fields's Moviola, sometimes working until 3:00 or 4:00 in the morning. He also dubbed the unusual sound track of garbled audio broadcasts. After twelve weeks, the film was done. "I didn't expect it to turn out so well," Lucas says modestly, but he knew exactly what he had done: *THX* had traveling shots, sophisticated graphics, and film optical processes never before seen in a college film. The student screening where it was finally shown turned into a madhouse, the cheering beginning when the opening title flashed on the screen: the USC logo turning from yellow to blood red.

Hollywood noticed, too. *Los Angeles Times* film critic Charles Champlin heard about *THX 1138:4EB* through the movie industry grapevine. "It was a period when there were a lot of good people at USC, but *THX* was an astonishing piece of student work. It wasn't brilliantly absorbing drama, but the whole sense of paranoia and freedom in a bleak, uncertain world was very, very impressive. It was obvious that Lucas was someone to watch." Ned Tanen, then a production executive at Universal Studios, had a similar reaction: "You looked at the movie and said, 'Jesus, who the hell did *this?* I don't know where he stole the footage, but he is someone very special.'" Tanen made a note to find out who the filmmaker was and to keep an eye on him.

Film students from other schools also attended *THX* screenings. A young filmmaker majoring in English at Long Beach State showed up for one screening at UCLA's Royce Hall and briefly was introduced to Lucas. Steven Spielberg recalls, "He reminded me a little bit of Walt Disney's version of a mad scientist. He was so unassuming when I first met him that I couldn't immediately associate him with the power of *THX*, which really moved and influenced me. I never had seen a film created by a peer that was not of this earth—*THX* created a world that did not exist before George designed it. It was hard to believe that here was somebody who knew this side of the camera as well as I thought I did."

Emboldened by his success, Lucas grabbed for the brass ring—a ticket to Hollywood. A student scholarship was offered by Columbia Pictures and producer Carl Foreman (*The Guns of Navarone*) for work on *McKenna's Gold*, a Western adventure starring Gregory Peck, Omar Sharif, Telly Savalas, and Lee J. Cobb, with veteran J. Lee Thompson directing. Two USC and two UCLA students were chosen to direct short films on the making of *McKenna's Gold* at its Utah and Arizona desert locations. There were no young people anywhere in the industry in 1967. Foreman paid for all the equipment and film used by the students and gave them $150 a week in expense money. In exchange, he wanted four promotional features for *McKenna's Gold* that could be shown in theaters or on television.

Lucas hoped to find out what Hollywood was all about: "I didn't really have much feeling about the place. I thought I'd see for myself and know why I disliked it, rather than just saying it out of hand." But he may have had ulterior motives, according to Marcia: "George wanted to direct. One of the reasons he did the Foreman project was to learn about directing and hopefully to make an impression on Foreman."

Lucas and Chuck Braverman from USC and David Wyles and David MacDougal from UCLA were chosen for the program, after extensive screenings of their films by selection committees at each school. (Foreman had been particularly impressed by *THX*.) They drove to Page, Arizona, where they operated as their own independent unit, with no direct supervision. The students had their own station wagon, camera, and lighting equipment, and a free schedule. Each one had to produce a ten-minute, 16-millimeter film that related in some way to *McKenna's Gold*. "Any attitude or approach you want, critical or worshipful," Foreman told them.

Lucas was excited about the money—he figured he could live on $25 a week of his salary and save the other $125 (by the time he arrived back in Los Angeles, he had saved $800). The students quickly chose topics for their films: Braverman did a featurette on Foreman; MacDougal chose director Thompson; and Wyles filmed the horse wranglers, the crew members in charge of the equine performers. Lucas had a different idea. He didn't want to do a film on *somebody;* he wanted to do a visual tone poem. Foreman, who had approval of each script, told Lucas to try something else, but George stood his ground. "I thought the whole thing was a ruse to get a bunch of cheap, behind-the-scenes documentary films made, and they were doing it under the guise of a scholarship," he says. "Well, if they were going to give a scholarship to make a movie, then I wanted to make a movie. I wasn't going to do some promo film to advertise the picture. I was a very hostile kid in those days."

Lucas went off and did his desert poem. Foreman remembers that the other students thought George was a loner. "There was resentment because they thought he was snubbing them," says Foreman. "The others were all helping each other out, acting as the crew, but Lucas was working on his own." Actually, Lucas says he got along well with his colleagues, especially with MacDougal. Still fond of numbers, Lucas called his film *6-18-67,* the day he completed filming it. A solitary exercise, the film begins with soft-focus pictures of desert wildlife and displays an acute awareness of the sights and sounds of the wilderness. There is the unearthly hum of giant power lines and transformers, the slow turning blades of a watermill, and speeded-up footage of clouds racing over a landscape. The contrast between the reality of nature and the artifice being created by the movie crew (which is seen only in long shots of the camera under an umbrella) is clearly established. The film ends with a glorious sunset.

Foreman had changed his mind by the time he finally saw *6-18-67:* "A lot of things were going on in the desert that we weren't paying any attention to. Life went on before us, and life went on after us, and that's what George's film was all about."

Lucas didn't care for what he saw of Hollywood. Although he enjoyed working with Foreman, he thought the whole idea of making a film like *McKenna's Gold* was asinine. "We had never been around such opulence, zillions of dollars being spent every five minutes on this huge, unwieldy thing. It was mind-boggling to us because we had been making films for three hundred dollars, and seeing this incredible waste—that was the worst of Hollywood." Lucas also realized how much in love he was with Marcia, whom he had begun living with before going to Arizona. He wrote her in June 1967: "This film is going to be a film about you because no matter what I'm photographing, I pretend and wish that it is you."[7]

Foreman was particularly impressed by an observation Lucas made to him one afternoon on the set of *McKenna's Gold.* The cast and crew were sitting around after the lunch break, waiting for the sun to come through the clouds. Lucas motioned Foreman over and said, "I've been here since eleven this morning and everyone's waiting for the sun. But they've never rehearsed the scene. I think they'll rehearse when the light comes, but they won't be ready to shoot and they'll lose the light." Foreman was mortified—the young intern was absolutely correct. The producer discreetly went up to director Thompson and asked if he had rehearsed the scene. No, Thompson had said, he hadn't. Foreman suggested he do so, and Thompson agreed it was a good idea. "I was both embarrassed and impressed," Foreman recalls. "That director hadn't done something that this kid knew to do."

Lucas felt he had accomplished something in Arizona and was really coming into his own for the first time. His confidence was further boosted by a series of prizes he won at the National Student Film Festival. The major showcase for student work was in its third year in 1967 when Lucas entered films in three categories: *THX 1138:4EB* for dramatic films, *The Emperor* for documentaries, and *6-18-67* for experimental works. The judges initially voted to award Lucas the first prize in all three areas; he would have made a clean sweep, except he hadn't entered an animated film, an award that went to John Milius for *Marcello, I'm So Bored*, which Lucas had edited. The judges had second thoughts about awarding so many major prizes to one student, however, so they ended up giving *THX* the dramatic prize, and honorable mentions to his other films. Lucas and Milius, along with the previous year's winner Martin Scorsese from New York University, were featured in a *Time* magazine article that Milius still recalls with amusement. It showed him sitting at an editing machine—"I couldn't even operate one of those damn things," he says with a laugh. "George did all the editing on my films."

Lucas decided to give Hollywood one more chance. Before going to Arizona for *McKenna's Gold*, he had entered a scholarship competition sponsored by Warner Bros. It enabled a student to observe the studio's operation for six months, picking a particular department to work in. The finalists were Lucas and Walter Murch, and on the afternoon of the last interviews they sat on the USC patio waiting for the decision. Murch recalls, "We made this kind of Huck Finn and Tom Sawyer bond that whoever got the scholarship, if anything came out of it, he would help the other guy and spread the wealth. The idea that anything *would* come out of it was so remote that we didn't take it very seriously."

Lucas won, intending to work in Warner's animation studio, famous for the Bugs Bunny and Looney Tunes cartoons. But the department was closed, a victim of Hollywood's economic depression in the 1960s. Only one production was shooting on the Burbank lot, a musical called *Finian's Rainbow*, based on the popular Broadway show of the same name. The director was a bearded young man named Francis Coppola, not much older than Lucas, who was a legend in the student film community. Lucas recalls, "Francis Coppola had directed his first picture as a UCLA student and now, Jesus, he got a feature to direct! It sent shock waves through the student film world because nobody else had ever done that. It was a big event." Lucas began to hang around the *Finian's* set and was impressed by Coppola's self-confidence. Coppola remembers, "I was working on the show and there was this skinny kid, watching for the second day in a row. You always feel uncomfortable when there's a stranger watching you, so I went up to him and asked who he was." Lucas explained his situation and asked Coppola if he could work with him.

"We started a conversation and a friendship," Coppola says. Their friendship endures to this day; it has had a vital and dramatic effect on the lives of both men as well as on millions of moviegoers.

4
COPING WITH COPPOLA

He's one of the best. He's outwitted the empire on numerous occasions, and he's made some very fast deals. One of his problems is that he gambles quite heavily and that's where he loses most of his money. He's tough and sharp, only somehow he never manages to scrape together enough to get any power. . . . He's slightly self-destructive and he sort of enjoys being on the brink of disaster. . . . You might meet him and he may be worth ten billion dollars, and the next time you meet him he's in debt up to his ears.

—George Lucas describing Han Solo

The day George Lucas walked onto the Warner Bros. lot to begin his apprenticeship with Francis Coppola on *Finian's Rainbow* was the day Jack Warner cleaned out his office and left. The venerable studio, started in 1922 by Harry, Jack, Albert, and Sam Warner, had been sold to a television packaging firm, hastening the departure of the last of the moguls. *Finian's Rainbow* was the final movie ordered under Warner's regime. Lucas became one of the first new employees of Warner Bros.–Seven Arts, signing an agreement on July 31, 1967, to be Coppola's administrative assistant. He was paid just over $3,000 for six months' work.

The Burbank studio, equipped with Western, turn-of-the-century, and contemporary one-dimensional streets, resembled a ghost town when Lucas arrived. *Finian's Rainbow* was the only activity. Visiting the animation department, Lucas found a lone executive sitting behind a huge desk, waiting for the phone to ring. Old Hollywood was dead. It seemed only natural for Lucas to gravitate toward the new Hollywood, in the person of

Coppola, the only man on the lot with a beard, a film school degree, and a birth certificate less than fifty years old. It was a fateful meeting: Coppola was to become the major influence on Lucas's career.

Lucas was twenty-two at the time, Coppola just five years older, but the similarities ended there. Coppola was burly, boisterous, and outspoken, a sharp contrast to the taciturn, self-effacing Lucas. Ron Colby, Coppola's assistant, remembers Lucas "standing there in his black chino pants, white T-shirt, and white sneakers, day in and day out. He had a little goatee and looked like a back-room engineer. He was just very quietly always there, watching, looking, and listening."

Coppola took an immediate liking to the diffident young man: "I was very grateful to have someone of my own generation around to discuss what I was trying to do as opposed to what I was able to do. I very quickly became aware of his superior intelligence." Lucas had his reasons for attaching himself to Coppola. He hoped to make a good impression on people he thought might be able to help him. His original plan was to spend six months at Warner Bros., go back to USC to complete his master's degree, and then move up to San Francisco to direct commercials and educational films, making personal avant-garde movies in his spare time. Lucas left himself a Hollywood escape hatch, however. Carl Foreman had responded favorably to his suggestion that *THX* be turned into a feature film and had advised George to write a story treatment which he would try to place with Columbia Pictures.

After two weeks of watching Coppola struggle with *Finian's Rainbow,* which starred Fred Astaire, Petula Clark, and a bunch of fat midgets in leprechaun costumes, Lucas felt he had seen enough. He thought that if he could scrounge up enough film, he could make his own small movie while at Warner's. Coppola was insulted by the idea of George walking away from his production. "What do you mean, you're leaving? Aren't I entertaining enough? Have you learned everything you're going to learn watching me direct?" Coppola yelled.

"There's nothing to do over here," Lucas responded, typically laconic. He explained his plans for *THX,* but Coppola was quick to warn him that the studios would only rip off a young filmmaker. "Francis was just beginning to flex his mogul wings then," remembers Lucas, one of the first directors taken under those wings. Coppola offered Lucas a permanent job on *Finian's* and on the next film he was planning, *The Rain People,* and promised to help on the *THX* screenplay. George agreed.

Ron Colby remembers seeing Lucas and Coppola together: "George was literally half of Francis—half the size, half the beard, half in every dimension." It wasn't difficult to overshadow Lucas—he was easily missed, tending to blend into the background. George was acutely aware that he didn't possess Coppola's glib patter or his ability to wheel and deal with the Hollywood power brokers.

The Rain People was a small, personal drama about a housewife (Shirley Knight) escaping suburban life by driving across the country; along the way, she picks up a brain-damaged hitchhiker (James Caan in his movie debut). Coppola began shooting the film without a deal for any studio to finance and release it. "Francis has a tendency to just *do* things," Lucas says. Coppola wrote the script in a couple of weeks while still directing *Finian's*. Lucas and several other Coppolytes dutifully went to New York that Thanksgiving to film flashback sequences of Caan's football games at Coppola's alma mater, Hofstra University. George was assistant cameraman, art director, production manager, and did most of the sound recording. This was *real* movie making!

Coppola was living the dream George had always nourished. Here was a man who had an idea for a film, wrote and directed it, then made it the way he wanted to, with no studio executive or producer, *no one,* telling him what to do artistically. Lucas was hopelessly smitten with the idea of the personal film. There was also something adventurous and roguish about striking across the country in a caravan of trucks and cars, invading locations and their cheap motels, waging art as an army might wage war. Sleeping four crew members to a room brought back Lucas's memories of his racing days, a favorite (and romantic) period in his life. He became the production's boy friday, the official sounding board for the stream of ideas constantly emanating from Coppola's fertile imagination.

Francis also made sure George worked on his *THX* script, which Coppola planned to take to Warner Bros. as part of a package of movie ideas. To prove his good intentions, Coppola had Warner Bros.–Seven Arts advance Lucas $3,000 as an option on *THX.* The payment also became George's salary for working on *Rain People.* Lucas laughs about it now: "I was making money for writing the screenplay rather than for working on the film, so in effect, Francis got a free crew member."

Lucas didn't mind working for nothing. He was impressed by Coppola's respect for artistic freedom and his enthusiasm for the all-for-one, one-for-all concept of film making. Coppola even passed out "unofficial certificates redeemable for original certificates good for one percent of the film's net profits" to each cast and crew member. (There were no net profits.) Tensions did arise; the twenty-three members of the *Rain People* company had to adjust to lots of time in Howard Johnson motels in the middle of nowhere. "It was very nerve-wracking," Lucas remembers. Coppola had ruled that no wives or girlfriends could accompany the group, but the director excluded himself from the restriction. Lucas remembers sitting in a motel room in Blue Ball, Pennsylvania, that had no phone, TV, or restaurant, while Coppola spent the weekend in New York. "I got a little angry about that," Lucas recalls. "Francis was saying all this 'all-for-one' stuff and then he goes off and screws around in New York. He felt he had a right to do that, and I told him it wasn't fair. We got into a big fight over it."

If there was trouble in paradise, it quickly blew over. Lucas was having the time of his life, and Coppola knew it. "We actually had a lot of fun on that trip," reminisces Lucas. "It was rugged, but for all us young clowns, it was a great time." The experience seemed perfect material for a documentary. Coppola was making a small, intimate film about real-life people. Lucas decided to make a small, intimate, *cinéma vérité* diary about the real-life people making *Rain People*. *Filmmaker,* the documentary that resulted, was designed as a personal statement about the daily strains and stresses of a movie production in constant motion. Lucas found an unused camera and asked Coppola if he could make a little behind-the-scenes film. The idea intrigued Coppola, who liked being in front of the camera almost as much as behind it. He paid for Lucas's film out of the movie's budget for still photographs and gave George the go-ahead sign.

But Lucas had to make his documentary without getting in the way. There were other problems, too. "George could not carry a sixteen-millimeter camera for very long," says Mona Skager, another Coppola associate who worked on *Rain People*. Skager often saw Lucas on the floor, shooting up through glass-topped tables. "It was basically because the camera was too heavy," she recalls with a chuckle. Lucas was a one-man band, his camera and his tape recorder at the ready. He devised a system of preparing his equipment so he could run over to the camera, pick it up, and immediately begin shooting.

Lucas had only $12,000 to make *Filmmaker,* not much for a professional-looking half-hour documentary. He experimented by shooting it without a light meter, testing whether he could gauge the available light with his naked eye. Coppola was tolerant of his ambitious assistant, although occasionally he would scowl at the camera when it invaded his privacy. Lucas wasn't afraid to film some tense confrontations between Coppola and actress Shirley Knight, but he ultimately rejected most of the footage. "I decided to be discreet," Lucas says with a smile. "I didn't want to destroy anyone's career."

Filmmaker remains one of the best documentaries about the production of a movie, as fresh and insightful today as it was in 1968. Subtitled "a diary by george lucas," the thirty-minute film has the fluidity and detail of a written journal coupled with a cinematic sense of movement as the *Rain People* company goes from location to location. The Coppola seen in the film is thinner than today's movie maverick, but his anguish over what he perceives as attempts to destroy his artistic vision is the same: "I'm tired of being the anchor when I see my world crumbling," he says at one point. Coppola emerges from *Filmmaker* a bearded prophet of doom for the dinosaurlike studio system—in one animated phone conversation with a Warner Bros. executive, Coppola shrieks, "The system will fall by its own weight! It can't fail to!"

Coppola's presence dominates *Filmmaker,* although at one point he seems to disappear from the movie. During a swing through the Southwest, the hirsute members of the crew, including Lucas, had to shave off their beards and trim their hair—this was 1968, after all. Without his tangle of a black beard, Coppola was unrecognizable, and Lucas had to add a voice-over narration explaining the sudden transformation. "That was a wonderful scene," says Walter Murch. "Nobody knew who he was or would listen to what Francis said when he didn't have his beard. It was like Samson's hair." Lucas also captures the spontaneity with which Coppola made *Rain People.* The director is shown frantically rewriting scenes to fit a patriotic parade the crew had stumbled on in Chattanooga, Tennessee. Stricken by the flu, Coppola describes how he had to keep running to the rest room in the bus station while filming the parade. He spent so much time there that he decided to film a key scene in the Greyhound station. This was hardly the stuff taught in film school.

The final shot of *Filmmaker* shows the cast and crew posed in front of a caravan of prop and equipment trucks, looking like nineteenth-century dramatic troupers coming home from a tour through the hinterlands. Standing atop one of the trucks, seen for the first time in the film, is George Lucas, wearing a white T-shirt and carrying a camera that looks bigger than he is. Inexplicably, Lucas stands out in the scene, a weird portent of things to come.

George and Marcia edited *Filmmaker* at their Portola Drive house. When they were finished, the film had the look of a professional movie, not the work of just another cinema graduate. *Filmmaker* is still used in USC classes as an example of a first-rate documentary. Lucas was proud of it, too—*Filmmaker* was his most ambitious effort to date, and it worked. It also helped advance his career.

There is disagreement between the way things are and the way I think things should be.[1]
—Francis Coppola, speaking at a February 1981 press conference

If there is a major influence on the way George Lucas lives, it is Francis Coppola. Through a combination of friendship and rivalry, Lucas and Coppola have interwoven their careers and personalities in a strange and sometimes sad saga. "My life is a kind of reaction against Francis's life," Lucas says—he is openly emotional about the subject. Coppola is impulsive and daring, Lucas is cautious and conservative; Coppola's gregariousness finds counterpoint in Lucas's reserve. "I'm his antithesis," Lucas says of the man he both admires and resents.

Their backgrounds could not be more dissimilar. Lucas came from the Midwest, transplanted to California; Coppola grew up in a New York Italian family of artistic gypsies; his father, Carmine, was a volatile and talented composer and musician. Lucas was dubbed the "seventy-year-old kid" by Coppola, who sees himself as a sixteen-year-old adolescent. Yet it is Lucas who has made millions from reshaping his childhood, and Coppola who has achieved less financial success with mature "message" movies. "All directors have egos and are insecure," according to Lucas. "But of all the people I know, Francis has the biggest ego and the biggest insecurities."

Francis became George's mentor and his closest friend in the movie business. His influence was total; he even inspired Lucas to grow a full beard, making him a junior Samson. Coppola once told Lucas, "If you grow a beard, people will respect you more." Lucas admired Coppola to the point of hero worship but never knuckled under to him for a second. "George always used to say, 'I'm watching Francis and trying to learn from all his mistakes,'" remembers Richard Tong, the accountant for first Coppola and then Lucas.

It was difficult for a young filmmaker to resist Coppola in the late 1960s—Francis was the latest Hollywood Svengali, luring young talent to his side with hypnotic ease. "Francis is very big in both George's and my lives," explains Carroll Ballard. "We owe him the fact that we're making films today, but he also laid a big power trip on both of us that we're still smarting from." Coppola has always engendered strong emotions among his friends and enemies. Some call him a lovable madman, others label him a megalomaniac. John Milius says, "As Talleyrand said of Napoleon, 'He's as great as a man can be, without virtue.'" For Willard Huyck and

Gloria Katz, "Being with Francis is tiring. Every time we work with him, we have to rest for a week."

No one disputes Coppola's talent, willpower, or determination. Stricken by polio at an early age, he grew up dreaming about making his own little movies and building a tiny sound boom out of wood. The dreams became real in the early 1960s when he apprenticed himself to Roger Corman, a low-budget movie producer who acted as an unofficial film industry guidance counselor/exploiter. Eventually Coppola directed a film, *Dementia 13,* in Ireland; he wrote the screenplay in three nights. Coppola was not afraid to work in Hollywood, which is why he took on *Finian's Rainbow.* He worked within the system only so he could take it over, however. Coppola didn't want to eliminate movie moguls—he wanted to replace them.

Coppola was the first bona fide Hollywood character Lucas had encountered. "He has charisma beyond logic. I can see now what kind of men the great Caesars of history were, their magnetism. That's one reason I tolerate as much as I do from Francis. I'm fascinated by how he works and why people follow him so blindly," Lucas says. From the outset of their relationship, George and Francis were an odd couple: the expansive, older Italian-American, hugging everybody in sight, surrounding himself with stimulating people; and the shy, small-town rube, fierce in his determination to be successful on his own terms. Their relationship thrived because they were opposites—Francis loved being in the spotlight, and George didn't mind standing in his shadow.

Coppola sees his relationship with Lucas (and now their respective film companies) as similar to the rivalry between UCLA and USC's film schools, the soulful poets versus the cold technocrats. Lucas knew Coppola lacked the technical sophistication he and Walter Murch brought to the editing of a movie. Lucas once told Murch, "Francis is really talented, but he needs *us.* He's great with actors and dramatic stuff, but his films need the other stuff that we do well." By combining their respective skills, Lucas and Coppola made a strong team. "There was a balance," Coppola said of the time he and Lucas worked closely together. "We can do more together than either of us can alone. One could fantasize what *Star Wars* would have been like had I produced it, or *Apocalypse Now* with him as producer."

Lucas agrees that he and Coppola "were like two halves of a whole. I was always putting on the brakes and he was always stepping on the gas. It was good for me, because it loosened me up and got me to take more chances. I realized that you can jump off the cliff and survive ninety-nine percent of the time. And the one percent of the time Francis didn't make it, he made it look like he did." Coppola never let Lucas forget who the senior partner was in their relationship, however. Coppola liked to think of himself as the real-life equivalent to Don Corleone, Marlon Brando's character in *The Godfather*, even to the point of printing up matchbooks inscribed, "Francis Ford Coppola: The Godfather." Deborah Fine, who worked for Coppola in the Zoetrope years, explains, "Francis loves the idea that he is the mentor and creator of the people he has given a start to, George being one of them. And he doesn't like to let go of that idea once they're on their own feet and successful. Francis loves the idea that they are *forever* in his debt because, after all, he gave them their start."

Aware of this, Lucas carefully kept his independence from Coppola. The complex relationship that evolved was made up of both gratitude and resentment, and it is shared by most of Coppola's protégés. "Somewhere along the line, Francis became worried about the competition, so he decided to become our father and steer our futures," Carroll Ballard says. "I think he feels we're all very ungrateful, ambitious assholes for abandoning him after he gave us our start." Lucas talks about the impression Coppola gives that "people disappear when they walk out of the room. He has no conception that people live their lives after they leave him. He finds it incredible that people do things he doesn't wish them to do, since he's controlling it all and they're all here for *him.*"

Coppola's defenders see his Godfather qualities in a more positive light. Ron Colby insists that "if it hadn't been for Francis, *THX* never would have gotten made anywhere, at any time, as a major feature, especially with George directing. The fact that George got a shot at directing can only be attributed to Francis. George would have ended up making documentary films for Northrup and Sperry-Rand for at least a decade before he got a shot at doing anything, if ever."

Comments such as Colby's raise Lucas's hackles and make him defensive and angry. "My feeling was and still is that if I was destined to make movies, I would have. I was going to make *THX* whether I did it with Francis or not. Francis helped me and gave me a chance, but at the same time, he made a lot of money off me. Francis has a tendency to see the parade marching down the street and to run in front of it with a flag and become the leader." Lucas prefers that no one lead his parade but George Lucas. Coppola's competitiveness has always put him off, and as Lucas notes, "I have a lot of very competitive friends."

But the similarities between the two men often exceed their differences. Both have retained a childlike quality that has made them movie vision-

A sunny disposition: George Lucas at age 2.

A rare Lucas family portrait, circa 1950, unusual for Dorothy's presence since she was often in the hospital or bedridden during this period. From left: Wendy (age 4), Dorothy, George, Sr., George, Jr. (age 6); kneeling are Kate (age 16) and Ann (age 17).

The car crash that changed the life of George Lucas and propelled him to success. This photograph, taken shortly after the accident on June 12, 1962, was featured on the front page of the local paper, Modesto Bee.

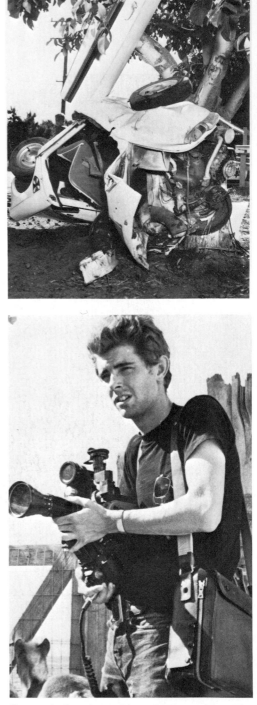

Portrait of the artist as a teen-aged punk: George in junior high school in 1959.

George during the making of Filmmaker, *his documentary about the filming of* Rain People, *which was directed by Francis Coppola in July 1968.*

George looking like the dashing, romantic moviemaker he never thought he could be, taken during the editing of Filmmaker *in San Francisco, February 1969.*

The New Hollywood in its 1970 incarnation, striking a dramatic pose atop the San Francisco headquarters of American Zoetrope. From left: *John Korty, Carroll Ballard, an unknown filmmaker, John Milius, Barry Beckerman, Zoetrope Vice-President George Lucas, Al Locatelli, Bob Dalva, Zoetrope President Francis Coppola. Kneeling (from left) are* THX *Producer Larry Sturhahn and Dennis Jakob. Courtesy of John Korty*

Gary Kurtz, coproducer, and George Lucas, director, on the set of American Graffiti.

George Lucas with his wife, the former Marcia Griffin, two years after their marriage, in front of their Marin County home in 1971.

Lucas and his friends clown around after visiting the shark for Steven Spielberg's Jaws *at Universal Studios in 1974.* From left: *Hal Barwood, Gloria Katz, Lucas, Gary Kurtz, Colin Cantwell (designer of the prototype spaceships for* Star Wars), *and Willard Huyck.*

The agony of writing Star Wars *is apparent in the grim features of Lucas as he did one final rewrite of the screenplay in Tunisia in March 1976. Filming was to begin in a matter of weeks.*

Peter Mayhew (Chewbacca) displays an understandable reluctance to descend into the muck of the garbage compactor, but Lucas is insistent. Mayhew's costume retained an unpleasant odor for the duration of the filming.

George Lucas and Mark Hamill (Luke Skywalker) confer on the desert wastes of Tunisia, April 1976. Lucas was already behind schedule, and none of the "gadgets" (like R2-D2) would work.

The dejected filmmaker: George Lucas ponders everything that's gone wrong on the Elstree Studios set of Star Wars, *June 1976.*

Lucas explains a scene to Mark Hamill (left) and Harrison Ford (Han Solo), who are in stormtrooper outfits in their attempt to liberate Princess Leia.

George and Marcia and a fake Jerba relax in front of the Space Cantina set in Tunisia, April 1976.

aries. They also share a love of technology and gadgets, adult playthings that are the equivalent of the train sets both played with as youngsters. Bunny Alsup, Lucas's secretary during the making of *American Graffiti,* remembers a Christmas dinner at the Lucases' home which the Coppolas attended. Lucas brought out his old Lionel train set, and he and Francis spent hours racing the engines over and over the track. "It was amazing to see George and Francis literally on the floor playing with toys," Alsup recalls. The toys have simply become more expensive: electronic editing systems, computer graphics, and film-to-video transfers. Lucas and Coppola were heading down the same track, even if they didn't know it.

The two young upstarts shared a heady feeling of rebellion in Hollywood in the socially turbulent late 1960s. "We would walk into the commissary and everybody would be just horrified because here were all these beards and hair," Mona Skager recalls of the times she accompanied Francis and George to lunch. Coppola may not have been the revolutionary he appeared to be, however. Lucas's resentment over the attitude Coppola displayed during the making of *Rain People* was the beginning of a moral disagreement over the right and wrong way to treat people. Lucas thought they should be treated with dignity, their self-respect encouraged, and their independence furthered. Coppola believed that the leader should be rewarded for his vision and expertise and that the less talented simply had to accept that value system.

The basic difference between Coppola and Lucas comes down to George's desire to redefine the rules of the game and Francis's desire to take over the game. Coppola is like a brilliant field general, a motivator and leader of people, while Lucas is more the chief petty officer, concerned with details and strategy. Today Lucas runs his company like a Fortune 500 corporation, while Coppola's Zoetrope Studios resembled an ensemble theater led by a mad director. "Francis and George are about the most opposite people who ever lived," says Haskell Wexler. It is the visionary versus the pragmatist and even their movies reflect these differences: Coppola's are cinematic opera, played on a grand and glorious scale; Lucas sees his films as dumb entertainments and sideshows. There are few pretensions to Lucas, whereas he recalls being very aware of Coppola inflating *Rain People* into Film Art.

"Francis depends on defying gravity through sheer will," Lucas observes. "That's why we didn't always get along. I was on the other side, looking at reality and saying that we were going to fall. I've always been in awe of that side of Francis and I still am. It's way beyond anything I can comprehend."

Another reason for the growing gulf between Coppola and Lucas was a basic difference in lifestyles. George and Marcia Lucas are quiet people who have dinner at home most nights, do little entertaining, and only occasionally travel. As for Coppola, Marcia wryly observes, "There's never a dull moment. There are always ten or twenty or thirty people around, with somebody sitting down and playing the piano in that corner of the room, and some kids dancing around in that corner of the room, and the intellectuals having a deep conversation about art in another corner of the room. His life is just in a constant state of upheaval." Marcia feels that for all his success and fame, Coppola lacks Lucas's calm sense of certainty. Coppola himself acknowledges this: "I bring to my life a certain amount of mess, and George, above all, is terrified to be embroiled in something like this. He wants his life to be orderly."

It's sort of romantic, like kids picking oranges in an old Jane Powell movie.[2]
—Francis Coppola on the marriage of George and Marcia Lucas

While George was with Coppola, first on *Finian's Rainbow* and then on *Rain People,* Marcia continued working for commercial production companies. Back in New York for the start of filming on *Rain People,* George missed her more than ever, and she finally joined him. "It was so wonderful and romantic and emotional to see each other in New York because we had been separated for a long time," Marcia recalls. Taking the train to the next location in Garden City, Long Island, on a rainy February day in 1967, Lucas proposed. Marcia accepted and they decided to get married as soon as *Rain People* was finished. "I was beginning to see where my life was going," Lucas says. "Marcia's career was in Los Angeles and I respected that. I didn't want her to give it up and have me drag her to San Francisco unless there was some commitment on my side."

The new bond was tested just a few weeks later. The *Rain People* troupe had settled in Ogallala, Nebraska, for five weeks, and editor Barry Malkin needed help organizing the footage. Lucas mentioned to Coppola that his girlfriend was a good assistant editor, and Francis agreed to hire her. George excitedly called Marcia with the news, only to be met with uncertainty on her part. Haskell Wexler wanted Marcia to come to Chicago as assistant editor on *Medium Cool.* Marcia found herself in a dilemma: if she went to Chicago, she would earn her first credit on a feature film, and *Medium Cool* promised to be a six-to-nine-month job;

George was offering her only five weeks' worth of work in Nebraska. When the company returned to Los Angeles, her services would no longer be needed.

"I'm really going to have to think about this," Marcia told George. "Don't you want to be with me? Don't you miss me?" he asked. Years later, Marcia reflected on her decision to join Lucas in Nebraska, which went against all her instincts. "I was poor, right? Financial security was very important to me. I wanted to make it my own way. But we were engaged, we were terribly in love, so I decided to go." It turned out that after she returned home, she still could work as an assistant editor on *Medium Cool,* and she ended up with a credit after all. She got the best of both worlds.

On February 22, 1969, George Walton Lucas, Jr., and Marcia Lou Griffin were married at the United First Methodist Church in Pacific Grove, just south of Monterey, California. Marcia's mother, Mae, was there, as were George's parents, his sisters, and a representative sampling of Lucas's Hollywood cronies, including Coppola, Walter Murch, Hal Barwood, Matthew Robbins, even Verna Fields. John Plummer was George's best man. Immediately after the reception, the newlyweds departed for Big Sur and a Northern California honeymoon. They visited Marin County and decided to settle there. Marcia found a hilltop house in Mill Valley for only $120 a month. "We were really happy and optimistic," Lucas recalls. The house was small, but George didn't care. "In our lifestyle there were only two rooms we used, the kitchen and the bedroom. We were in either one or the other," he explains.

Marcia was glad to be in San Francisco, even though her family and friends were in Southern California. She had hoped to find work quickly, but no jobs turned up, and she soon found herself lonesome and homesick. Marcia was ready to have a baby, but George balked at the idea. They had only been married a short time, he didn't have a steady income, and he wasn't sure he would get the opportunity to direct a feature film. "He didn't want the extra responsibility at that time because he might be forced into taking a job that he didn't want to take," Marcia explains.

Marcia tried to busy herself as best she could. She tended their little house and encouraged George as he and Coppola began the arduous task of setting up American Zoetrope. The Lucases were the picture of domesticity—George's parents remember a visit from their son and new daughter-in-law during which George playfully ordered Marcia around. "Wife, do this, do that," he commanded. "He was just playing, but they had a wonderful relationship," Dorothy Lucas explains, contentment in her voice. "Marcia spoiled George terribly when he was making films. She'd bring him breakfast in bed after the nights he worked late."

Marcia's opportunity finally came. Michael Ritchie, another Hollywood director who had moved to San Francisco, offered her a job as an assistant editor on *The Candidate,* which starred a young actor named Robert Redford. Ritchie found Marcia to be skillful, reliable, and creative, and recommended her to his friend, director Martin Scorsese. Marcia became the editor on Scorsese's movies *Alice Doesn't Live Here Anymore* and *Taxi Driver.* Both were difficult jobs, given the tremendous amount of footage Scorsese shot, but Marcia became more confident about her editing skills when the movies were released to critical raves. The only drawback was working in Los Angeles while George was in Mill Valley; although Scorsese usually filmed his movies in New York, all the editing and postproduction work was done in Hollywood.

"What Marcia was doing was very difficult," says Willard Huyck who, with his wife Gloria Katz, is among the Lucases' closest friends. "George wasn't going berserk or anything, but he wasn't very happy about the situation." Gloria Katz chimes in: "That was actually a very big step for George; it was consciousness raising." It was not in the Lucas family tradition to allow a wife to build an independent career of her own. George hated cooking and cleaning in Marcia's absence and soon hired a housekeeper. He was happy to see his wife working, but his frustration about his own career was mounting. The dream of American Zoetrope had become a reality—and it was beginning to turn into a nightmare.

The essential objective of the company is to engage in the varied fields of filmmaking, collaborating with the most gifted and youthful talent using the most contemporary techniques and equipment possible.[3]
—From the announcement of the formation of American Zoetrope

The vision was so romantic: a film community composed of participants aged thirty and under, sharing ideas and equipment in the green solitude of Marin County, establishing a peaceful alternative to the barren wastes of Hollywood. The goal was to create a haven where contracts were immoral and agents were immaterial; a homey, rural base, not a sterile reflection of the emptiness of Los Angeles; a Camelot where young and untried moviemakers could follow the philosophy according to Saint Francis Coppola: "Film is the ultimate form of expression."

The dream had its genesis in the unlikeliest of places, the Lakeway

Lodge in Ogallala, Nebraska, during the making of *The Rain People*. Coppola and his cast and crew discussed a simple idea: movies can be made anywhere. You don't have to be under the thumb of a big studio. The city fathers of Ogallala, enjoying their brief flirtation with Hollywood, good-naturedly offered to turn an abandoned grain warehouse into a sound stage. Silly as the idea seemed, it added impetus to the thoughts shared by Lucas and Coppola. "We started fantasizing about the notion of going to San Francisco, to be free to produce films as we had done on *Rain People*. It was a beautiful place to live and had an artistic, bohemian tradition," Francis says.

Lucas missed the camaraderie he had known in film school and saw Zoetrope as a means of reuniting the participants and reviving the spirit from USCinema's patio. He became a confirmed believer when he substituted for Coppola at a 1968 San Francisco forum for high school English teachers on "Film in Relation to the Printed Word." It's difficult to think of a poorer choice than George Lucas to speak about the relation of anything to the printed word, especially in front of eight hundred English teachers. But his appearance proved fortuitous as John Korty, the only filmmaker actually making a living in San Francisco in 1968, was also on the panel. Korty had started as a documentary director, moving to Stinson Beach, a particularly secluded area of Marin County, in 1961. There he made three feature films in four years for a total cash outlay of $250,000—*Crazy Quilt, Funnyman,* and *Riverrun*—making him one of the most successful independent directors in the country.

Lucas sat enthralled as Korty outlined his maverick career; as soon as the seminar ended, he pulled Korty over to a pay phone and told him that he must speak to Coppola. When George reached Francis in Ogallala he was so excited he could barely speak. "Francis, you've got to talk to John Korty," he yelled over the phone. "He's *doing* what we've been talking about." Coppola, Lucas, and Ron Colby agreed to meet Korty at his Stinson Beach studio on July 4, when *Rain People* would be finished, and sure enough, they turned up at the door of the big gray barn on Independence Day. "Their mouths just dropped open," Korty remembers of his guests' reaction to his well-equipped facility. "They said this was exactly what they had fantasized. They hadn't realized anyone could actually do it."

After delivering *Rain People* to Warner Bros., Coppola and Colby visited Lanterna Films, a small film studio in Denmark that had one of the most complete collections of magic lanterns and other early film projectors. The studio was located fifty miles outside of Copenhagen, occupying a beautiful mansion in a grassy setting. The bedrooms had been transformed into editing rooms with the latest equipment, and in a barn to the side of the house was a sound-mixing facility.

Coppola and Colby had lunch on the huge lawn and decided that this was the environment they would re-create in Marin County. Coppola was particularly taken with the expensive equipment he saw at Lanterna: "I had this notion that the new technology was going to be the magic ingredient that would enable us to succeed. We had the naive notion that it was the equipment which would give us the means of production. Of course, we learned much later that it wasn't the equipment, it was the money." Bitten by the technological bug, Coppola stopped at a film trade show in Cologne, Germany, where impulsively he bought a complete sound-mixing studio for almost $80,000. He didn't have the money, he didn't have a place to put the equipment when it arrived, and he didn't have any films to mix.

In June 1969, Coppola, George Lucas, Ron Colby, and Mona Skager arrived in San Francisco to look for a large Victorian house that would duplicate the Lanterna setting. The company's name reflected Lanterna's influence, too: a Zoetrope was a device that projected moving images as its cylinder was spun; Coppola had been given one as a gift. The Greek root of Zoetrope means "life movement," and Coppola felt it was the perfect symbol for his dynamic young film company. Together with John Korty, the newcomers scoured the small Marin towns of Ross, Inverness, and Tomales Bay for a suitable location, with little luck. Bids on three houses all fell through, and Coppola was getting worried—the equipment would soon arrive from Germany.

A disagreement developed between Coppola and Lucas over the setting and philosophy for the new company. Coppola wanted Zoetrope to be a full-fledged studio, complete with landing pads for helicopters and parking lots for mobile production vans. Lucas wanted "a nice little house to work in." Coppola was putting up the money, however, by selling his house and pooling what few assets he had. When a warehouse became available in downtown San Francisco, Coppola immediately signed a long-term lease. American Zoetrope was born, not in the bucolic splendor of Marin County but in a warehouse loft at 827 Folsom Street. Lanterna Films it was not.

Yet the goal had been achieved. "We wanted to get away from what we all viewed then as the oppressive atmosphere of Hollywood," Ron Colby explains. "It seemed like a good idea to go off and be autonomous. There wasn't the feeling that you were showing up at the factory every day. In any event, it was our factory." Coppola believed Zoetrope could become the new elite of the film business. Lucas saw it as a regrouping of the Dirty Dozen; he invited John Milius, Matthew Robbins, Hal Barwood, Willard Huyck, Gloria Katz, and Walter Murch to join him in the venture.

Lucas wasn't pleased with the dingy building—he had hoped for something more countrified. But he loved the idea of a guild of filmmakers removed from the moral squalor of Los Angeles. The editing equipment soon arrived from Germany, in the midst of the extensive renovation work being done to the warehouse, and was set up in the hallway. Lucas recalls of Zoetrope's early days, "It was like trying to put together a bicycle for Christmas when the kids will be up in an hour—you've got to get the whole thing together quickly, things are going wrong, and there are no instructions."

Lucas had suggested calling the company Transamerican Sprocket Works, but Francis had plans to go public and wanted the name to be on top of the New York Stock Exchange board. He also thought George's suggestion was too whimsical and would put off potential investors. Not that the investors were lining up when the papers for American Zoetrope were filed on November 14, 1969. The company's sole shareholder, Coppola, was also its president; Lucas was vice-president, and Mona Skager was secretary-treasurer. It was an unusual board of directors: Coppola bubbling with enthusiasm, Skager coolly skeptical, and Lucas— "a very sweet, shy, serious-minded person, rather unassuming," Skager recalls. No one had much money, although some was due when *Rain People* was released by Warner Bros. The carpenters worked side by side with the sound mixers, building separate offices of equal size for Coppola, Lucas, and Korty, who became Zoetrope's first official tenant. By the time construction was finished, Zoetrope did indeed resemble a ministudio, lacking only a film lab. The feeling of accomplishment was heady. "We were all, I thought, independent filmmakers pooling our resources," says Korty.

Coppola's democratic philosophy nagged at Lucas as Zoetrope began to attract other filmmakers. "Francis would give a camera to the guy sweeping floors if he had expressed the desire to use one," George says, exaggerating only slightly. Lucas felt Coppola exploited cinema school graduates because of their eagerness to learn and was especially resentful of Coppola's oft-stated determination to sign the Zoetrope family of filmmakers to long-term contracts. The man who once had called "contract" a dirty word had come full circle in his thinking. Coppola used to think that Roger Corman had made a mistake by not putting talented young filmmakers under contract and holding on to them, ending up with great directors working for free, more or less. "Francis saw Zoetrope as a sort of alternative *Easy Rider* studio where he could do the same thing: get a lot of young talent for nothing, make these movies, hope that one of them would be a hit, and eventually build a studio that way," Lucas says.

Despite Lucas's reservations, Coppola's enthusiasm was infectious. The message went out on the USC and UCLA grapevines that Zoetrope was where the future was taking shape. Coppola's real strength was in making deals. He took ideas for seven movie projects to Warner Bros., one of which was the feature version of *THX*. The studio was now the property of a parking lot company, Kinney Services, and a former agent named Ted Ashley was in charge. As usual, Coppola tried to bluff his way into a deal; he sent a telegram to Ashley's assistant John Calley, announcing that he had a film ready to go and demanding that Warner's put up the money. In reality, *THX* was still in the rough draft stage, but the studio agreed to put up $3.5 million to develop five scripts, including *THX*. Ashley drove a hard bargain, too—any money expended would have to be repaid by Coppola and Zoetrope if the screenplays and film did not live up to expectations. If even one of the films proved to be a commercial hit, everyone would come out well. Warner's was worried about *THX 1138*, but Coppola assured them that the movie would look expensive in spite of its projected under-$1 million budget.

THX had continued to fascinate Lucas after he finished the student version in 1967. He knew a feature had to differ from the student movie in both theme and scope, while keeping within the modest budget. (Coppola encouraged Lucas to try something different, although some of his own ideas were bizarre: Francis wrote George from London that he had discovered a new 3-D process with which to make *THX*.) Coppola had no plans to pay for a screenwriter so he gave Lucas a valuable lesson in discipline: if he was going to make it in the movie business, he was going to have to learn how to write.

"So I wrote it, and I turned it in to Francis, and I said, 'This is terrible,'" Lucas remembers. "He read it and said, 'You're right.'" Coppola tried to rewrite the script, but he and Lucas didn't share the same concept of the movie. Warner Bros. didn't like the script either, so Coppola gave in and hired Oliver Hailey (now a successful film and TV writer) to work with Lucas. They had daily story conferences, but when Hailey turned in his screenplay, it wasn't the movie Lucas wanted to make.

When Walter Murch arrived in San Francisco to edit the sound effects on *Rain People,* Lucas solved his problem. He and Murch were accustomed to working together, and Murch brought a spacey insight to Lucas's visual imagination. They prepared a new script. "We just threw everything up in the air and watched it come down," Murch recalls with a smile. There were layers of themes in the screenplay. Lucas explains, "In one sense, we were making a very two-dimensional kind of movie, with a flat, graphic look. Then we planned to have the audio vision on the sound track, and the dramatic vision laid over that." George wanted to experiment with the aesthetics of a film. Since he was going to construct an imaginary society, he might as well have fun making up its rules, even if they didn't always make sense. "I didn't want to alter things for the convenience of drama," Lucas says. That was not a statement designed to make studio executives happy.

By this time it looked as if *THX* would never get off the ground. Lucas went to John Milius and suggested they resume work on the Vietnam project they had discussed in college. Lucas and Milius began work on a story treatment for *Apocalypse Now.* But Coppola hadn't given up on *THX.* He prepared an impressive display of Lucas-designed graphics and showed executives at Warner Bros. some of the footage from the student version. He also concocted an extremely low budget for the film, a mere $777,777.77 (seven was Coppola's lucky number). To further impress Warner Bros., Coppola tossed Lucas's Vietnam movie into the deal, a movie to which Coppola had no link other than the fact that Lucas had told him about it.

When Warner's said yes to both projects, Coppola hurried to tell Lucas the good news. "I was shocked," remembers George. "It was great about *THX,* but Francis hadn't even asked me or talked to me about *Apocalypse*—he just went off and made a deal for the movie. But it seemed that Zoetrope would be this great company and we young filmmakers were going to take over the world, so I was pleased." Coppola was proud of his protégé, whose ability and talent had responded to Francis's prodding. He also knew that with an actual movie to make, Zoetrope was in business.

Lucas didn't get the greatest deal in Hollywood. He was paid only $15,000 to write and direct *THX 1138,* although Coppola promised him that his salary would rise to $25,000 on *Apocalypse Now.* George, Sr., and Dorothy were stunned when they heard Warner Bros. was giving little Georgie almost a million dollars to make a movie. "We got off the phone and said, 'My God, they're giving a twenty-three-year-old kid all that money!'" Dorothy recalls.

Lucas recognized his opportunity: "I realized that I might never get the chance again to make this totally off-the-wall movie, without any real supervision. Once I did this, I thought they would never let me in the film business again." George wasn't totally unsupervised in the making of *THX,* however; Warner Bros. insisted, and Coppola agreed, that a line producer be hired, someone to ensure that Lucas shot the film within its allotted budget and schedule.

Lawrence Sturhahn, who had worked on *You're a Big Boy Now* with Coppola, was given the job, much to Lucas's displeasure. "Sturhahn was assigned to *THX* so George would have someone to hate," explains Matthew Robbins. "Francis felt it was necessary to get a producer in opposition to the director, and it worked perfectly." Maybe for Coppola, but not for Lucas. He resented Sturhahn, who spent most of his time on the phone. Lucas wanted a producer to help with the logistics of the movie; what he got was someone happy to let Lucas do all the work. Lucas didn't like his first encounter with the bureaucracy of a Hollywood studio. "The more he had to deal with grown-ups, the less he liked it," says Matthew Robbins.

Lucas grew up quickly during the making of *THX.* He had only a ten-week shooting schedule, the same period of time he had needed to make the student version. He used a local crew because Coppola didn't want to incur the high cost of Hollywood labor. Lucas couldn't even join the Directors Guild because the initiation fee was too high. But his mind was bubbling with ideas.

George had decided to shoot *THX* in Techniscope, an older film process he had learned about at USC that uses half as much film and yields a wide-screen effect with normal camera lenses. Techniscope was also cheap and could be set up quickly, two requisites for the making of *THX.* Lucas planned to use existing light wherever possible, so he could get in and out of his locations quickly. Every aspect of *THX* was planned in detail, and each shot was virtually edited into the movie before being photographed.

The plot of *THX 1138* elaborated on the student version, although the setting was still a computer-controlled subterranean world populated by citizens permanently sedated with tranquilizing drugs. "Work hard, increase production, prevent accidents, and be happy" is the reigning philosophy, articulated by OMM, the unemotional God of the future. The drugs are effective enough to have eliminated all sex and most of its differentiations—men and women have shaved heads and wear identical white clothing. Policeman-robots with polished-steel faces and wicked-looking batons enforce the rigid laws, while the minions of OMM monitor everyone with two-way TV screens inspired by George Orwell's novel *1984*.

The main characters are THX 1138 and LUH 3417 (Lucas's fondness for numbers still lingered), roommates who feel the first stirrings of sexuality. Abstaining from their medication, they make love and conceive a child. THX's aberrant behavior is reported by SEN, his jealous supervisor who wants THX as his own roommate. THX is tried and found guilty of drug evasion and sexual perversion.

The movie's major setting is the White Limbo, the prison where THX is sent. It has no boundaries other than its inmates' fears, and no one has ever escaped. THX becomes the first by simply walking into the limbo, where he is joined by a black hologram, a lifelike image that seems to be real but is actually electronic. Together, they steal powerful jet-cars and race through the civilization's underground tunnels, just ahead of the robot police. The hologram is killed in a fiery crash, but THX eludes his pursuers, fends off an attack by hairy dwarfs who live in the superstructure (they evolve into Jawas in *Stars Wars*), and discovers a ladder leading to the surface. The final shot is of THX frozen before a blinding column of light as the sun rises, shedding its first rays on his new world.

(Lucas likes putting sunrises and sunsets in his movies because it gives the audiences a sense of real time. After a screening of *THX 1138*, Jim Bloom, now one of Lucas's producers, went up to George and Walter Murch and asked them what the significance of the sunrise was in the final shot. "George sort of looked at me, and Walter looked at me, and he and Walter looked at each other, and George looked back at me, and he said, 'Well, it's just a sunrise.' And that was it.")

Limited by time and budget on *THX,* Lucas used existing locations that required little modification. He shot as much film as he could of each sequence, using one camera for closeups, a second for the master shot of the entire scene, and sometimes a third camera for another angle. Lucas rarely filmed a scene several times—occasionally he would film the rehearsals and print them. "I'm very documentary in style, just set up all the cameras and shoot the scene," Lucas says. "I like the actors to play against each other and not the camera, so I put the cameras off in the corner where they won't be intrusive." Lucas and his crew zipped around the San Francisco area, using the half-completed tunnels for the new San Francisco rapid transit system as their major set.

Directing a movie means responding to a thousand questions every day, a concept foreign to Lucas. He couldn't believe he had a career that demanded interaction with large groups of strangers. Lucas once told

Walter Murch that his emotional state while directing a film was like watching the needle on a sound meter. The needle should move back and forth depending on whether a loud chase scene or an intimate conversation is being recorded. What happens internally to him, Lucas said, "is the needle starts out at zero, and two days into shooting it's up in the red—and it just stays in the red." Yet Lucas projected a quiet detachment that intimidated his cast and crew. "I'm not very good with people, never have been," admits Lucas. "It's a real weak link for me."

Coppola was aware of Lucas's shortcomings. He told Ron Colby to cast the film carefully with actors capable of inspiring their own performance. Veteran British actor Donald Pleasance was cast as the heavy, SEN, while the title role went to Robert Duvall, whom Lucas knew from *The Rain People*. San Francisco actress Maggie McOmie played LUH, and the cast also included comedians Marshall Efron and David Ogden Stiers, later the costar of the "M*A*S*H" TV series, playing Major Charles Emerson Winchester.

"I had it instilled in me that the first thing to do when you're directing is to get the very best actor for your lead, somebody who's good for the role and is also a nice guy," Lucas says. "My life is too short to put up with a lot of trouble from my cast." The female roles were more difficult because McOmie and the other women had to have their heads shaved. (It became a problem to get people to shave their heads; eventually Colby got extras from Synanon, a local drug rehabilitation program.) There were also fairly explicit sex scenes between THX and LUH, which Lucas filmed on a closed set at a small local studio.

THX was not without its other problems. The equipment was crude, almost primitive; a crew member, Ted Moehnke, wheeled around his props and special effects in two Sears garbage cans. Lucas was amazed to find out that the pros weren't any better than the film students. "They still put the film in backward and screwed up," he says. "Only in the professional industry, you pay for it—enormously. What a realization that was for me and my friends." What his crew lacked in experience was made up in enthusiasm, and Lucas had his best time as a director on *THX*.

"It was the only movie I really enjoyed doing," he says wistfully. "It's always a big thrill doing your first film because you haven't gone through the other end of it, all the criticism, anguish, and failure. That doesn't even occur to you because you don't know what can go wrong. It's all fun." Coppola occasionally dropped by the set, often accompanied by a Warner executive or some other visitor from Hollywood. *THX* was his showcase, the proof that Zoetrope was working. Lucas became even more determined to bring the film in on time and under budget, validating Francis's confidence in him.

Lucas's secret weapon was his ability to improvise. He built one miniature set by himself using model parts and a $10 fireworks assortment for explosions. Lucas had definite ideas on how every scene should look. When a key sequence in *THX* required a roomful of bottled human embryos, Ted Moehnke arranged with the University of California to get a mold of a dead embryo in exchange for a needed piece of medical equipment, which Zoetrope donated to the university. He filled the mold with latex rubber and turned out embryos amid the renovation of the Zoetrope warehouse.

At the end of the shooting, Coppola decided to have a group therapy session involving the producers, the director, and the crew. George impatiently listened as the crew complained that he never talked to them, confided in them, joked with them, or related in any sort of a personal way. "It was one of those feely-talky therapy sessions," Lucas says with a snort. "Lucky they hadn't invented hot tubs yet, or we'd all have been in one." But the criticism touched a nerve; Lucas knew he had to confront his difficulty in communicating with people, even if it ruined a lot of his fun in making movies. "Being a director is a very draining job," Lucas is convinced. "It's like being head of a very big family, and you have to give every little kid your attention." Lavishing attention on insecure show people was not Lucas's idea of a good time.

THX was difficult to film; it is also difficult to understand. The short film was almost unintelligible, although Lucas and Murch greatly improved on the story line in the feature version. *THX* is Lucas's most complex film, his one attempt at a "message" picture that he hoped would induce people to take some measure of their own lives. Unfortunately, the message is sometimes as scrambled as poor THX's brains after they've been electronically fried by the mind controllers.

The themes are familiar: the relationship between men and machines; the necessity of escaping a restrictive environment; and the acceptance of responsibility in relationships and in broad moral terms. Lucas wasn't trying to remake *Brave New World* or *1984;* he was suggesting that people didn't have to participate in a repressive society—"You could just walk out." That was also the reigning philosophy on college campuses in the late 1960s. Lucas had tapped into the mass psychology of his generation; unfortunately, in 1968, this group could not turn a weird science-fact movie into a blockbuster hit.

The political content of *THX* is unusual in light of Lucas's reputation as a noncontroversial filmmaker interested only in entertaining movie audiences. Ron Colby, who worked on *THX,* remembers being angry at Lucas's blasé response to the political struggles of the late 1960s. Lucas describes his beliefs of that time as "left-of-the-middle." "The central thing in my life was that I wanted to make movies," he explains. "I didn't want the distraction of causes, much as I believed in them." That is precisely the criticism most often leveled at Lucas, that he excludes the real world from his films, opting instead for harmless fantasy. But *THX 1138* is as political as any American movie released by a major studio in the late 1960s. Lucas portrays a repressive government that sedates its citizens, manufactures its future generations in the laboratory, and relegates minorities to the status of nonhumans. "Modern society is a rotten thing, and by God, if you're smart, you'll get out now and escape. Start an alternative civilization above ground, out of the sewer you find yourself in," is Lucas's summation of the message he was delivering in *THX.* Not exactly the stuff of childhood fantasies.

THX demonstrates that problems aren't solved by talking about them—in the White Limbo sequences, the prisoners spend all their time discussing the *concept* of freedom but never do anything about it. THX *achieves* freedom by walking into the white infinity; he takes action and accepts its consequences, which can include death. "I felt that society had drifted to a point where everything was being talked about and nothing was being done," Lucas says. "I still feel that way."

What kind of solution does running away offer, though? Lucas seems to embrace the hippie homily, "Turn on, tune in, and drop out," although *THX* carries a strong antidrug message by equating sedation with repression. Once THX is weaned from drugs by his love for LUH, he realizes that he can leave both the void and his fear behind. "The fear of the unknown is what keeps people in line," Lucas believes, a concept he put to better use in *Star Wars.* "You've got to take responsibility for the way things are, and for making them change."

THX also contains the only erotic sequences in Lucas's films, including a televised nude striptease by a buxom black woman. The channel switches, and THX passively watches a man being brutally beaten by two robot policemen. "I feel violence can be a positive, therapeutic thing [in films] if handled correctly," Lucas says. "Whether I'm handling it right or not, I don't know," he adds. Lucas's indecision about violence in *THX* is reflected in one scene in which two "doctors" experiment with THX's nerve reflexes. Banal electronic shoptalk ensues while THX is jerked around like a spastic doll, tortured by electronic probes. Despite how uncomfortable the sadism makes the audience feel, Lucas considers this one of the funniest scenes in the film, and his personal favorite—it's his revenge on the medical procedures he was subjected to following his car accident.

The sex scenes in *THX* were explicit enough to warrant a feature on the movie in a soft-core pornographic movie magazine called *Adam Film World*. Describing the lovemaking sessions between LUH and THX, the magazine leers, "Seems good old-fashioned sex play leads right to the old-time physical orgasm, and you know they're never going back to that futuristic mental stuff."[4] Lucas claims that he left even sexier footage out of the movie at the request of Robert Duvall.

"I'm not a prude," Lucas says with defensive pride. "The fact that I've become well known for children's films seems to force me into that prudish niche, but it isn't so." Lucas's marriage to Marcia took place just before *THX* was made, and the film reflects both his physical passion and his strong feelings about the necessity of love for survival. The love relationship between LUH and THX is genuinely affecting, given the movie's reputation as a cold, mechanical exercise.

The most unsettling relationship in *THX 1138* is the one between THX and SEN, the supervisor who seems to have designs on THX. As played by Donald Pleasance, SEN displays homosexual characteristics in a sexless society. Lucas insists that homosexuality does not exist in THX's world, and even if it did, he didn't design SEN to be gay. But he acknowledges that even Pleasance had trouble understanding his character. Lucas explains away the loose ends in *THX* by saying that he wanted to make the equivalent of a foreign-language movie, where the audience doesn't really understand the social patterns they're watching until the film is over.

THX was perceived as a bleak, depressing film upon its release, in keeping with its creator's personality. "In those days, George was a much more negative, darker person," says Bill Neil, Coppola's brother-in-law, who worked on *THX*. Even its admirers consider the movie to be austere and unemotional. ("The fact that it was an emotionless society didn't give me much to work with," Lucas says.) But the craftsmanship with which *THX* was made offered indisputable evidence of Lucas's film-making ability.

There are sophisticated graphics in *THX* for a young director making his feature-film debut on a shoestring budget. The crowd scenes with hundreds of bald-headed, white-robed zombies streaming down the city's corridors are scary and effective, as are the White Limbo sequences.

Lucas cut in an exciting chase scene with THX and the robot police on their jet bikes that works because of the pacing. Even the sound effects, which Walter Murch designed and recorded, were revolutionary for their time. They let the audience know it was entering a different world. *THX* is one of the few science-fiction films that seems more *from* the future than *about* the future.

Not everyone enjoyed the challenge. Marcia Lucas wasn't fond of *THX* except for its graphics. It never worked for her dramatically: "When I was a viewer watching the film, I never got emotionally involved in it. And I like to be emotionally involved in films." Many of Lucas's friends felt that the film did not have a strong enough plot and that *THX* left the audience depressed rather than hopeful.

The reviewers generally were kind, but the director became angry at reading criticism of his motives and intentions: "Critics are the vandals of our time, like spray-painters who mess up walls. You realize they spend two hours seeing a movie once and two hours writing about it—they spend less than one day in their whole life thinking about that particular film, whereas most filmmakers spend at least two or three years planning and making a movie. I basically said, 'To hell with reviews.'" What disturbed Lucas most about the critical reaction to *THX* was that he was perceived as a cold fish, a label he rejects to this day. "I do have emotions, and I'm not a weird sci-fi kind of guy," he says.

Lucas learned from the critical and popular reaction to *THX* that if he wanted to change the world, showing how stupid and awful society could be was not the way to proceed. Audiences like positive stories, not negative diatribes. It was a mistake he wouldn't repeat.

Lucas's problems with *THX* began when he finished the movie. Coppola gave him a year to work on the postproduction, which Lucas did in the attic and extra bedroom of his Mill Valley house. George and Marcia edited all day, then Walter Murch came over and cut sound all night. At 6:00 A.M., Lucas and Murch changed shifts. George achieved almost everything he wanted with his first film: he was able to write, direct, edit, and control his vision, a total "hands-on" experience that he loved. For those reasons, he still considers *THX* his most satisfying film in terms of his personal goals.

Lucas's inexperience with the ways of Hollywood ended when *THX 1138* was delivered to Warner Bros. Coppola came by the Mill Valley house on the evening before he was to take the film down to Burbank. Murch showed him a reel, and all Coppola murmured was, "Strange, strange."

The statement was prophetic. When Ashley and his management team saw *THX,* they were puzzled by its abstract imagery, eerie sound track, and incomprehensible plot. Ashley was convinced that the film was a stiff and ordered Coppola and Lucas to turn the negative print over to Rudi Fehr, a veteran in-house editor at Warner. (It was said to be the first time the studio physically took a picture away from its director and producer.) "They had all the marbles, they owned the film," Coppola says of his capitulation to Ashley and company. He waited until he returned to San Francisco before telling Lucas the bad news.

Bad news it was, indeed. Coppola had taken the next seven American Zoetrope projects down with him for the *THX* screening, among them two films Coppola himself would later make, *Apocalypse Now* and *The Conversation.* Ashley was so upset after seeing *THX* that he canceled the entire Zoetrope deal, refusing to consider the merits of the other scripts. The day became known as Black Thursday, a blow from which Zoetrope never recovered. Lucas was devastated; his film had been ridiculed and taken away from him, and he felt responsible for the demise of Zoetrope. Coppola fled to Europe to lick his wounds; since Lucas was unable to reach him, his anger at Warner Bros. simmered within. Fehr cut only four minutes from *THX,* mostly scenes in the White Limbo and some of Lucas's bizarre attempts at humor, but the blow to his creative freedom wounded George.

"The cuts didn't make the movie any better; they had absolutely no effect on the movie at all," he says. "It was a very personal kind of film, and I didn't think they had the right to come in and just arbitrarily chop it up at their own whim. I'm not really good with authority figures anyway, so I was completely outraged." Coppola insists that *THX* was barely cut, but to Lucas, they might as well have chopped up the entire movie into little pieces. It took eleven years for him to speak again to Ted Ashley. During negotiations to release *Raiders of the Lost Ark,* Ashley had to apologize and admit he had been wrong before Lucas would forgive him. (Even so, Paramount Pictures released *Raiders.*) Recalling the reconciliation he arranged between Lucas and Ashley, attorney Tom Pollock says, "It was right out of the Vatican."

THX 1138 opened well in its initial commercial engagements, but business quickly fell off and the movie was relegated to cult film status, playing midnight screenings at art theaters. Eventually it earned $945,000 in rentals, the part of the ticket sales returned to Warner Bros. by theater owners, but it still ended up in the red. Warner Bros. rereleased the movie after the success of *Star Wars,* with the excised footage restored, but *THX* again failed to catch on with a mass audience. It remains Lucas's biggest commercial failure and, at the same time, his favorite film. The experience was frustrating and character-building for Lucas, who had spent the better part of two years making a very personal movie that had been dumped into the marketplace without attention or care. Marcia Lucas saw only a positive benefit from the personal ordeal she and George had undergone: "Directing that movie was a great thing for George. It was a breakthrough. Now he was really a filmmaker."

5
ROCKING AROUND THE CLOCK

Zoetrope just never got off the dime. Only now, a generation later, are all these people having successful careers.

—Agent Jeff Berg

On November 21, 1969, two workmen arrived at the Warner Bros. studio in Burbank carrying a huge, black coffinlike box. They strained as they lifted it up the curved staircase to the office of Warner president Ted Ashley. Inside the box were seven screenplays in fancy black binders embossed with the Zoetrope logo, the early projection device that symbolized the dream of a new cinema. In just a few hours, the black box was headed back down the stairs. Ashley had rejected its contents and thus nailed the coffin shut on the plans of Francis Coppola, George Lucas, and the group of young filmmakers they had brought together in San Francisco.

Lucas and Coppola were more than devastated by Warner's summary dismissal—they were financially liable for roughly $300,000, the money the studio had spent developing the scripts. Within the crumbling Zoetrope organization, there was uncertainty about Coppola's leadership. Bills piled up, equipment disappeared, accountants took one look at the company's books and walked away. Lucas panicked—this was just the kind of situation his father had warned him about, crazy creative types spending money like there was no tomorrow, not bothering to worry about the financial consequences.

Internal dissension also racked Zoetrope. Several socially active film-makers had joined the company and formed a radical union that sued the established San Francisco unions for jurisdiction over Zoetrope productions. Lucas vehemently opposed the transformation of Zoetrope into a political battleground and slowly withdrew from the company. The matter was eventually resolved, but it cost Coppola and Zoetrope $40,000 in legal fees. Coppola has especially unpleasant memories of the period: "Zoetrope was picked clean. Everyone had used it, no one had contributed, and there was a time when I literally was staving off the sheriff from putting the chain across the door." Even stalwarts like John Korty departed when his office rent skyrocketed from $200 to $1,000 a month as Coppola desperately tried to raise cash.

Typical of the waste at Zoetrope was an invitation Coppola sent to George and Marcia asking them to attend a reception at the San Francisco Film Festival in 1970. Printed on fine bond paper and embossed with the Zoetrope logo, the invitation carried a personal note from Coppola at the bottom: "This letter cost $3 to print, type, and send to you." Lucas detested this sort of meaningless extravagance, and it led to a deepening rift between the two men. "George became very discouraged by my 'bohemian' administration," acknowledges Coppola. "I have an ability like a pied piper to get everybody's dream going, but in the end I was vulnerable and got wiped out. George was very concerned to get an operation going that wouldn't be as loosely run as mine."

At his bleakest moment, Coppola was approached by Paramount Pictures to direct the film version of Mario Puzo's potboiler novel about the Mafia, *The Godfather*. Coppola was reluctant to reenter the Hollywood system, but Lucas urged him to take the job, if only to pay off Zoetrope's debts. Lucas had learned the drawbacks of being the protégé of a master who occasionally stumbled.

Other Zoetropians also felt they were on a roller-coaster ride of high hopes and depressing results. "They were wonderful years and I learned a lot," says librarian Deborah Fine. "But personally they were very tough on me. The feeling from working for Francis is tough shit if you don't think you're getting paid enough or if you don't think your working conditions are good enough. There's a million people out there that would kiss the ground to work for him for nothing."

If Lucas was ever in a similar position, he felt he knew exactly what *not* to do. He maintained his friendship with Coppola and helped him film montage scenes of the gang wars in *The Godfather*. But he looked elsewhere for work, too. Documentary maker David Maysles hired Lucas as a cameraman for the infamous Rolling Stones concert at the Altamont Speedway outside San Francisco in 1969. It may have been Lucas who captured the stabbing death of a concertgoer by a Hell's Angel, but he says he can't remember. The event made no special impression on him.

During this period Lucas got to know Gary Kurtz who had attended USCinema and had worked on a few Roger Corman pictures. He served for four years in a marine photography unit, although he was a Quaker and refused to carry a gun. Kurtz was a solemn, bearded man who made Lucas seem like an extrovert. They struck up a friendship and Kurtz agreed to produce Lucas and Milius's film about the Vietnam War.

Lucas proceeded apace with his ambitious career plans, despite the stillbirth of *THX 1138*. He had enjoyed feature-film directing and was no longer interested in industrial films and commercials. But for his second film he was going to have to make something more professional and, he hated to admit, more commercial. He had acquired the appendages of an up-and-coming director: a lawyer, Tom Pollock, and an agent, a young Berkeley graduate named Jeff Berg. He was with Creative Management Associates, one of the new breed of Hollywood talent agencies, which also represented Lucas's friends John Milius, the Huycks, and Matthew Robbins.

Lucas wanted to make a movie that would dispel his image as a technobrat, a cold, mechanical filmmaker devoid of warmth and humor. The vehicle was a rock 'n' roll movie in which the music was as important as the story and the characters. Lucas didn't think he was any good at telling stories, but he didn't have to worry with *American Graffiti*—the songs sufficed, summoning a tidal wave of memories for the audience. What was more commercial than a sound track of Top 40 hits?

Lucas knew that one good film idea wasn't enough. If a studio didn't care for a concept, it was best to have a second one ready, about which you could be equally enthusiastic. Lucas had long dreamed of making a space movie that would evoke the Flash Gordon and Buck Rogers serials he watched on TV as a child. He tried to buy the movie rights to Alex Raymond's Flash Gordon books, but discovered that Italian director Federico Fellini had already optioned them. (*Flash Gordon* eventually was made by producer Dino De Laurentiis in 1980, with poor box office results.) Forced to come up with his own story, Lucas decided to research mythology and fairy tales for possible ideas, but concentrate first on his musical.

THX hadn't furthered Lucas's self-confidence as a writer, but he pushed ahead with a five-page bare-bones story about four young men on the brink of adulthood who go their different ways. Jeff Berg peddled it to the major studios, where there was a unanimous lack of enthusiasm. Most executives thought the idea was weird and expected the music rights to cost a fortune. One of the few executives initially intrigued was a production vice-president at United Artists, David Chasman. But he too thought the project risky, and passed.

Chafing at the delays, Lucas decided to go to Europe and the Cannes Film Festival, where *THX* was chosen for the Directors' Fortnight, a new showcase for young filmmakers. Marcia had just finished a job as assistant editor on *The Candidate* for Michael Ritchie and was eager for a vacation. There was going to be a stopover in New York before the flight to London and Lucas decided to gamble by going over Chasman's head, directly to United Artists president David Picker, who was based in New York. Perhaps if he pleaded his case personally, Lucas thought, Picker might see potential in *American Graffiti,* the title George had come up with on a weekend trip to Modesto.

Before George and Marcia left, Lucas went with Milius and Robbins to see *THX* at a Hollywood Boulevard theater, the first time George saw his movie with a paying audience. His heart was pounding as he took his seat, but the response was enthusiastic: "They loved it—they jumped and laughed in all the right places. I was *really* feeling good. I didn't care whether I had a hit or not, because I never thought it would be a hit. But at least I sat in a theater with my film and an audience, and they liked it. That was enough for me." It wasn't enough for Warner Bros.—the studio had no intention of sending Lucas to Cannes. George and Marcia's savings amounted to $2,000, but Lucas said, "What the hell, let's go." So off they went, backpacks and sleeping bags in tow. It was to be their first and only vacation for the next seven years.

David Picker was surprisingly receptive to Lucas's idea when they met in New York. He asked if there were other projects the young filmmaker had in mind, and when he heard a rough story outline of what would become *Star Wars,* suggested a possible two-picture deal. Picker agreed to read the short treatment on *Graffiti* and to call Lucas with his decision.

Lucas got a call from Picker in London on his twenty-sixth birthday. Someone was going to make his movie! But Picker was wary enough to structure the deal so that any profits that resulted from one picture could be applied against the possible losses of the other. Picker also insisted that Lucas improve the story and come up with a full screenplay, for which United Artists would pay $10,000. Lucas knew he needed help and called Willard Huyck and Gloria Katz, the rival film school graduates with whom he had become close friends. The Huycks reluctantly informed him that they had been offered a low-budget horror movie of their own to make in England. Lucas urged them to take the job and hung up the phone in a daze. He was five thousand miles from Hollywood and had no idea whom to hire as a replacement.

Lucas had asked Gary Kurtz to produce *Graffiti* if and when he got a deal, and Kurtz began the search for a new screenwriter. George remembered a former classmate at USC, Richard Walters, and he agreed to have a first-draft screenplay done by the time Lucas returned from Europe. In Cannes, Lucas met Picker in the executive's suite at the posh Carlton Hotel and cemented the deal for *Star Wars,* which George described as "this big sci-fi/space adventure/Flash Gordon thing." As a bonus, Picker left Lucas his reserved tickets for the Cannes film premieres, and George and Marcia saw the festival in style.

THX 1138 emerged as one of the sleeper hits at Cannes, selling out both of its screenings. A press conference was scheduled so the French critics could meet this innovative young director, but typically, Lucas never knew about it. "I was barely able to get into my own picture, let alone go to a press conference," he recalls with a laugh. "But for a number of years, the French thought I was this real snob." George and Marcia purchased a Eurailpass and spent the summer on their own Grand Tour, covering the European racing circuit from Le Mans to the Monaco Grand Prix.

Lucas couldn't wait to read Walters's script on his return; not unexpectedly, he was disappointed. It didn't reflect his vision at all: Walters's version was overtly sexual and Lucas considered it to be in bad taste. He was even more upset when he discovered that Kurtz had agreed to pay Walters the entire $10,000 for just a first draft. Lucas now had a deal, no script, no $10,000, and just $500 in the bank.

Lucas did receive offers to direct other movies following *THX.* Tomorrow Entertainment, an independent production company that Jeff Berg had tried to interest in *Graffiti,* wanted Lucas to make a low-budget caper movie, *Lady Ice,* starring Donald Sutherland. The more Lucas turned down the producers, the more desirable he became, until the offer stood at $100,000 and 15 percent of the film's net profits. It was tempting—Lucas was desperate for cash to develop a new *Graffiti* script. He had a long talk with Marcia before deciding to say no. The decision was a turning point— Lucas was determined to stay true to *his* vision and not be deflected from his goals. Michael Ritchie was impressed by Lucas's independence. "All of the rest of us have had to make films we really didn't want to make," Ritchie points out. "George never did."

Lucas's decision to pass up *Lady Ice* (the film was finally directed by Tom Gries and proved to be a box office disaster) looked even more foolish when United Artists backed out of the deal for *Graffiti* and *Star Wars*. Picker was not impressed with the screenplay Lucas had hurriedly written himself after rejecting Walters's screenplay and declined to invoke the contract's second stage, which triggered additional money for a rewrite. If Lucas wanted to work on *Graffiti* using his own money, Picker said United Artists would be happy to take another look at it. Otherwise, the deal was off. Lucas was furious—he felt the studio was too cheap to pay for a rewrite. He went back to the typewriter and turned out two more drafts of *American Graffiti*. They were turned down by every studio in Hollywood.

Lucas was becoming desperate. He and Marcia were heavily in debt, having borrowed several thousand dollars from George's parents, other relatives, and friends. Like his father, George hated owing money, even to members of his family. Tom Pollock had set up a company to contract Lucas's services as a director and thereby reduce his tax burden. George called it Lucasfilm Ltd., not because it sounded English—he just liked the alliteration and the inclusion of his own name, a revealing bit of vanity for a supposedly modest man.

No one seemed interested in Lucas's services as a director or a corporation. He was still struggling with his concepts for *Star Wars* when he met with NASA illustrator Ralph McQuarrie to help him work out his ideas. But Lucas felt he wasn't making any progress. He had been the first of his group to make a feature film and now it seemed he might be the last to make a second one. Was his career over already?

Making a film is a cross between a circus, a military campaign, a nightmare, an orgy, and a high.[1]

—Norman Mailer

Lucas never lost his conviction that the time was ripe for a film like *American Graffiti*. Speaking to a Modesto Rotary Club meeting at his father's request after the movie was finished, Lucas told the local businessmen, "I decided it was time to make a movie where people felt better coming out of the theater than when they went in. It had become depressing to go to the movies." To the amusement of his hometown audience, Lucas added that he had spent four years cruising 10th Street in Modesto, time his father considered worthless. "I made *American Graffiti* to prove him wrong," Lucas said, only half-joking.

Obtaining studio financing for *Graffiti* was proving difficult. The lack of box office success for *THX* had marked Lucas as a noncommercial director, and the unusual concept behind *Graffiti* hardly reassured conservative studio executives. In the story treatment for the film, Lucas pasted in the word "musical" in big block letters and as a part of the presentation included, *"American Graffiti* is a MUSICAL. It has singing and dancing, but it is not a musical in the traditional sense because the characters in the film neither sing nor dance." The silence from 20th Century-Fox, MGM, Paramount, and American International Pictures was terminal. Even his friends thought Lucas was making "a silly kids' movie." Only Marcia was solidly behind him.

Few executives bothered to read the rest of the story outline and thus missed Lucas's point. The music wasn't the problem with *American Graffiti,* it was the solution. George's junior college studies in anthropology and sociology had made him aware that the 1950s culture that had nurtured him was fast disappearing in the socially turbulent 1960s. Instead of cruising, kids were getting stoned on pot. Lucas knew that if he could re-create his era, he would strike a chord in the generation that was becoming the mainstay of the movie audience.

Bill Huyck and Gloria Katz had completed their movie and were eager to begin work on *Graffiti.* Lucas outlined the plot structure, a complicated arrangement in which each character was involved in several subplots along with the main story line. He calculated that each scene would run the length of a popular song, about two and a half minutes, or two and a half screenplay pages. If *Graffiti* was ninety minutes long, it would require forty-eight scenes, or twelve for each major character. The Huycks were confused at first, but as they began writing, they realized George's goal was to keep the story constantly moving; each of the subplots added momentum and built toward the movie's conclusion.

The Huycks' main task was to bring to life the four prototypes Lucas had created: Curt the rebel, Steve the stolid citizen, Terry the nerd, and Milner the king of the road. "They were cardboard cutouts in my script, nonpeople," admits Lucas. "Bill and Gloria made it one hundred percent better with a combination of wit, charm, snappy one-liners, and punched-up characters." The Huycks wrote quickly, turning out ten pages a day which Lucas would rewrite and then return to them for yet another revision. *American Graffiti* was drawn from Lucas's own adolescence in Modesto, but Huyck and Katz had little trouble relating to the story—both grew up in Southern California. "A hamburger in Modesto is the same as a hamburger in the San Fernando Valley," Huyck explains.

By meshing their individual high school experiences, the Huycks and

Lucas achieved a successful collaboration. Lucas supplied most of the character names and served as the partial model for Terry the Toad, Curt, and Milner. The Huycks envisioned *Graffiti* taking place during one endless surreal night, but Lucas insisted the movie be grounded in reality, giving *Graffiti* immediacy and depth. Lucas made the final script decisions—even the Huycks were not permitted to tamper with his vision. Bill and Gloria did not feel strongly about the material, so there were few creative conflicts. Huyck recalls, "We never thought anything would come of it. It was just a little movie, and that made it easy. We were having fun."

There was a disagreement over the ending of *Graffiti*. Lucas insisted that the final image be a title card detailing the fate of the characters, including the death of Milner and the disappearance of Toad in Vietnam. The Huycks found that ending to be depressing and were incredulous that Lucas planned to include only the male characters. "We were upset by that and we really fought him," remembers Huyck. "We said, 'George, if you've got to have a postscript, you should at least tell the fate of the girls.'" Lucas argued that mentioning the girls meant adding another title card, which he felt would prolong the ending. "It was purely a filmic decision," he emphasizes. "It's a movie about the four guys." With hindsight, he concedes he should have added the women. The men-only ending gave critics like Pauline Kael the opportunity to accuse Lucas of chauvinism, a charge he hotly disputes. "It's just my usual problem of sacrificing content for form," he explains.

Lucas denigrates his own contributions to the final *Graffiti* screenplay, but his quirky "goofball" sense of humor is best seen when Toad tries to buy liquor to impress Debbie. He asks several people walking into a liquor store to make the purchase for him, but something always goes wrong: a businessman intimidates him and a wino rips him off by sneaking out the back door. When Toad enters the store himself, he fails to muster up the courage to ask for the booze. Finally a young man agrees to make the buy and tosses the bottle to Toad as he flees the store, which he has just robbed. The scene is one of the funniest in the film, but it goes by quickly, as if Lucas was embarrassed to reveal his "silly" side.

Jeff Berg made one final attempt to place the rewritten *Graffiti* at Universal Studios, where a young production executive named Ned Tanen had initiated a program of low-budget films like *Two Lane Blacktop* and *Diary of a Mad Housewife*. The movies didn't make much money, but Tanen was about the only executive in Hollywood willing to give young talent a chance. He remembered Lucas's student version of *THX* and met with George, Berg, and Pollock. Lucas came armed with his new screenplay and a cassette of songs culled from his extensive collection of 45s. He was adept at talking up a project he believed in—his shyness disappeared and his enthusiasm was infectious. After several tough negotiating sessions, Universal agreed to finance and release *Graffiti,* with some strings attached.

The studio budgeted only $600,000 for the entire production, a small sum even in the early 1970s. Columbia Pictures had passed up *Graffiti* because it estimated the music rights alone could cost $500,000. Universal insisted that the $600,000 budget include all the music rights, the salaries for the cast, Lucas's $50,000 fee for writing and directing—*everything.* Berg managed to get the amount raised to $750,000, but that was Universal's only concession. "I don't think it was a question of a good deal or a bad deal," Berg says. "It was *the* deal."

Kurtz was Lucas's choice to produce the film, but Universal insisted on a more prominent producer who could ensure that things wouldn't get out of control. A list of names acceptable to the studio was prepared, but Lucas felt comfortable with only one: Francis Coppola. *The Godfather* had just opened to critical raves and outstanding grosses, and Coppola was looked upon as the new savior of the movie business. Universal executives could already see the advertising copy for *American Graffiti:* "From the man who brought you *The Godfather.*"

Tanen flew to San Francisco and begged Coppola to produce the movie, telling him it was the only way Lucas would be allowed to direct it. Being reunited with Francis was awkward for George. After the failure of Coppola to back him in his struggle with Warner Bros. over the cuts in *THX,* Lucas had reduced his professional relationship with him, although they remained close personal friends. George knew Francis was hurt when he didn't take *Graffiti* to him first. "When I had to come back to him and ask him to produce *Graffiti,* Francis was feeling very good," Lucas recalls. Coppola was so enthusiastic about the movie that he tried to arrange his own financing but was unsuccessful. Reluctantly, Coppola agreed to Universal's terms, including the studio's insistence that he act as line producer, watching over all the details. Lucas knew that Coppola would leave him alone—Coppola had no intention of showing up on the set every day.

Universal also optioned Lucas's second picture, *Star Wars,* an idea that had piqued Tanen's interest. The executive had a hunch that backing Lucas was going to prove a shrewd investment for the studio. "There was something unique about George that I didn't really understand," remembers Tanen. "You could just feel something big was going to happen to him."

Francis and Universal immediately wanted to change the film's title—they feared *American Graffiti* sounded like an Italian movie about feet. Coppola suggested *Rock Around the Block,* but Lucas refused to abandon *Graffiti,* which he thought evoked memories of a bygone civilization.

The major battle with Universal came over the budget. Lucas was given less money to make *Graffiti* than he had for *THX* three years earlier, and he figured he'd have to make what he called a Sam Katzman picture, a reference to the famous producer of 1950s B movies like *Rock Around the Clock.* Lucas wanted enough money to guarantee wall-to-wall music, the right cast of young actors, and the ability to shoot at night on location. He also wanted Universal to give him final cut of the film so his unhappy experience with *THX* would not be repeated. But he did not have the clout to win that provision, which went only to top Hollywood directors. It would prove a costly omission.

The deal for *American Graffiti* almost fell apart when it came time to license the rock 'n' roll songs. The music cost almost $90,000, more than 10 percent of the entire budget, and Universal pressured Lucas to cut the sound track down to five or six songs. He refused. Lucas was aware that with the exception of thirty-two-year-old Tanen, he was up against an older generation of studio executives, to whom the idea of sitting through ninety minutes of rock music was unbearable. Lucas believed that even if the movie failed, the young audience would still get a procession of rock classics. As usual, his instincts were correct. The vintage rock 'n' roll songs did slam viewers back to the moment in their lives when they had first heard them. Few people grew up in a town like Modesto, but everyone listened to the same music—Lucas has the gift of making the general out of the specific.

Lucas winnowed his original list of eighty songs to forty-five and eliminated the Elvis Presley tunes. Kurtz knew Dennis Wilson of the Beach Boys from a movie they had done together, and Wilson licensed the production two of the group's songs, "All Summer Long" and "Surfin' Safari," at nominal rates. Tom Pollock negotiated a deal with the other music publishers that prohibited one composer from receiving a higher license fee than any other. Once the Beach Boys were in hand, the other songs quickly fell into place. It was painful for Lucas to eliminate almost half of his original selections, but the sacrifice was hardly appreciated. Kurtz took the list to the head of Universal's music department. "He just about had a heart attack," Kurtz remembers. The studio was nervous enough to make Coppola responsible for the music costs—anything over the $90,000 budget had to come out of Francis's pocket. Lucas felt compromised, but he had protected the best songs: "I Only Have Eyes for You," "See You in September," "Why Do Fools Fall in Love," "The Great Pretender," "Smoke Gets in Your Eyes," and "Get a Job." Lucas enjoyed the irony of the final song—he finally had one.

It's hard work making movies. It's like being a doctor: you work long hours, very hard hours, and it's emotional, tense work. If you don't really love it, then it ain't worth it.[2]

—George Lucas

Universal Pictures Production #05144, also known as *American Graffiti,* started filming on June 26, 1972. Ten years earlier, George Lucas had been in a Modesto hospital bed, fighting for his life. Now he was being given twenty-eight shooting days to re-create the four years that had led up to his fateful accident. If he shot from 9:00 P.M. to 5:00 A.M. on locations in close proximity to Marin County, Lucas estimated that he just might make it. But it was imperative that everything be organized and ready to go, a task that fell to Gary Kurtz. He was the nuts-and-bolts man, content to let Lucas direct the picture while attending to the myriad problems of location shooting.

Kurtz had worked as a lab technician, electrician, writer, cameraman, director, editor, sound mixer, production manager, and associate producer; his wealth of experience reassured Lucas. George trusted Kurtz to take care of the questions that distract a director, and Kurtz was happy to stay in the background. "He did his job, I did my job, and we sort of complemented each other that way," Lucas says, a curt summary of a twelve-year relationship. Kurtz was Lucas's buffer from the outside world, responsible for smoothing over egos ruffled by Lucas's abrupt professional manner. Kurtz also didn't instruct Lucas on how to make the movie— George didn't like people who told him what to do or how to do it.

Fred Roos, a longtime Coppola associate, was hired to cast *Graffiti.* Lucas felt it was essential to people the film with performers who could *become* the characters. Lucas, Kurtz, and Roos conducted an old-fashioned Hollywood talent search for young, fresh performers, going from drama schools to Bay area community theaters. George eventually selected four or five hopefuls for each of the major roles and videotaped them at Haskell Wexler's commercial production studio in Hollywood. He was one of the first directors to use video tests to audition his actors.

Lucas wanted a group of compatible actors—without the right chemistry, the film wouldn't work. Lucas insisted on looking at every performer, demonstrating a stamina few directors possessed. Roos and Lucas sat through hundreds of interviews, while George made tiny notations that no one else could read on yellow legal pads. Finally, they decided on a cast.

What a cast it was. *American Graffiti* introduced more stars than any other recent Hollywood production—the credits read like a "Who's Who" of film and television actors of the 1970s and '80s: Richard Dreyfuss, Harrison Ford, Cindy Williams, Suzanne Somers, Ron Howard, Mackenzie Phillips, Candy Clark, Paul LeMat, Charles Martin Smith, Bo Hopkins, Kathleen Quinlan, Kay Lenz—the list is astonishing. Fred Roos just shrugs his shoulders in explanation: "I had my finger on a whole range of hot young people that I thought had a future, but no one expected this cast to do what they've done."

Lucas didn't always glimpse the potential talent in each cast member. He had to be persuaded to hire twelve-year-old Mackenzie Phillips as Carol—California child labor laws limited how many hours she could work, and Kurtz had to become her official guardian for the duration of production. Charlie Martin Smith was a last-minute choice when Lucas's original selection looked terrible on videotape. Steve's girlfriend Laurie was originally conceived of as a blonde, not the brunette played by Cindy Williams. Lucas simply transferred his penchant for blondes to the Teen Angel character, who had no dialogue. Roos selected a former model named Suzanne Somers—*Graffiti* was her first professional acting job.

Cindy Williams, a good friend of Roos's, was twenty-five and despaired of getting the role. She came to her audition "dressed real high school" and won the part of Laurie. Ron Howard was eighteen but was still saddled with a child actor reputation from his years as Opie on "The Andy Griffith Show." No one had ever thought to cast him as a teenager. Paul LeMat, a onetime professional boxer, had lost a role in John Huston's *Fat City*, but he was just the type Lucas was seeking to play Milner, right down to the white T-shirt with a cigarette pack rolled up in the sleeve. Harrison Ford was a struggling actor who earned most of his income as a carpenter building and repairing homes for the Hollywood community. Richard Dreyfuss, a cocky New York actor who hadn't yet appeared in a movie, seemed an unlikely choice to portray a small-town California teenager, but Lucas liked him immediately and offered him his choice of roles, Curt or Toad. Dreyfuss chose Curt because he, like Lucas, had fantasized being the kid who always had a quick answer.

Lucas did not make much of an impression at the auditions. Cindy Williams thought he looked like her little brother. Roos did most of the talking, while Lucas nodded, smiled, and mumbled, "Okay, great."

Lucas knew he was going to have to choose his cast carefully because the actors were all playing parts of himself. And on the whole, he got along well with them. Lucas has been fortunate as a director: "I've had wonderful casts that were fun to work with and put up with me without too much complaining." But Lucas keeps a careful distance between himself and his actors. He knows they need his approval and feedback, but he also knows he's incapable of giving it—it's simply not in his nature.

Lucas tried his best to play the role of the concerned director. When Cindy Williams finished a scene, she would often ask George how she had done. Lucas, looking startled, would usually mutter, "Great! Terrific!" Reassured, Williams worked with renewed confidence—until Dreyfuss and LeMat let her know that Lucas said the same things to them. It was his *only* response.

The actors appreciated their freedom. Lucas made them feel they were contributing to the picture. They could change their dialogue if they were careful not to change the concept behind the scene. Dreyfuss came up with the idea of trying to unlock his old high school locker, only to discover that the combination had been changed, a scene Lucas used in *Graffiti*. Williams remembers that above all, George seemed grateful that everyone was trying so hard: "He was happy to get whatever he could from us, like a guy on his first date." Dreyfuss teased Lucas incessantly about his taciturn demeanor. "George, will you shut up?" Dreyfuss would taunt. "I can't get a word in edgewise."

Lucas didn't have time to talk. He wasn't a night person, but he had to become one for the filming of *Graffiti*. Since all the action took place after sundown, he couldn't begin shooting until 9:00 P.M., when the darkness looked convincing on film. He had to stop at 5:00 A.M. when the first rays of sunlight appeared. Lucas had trouble getting used to sleeping during the day and working all night; he would usually doze for two or three hours before watching the footage from the previous night's shooting. He made editing notes for Marcia and Verna Fields who were cutting *Graffiti*. After dinner, Lucas planned the night's shooting until it was dark enough to begin.

Graffiti did not get off to the best start. The day before filming began, a key member of the crew was arrested for growing marijuana. The first night's shooting was scheduled for San Rafael, a pleasant small town in Marin not far from Lucas's Mill Valley home, where more bad luck beset the company. Lucas couldn't get the cameras mounted on the cars and didn't get his first shot until 2:00 A.M. He already had lost half a night on his tight schedule.

111

Lucas intended to shoot most of the outdoor footage in San Rafael, even though the city was charging him $300 a night to block off the main commercial thoroughfare. When the cast and crew assembled for the second night of filming, the police told them to go home—the city had revoked their permit. A bar owner had complained that the filming hurt his business by blocking off the street, and he was threatening to sue the city if it happened again. Kurtz finally negotiated a compromise: *Graffiti* would film for three more nights in San Rafael and then leave for Petaluma, a town twenty miles to the north that Lucas had rejected because he thought it looked too dark on film. There was still a key scene to be shot that night and George already felt the pressure of having to make up lost time.

An hour after shooting got under way, Lucas heard the wail of fire engines, a sound effect that was not in the script. A restaurant was in flames and the fire trucks roared to the five-alarm blaze, sirens wailing. Lucas saw his carefully planned shooting schedule go up in smoke. He tried to film around the traffic jam, shooting on back streets with some of the vintage 1950s cars he had recruited from all over Northern California. As Lucas sat on the back of a camera truck filming Milner's deuce coupe, the assistant cameraman slipped off the trailer and was run over by the car. Barney Coangelo was rushed to the hospital and although he was not seriously hurt, his injury sobered the crew and director. Lucas wondered what else could go wrong. "I figured this movie's gonna be a disaster. It was written all over my face," he recalls.

The move to Petaluma cost Lucas an additional $15,000, but the production went smoothly in the town famous for its chicken ranches. Desperate to make up lost time, Lucas listed the shots he planned to film, then eliminated five of the less important scenes. He photographed only the minimum footage he needed to edit *Graffiti*. Lucas was making himself physically ill from the long hours he was spending on the film—he had frequent headaches, a queasy stomach, and was prone to colds. Coppola became concerned and told George not to worry so much about the schedule and budget. "Take as much time as you want," Coppola advised. Bleary-eyed from lack of sleep, Lucas snapped back, "Francis, I will *not* do that, by God! If this is going to be a turkey movie, at least I will have brought it in on time!"

Other problems cropped up. In an attempt to save money, Lucas had hired two local cameramen with little feature-film experience—he thought he could oversee the photography himself. But he drastically underestimated his responsibilities as a director and quickly realized he needed professional help. Coppola asked Haskell Wexler to come to Lucas's aid; they wouldn't be able to pay him a salary (there was no money left in the budget), but Coppola suggested giving Haskell a percentage of *Graffiti*'s eventual profits. The money didn't matter to Wexler, who showed up on the set each night although he was filming commercials during the day in Los Angeles. "I guess I wanted a little adventure," Wexler recalls with a smile.

Wexler flew from Los Angeles to San Francisco after dinner, where he was met by a helicopter that took him to Sausalito, just on the other side of the Bay. There a car picked him up for the drive to Petaluma. Like Lucas, he averaged only two or three hours of sleep, but Wexler was recharged by the enthusiasm on the set. Lucas wanted *Graffiti* to have the ugly neon look of a garish jukebox, not an easy effect to achieve. Wexler had to devise ways to light the actors while they were *inside* their cars, cruising down the street. He purchased recreational-vehicle lights, which give off a soft glow, and taped them up and down the inside of the car roofs. He used a jacked-up truck's headlights to give the illusion of passing lights on the actors' faces.

The *Graffiti* crew went all out for Lucas, but the director never let them know what he was thinking. He never tore his hair out, screamed, or stomped, although he could lose his temper on occasion. Early one morning, just as the sun came up and Lucas hurried to get in his final shot of the night, a sound man walked right into a dramatic scene. "Boy, did I blow my top!" Lucas recalls. "I started screaming and yelling, and the whole cast just stopped still and said, 'My God, he yelled!' The crew was amazed. It had never happened before, and it was a huge event."

Lucas had one more blowup that reflected the pressure he felt. He was filming a scene with Ron Howard and a waitress who tries to seduce him at Mel's Drive-In. Lucas, ever the stickler for detail, insisted that the prop man find an authentic 1960s Coke bottle for the shot. About to call "Action," Lucas noticed that the bottle was new. He exploded, firing the man on the spot. When *Graffiti* completed photography, the crew presented George with an old-fashioned Coke bottle specially inscribed "Bottled in Modesto, California."

Any movie whose only required prop one day was a bra could expect to have its rowdy moments. Jim Bloom, a young production assistant, had rounded up four hundred cars popular in the late 1950s and early '60s, including Milner's 1932 deuce coupe, Studebakers, Chevys, Fords, and Mercurys, and a white 1956 Thunderbird for the Teen Angel. Bloom offered car owners $25 a night to bring in their automobiles, but the drivers were not easily parted from their Dagoed, torched, and tuck-and-rolled machines. Hundreds of latter-day greasers watched the shooting each night. When they weren't gawking, the car freaks drag-raced through the back streets of Petaluma, chugging beer and acting like the real-life versions of their fictional *Graffiti* counterparts.

In spite of the carnival atmosphere, Lucas managed to film six to ten pages of the script, or fifteen to twenty camera setups, a night. It was a quick pace by Hollywood standards, where five to ten setups was considered fast. Lucas suffered the usual pitfalls of location filming: cameras jammed and toppled off their tripods, cars blew gaskets and gears, and a light rain completely ruined one night's shooting. The plane that was to carry Curt to college at the film's end had a flat tire during takeoff and didn't leave the ground. Some of the difficulties Lucas encountered were comic. Kurtz, a lifelong vegetarian, hired an organic-food caterer for the production. But the teamster drivers and other crew members threatened to walk off the picture if they weren't served meat for dinner. Kurtz had to bring in a second caterer, and the movie company split into two camps, the carnivores and the vegetarians. Paul LeMat had a vegetarian dinner one night with Lucas just before filming one of his most important scenes as Milner. Immediately after eating, LeMat became violently ill and was rushed to the hospital. He was allergic to walnuts, which had been used in the Waldorf salad. LeMat ate in the meat line after that.

Lucas didn't find it easy to cope with these mishaps on three hours' sleep. An enduring memory of the *Graffiti* actors is of George falling asleep in the back of the camera truck, bundled up in Gary Kurtz's down jacket that was four sizes too big for him. "Nobody could really tell whether I was asleep or awake," Lucas says in his own defense. But he always managed to wake up by the end of the scene, in time to say, "Cut," or, "Well, why don't we try it once more?" The latter phrase became the actors' anthem on *Graffiti,* the slogan for what Cindy Williams calls "a great summer camp where we were all working against the clock and having fun." Harrison Ford, the oldest of the leading players, served as unofficial "den daddy" to the group, although at times he stirred up more trouble than he prevented.

Ford, LeMat, and Bo Hopkins were the ringleaders for the good-natured chaos that accompanied the filming of *Graffiti*. They drank large quantities of beer while waiting between takes in their cars, urinated in the motel ice machines, and conducted climbing races to the top of the local Holiday Inn sign. Lucas remembers one of the actors setting fire to his room one evening. Another time, LeMat threw Dreyfuss into the motel swimming pool, leaving a big gash across the actor's forehead on the day before his closeups were to be filmed. Lucas had other problems with Dreyfuss—Richard didn't want to wear the Bermuda shorts and garish shirt Lucas had chosen for Curt. Dreyfuss called his shirt the "Test Pattern"—"Whenever Haskell needed to focus his cameras, he'd just have me stand in front of them wearing that shirt."

Lucas displayed the same natural technical ability in directing *Graffiti* that he had shown with *THX*. Coppola visited the set one evening when Lucas was churning out setup after setup, shooting and printing first takes, doing everything in an efficient hurry. Coppola, who had spent entire days designing the elaborate camera angles used in *The Godfather*, was amazed by Lucas's breakneck pace. "I go to great lengths to get interesting compositions for *The Godfather*, and the kid here comes over, sets up the camera, puts everybody up against the wall, and just shoots," Francis complained. Instead of shooting from intricate angles, Lucas concentrated on making his actors feel that they were part of the scene. His strong card was still his visual sophistication, but he was learning more about the dramatic, rather than just the graphic, structure of a scene.

Lucas's overriding concern was money. Ned Tanen recalls that one of the car stunts in *Graffiti* didn't work at first, and he got an urgent call from Kurtz asking for an additional $5,000 to restage it. "I literally had no authority to give him that money," Tanen remembers. "So I just told him to go ahead and do it without ever clearing it." The financial pressure was constant and acute. Lucas refuses to make excuses for *Graffiti*, although he knows that with more time and money he could have made a more polished film. "It's what's on the screen that counts," he says. "The job in film is to do the impossible every day, and you get thrown things from left field all the time. The job of the director is to go with the punches—you just keep doing it until the film is finished." Privately, Lucas considers *Graffiti* to be crude. But its lack of technical sophistication does not detract from the audience's enjoyment.

American Graffiti is filled with private jokes between Lucas and his friends. Milner's deuce coupe bears license plates that read "THX 1138." The local movie theater in the film is playing *Dementia 13*, the first feature-length movie directed by Francis Coppola. By the end of production, however, Lucas was no longer in a joking mood. He had yet to film *Graffiti*'s climactic car crash that follows the drag race between Milner and Bob Falfa, played by Harrison Ford. The elaborate car stunt required Falfa's vehicle to go off the road and roll several times end over end, exploding just after the stunt doubles for Ford and Cindy Williams stumble out. The first attempt at the stunt failed because the car's axle rod broke. A second attempt was made, only to have the other axle break. On the last day of shooting, August 4, 1972, the car stunt again failed, this time causing a near-tragedy.

Two camera operators were lying on the road, their cameras at ground level to film Falfa's car as it roared toward them and then veered off the road. This time, the car never veered—it headed straight for the cameras. "We all thought those two guys were dead, no kidding!" Richard Dreyfuss recalls. "That car missed one camera by inches, and the cameraman panned right with it! We were all shitting in our pants by that time." A few days later, Lucas took *four* cameras out to the deserted country road and filmed the stunt. As he returned to the production office, *Graffiti* finally in the can, Universal's Ned Tanen was there to congratulate him. "You really don't like doing this, do you?" Tanen asked Lucas, who looked totally exhausted. George shook his head. "I'll finish it, but I don't ever want to have to go through this again."

It's like taking your little kid and cutting off one of her fingers. "It's only a finger, it's not that big a deal," they say. But to me, it's just an arbitrary exercise of power. And it irritates me enormously.[3]
—George Lucas on Universal's editing of *American Graffiti*

Lucas was lucky to have survived *American Graffiti*. Gary Kurtz says that if filming had continued much longer "we'd all have been dead." Kurtz was so overworked that his back went out; for a few weeks he hobbled around with the aid of a cane. Lucas was looking forward to editing the movie, even if he didn't have the strength for it. He put together a twenty-minute assemblage of scenes for the cast party celebrating the end of shooting. When the lights came on, Harrison Ford turned to Cindy Williams and yelled, "This is great!"

George wanted Marcia to edit *Graffiti*, but Universal pressed for a more experienced editor. Lucas's old employer Verna Fields had just finished cutting another young director's movie for the studio, Steven Spielberg's *Sugarland Express*, and Universal was pleased with the results. Lucas, hoping Fields would be a buffer between him and the studio, agreed to hire her. Fields edited for only ten weeks, long enough to finish the first rough cut of *Graffiti*. Coppola had purchased a house in Mill Valley at Lucas's urging, and the two-story garage behind it became the editing studio for *Graffiti*. Coppola worked in the adjacent house on his screenplay for *The Conversation,* another of the abandoned Zoetrope projects. There were frequent Italian boccie bowling games on the lawn, along with picnics and sunbathing. "It was the closest we ever got to the original dream," Coppola says wistfully.

Every day Lucas looked at *Graffiti* footage and explained what he wanted from Marcia and Verna. It was the only time he ever saw and spoke to his wife during the hectic postproduction period. George asked Walter Murch to join the team as sound editor, and together they performed the painstaking task of cutting the music to fit each scene. The music was critical to the impact of the movie, acting as counterpoint to and reinforcement for the classic teenage situations depicted on screen. Lucas wanted to match the songs to the scenes on the basis of mood and melody rather than lyrics, not wanting to ape the actions of his characters.

The most difficult job was establishing the rhythm of the movie, moving the sequences smoothly from one character to another. Lucas originally planned to repeat a progression: Curt segues to Toad, who leads to Milner, then to Steve, and back to Curt. But the structure proved too rigid; the characters had no freedom. Marcia and George argued over the approach and eventually he abandoned it. When the first cut of *Graffiti* was finally completed, everyone was pleased: "I thought we had one hell of a picture," remembered Verna Fields. But at two and three-quarters hours, it was an hour too long. The Lucases and Murch (Fields had since gone on to another film) spent the next six months trimming footage. The story was so interwoven that removing one or two scenes disrupted the entire flow of the film. Lucas now realized how important editing actually was: "You literally can have a film that works fine at one point, and in one week you can cut it to a point where it absolutely does not work at all."

That description applied to the second version of *Graffiti,* which was twenty minutes shorter and just awful. Marcia had patiently listened to George, but now she took over and deftly recut the movie. While Marcia trimmed and spliced, George and Walter improved the sound concepts they had first introduced in *THX 1138.* In *Graffiti,* the sound established moods and amplified the atmosphere. The music track overwhelmed the usual sound effects, but Murch created a natural range of background noises that gave the film a rich texture.

American Graffiti finally was whittled down to just under two hours and was ready to be submitted to the studio. Universal had left Lucas alone during the filming, other than an occasional visit from an executive shepherded by Coppola. Lucas wanted a carefully selected audience of young people to preview the movie in San Francisco. He hated the idea of a Hollywood sneak preview, populated by movie-industry types and cynics; he wanted to gauge a real audience's reaction to his film. Universal hadn't seen *Graffiti* at all; for that matter, Coppola had only seen bits and pieces of it. Everyone awaited the debut of *Graffiti* with mixed anticipation and apprehension.

The preview took place Sunday, January 28, 1973, at 10:00 A.M. in the Northpoint Theater in San Francisco. Lucas was told he was crazy to preview a comedy on a Sunday morning, but he figured Universal was going to have to see the movie some time. As the Lucasfilm Ltd. logo came on the screen for the first time, George and Dorothy Lucas, among the invited guests, grinned with pride, unaware what they were about to witness. Kurtz was ready to tape-record the audience to see which scenes drew the most laughter.

The Northpoint screening of *American Graffiti* has become part of modern film lore, a mythical event that symbolizes the difference between the old and the new Hollywood. Like the crime depicted in the Japanese movie *Rashomon,* directed by Lucas's hero Akira Kurosawa, the *Graffiti* preview was seen by each eyewitness in a totally different light. The controversy that ensued at the film's conclusion has added to the screening's mythic qualities—those who were present are proud of their special status, because they, too, have become part of the legend.

There is no disputing the audience's reaction—they loved it. The film broke twice in the first ten minutes and the sound wasn't properly synched, but nothing could dampen the enthusiasm at the Northpoint: more than eight hundred people laughed, cheered, and applauded. Ned Tanen was there representing Universal; he had flown to San Francisco that morning with Hal Barwood, Matthew Robbins, and Jeff Berg. All three remember that Tanen was not in the best of moods—his stomach was upset and his anxiety about *Graffiti* seemed palpable. "Ned wouldn't sit with us on the airplane and he wouldn't share a cab to the theater," remembers Robbins. "He was furious before he even saw the movie."

As the final credits rolled by, an ashen-faced Tanen got out of his seat and rushed to the back of the theater, where there was a dimly lit walkway between the seats and the wall. The applause continued as Tanen and Gary Kurtz stepped into the alley behind the Northpoint. The words tumbled out of the raging executive: "This is in no shape to show to an audience," Tanen sputtered. "It's unreleasable!" Tanen scolded Kurtz for publicly previewing the movie—it should have been shown privately to the studio first. Now everyone would know what a dog the film was. Kurtz stood in stunned silence. He thought *Graffiti* had been a rousing success.

He went back into the theater, found Lucas, and quickly whispered that Tanen hated the movie.

Tanen reentered the theater as the houselights came on and the audience began to file up the aisles. The first person he encountered was Francis Coppola, who asked innocently how Tanen had liked the film. Ned responded that he had a lot of problems with *Graffiti* and he didn't think it worked at all. "You boys let me down," he told Coppola. "I went to bat for you and you let me down." Tanen looked at Lucas as he said this and remembers that George had a dazed expression on his face. "I was in shock," Lucas confirms.

The nightmare Lucas had experienced on *THX* was recurring—he was about to lose control of a movie again. Coppola felt Lucas's pain and lashed out at Tanen. "You should get down on your knees and thank George for saving your job," Coppola bellowed. "This kid has killed himself to make this movie for you. And he brought it in on time and on schedule. The least you can do is thank him for doing that!" Tanen tried to explain, but there was no stopping Coppola, who lectured Tanen about his insensitivity to Lucas's feelings. Lucas watched in amazement, reveling in the exchange between the leading Young Turk movie director and one of Hollywood's brightest young studio executives. The crowd surrounding Coppola and Tanen as they screamed at each other included Barwood, Robbins, Berg, Michael Ritchie, Walter Murch, and Marcia Lucas, all of whom were dumbfounded by the unusual public display of emotion.

If Tanen didn't want the film, Coppola sneered, then *he* would be happy to buy it. Coppola remembers offering to write a check for *Graffiti* on the spot, an offer Tanen steadfastly denies was ever made. (Mona Skager notes, "Francis doesn't carry checkbooks.") But Coppola *did* offer to buy the film. He was making up for his lack of courage in standing up to Warner Bros. over the cutting of *THX*. "This movie's going to be a hit! This audience loved this movie! I saw it with my own eyes!" Coppola yelled. The confrontation was etched indelibly in the memory of those present. "I wish I'd been there to see it myself, because it's the best story to come out of Hollywood since the late 1940s," says Steven Spielberg.

Kurtz tried to calm everyone down by suggesting Tanen and Lucas meet the next day at Zoetrope's San Francisco studio. Lucas and Kurtz would make a list of possible changes based on the preview audience's reaction, and Tanen could go over the film reel by reel and make his own suggestions. The ploy worked—the next morning, Tanen's attitude was much improved. Lucas, however, was morose and depressed, feeling that he already had lost control of *Graffiti*. Tanen justified his initial reaction by insisting that several changes be made. Looking back, Lucas and Tanen recognize and sympathize with each other's position. Lucas acknowledges the pressures under which Tanen was operating, and Tanen says he probably should not have taken the film away from Lucas. "Life is hard and we all do things maybe we shouldn't do," he says softly.

After the screening, Lucas went home and bitterly complained to Marcia. He really had tried to give the studio a good film, and Tanen wouldn't even recognize his efforts. He didn't have to defend himself, George said, because he was right and Tanen was wrong. Marcia was more realistic: "George was just a nobody who had directed one little arty-farty movie that hadn't done any business. He didn't have the power to make people listen to him." Marcia was irritated by George's unwillingness to fight for his movie. She had confidence in *Graffiti*, but George didn't seem to share it. Lucas called his parents and asked them how much longer he had to compromise his beliefs. "Only to the point where you still feel comfortable," answered George, Sr.

Lucas's basic reaction was to pout and sulk. He ranted and raved in the privacy of his office, but he let Kurtz handle the difficult negotiations with the studio. George's distaste for confrontations once again outweighed his artistic outrage. Lucas spent the next month remixing and recutting the picture, ignoring Tanen's suggestions unless he agreed with them. He and Kurtz took the movie down to Los Angeles in March 1973 for Tanen's approval. But the executive became upset all over again when he saw the reedited version. Lucas had ignored his advice. Unless the changes he had outlined were made immediately, Tanen threatened to turn the movie over to Bill Hornbeck, Universal's veteran editor.

"I got real angry," Lucas recalls. "And when I get angry like that, I get very quiet, so everybody knows how angry I am. Francis yells. I'm just the opposite." Lucas realized he was in a no-win situation. He had hoped to get at least one finished print of his version of the movie, but now that seemed impossible. Universal, in effect, was reclaiming *American Graffiti*, and they had the right to do whatever they wanted to it.

Lucas's dispute with Universal over *Graffiti* coincided with a strike called against the movie studios by the Writers Guild of America. Prohibited from working on his unreleased film or from crossing the picket lines at the Universal lot in Studio City, Lucas met with Coppola and Kurtz at the nearby Universal Sheraton Hotel. They asked Verna Fields to rejoin the picture and intercede on their behalf, figuring the studio trusted her. Feeling a little more hopeful, Lucas and Coppola returned to San Francisco, leaving Kurtz and Fields to battle Universal. Marcia believes that Coppola should have stayed and fought for the film, but Jeff Berg recalls that Francis effectively lobbied for *Graffiti*'s integrity from San Francisco.

Coppola claims that due to his intercession, the cuts finally made in *Graffiti,* totaling about four and a half minutes of footage, were minimal. They included three scenes: one featuring a used-car salesman giving a pitch; another in which Steve tells off a fuddy-duddy old teacher at the school sock hop; and an ad-libbed rendition of "Some Enchanted Evening" by Harrison Ford. (To use the song, Universal would have had to obtain the permission of Richard Rodgers and of Oscar Hammerstein II's estate, which took one look at *Graffiti* and indignantly refused.) Tanen also wanted to cut a fourth scene, Milner's moving soliloquy in the automobile junkyard, but Kurtz talked him out of it. However, Tanen was adamant about excising the salesman and the song.

Lucas was kept apprised of the editing changes via phone. The idea of knuckling under to Universal enraged him, even at the distance of four hundred miles: "They were simply coming in and putting a crayon mark on my painting and saying, 'Hey, don't worry about it. It's just a crayon mark.'" *Graffiti* was a watershed for Lucas—he vowed never to give up control again. If his films did not reflect his vision, then he would rather not make them at all. Lucas considered himself to be a rational person, capable of accepting constructive criticism. But he *knew American Graffiti* worked with an audience—he had seen it himself.

Lucas acknowledges that the used-car salesman and "Some Enchanted Evening" scenes were not crucial to the movie, but he was fond of them. "It was self-indulgence, but I think a filmmaker should be allowed a little self-indulgence, as long as it doesn't destroy the whole movie," Lucas says. "I mean, you've got to get something out of it." Lucas didn't care how slight the alterations were. He felt he had been trifled with and deceived, and in the morally righteous world of George Lucas, that was unpardonable. Underneath his mild-mannered exterior, Lucas is a highly emotional person with deep rages. There are no subtle gradations in his judgment of events in his life; instead things are always "infinitely" better or "infinitely" worse. Such extreme metaphors reflect the wild swings of his inner personality. "He characterizes things as being either totally dark or totally light," says John Korty.

Thus, the mutilation of *American Graffiti* was a totally black incident for Lucas, representing Hollywood's perfidy and crassness. It left him with an abiding resentment that has deepened over the years. Ned Tanen says that he and Lucas are now friendly acquaintances, but George has wounded the executive with published comments about the sleazy denizens of Hollywood, presumably including Tanen as the prime specimen. "I was really angry," Lucas said of the cutting of *Graffiti* to *Rolling Stone* magazine in 1980, "and I remain angry to this day."[4]

Reediting *Graffiti* did not solve Tanen's problems. He still had to get the studio to release a film that was perceived as a giant headache. He scheduled another preview screening for May 15, 1973, this time at the Writers Guild Theater in Beverly Hills. He called Wolfman Jack, one of the film's stars, and asked him to pack the house with kids. Most of the cast also attended the screening, although Richard Dreyfuss and Harrison Ford slunk out of the theater, each embarrassed by his first big-screen performance.

Everyone else present loved the movie—several people remember it as the most exciting Hollywood preview they have ever attended. People yelled, screamed, stood, and clapped from the opening scenes, singing along with the sound track. One attendee called it "a love riot." Steven Spielberg has seen exciting previews of his own films, including *Jaws* and *Close Encounters of the Third Kind,* but he insists that the *Graffiti* screening was the most powerful he has ever witnessed. "It hit a chord of nostalgia, because it was such a warm nod backward. It was for George's, mine, everybody's generation," he says. Ned Tanen *still* didn't like *Graffiti,* however. As he walked out of the theater with his date, Tanen looked morose and his companion asked what was bothering him. "I didn't think it played well," Tanen said in a dejected voice. The woman looked at him in amazement: "It was such a good movie, you couldn't even hear it! What are you talking about?" Tanen sighed and shook his head. "I'm basically manic-depressive by nature, so I guess I just didn't get it," he admitted.

The screening accomplished Tanen's purpose, however. Universal could no longer ignore that audiences loved *American Graffiti.* The studio's enthusiasm quickened when 20th Century-Fox and Paramount Pictures put out feelers to release *Graffiti* if Universal wasn't interested. Universal panicked and decided to release it immediately, which meant dumping *Graffiti* in hundreds of drive-in theaters. After protests by Kurtz and Coppola (Lucas remained in San Francisco in a huff), Universal agreed to open the film first in New York and Los Angeles, then across the country two weeks later.

The theater chosen for the Los Angeles premiere was the Cinerama Dome in Hollywood, designed for the wide-screen Cinerama movies of the early 1960s. Lucas had filmed *Graffiti* in Techniscope, and the blown-up images on the Dome's curved screen looked like a Bromo-Seltzer commercial, recalls Tanen. "I was hysterical to get it out of that theater. I screamed and yelled at everybody. I stood in front of the screen waving my arms and said, 'Get this goddamn thing out of here, it looks terrible!'" The film was moved to Westwood, the bastion of youthful Los Angeles moviegoers located next to the UCLA campus.

Cindy Williams drove through Westwood on the night *American Graffiti* opened, August 1, 1973. She was stunned by the long lines snaking around the Avco Theater: "I never thought I'd be in a movie that had lines around the block!" *Graffiti* didn't set box office records in its first week in New York and Los Angeles—this was before the blockbuster openings of movies like *Star Wars, Superman,* and *E.T.* But to Universal's surprise, *Graffiti* did well *everywhere:* the big cities and small towns, the East Coast and Southwest, the art theaters in New York and the one-marquee towns. Tanen is still amazed by the movie's steady drawing power: "It didn't actually explode, it was never that huge of a hit. It just stayed in theaters for, like, two years. They had birthday parties for it. It just ran and ran forever."

It took six months for Universal, Kurtz, and Lucas to fully realize what a big hit they had. *Graffiti* proved to be the most profitable film investment a Hollywood studio ever made. The direct cost of the film was $775,000 and another $500,000 was spent for prints, advertising, and publicity. Universal took in film rentals (the portion of ticket sales returned to the distributor) of *$55,886,000.* For every dollar invested, Universal saw more than $50 in profits, a ratio that even *Star Wars* could not equal.

Graffiti currently rests at the number 18 spot on *Variety*'s list of all-time movie hits, having sold more than $117 million in tickets throughout the world. It was less successful outside the United States, which is no surprise. The film achieved a cult reputation in France but was too American for most overseas audiences. It made less than $5 million in rentals outside the United States and Canada.

As the money poured in, the only unhappy person was Coppola. Lucas smiles as he recalls how "Francis was kicking himself forever for the fact that if he had just financed the film himself, he would have made thirty million dollars on the deal. He never got over it." No one expected *Graffiti* to enjoy the success it did, least of all Lucas: "I had never been interested in making money, just in making movies. I became rich and successful by accident. The only thing I worried about was that the studio might lose money. As long as the film broke even, I felt I had done my job. Believe me, I did not set out to make a blockbuster movie with *Graffiti.*"

But of course Lucas *had* set out to make a commercial movie—it was by conscious design that he changed his approach from the esoteric weirdness of *THX 1138.* He and Jeff Berg had projected that *Graffiti* could earn as much as $30 million in rentals. Richard Dreyfuss was one of the few who had no faith in the film's box office potential: "I didn't think it was going to make sixty *dollars.* I am on record as being the only one on that set who didn't know. I just thought it was a little movie."

Movie directors pray for the rave reviews *American Graffiti* received. Tanen was struck by the intense media interest in Lucas even before the film opened: "Why is he getting this kind of treatment? He's another kid making a rite-of-passage movie. It wasn't the first one, certainly not the last." Lucas received a kind of worshipful respect that few top directors were accorded. Something came across to reviewers in Wichita or Philadelphia. Charles Champlin of the *Los Angeles Times* recalls, "It was the kind of film you wanted to root for."

The positive reviews meant nothing to Lucas because of a damning critique in the *San Francisco Chronicle.* He was hurt and embarrassed—the *Chronicle* was read by his parents, relatives, and friends. "It was the first time I had a film that I thought was good, and as far as my family and friends were concerned, it was a turkey, because that was the only paper they read. Whatever triumph there was was muted enormously," Lucas remembers. Most of his colleagues loved *Graffiti,* although Haskell Wexler, who photographed it, thought it looked like a television show. Lucas's friends most enjoyed the revelations *Graffiti* gave them about George himself. Carol Titelman, who later worked for Lucas, did not particularly like *Graffiti.* But when she met George, she was surprised by how shy and repressed he seemed. "God, he must have such an incredible inner life to have produced this crazy film full of music, action, and teen-aged passion," she mused.

The popular success of *Graffiti* was validated by the annual series of critical awards. The movie received 1973 Academy Award nominations for Best Picture, Best Direction (Lucas), Best Original Screenplay (the Huycks and Lucas), Best Supporting Actress (Candy Clark), and Best Film Editing (Marcia Lucas and Verna Fields). It won the Best Screenplay award from both the prestigious New York Film Critics Association and the National Society of Film Critics. The Hollywood Foreign Press Association gave *Graffiti* a Golden Globe award as the Best Comedy Picture of the Year. All this helped Universal develop a new respect for the movie. When the Academy Award nominations were announced on

January 4, 1974, Lucas received a telegram from Universal president Sidney Sheinberg, Ned Tanen's boss: "I personally consider the film an American Classic." Lucas was not mollified.

Lucas never expected *Graffiti* to win any Academy Awards, and he wasn't surprised when it did not. Until *Annie Hall* triumphed over *Star Wars* four years later, a contemporary comedy had not recently won the Oscar for Best Picture. *Graffiti* was, as Lucas describes it, "a little, tiny, out-of-town, nobody kind of movie, successful but still small and low-budget," an unlikely candidate for Oscar recognition. The film that swept the 1973 awards was *The Sting*, a big-budget, star-laden (Robert Redford and Paul Newman) commercial movie more in keeping with Hollywood tradition. Lucas was only slightly disappointed, Kurtz more so, and Marcia cried. She badly wanted to win. George just didn't care.

From being a struggling, starving filmmaker to being incredibly successful in a period of a couple of years is quite a powerful experience, and not necessarily a good one.

—George Lucas

Few people were less prepared for success than George and Marcia Lucas. Their combined income had never exceeded $20,000 a year prior to making *Graffiti,* and during the lengthy development process on the film, their slender resources were stretched to the limit. Accountant Richard Tong prepared the Lucases' tax returns in 1973, consisting of Lucas's directing fee ($50,000), Marcia's two W-2 statements from her editing work, and some interest on their bank savings. Lucasfilm Ltd. was George's production company, but his directing services were loaned to Universal and *American Graffiti* via a separate company, of which he was the sole shareholder for tax purposes.

At the time of *Graffiti*'s release, Lucas was dead broke. He had borrowed money from his parents, from Coppola, and from his lawyers Doug Ferguson and Tom Pollock. Then came the deluge of profits, and George and Marcia didn't know how to react. "Part of it was having to break loose after being so poor for so long," George explains. "It took me a long time to realize that I could buy things." He and Marcia enjoyed their modest lifestyle—living in their small home, driving the silver Camaro, wearing unisex blue jeans and work shirts.

Now, to George's amazement, his once-stated vow to become a million-aire by age thirty was fulfilled, two years ahead of schedule.

His closest friends saw few obvious changes in Lucas. John Milius made almost $90,000 a year writing original screenplays and doctoring others for the movie studios. Coppola had made millions from *The Godfather.* Barwood and Robbins were doing well from their various development deals. His friends' success coincided with the period when Lucas was struggling. "I think that gave him a real desire to be rich," says Milius.

Lucas's eventual share of the *Graffiti* profits was more than $7 million; after federal and state taxes, he and Marcia were left with almost $4 million in cash. Marcia could hardly believe it—this was a far cry from a childhood of two new dresses a year. George immediately repaid his outstanding loans, taking particular pride in giving $2,000 back to his parents. George, Sr., was standing so straight and tall that it seemed as if he might topple over backward—his little Georgie had earned ten times more than his damn movie cost!

Adhering to his father's small-town economic philosophy, Lucas chose the most conservative investments for his financial windfall: land, tax-exempt municipal bonds, savings accounts. He made some investments in the stock market, but quickly withdrew from them after turning a small profit. Lucas now had his nest egg, a guarantee that he and Marcia never would be poor. He also had the money to ensure that his artistic freedom never would be violated again.

The burden of wealth had a negligible effect on Lucas's business activities too. Lucy Wilson was hired in 1974 as Lucasfilm's first book-keeper, now that there were books to keep. One of her duties was to cash checks for George. "He'd keep one check at a time in his wallet, and the only way I noticed his getting wealthier was that it used to be made out for fifty dollars and then it turned into a couple of hundred dollars," Wilson recalls. Lucas had no idea of how much money was in his bank accounts and he refused to balance his checkbook. "Money just didn't seem to matter to him," Wilson says.

Lucas made one important purchase: a Victorian house in Marin that represented his version of the Zoetrope dream. He and Marcia had moved from Mill Valley to the small Marin town of San Anselmo when *Graffiti* was released. Their new home on Medway Street was small, and Lucas wanted a separate office where he could work on *Star Wars.* Marcia discovered a dilapidated Marin landmark for sale, a wood frame residence built in 1869. Lucas bought it for $150,000 in December 1973 and had a screening room built in the back. The bedrooms were turned into offices, which friends like Barwood and Robbins, Michael Ritchie, and Carroll Ballard occupied for little or no rent. The Lucasfilm staff—George, Gary

Kurtz, Bunny Alsup, and Lucy Wilson—also moved to Parkhouse, which was the name Marcia gave to the sagging structure.

Privately, George enjoyed his newfound success. John Korty remembers that "There was a kind of sweet revenge in having gone into the Hollywood arena and done things better than they ever did them, then coming away with seven million dollars and saying, 'Screw you.'"

Lucas had peculiar notions about success by Hollywood standards. He shared his *Graffiti* wealth with the people he felt had contributed to it. To do otherwise would be immoral, George believed. He gave new cars to his secretary, Bunny Alsup, casting director Fred Roos, and editors Verna Fields and Walter Murch, along with $10,000 in cash and gifts to other crew members. Small profit "points" (percentages of the movie's net profits after studio deductions for making and distributing the film) were given to the Huycks, Gary Kurtz, and Tom Pollock. Legend has it that Lucas made twelve millionaires from handing out points on *American Graffiti,* but the number is closer to three or four. Still, how many twenty-eight-year-old filmmakers can make the boast at all?

The recipients of Lucas's generosity were impressed, mostly by the spirit in which it was given. Lucas split one point ten ways for the principal cast members and gave one point to cinematographer Haskell Wexler, who was not paid any salary. (Coppola gave him two more points.) "My view is that even if George knew it was going to be the big success that it was, I believe he still would have given out the percentages," says Wexler who, to date, has seen almost $1 million from *Graffiti*. Richard Dreyfuss has seen his $5,000 salary dwarfed by the nearly $70,000 he has received. "It was such a pure thing," says Dreyfuss. "Everyone was so venal in that rotten world and here was this free gift, a really great gesture."

Not everyone was satisfied, however. Lucas complained to accountant Richard Tong that some of the recipients of cars had complained about not getting more cash instead. George was disturbed by the greed of some people and told Tong that he would never do it again. "I thought he meant that's the last time he would share," Tong says with a laugh. "But no, he just meant no more cars."

Lucas was surprised by the ingratitude of some recipients of his generosity, but he became upset over Francis Coppola's reluctance to meet what Lucas thought were his obligations. They had agreed to split the profits from *Graffiti* in half, each getting 20 percent. Out of his half, Coppola was to give producer Gary Kurtz 5 percent. Out of Lucas's share came points for Huyck and Katz, the actors, and Pollock. Coppola resisted the idea of sharing his profits with Kurtz from the outset. He hadn't hired Gary—Lucas had—and Francis felt George should take care of it. The disagreement reached a climax over the profits due Wexler, who joined *Graffiti* after the initial profit split was worked out. Coppola, who planned to do his next film with Wexler, proposed giving Haskell three points: he would pay two and Lucas could pay the remaining 1 percent. When the money started to come in, Lucas promptly paid his share, but Coppola balked at giving profits to Kurtz and Wexler. Lucas accused him of reneging on his promise, and only after intense negotiations were Kurtz and Wexler paid by Coppola. Coppola ultimately recieved 13 percent of *Graffiti*'s profits, amounting to almost $3 million. Lucas ended up with 15 percent of the profits and strong feelings over Coppola's behavior. "Francis was questioning my honesty," Lucas says of the dispute over what was owed to whom. "He thought that I was operating the same way he was operating. He was accusing me of being like him, and that upset me."

The argument was not over the division of spoils—there was enough money from *Graffiti* to make both men wealthy. But the dispute summarizes the unusual relationship between Coppola and Lucas—even now, each man believes he was right and the other person was misguided. The disagreement over profit-sharing reveals the essence of each man: George's sense of moral obligation and Coppola's laissez-faire attitude. "We really didn't have any kind of giant falling out," Lucas says of the post-*Graffiti* recriminations. "But it was one of the reasons we drifted apart, more than anything else."

The dream was over. Coppola felt excluded from *Graffiti* by Lucas—there was no room for Francis in George's movie. Lucas had gone to Coppola to produce *Graffiti* only at Universal's insistence. Because of that, Coppola thinks Lucas wanted to make the most money from the film. Lucas sees things differently, convinced that Francis had to dominate him, if not in the making of *Graffiti*, then in the division of its spoils. Lucas used to rationalize Coppola's behavior by assuming that Francis simply didn't know any better. But after the arguments that followed *Graffiti*, Lucas saw Coppola as immoral. That sort of behavior was *just not right*.

I've had a very volatile relationship with Francis. It's on both sides, like we're married and we got divorced. It's as close a relationship as I've had with anybody.

—George Lucas

The divorce, when it came, was painful. Since his days at USC, Lucas had wanted to make a movie about the bizzare media circus the Vietnam War had become. John Milius had also worked on the idea at USC, going so far as to interview returning veterans who told him fantastic and colorful stories. "Surfing and bombs" became the theme of the movie Lucas and Milius discussed over the years. *Apocalypse Now,* the title given the project, was a reflection of Milius's right-wing politics, about shitkicking the enemy whether it was justified or not. Lucas saw the movie as an updated *Dr. Strangelove,* a case of trying to kill an ant with a sledgehammer, only to discover that the ant is winning.

Lucas suggested to Milius that the purpose of the movie be a trek to a goal. Milius had envisioned a helicopter journey, but Lucas suggested a simple boat ride up a river. An intelligence officer is dropped off with a secret mission to "terminate with extreme prejudice" a Special Forces commander who has lost his mind and "gone native."

Apocalypse Now was one of the first projects Lucas mentioned to Coppola during Zoetrope's formation, but it was discarded by Warner Bros., with the rest of the Black Thursday screenplays. After Coppola repaid Warner's for the development money, he owned the rights to all the Zoetrope projects. Lucas remained determined to get *Apocalypse* off the ground, and after finishing *American Graffiti,* he made a development deal with Columbia Pictures for it. Gary Kurtz made a trip to the Philippines to scout locations; he and Lucas were convinced *Apocalypse* could be made cheaply using documentary-style 16-millimeter cameras, real soldiers as extras, and a budget of under $2 million. While Kurtz was gone, Lucas and Milius worked on a story treatment, and soon Milius had the screenplay completed.

Lucas was feeling frustrated in his efforts to get *Star Wars* in manageable shape and saw *Apocalypse* as the next logical step in his career. He went to Coppola in early 1973 and said, "I've got a chance to make this [film], Francis." But if *Apocalypse* was to be made, it was with Coppola as producer and owner of 25 percent of the profits, twice as much as Lucas, who split his 25 percent with Milius. That didn't seem fair to George, who was still smarting from the profit wrangles over *Graffiti.* "I couldn't possibly have made the movie under those conditions," Lucas says, so he turned back to *Star Wars.*

A year later, Coppola approached Lucas about *Apocalypse.* Francis had the idea that if the film were released simultaneously with the American Bicentennial, it could have a huge impact. It was 1974, and Francis was ready to go; with George directing again, they could do better than they did on *Graffiti.* But Lucas, who had just closed his deal with 20th Century-

Fox on *Star Wars,* felt he had to finish the job at hand. Lucas was at first incredulous and then furious when Coppola persisted, offering him a directing fee of $25,000 and 10 percent of the profits, the deal agreed upon six years earlier for Lucas's second Zoetrope project. Lucas was being paid $150,000 to write and direct *Star Wars.* Lucas asked Coppola to wait until *Star Wars* was finished—he very much wanted to direct *Apocalypse.* But Francis was adamant that the movie come out in 1976. Coppola recalls, "At one point, I just said, 'What the hell, I've got it [*Apocalypse*]. Let me do it, just to get it off the boards." Lucas was tired of hassling with someone he both loved and hated. "If you want to make it, go make it," George said resignedly. Francis tried to get Milius to direct *Apocalypse,* but John also spurned the low terms. Eventually, Coppola directed the film himself.

The making of *Apocalypse Now* took more than two years, cost $36 million, and nearly broke Coppola in mind and spirit. Francis gave George a couple of profit points in the movie at its release in 1979, and although the film surprised skeptics by earning most of its money back, it has yet to return any profits to George. Lucas was deeply hurt by Coppola's refusal to wait for him to direct *Apocalypse.* George felt he had invested six years of his life in the project, only to see his original concept distorted by Coppola's fervid imagination. "It was *my* picture, and I didn't have any control over the situation," Lucas now says. "I don't hold anything against Francis, though. He had every right to make it; he owned it. But I was quite upset at the time."

Lucas felt he had been ripped off. This time it was just too much—it was the last affront. He disassociated himself from Coppola both professionally and personally. The onetime close friends still see each other at holidays, and their meetings are always friendly, if strained. But their consecutive disputes over the *Graffiti* profits and *Apocalypse Now* have dissolved their professional relationship. As usual, Coppola had the last word. Harrison Ford appeared briefly in one scene in *Apocalypse,* playing an intelligence officer at a briefing. As the Ford character removes his glasses, Coppola zooms in for a closeup of Ford's green army shirt. The name tag clearly reads, "Col. G. Lucas."[5]

6
THE VISION OF
STAR WARS

I have a bad feeling about this.
                                    —Sentiment often expressed in *Star Wars*
                                    by Luke Skywalker, Han Solo, and C-3PO

The weather was wretched in Tunisia. George Lucas hated the searing winds and the bitter cold of the Sahara Desert. On March 26, 1976, the day after *Star Wars* started production, it rained. It hadn't rained during the Tunisian winter in fifty years. There were mudholes everywhere and the first location was supposed to be a *dry* lake bed, the Chott Djerid.[1]

Lucas's problems were just beginning. The two actors in the initial scene were having trouble. Anthony Daniels was inside C-3PO (See-Threepio), a gold-burnished robot whose suit was getting its first real test. Daniels was cut and bruised from the sharp plastic edges of the ill-fitting costume; he could hardly move. Kenny Baker occupied a three-foot-high metal "droid" called R2-D2 (Artoo-Detoo). It didn't work at all.

R2-D2's electronic controls were designed to enable him to shuffle forward, turn, and move laterally, but they only succeeded in picking up Tunisian radio signals. Baker, three feet, eight inches tall, could do little to control the robot. His elbows were stuck to his sides, barely allowing him to reach the switches that activated his lights and power. It was so noisy inside R2-D2 that Baker couldn't hear Lucas call "Cut"; a crew member had to hit his shell with a hammer to stop him. Lucas finally removed

Baker and pulled the empty R2-D2 across the sand on a thin wire. The robot promptly fell over. "Everything was constantly going wrong," George grunts. "Typical."

Lucas was on a tight schedule. He had ordered a chartered jet to pick up the cast and crew exactly eleven days after they arrived in North Africa—if they weren't ready, the airline would charge the production $1,000 per hour in penalty fees. Back in Hollywood, 20th Century-Fox was betting almost $10 million that the thirty-one-year-old filmmaker could deliver a "space fantasy" that would prove profitable, although the final form of *Star Wars* was indecipherable to everyone but Lucas. The screenplay had been examined by the Tunisian authorities, who approved it after finding no political implications in the story.

Tunisia had the Moroccan architecture and settings Lucas needed for his scenes on Tatooine, the desert planet. In Nefta and nearby Jerba, he found the white-domed structures that become the compound where Luke Skywalker lived with his Uncle Owen Lars and Aunt Beru. In the village of Matama people live in deep caves off a central open hole that protects them from the frequent sandstorms. Lucas liked the otherworldly look of the caves, and one sunken dwelling became the breakfast nook of the Lars household. George sent Marcia a picture of himself in front of Obi-Wan Kenobi's cave and inscribed it: "Are you sure Orson Welles started this way?"

Orson Welles never encountered the misfortunes awaiting Lucas. An entire day was spent filming R2-D2 moving a yard or two. The prefabricated sets from England were so big that it took the British and Tunisian crew four days to move them thirty miles into the desert from the production base at Nefta. The sandcrawler in which the Jawas transported C-3PO and R2-D2 stood two stories tall and was ninety feet long. The night before Lucas was ready to shoot the Jawas' scene, a ferocious sandstorm raged across the desert and blew the giant sandcrawler apart. It took a day to put it back together and an additional day to shoot the scene. The sandcrawler was then transformed into a burned-out hulk, which took another day. There was barely time to break it apart, pack it up, and ship it back to England.

The wind was bitterly cold in the desert and the camera lenses became pitted by sand. R2-D2, still incapable of walking, was mounted on sand-colored skis and pulled along a fiberglass line. Luke's land speeder, which was supposed to skim above the sand, also never functioned. Lucas filmed some long shots of the useless machine, knowing he would have to redo the sequences back home.

George drove his cast and crew unmercifully; he set an example by getting only four or five hours of sleep a night. Goggles were standard issue, as sandstorms erupted without warning. Those who survived the freezing temperatures and mud were felled by dysentery, an affliction that persisted despite the crew's reliance on bottled water and canned food.

Of the major cast members, only Mark Hamill and Alec Guinness had made the trip. There was also a full complement of Jawas, tiny creatures whose faces were shrouded by brown hooded garments, except for two yellow eyes. Beneath the costumes were five Tunisian children, an English midget, a French-Tunisian midget, and producer Gary Kurtz's two daughters.

Tunisia was the perfect location for *Star Wars*. "It was really like being on Tatooine. There are no sound stages, and you really become intent on the action," Hamill remembers. For all his problems, Lucas accomplished what he set out to do: the characters of C-3PO and R2-D2 were firmly established as the electronic equivalent of Laurel and Hardy.

The *Star Wars* company left enough artifacts in Tunisia to puzzle future archeologists, including a few trucks and giant prop bones for a bantha skeleton. The rocky gully where R2-D2 is zapped by the Jawas is now officially known as the *Star Wars* canyon—Lucas used it again in *Raiders of the Lost Ark*. And tiny Matama, where people live in holes in the ground, features a small sign in the center of town: "*Star Wars* was filmed here."[2]

Every single deal we've done has been a trade-off of dollars for control, because that's what George has always wanted. The whole history of the *Star Wars* negotiations was dollars versus control.

—Tom Pollock

George Lucas was ready to retire from directing after the rigors of making *American Graffiti*. The physical toll it took on him wasn't worth the reward. But the idea of a space fantasy nagged at him—*THX 1138* had whetted his appetite for the movie he really wanted to make. Before he folded up his director's chair, he wanted to film one big picture on sound stages with elaborate sets and great special effects.

George had been waiting since childhood to see a romantic-fantasy-adventure story set in a distant time and place. But Hollywood churned out a steady stream of predictable, clunky, and silly science-fiction films, with only an occasional gem like *Forbidden Planet*. Lucas correctly sensed a void in the movie marketplace: audiences had tired of cinematic sex and violence in the late 1960s and early '70s; they wanted comedies and action-adventure films like the Hollywood classics.

When he finished editing *American Graffiti* in February 1972, Lucas went right to work on his idea. He wrote each morning and spent the rest of his time researching fairy tales, mythology, and social psychology. He was looking for a way to blend modern technology with the traditional story elements that were attractive and meaningful to children. "I was trying to get fairy tales, myths, and religion down to a distilled state, studying the pure form to see how and why it worked," Lucas says.

He became a voracious science-fiction reader, devouring Isaac Asimov's contemporary novels and classic sci-fi authors like Edgar Rice Burroughs and Alex Raymond. Like the wood and dirt "environments" he had constructed as a child, Lucas was building *Star Wars* from scratch.

As usual, George had difficulty getting his ideas on paper; he decided to write a story treatment (an expanded synopsis), rather than a complete screenplay. By May 1973, he had completed a bewildering thirteen-page plot summary. Handwritten on blue-lined paper, it tells "the story of Mace Windu, a revered Jedi-bendu of Opuchi who was related to Usby C. J. Thape, padawaan learner to the famed Jedi." With that as its opening sentence, it is not surprising that *Star Wars* elicited little enthusiasm. "I knew more about the story based on what George had told me than what was in that brief treatment," says Jeff Berg.

The first treatment resembles the early draft of a novel—it's fascinating to see how some elements were kept intact and others radically transformed or abandoned. Lucas set his story in the twenty-third century, a time when Jedi-Templar warriors, like their medieval counterparts, swore fealty to the Alliance of Independent Systems. Three locales were described: jungle and desert planets and a gaseous world with a city suspended in the clouds. Every person, beast, and structure was exotically named and described in detail.

The story was complicated: Leia Aguilae, a rebel princess accompanied by her family and retainers, flees from an evil sovereign who has taken control of the Alliance and declared himself emperor. General Luke Skywalker, one of two surviving Jedi knights (along with his friend Annikin Starkiller), leads Leia on a dangerous escape route. Along the way, they take two Imperial bureaucrats hostage, who add comic relief to the film. A rebel band of ten boys, aged fifteen to eighteen, also join the group. Pursued by Imperial troops, the rebels are chased across space and hide in an asteroid belt. They eventually escape in a stolen space freighter to a jungle planet where they are attacked and the princess is captured. The boys, trained by General Skywalker to fly one-man "devil fighter" planes, free the princess, engage in a laser-blasting dogfight in space with the Imperial fleet, and escape again into deep space. In the final scene, the general and his small band are rewarded by the princess on her home planet, where she reveals her true "goddesslike" self. The two bureaucrats get drunk and stumble off into the darkness, "realizing that they have been adventuring with demigods."

The characters in *Star Wars* remain surprisingly faithful to their inception, although Skywalker became a teenager, as did Leia. Two "workmen" named SeeThreepio and Artwo Detwo are finally combined with the bumbling bureaucrats to become Lucas's favorite robots. Also present in the story treatment are Han Solo, friend to the Jedi knights; Chewbacca, a Wookiee prince on the jungle planet pictured as "a giant furry alien"; and two villains, General Darth Vader and Valarium, the Black Knight. Lucas also described sleek white vehicles called land speeders.

The response to Lucas's treatment from his agent and lawyer was one of polite puzzlement—Berg and Pollock couldn't understand a word of it, but they did agree to help him sell the movie. Two things were important to Lucas in any deal with a studio: creative control, including the final editing cut of the movie, and ownership of the sequel rights. Lucas knew that *Star Wars* was too big for one film—he could make several movies from his massive story.

Star Wars first had to be submitted to United Artists, which had never formally dropped the second part of its *Graffiti* deal three years earlier. David Picker took one look at Lucas's treatment and estimated that the movie would cost a fortune, with no guarantee that the special effects could be done. Picker passed on the project.

Jeff Berg arranged for another studio executive, Alan Ladd, Jr., to see *American Graffiti* before it opened. A print was smuggled to him at 20th Century Fox. The son of the famous actor Alan Ladd, he had his father's dark good looks; he had entered the movie business as an agent in the early 1960s. After a stint as a producer, Ladd was one of several production executives at Fox in 1973; like his counterparts, he was in constant pursuit of hit movies.

Ladd was impressed by Lucas's directing skill in *THX 1138,* a tough assignment for a novice. The moment *Graffiti* illuminated the screen in the Fox theater, Ladd knew his instincts were correct: "I thought it was a terrific movie; I felt that I was seeing the work of a very talented man." Ladd met with Lucas, who told him the story of *Star Wars*. Ladd couldn't grasp the concept, but he desperately wanted to be in business with George. He even went so far as to inquire whether Universal was planning to release *Graffiti;* his interest helped spur Universal into action.

Ladd and Lucas agreed on a deal in principle at their meeting, but *Star*

Wars had to go to Universal first, who also held an option as part of the *Graffiti* deal. "We were pretty sure it would pass there, too, because it was right in the middle of Ned's most angry period," remembers Tom Pollock. "It was not submitted with enthusiasm." It wasn't met with enthusiasm, either—Universal declined to develop *Star Wars* just a month before *American Graffiti* became the studio's biggest hit in years.

Ned Tanen doesn't sleep any better after having passed up *Star Wars* (nor does David Picker, for that matter). Every movie studio has given up on films that go on to become big hits elsewhere; the mistake is not unusual, but the consequences in this case were enormous. "For the record, I didn't turn *Star Wars* down," Tanen states in a voice weary from repeating this explanation. "The company turned *Star Wars* down. I had a very tough time understanding the treatment. I would ask most people in the world to visualize what See-Threepio means from reading a thirteen-page treatment of *Star Wars*." Universal had only to pay Lucas $25,000 to develop a screenplay from his obtuse treatment, but the studio decided to save the money. The decision ultimately cost it more than $250 million.

Ten days after Universal said no, Alan Ladd, Jr., said yes, on behalf of 20th Century-Fox Film Corporation. His yes was qualified in a deal memo, not a contract.[3] Lucas was paid $50,000 to write and $100,000 to direct. Gary Kurtz got an additional $50,000 to produce *Star Wars,* and Lucas's own company, the Star Wars Corporation, was given 40 percent of the movie's net profits. An initial budget was set at $3.5 million. Lucas knew *Star Wars* could never be made for so little money, although it was five times what he spent on *Graffiti.* George worried that if Ladd knew what *Star Wars* would really cost, he'd back out of the deal.

The *Star Wars* deal memo, a seventeen-page abbreviated legal document—the Hollywood equivalent of a binding handshake—had one other crucial provision: all unresolved questions, including sequel and merchandising rights, had to be negotiated before the movie began production. The memo gave Fox, the movie's financier and distributor, all the legal advantages. But it allowed Lucas the opportunity to renegotiate several key provisions.

When *American Graffiti* opened to rave reviews and solid business three weeks later, Ladd looked very smart. He had gambled on his gut reaction and it paid off. He liked Lucas immediately, finding George intelligent, inventive, and knowledgeable about films. Lucas described *Star Wars* as an amalgam of *Buck Rogers* and *Captain Blood* and *The Sea Hawk,* two Errol Flynn swashbucklers. Ladd had grown up with the people who starred in and made these movies and was willing to take a chance on Lucas.

The success of *Graffiti* gave George the opportunity to renegotiate his contract and really stick it to Fox: Berg told him he could probably get $500,000 more in salary as well as gross (not net) profits from *Star Wars*, before the studio subtracted its distribution costs. Lucas could have received whatever he asked for; suddenly he was the hottest filmmaker in Hollywood. But George surprised everyone by not asking for more money. He had agreed to the Fox deal because he trusted Ladd, who had since become head of production at the studio. Lucas only wanted to make sure that *Star Wars* remained *his* movie: he asked for control, not dollars. He was prepared to accept his original salary, but he wanted everything that had been left unresolved.

Lucas was now taken seriously as a director. If he didn't make his move for creative control soon, he might never get the chance again. He wanted *Star Wars* to be produced by his own company, not Fox, so that he could check the costs charged to it. He wanted to control the merchandising and receive a portion of its profits. He wanted to own the publishing rights to the novelization of *Star Wars* and any other books inspired by the movie. He wanted the music rights and the income from a sound-track album. And most important, he wanted to control the sequel rights.

The business affairs executives for Fox couldn't believe their ears. This kid wasn't asking for the extra $500,000 up front; and he was entitled to it, given the success of *American Graffiti*. Instead he wanted the "garbage" provisions of the contract. Merchandising was considered worthless by movie studios—it took eighteen months to get toys designed, manufactured, and distributed; by that time, a film had usually disappeared from theaters. No one knew what the music would be, and the sequel rights didn't mean a thing unless the film was a big hit. Based on Lucas's thirteen-page treatment, *Star Wars* did not look like the studio's next blockbuster.

The deal was closed, saving Fox almost $600,000. Ladd concurred in the decision, and the contract was drawn up. Not everything went Lucas's way, however: he wanted final cut and didn't get it; like Warner's and Universal, Fox technically could recut his movie. He wanted ownership of the sequel rights, but he had to give Fox first crack at distributing any subsequent movie. And Fox retained ownership of the copyright to *Star Wars*. Lucas could make his own merchandising deals (of which Fox kept a percentage), but ultimately Fox owned the story, the characters, and the movie itself. Lucas opted for the long term, and he won; Fox took the short term, and they lost.

137

The script is what you've dreamed up—this is what it should be. The film is what you end up with.[4]

—George Lucas

When his first $10,000 check from 20th Century-Fox arrived in September 1973, Lucas was relieved. *Graffiti* was a hit, but it would be some time before his share of the profits trickled in. Meanwhile, Marcia's career was taking off. After *Graffiti* was released, Martin Scorsese asked her to edit *Alice Doesn't Live Here Anymore,* her first opportunity to gain solo recognition. Most of Hollywood assumed that Verna Fields had really cut *Graffiti;* Marcia was thought to be along for the ride as George's wife. While Lucas was writing his first *Star Wars* draft, Marcia was in Los Angeles, cutting film for Scorsese and loving it.

George encouraged Marcia but he didn't like being separated from his wife. When Marcia cut *Alice* at the film's Arizona location, Lucas joined her. He sequestered himself in a hotel room and thrashed out ideas for *Star Wars.* He was financially dependent on his wife; he had almost no money left from his first $10,000 payment from Fox, and he had no screenplay. Typical.

The next two and a half years were the worst years of Lucas's life. "He could not write that stupid script," remembers Pollock. George was permanently seduced by the idea of *THX:* "I was fascinated by the futuristic society, the idea of rocket ships and lasers up against somebody with a stick. The little guys were winning and technology was losing—I liked that." He wanted now to add heroes, villains, and other fairy-tale elements. But the message that technology cannot replace mankind had to be clear; the human element must ultimately prevail.

Lucas had a long-standing interest in the space program and in exploration of the unknown. He hoped to interest children in space travel with a romantic larger-than-life story. He remembered the lump in his throat as he watched the first NASA flights on TV—he wanted to recapture the emotional impact they had had on him. *Star Wars* wasn't designed to be propaganda for the space program, Lucas insists: "It was a subtle suggestion that opening the door and going out there, no matter what the risk, is sometimes worth the effort." The premise of *Star Wars,* according to Lucas, is that "you can't avoid tough decisions."

George had long been intrigued with the idea of creating a modern fairy tale. After seeing the reaction to *American Graffiti* from a lost generation of teenagers, he was more convinced than ever that America (not to mention the world) needed *Star Wars.* "There's a whole generation growing up without any kind of fairy tales," Lucas says. "And kids need fairy tales—it's an important thing for society to have for kids." Lucas wanted to return to more traditional values that held a special appeal for our rootless society. He needed a timeless fable that could demonstrate, not pontificate on, the differences between right and wrong, good and evil, responsibility and shiftlessness.

"Basically, George is for good and against evil, but everyone has his own interpretation of what that means," says Lawrence Kasdan. Seeing Lucas's religious philosophy unfold in *Star Wars* tells us as much about the man as the movie. Ugly ducklings are turned into heroes, desert rats become wise wizards, an evil monster is revealed to be the hero's father. Simply and essentially, *Star Wars* is the classic fairy tale. "A long time ago in a galaxy far away" is Lucas's version of "Once upon a time" and makes his purpose clear. Children get the message—they know eventually they'll have to leave home, take risks, submit to trials, learn to control their emotions, and act like adults. What they don't know is *how* to do these things. *Star Wars* shows them.

Even the *Star Wars* characters are fairy-tale prototypes. Luke is the traditional young hero at the painful time of adolescence, trapped between childhood and maturity. He undergoes an initiation common to mythological heroes: he is struck by tragedy (the death of his aunt and uncle), given a mission to accomplish in which he defies supernatural forces, and scores a decisive victory. In the end the threat of annihilation, crucial to the fairy tale's believability, is eliminated. Children see life as a never-ending series of challenges and obstacles, in which they always seem to be doing the wrong thing at the wrong time, with ultimately fatal consequences. Luke shares those feelings at first, but in the course of the movie he grows up and realizes his potential. It's a ray of hope for kids who fear they'll be little forever.

Children are not the only ones influenced by *Star Wars*. Audiences share a subconscious emotional reaction to a movie—when it's as popular as *Star Wars,* the shared emotion becomes a cultural force. People also saw what they wanted to see in the film. At various times it's been described as a metaphor for the tenets of Christianity, Buddhism, Judaism, and Islam. Lucas wanted to instill in children a belief in a supreme being—not a religious god, but a universal deity that he named the Force, a cosmic energy source that incorporates and consumes all living things.

The message of *Star Wars is* religious: God isn't dead, he's there if you want him to be. "The laws really are in yourself," Lucas is fond of saying; the Force dwells within. The major theme in *Star Wars,* as in every Lucas film, is the acceptance of personal responsibility, "the fact that you can't run away from your fate." What Lucas seems to be saying is that we can't run away from our calling or mission in life but have a duty to do what is expected of us. Hard work, self-sacrifice, friendship, loyalty, and a commitment to a higher purpose: these are the tenets of Lucas's faith. "I mean, there's a reason this film is so popular," he says. "It's not that I'm giving out propaganda nobody wants to hear."

Lucas knew what had gone wrong with *THX* and was determined not to repeat his mistake. It did no good to show how awful things are; he had to give audiences hope, make them believe things *are* going to get better. "I realized that for a film to have an impact, you have to come at things sideways," Lucas says. "Head-on is the attractive way to do it, but it doesn't have any effect unless you're very lucky. When you're going sideways, you can influence things more subtly because you're not attacking them."

The key to Lucas's sideways approach was the Force, something simultaneously tangible and ethereal. Obi-Wan Kenobi defines it as an energy field created by all living things that binds the universe together. When people die, their life spirit is drained from them and incorporated in a huge energy force in the sky. The Jedi knights are trained to tap into this collective energy, which gives them the status of magician/warriors.

The Force embraces passive Oriental philosophies and the Judeo-Christian ethic of responsibility and self-sacrifice. Yoda's philosophy is Buddhist—he tells Luke that the Force requires him to be calm, at peace, and passive; it should be used for knowledge and defense, not greed and aggression. The Force demands optimism, not the pessimism that characterizes Luke (and Lucas). In *American Graffiti,* adolescence was the Force— hard to understand, even harder to control. "This is a dangerous stage for you, Luke," Ben warns another teenager. "You are now most susceptible to the temptations of the dark side [of the Force]." To Lucas, the Force means looking into yourself, recognizing your potential, and the obstacles that stand in your way. He had undergone just this kind of introspection following his car accident—it was his religious conversion, and he wanted to share it with everyone.

Lucas's concept of the Force was heavily influenced by Carlos Castaneda's *Tales of Power,* an account of a Mexican Indian sorcerer, Don Juan, who uses the phrase "life force." Lucas turned him into Ben Kenobi, the familiar wise man who aids the hero in his difficult mission. Lucas chose a stark symbol for the dark side of the Force: Darth Vader is the embodiment of evil and its proselyte. His goal is to turn Luke to the way that is easier, quicker, and more seductive (just like Hollywood). Ben warns Luke that "the Force can have a strong influence on the weak-minded." Even when employed for good, the Force is addictive. If used to excess, it will turn on the user and bring out his bad, aggressive side. Darth Vader may be the legendary monster, but Lucas makes it clear that he thinks the dark side is in all of us. He offers redemption for our original sin, however. Vader does not triumph; Luke does.

I am simply trying to struggle through life; trying to do God's bidding.

—George Lucas

These were heady thoughts for a young man now lionized by the press and movie industry because of the success of *American Graffiti.* Lucas was a hero, they said, who was single-handedly saving the movie business from extinction. Success was wonderful, crazy, and terrifying to Lucas all at the same time. But the temptation evoked the self-denial instilled by his father: Hollywood's inducements were best turned down, quickly and decisively. Lucas may have bought a new car and a bigger house, but he was determined to keep himself, his family, and his career isolated from the alluring sirens in Los Angeles.

The way to do that was through work. Lucas confined himself to the writing room he had built in the back of Parkhouse. He spent eight hours a day there, five days a week, writing draft after draft. It was worse than being in school. His smooth features grew haggard, the brown eyes behind the horn-rimmed glasses became bleary, and his scraggly beard went untrimmed. His writing room was tastefully furnished, with a large photograph of pioneer film editor Sergei Eisenstein on one wall and a poster from *THX* facing it from across the room. Lucas's prize 1941 Wurlitzer jukebox, a garish pink-and-purple creation resembling a neon gas pump, dominated the room. George had a self-imposed rule: no music until his daily allotment of script pages was completed. Some days he wrote nothing at all and slammed the door behind him in frustration when it was time for Walter Cronkite and the "CBS Evening News," his traditional quitting time.

Star Wars ruled Lucas's life. He carried a small notebook in which he jotted down names, ideas, plot angles—anything that popped into his head. On the first page in the notebook was a notation scribbled during the sound mixing of *Graffiti*. Walter Murch had asked him for R2, D2 (Reel 2, Dialogue 2) of the film, and Lucas liked the abbreviated sound of

R2-D2. Soon the notebook was filled with cryptic words like Jawa, Wookiee, and Aguilae.

Lucas returned from the local newsstand each weekend with a large collection of science-fiction magazines and comic books. Marcia wondered what was going on, but George told her not to worry, he was making a movie that ten-year-old boys would love. Marcia still didn't understand, but as she put it: "George knows who his audience is." Lucas thought of *Star Wars* as a "Tinker toy movie," set in a time that was neither future nor past. It was crucial that the audience not think it was science fiction; *THX* had been hurt by Warner's sci-fi advertising campaign. Nevertheless, he thoroughly researched the science-fiction field from Buck Rogers and Flash Gordon to Stanley Kubrick's watershed film, *2001: A Space Odyssey,* made in 1968. Lucas was in awe of Kubrick's technical craftsmanship, but the movie was too obscure and downbeat for his tastes. *Star Wars* was to have heroes and heroines, villains and rogues, robots and romance. Lucas learned from Kubrick that the believability of a film set in another place and time depends on the atmosphere the writer/director creates. Lucas thought *2001* was the ultimate sci-fi film; he had to come up with something completely different.

Lucas looked *everywhere* for ideas for *Star Wars,* which is at the same time derivative and original. The major influence on *Star Wars* is *THX 1138:* the hunchbacked shell dwellers become Jawas, the robot policemen are transformed into stormtroopers, and OMM is a beneficent version of the Emperor. THX, the hero who makes good his escape and faces the unknown responsibilities of a new existence, has become Luke Skywalker.

Lucas also borrowed liberally from the Flash Gordon serials he had watched as a child, transplanting video screens, medieval costumes, art deco sets, and blaster guns to *Star Wars.* The acting in the serials was awful and the special effects were cheap and crude, but there was constant action, a quality he wanted in *Star Wars.*

Lucas used Ming, the evil ruler of Mongo in the Flash Gordon books, as another model for his emperor. Alex Raymond's *Iron Men of Mongo* describes a five-foot-tall metal man of dusky copper color who is a trained servant and speaks in polite phrases. From *John Carter on Mars* came banthas, beasts of burden in *Star Wars;* Lucas also incorporated into his early screenplay drafts huge flying birds described by Edgar Rice Burroughs. George watched scores of old films, from *Forbidden Planet* to *The Day the World Ended,* and read contemporary sci-fi novels like *Dune* by Frank Herbert and E. E. "Doc" Smith's *Lensman* saga.

But Lucas still had to write the script, an anguishing process: "You beat your head against the wall and say, 'Why can't I make this work? Why aren't I smarter? Why can't I do what everybody else can do?'" His creative limitations were his own limitations as a person: his inability to express emotions crippled him as a writer. *Graffiti* came out of his life experiences but he had to invent *Star Wars*. He was so tense that he often felt incapable of writing a clear sentence or following a single train of thought. "I don't let out my anger and fears very well," Lucas acknowledges. Instead, he suffered stomach and chest pains and headaches until the script was finished.

Lucas tried all kinds of approaches to writing. He organized the screenplay by writing so much description, a short patch of dialogue, then more description in the hope that everything would balance. George was a perfectionist—all his *Star Wars* drafts (along with those for *THX*, *Graffiti*, and his subsequent screenplays) were written in longhand on carefully selected blue-and-green-lined paper. Lucy Wilson bought reams of paper for her boss, but he complained about the number of lines and the color, and lectured her on the importance of obtaining exactly the right kind of paper. He used only No. 2 hard lead pencils, making his tiny printing almost impossible to read. Lucas's strangest quirk was to snip off his hair with a pair of scissors when he felt frustrated: "I came in one day and his wastebasket had tons of hair in it! It was driving him that crazy," remembers Wilson.

It's a wonder Lucas didn't go bald. He was struggling to create a new universe, a reality that did not exist outside of his imagination. George structured his story in traditional Hollywood style: a clear beginning to introduce the characters, a middle section that establishes the conflict, and an ending that resolves it. Each of the characters had a purpose, and was readily identifiable. Lucas wanted his setting to be different from any that movie audiences had ever seen, while still remaining realistic. The story and format were important, but he did not want them to interfere with his goals. George had been weaned on television, but ultimately had no respect for it—"Kojak" was a far cry from the Brothers Grimm. Lucas thinks that TV is amoral; its only values are those of the products it advertises. He prefers film, which he thinks imparts real values with larger-than-life dimensions.

Lucas wanted to present positive values to the audience. In the 1970s traditional religion was out of fashion and the family structure was disintegrating. There was no moral anchor. Lucas remembered how protected he had felt growing up in the cocoonlike culture of the 1950s, a feeling he wanted to communicate in *Star Wars*.

"I wanted to make a kids' film that would strengthen contemporary mythology and introduce a kind of basic morality," Lucas explains. "Nobody's saying the very basic things; they're dealing in the abstract. Everybody's forgetting to tell the kids, 'Hey, this is right and this is wrong.'" Lucas was imposing his values on the rest of the world, but he felt they were the *right* values.

The true art of a warrior is to balance terror and wonder.[5]
—Don Juan in *Tales of Power* by Carlos Castaneda

Infusing a fluid, dramatic movie with a moral structure was a task Lucas dreaded. He had dozens of story elements, but no cohesive plot. His characters evolved and adapted like proto-organisms. He couldn't decide where to begin and where to end *Star Wars*. Morality was the least of his problems.

The hero of *Star Wars* begins as an elderly general, already a Jedi knight, but Lucas saw there could be more character development if Skywalker was a younger man who gradually becomes a Jedi. The character originated in Lucas's own dual nature: the innocent, idealistic *naïf* combined with the cynical pessimist (the latter became Han Solo). Princess Leia dominated the early screenplay drafts but was never the traditional damsel in distress. As Luke's character grew, Leia's receded, and she was given a love interest with Han Solo to keep the audience interested in her. Lucas wanted the sexual rivalry between Han and Luke over Leia to duplicate the classic screen jealousy of Clark Gable and Leslie Howard over Vivien Leigh in *Gone With the Wind*.

Obi-Wan Kenobi and Darth Vader also started as one character until Lucas separated them into the good and bad fathers. Vader became more of a machine than a man; his incredible strength and armored visage made him the perfect symbol of rapacious technology. Vader had to be terrifying, but still a man—Lucas insisted that his characters remain human. Ben Kenobi evolved from the elderly general to a crazed desert hermit, and finally, to the long-suffering, dignified Jedi master played by Alec Guinness.

These transformations were slow in coming. Lucas's first draft screenplay took a year to complete, until May 1974. The story pits the Jedi Bendu, formed one hundred thousand years earlier as the Imperial Space Force, against the evil Knights of the Sith, a sinister warrior sect. The hero is Anakin Starkiller, eighteen, sought by his older brother Biggs to help rescue their father, Kane. The reunited family opposes the fascist regime of the Emperor, and Kane's daughter Leia is sent to a distant galaxy for safekeeping.

Kane Starkiller and Luke Skywalker, a general in his early sixties, are the only surviving Jedi—the rest have been hunted down and exterminated by the Sith knights. Starkiller and Skywalker share a belief in "the Force of Others," a mystical bond between Jedi that gives them miraculous powers. The Jedi nemesis is Prince Valarium, the Black Knight of the Sith, aided by a tall, grim-looking general named Darth Vader. There are also two battered construction robots, Artwo Detwo and SeeThreepio, both of whom speak, and eight foot tall rebel pilots with gray fur called Wookiees, who live on a jungle planet. Han Solo makes a brief appearance as a huge, green-skinned monster with gills and no nose—it's doubtful Harrison Ford would have taken the part in this form.

As in the final version of *Star Wars*, the ending shows the destruction of the Death Star, the Empire's ultimate weapon. The Jedi knights deliver a samurai-warrior yell as they dispatch their enemies with laser swords. The Emperor is an elected official who is corrupted by power and subverts the democratic process—Lucas modeled him after Richard Nixon. Owen Lars, later to become Luke's ill-fated uncle, was an anthropologist studying quaint Wookiee customs.

Lucas knew the script was a mess. He turned the two brothers into Luke and Han Solo, Ben Kenobi emerged from Kane Starkiller, and Vader became the single all-purpose villain. If *Star Wars* was to have the emotional impact Lucas hoped for, the characters had to propel the story. George wanted a movie that would make people laugh and cry, two of the hardest responses for him to elicit.

There was progress by the time the second screenplay was finished on January 28, 1975. It had a title, *Adventures of the Starkiller, Episode One of the Star Wars,* and was set in the Republic Galactica, which was convulsed by civil war and "lawless barbarism." There was a quest now for the Kiber Crystal, which controlled the Force of Others, "a powerful energy field . . . that influenced the destiny of all living creatures." The screenplay promised: "In the times of greatest despair there shall come a savior, and he shall be known as 'The Son of Suns.'"

The Force now had a good side called Ashla (reminiscent of Aslan, the lion and Christ symbol in author C. S. Lewis's famous *Narnia* books), and the Bogan, or para-force, representing evil. The Jedi Bendu, led by the legendary Skywalker and his twelve children, controlled the Ashla Force, but they were being eliminated by Lord Vader, a seven-foot-tall black-hooded knight. If Vader was the Devil, Starkiller was God, complete with long silver beard, flowing white robes, and penetrating eyes. They waged a bitter struggle for control of the Kiber Crystal, a small diamondlike object that intensified the power of the Force, good or bad.

Luke Starkiller, now a young boy, rescues his older brother Deak from the clutches of Vader. Leia is the daughter of Owen Lars and his wife Beru and seems to be Luke's cousin—together they visit the grave of his mother, who perished with his father on a planet destroyed by the Death Star. Han Solo has become a young Corellian pirate, formerly a cabin boy; he is burly, bearded, and flamboyantly dressed, a thinly disguised version of Francis Coppola. Han also has a girlfriend, a five-foot-tall cross between a brown bear and a guinea pig called Boma. Chewbacca, Han's two hundred-year-old Wookiee companion, has baboonlike fangs and large yellow eyes and wears bandoliers, a flak jacket, and brown cloth shorts. The robots begin to resemble their final form, as they aid Luke in the search for his brother—R2 is now beeping, not talking.

Lucas tightened his narrative with more plot twists and character development. An Imperial warship chases a rebel cruiser across space in the opening scene, introducing immediate action. Ben remains a nameless seer who gives Luke advice via the Force's mental telepathy. The Jawas make their debut, and promptly zap R2-D2. There is a much-improved space battle for the finale, as Luke aims at the weakness in the Death Star's construction. The script ends with a teaser about the next chapter of the *Star Wars* saga, in which the Lars family is kidnapped and a perilous search ensues for "the Princess of Ondes." Lucas now had enough material for three movies. He pared his story, blended characters, and introduced new environments. Finally, he cut his first screenplay in half: "It killed me to cut out things that I really loved, so I decided I would just postpone them a bit," he explains. "It was my rationale to get through the script and get the damn thing done."

George was creating an esoteric world that only he understood. He started anew with the middle story. It had the most action and starred Luke, the character with whom he felt most secure. The first trilogy told the story of young Ben Kenobi and Luke's father and was set twenty years before *Star Wars*. The final three movies feature an adult Luke and the ultimate confrontation between the rebels and the Empire. The entire saga spans more than fifty-five years; C-3PO and R2-D2 are the only element common to all the films.

Even in its reduced form, the script still contained two movies: the rescue mission to save someone from Darth Vader and the subsequent battle to destroy the Death Star. "I sort of tacked the air battle on," admits

Lucas, "because it was the original impetus of the whole project." Lucas also was uneasy about using the robots as his narrative thread. In the early *Star Wars* drafts, they dominated the first thirty pages. How would audiences react to a story in which people were incidental?

George turned to his friends for advice. He'd finish a script draft, let everyone read it, and then tape-record their comments and criticism. Michael Ritchie, whose office was at Parkhouse, was baffled by the early versions of *Star Wars*. "It was very difficult to tell what the man was talking about," he remembers. Matthew Robbins and Hal Barwood felt the opening sequence with the robots meant the return of Lucas the mechanical director. Chagrined, George rewrote the beginning, introducing Luke sooner to reassure the audience of a human presence.

Lucas also showed *Star Wars* to Coppola, who had just the opposite reaction. Francis liked George to take chances, like making Leia an eleven-year-old princess. "George became frightened of some of his own good ideas," believes Coppola. "I think he shied away from his innovations somewhat."

Other friends thought Lucas was ruining his career with his obsessive belief in *Star Wars*. They urged him to give it up, or at least to hire a professional writer to finish it. Lucas knew that if he couldn't write the movie, he would never be able to make it.

Marcia's faith never wavered—she was at once George's most severe critic and his most ardent supporter. She wasn't afraid to say she didn't understand something in *Star Wars* or to point out the sections that bored her. Lucas got angry, but he knew Marcia was articulating his own suspicions. "I'm real hard," Marcia says, "but I only tell him what he already knows."

She was also the only person to whom Lucas could vent his frustration. "A marriage where both people are in the same business and both are very strong is a challenge. You've got to go through a lot of changes," says George. Marcia's suggestions were among the few Lucas took seriously— he paid no attention to the creative ideas of the people who worked for him, especially the secretaries. "What it boils down to is he's a male chauvinist pig," says Bunny Alsop with a laugh.

Lucas vehemently rejects the chauvinist label—it upsets and hurts him. He does not go around saying that the female of the species is inferior, and he has given more women management positions than most Hollywood studios. Lucas insists he ignores the opinions of people for whom he has no respect, both men and women. "I just don't want my vision muddied," he says.

Alsup's comments may betray her frustration in preparing the *Star Wars* screenplay drafts. Lucas had never learned proper spelling or punctuation, and Alsup and Lucy Wilson were horrified by his grammar. There were often four or five misspellings in a single sentence—Lucas spelled Chewbacca differently each time. Finally Alsup devised her own spellings for the exotic names and places and checked them out with George. Lucas occasionally acted out scenes for his typists—he was a natural storyteller, and his spontaneous dialogue was much better than his writing. "If I had gotten a script of *Star Wars* as opposed to hearing George tell it, I might have been reluctant to put it on the screen as well," says Alsup.

Lucas sent Alan Ladd, Jr., a synopsis of his second draft on May 1, 1975. "The Star Wars" was now episode four in the *Adventures of Luke Starkiller,* "an engaging human drama set in a fantasy world that paralyzes the imagination. . . . A story not only for children, but for anyone who likes a grand tale of wonder on an epic scale . . . filled with marvels and strange terrors, moral warmth and, most of all, pure excitement."

The third version was delivered August 1, 1975. Luke has become a farmboy, son of the famous late Jedi knight, Anakin Starkiller. Owen Lars is Luke's bitter uncle who steals his nephew's savings to keep his farm going. A hologram of Princess Leia, now sixteen, begs for help in delivering R2-D2 to the rebel stronghold on a faraway planet, because he contains the plans of the feared Death Star. Luke searches for General Kenobi, his father's comrade, but is captured by sand people.

Ben Kenobi, "a shabby old desert rat of a man," saves Luke, but has to be persuaded to aid the rebels. They meet Han Solo, a "tough James Dean-style starpilot, a cowboy in a starship: simple, sentimental, and cocksure." Solo and his copilot, a Wookiee named Chewbacca, agree to transport the two passengers and their robots to the rebel planet on their space freighter, usually used for smuggling.

The Kiber Crystal is still the symbol for the Force, but Lucas more clearly establishes the dichotomy between good and evil: black-garbed Darth Vader versus white-haired Ben Kenobi. For the first time, the phrase "May the Force be with you" is heard, a variation of the Christian phrase "May the Lord be with you, and with your spirit." Leia, who has the mind-control powers of a witch, is captured and tortured by Vader until rescued by Han and Luke. Ben searches for the Kiber Crystal and encounters Vader, with whom he has a fierce light-saber duel. Ben is wounded but saved by Han and Luke in time to pass the powerful crystal to Luke. With its aid (not that of the Force), Luke attacks and destroys the Death Star.

The dialogue in *Star Wars* was still crude and clichéd, lacking wit or insight. But Lucas was on the right track, and his fourth attempt, completed eight months later, was a great improvement. Luke Skywalker resided on the desert planet of Tatooine; Owen Lars was his gruff, if no longer treacherous, uncle; and former brother Biggs was now an older friend and role model, a graduate of the Space Academy and an incipient rebel. (Biggs survived every screenplay draft, only to end up on the cutting room floor during the final editing of the movie.)

The screenplay still failed to reflect the dramatic visual impact Lucas wanted. Three years earlier, when he first conceived of *Star Wars*, Lucas had met with Ralph McQuarrie, an illustrator for Boeing Aircraft who had animated the Apollo space missions. He was still in Los Angeles, and Lucas contacted him.

Lucas gave McQuarrie the third draft script, comic book pages, and illustrations from the Flash Gordon books. He said he wanted a look that was graphically bold and highly imaginative. McQuarrie was commissioned initially to paint five scenes: the two robots crossing the desert, the light-saber duel between Ben and Vader, a stormtrooper assault with blaster guns, the climactic attack on the Death Star, and a group portrait of the major characters. Lucas had chosen well. McQuarrie loved to draw machines; at Boeing he illustrated the parts catalog. He brought an uninhibited, relaxed style to his work and an incredible attention to detail, qualities Lucas shared and admired. McQuarrie thought *Star Wars* would be hard to make, but the assignment was fun. He was free to invent whatever he thought appropriate, with George as his creative collaborator.

Lucas demanded finished paintings rather than the usual rough production sketches—*Star Wars* had to come alive visually. "He wanted people to look and say, 'Gee, that looks great, just like something on the screen,'" McQuarrie explains. Each painting measured twenty-two inches by ten inches; they had a startling impact when lined up together. "George spent his money wisely on *Star Wars* by developing the art," says Miki Herman. "Ralph McQuarrie's illustrations sold the movie to Fox."

McQuarrie's paintings also helped Lucas visualize how his creations would look on screen. Was Darth Vader menacing in fluttering black robes? McQuarrie thought not; he wanted Vader to be heavily armored. Lucas gave Vader armor *and* a cloak, and hoarse mechanical breathing. McQuarrie's Chewbacca was more frightening than friendly, with bright yellow eyes and sharp little teeth. Lucas softened the creature's menace and, at McQuarrie's suggestion, eliminated the Wookiee's clothes, but left the crisscrossed cartridge belts.

Lucas told McQuarrie that the robots had to be a team, while remaining distinctly different. George cited the robot in the classic silent film *Metropolis* when he described the metallic art deco look he wanted for C-3PO. McQuarrie made the robot fully jointed and added the essential touch of weary elegance. McQuarrie thought R2-D2 should be sort of cute. He gave him three legs, a round swivel top on his cylindrical metal body, and a squat demeanor.

The other element critical to the success of *Star Wars* was the casting. As always, the characters came out of Lucas's personality and he felt proprietary about them. He wanted little-known actors who would bring a freshness to their roles, so the audience wouldn't wonder who was in the costumes. Fox wanted at least one or two "bankable" stars in the lead roles, performers with proven drawing power. Lucas ignored the studio and proceeded with the same exhaustive casting approach he had used on *Graffiti*. He interviewed hundreds of actors until he found the ones he felt comfortable with, not caring whether they were stars. "There was great concern about that at Fox," Ladd confirms. "But there never was a demand from the studio to get some names in there. In my own mind, I thought, 'Who's a name to play Luke?' I couldn't think of anybody." Ladd trusted Lucas's eye for young talent: members of the *Graffiti* cast were already becoming stars. If Fox was going to gamble on the script and the director, it might as well put everything on the roll.

Marcia was editing *Taxi Driver* for Scorsese in Los Angeles when George went there to begin the interviews. For the first time, she was concerned: "I knew he was going to be looking at the most beautiful eighteen- and nineteen-year-old girls in Hollywood for Princess Leia, and I felt so insecure. I said, 'George, are you going to be a good boy when you're down there?'" Marcia didn't have to worry—Lucas had absorbed his father's moral dicta, and he and Marcia had always promised each other to disclose any transgressions. Both knew full well that having to tell about an affair would be worse than the affair itself. George had no plans to stray: "My first vow when I came to a film studio was never to date an actress. You're just a funny kid, and someone like a Playmate of the Month is coming after you—life is just too short for that."

Lucas joined forces with director Brian De Palma to minimize the strain of scrutinizing hundreds of hopefuls. De Palma was preparing *Carrie,* a horror film that required the same age group Lucas was seeking. De Palma was talkative and outgoing and let Lucas fade into the background during the interviews. For the next two months, operating out of the old Samuel Goldwyn Studios, they saw between thirty and forty actors a day;

each performer spent five minutes with the two directors. Lucas made notes on each actor and wrote the names of those who impressed him on a separate call-back list.

Mass interviews are nicknamed cattle calls, and Mark Hamill shudders as he remembers the experience. "There were guys literally everywhere, in age from sixteen to thirty-five," he recollects. "They weren't going to let us read, you had to look right first. So I walked in, and they were both sitting there. Brian said, 'So tell us a little bit about yourself.' And I went through the litany. George didn't say anything. I thought he was Brian's gofer or something. In fifteen minutes, it was all over." Almost fifty actors were invited back to do readings on videotape, Hamill included. Lucas finally emerged with four trios for Luke, Leia, and Han Solo, which he mixed and matched in the hope of finding the right on-screen chemistry. Harrison Ford was working as a carpenter at the Goldwyn Studios, installing a door for Francis Coppola's new office, and saw George for the first time since *Graffiti*. Ford knew about *Star Wars*, but he also knew that Lucas had said he didn't want to use anyone from *Graffiti*. Lucas felt comfortable with Harrison, however, and got him to read the male parts when George tested actresses for Leia's role. Ford obliged but soon grew irritated at being asked to read a part which he could never play. His churlishness helped win him the role of Han Solo.

At first, Lucas had some radical casting ideas: he considered Japanese movie star Toshiro Mifune for Ben Kenobi and thought of having a Eurasian girl play Leia. He interviewed several black actors for Han Solo and almost chose a young performer named Glynn Turman. Lucas was aware that if he developed the love interest between Han and Leia, an interracial romance could cause problems. "I didn't want to make *Guess Who's Coming to Dinner* at that point, so I sort of backed off," he acknowledges.

It was difficult to measure an actor's effectiveness from the scenes Lucas asked them to play for the auditions. "The dialogue for the test was even more difficult than the dialogue that ended up in the film," remembers Carrie Fisher, eighteen at the time and one of the first actresses tested. "It was space triple-talk, killer lines." George refused to allow the actors to read a complete script until they were signed for the movie. Cindy Williams auditioned, too, but was rejected because Lucas wanted an adolescent. "I heard one day that they were looking for a 'young Cindy Williams,'" she remembers. "I just about died—every actress waits in anticipated horror to hear those words."

It finally came down to two ensembles. In one group were Christopher

Walken as Han Solo and Will Selzer as Luke; a former *Penthouse* Pet named Terri Nunn was a possible Leia. The other group consisted of Harrison Ford, Mark Hamill, and Carrie Fisher. (Nick Nolte and William Katt were rejected for Han Solo, as were Amy Irving and Jodie Foster for Leia. De Palma cast Irving and Katt in *Carrie,* and both became stars.) Fred Roos, whose advice Lucas sought, lobbied for Ford, whom he had used in Coppola's film *The Conversation.* Fisher was passed over by Lucas initially, but Roos persuaded him to call her back for a videotaped test.

The daughter of Debbie Reynolds and Eddie Fisher, Carrie grew up in the shadow of their notoriety when Fisher left Reynolds for Elizabeth Taylor. Determined to be an actress, she had studied at London's Royal Academy of Dramatic Art, with her mother's encouragement. Her film experience was brief, but Roos was struck by her mature, worldly-wise quality. Lucas wanted Leia to be a sixteen-year-old princess, however, not a sophisticated, husky-voiced woman. Nunn looked great on screen, but she had a tough quality that did not suit Leia. Fisher got the role.

That left Luke, the creator's namesake. George liked Mark Hamill immediately. He didn't remember that Hamill, nineteen, had gone through a similar cattle call on *Graffiti* and never got beyond the first meeting. Since then, Mark had made more than a hundred TV appearances, in everything from soap operas to commercials. Lucas was also impressed by Selzer, another young actor with a more mature, intellectual presence, qualities Lucas had always wished he possessed. Hamill won because "he was more a gosh and golly kid, which was really what I wanted Luke to be," says George.

Lucas's casting choices were not popular. No one at the studio had ever heard of these people, and even Coppola felt Lucas had made a mistake by hiring untried actors. "I disagreed with George's casting, but it was not for me to say," Coppola says. "I think had I been invited to be involved, as I was on *Graffiti,* he would have had a different cast." The unspoken implication is that *Star Wars* would have had a *better* cast, but Coppola's ideas were irrelevant. Lucas consciously isolated Francis from the film that marked his graduation.

Lucas still had to fill the character roles of Ben Kenobi, the robots, Chewbacca, and Darth Vader. He had always pictured Obi-Wan played by someone like Alec Guinness, and to Lucas's surprise, Sir Alec was in Los Angeles in 1975, filming *Murder by Death.*

An unsolicited script arrived in Guinness's dressing room one day, with a cover drawing of a young man brandishing a sword. Guinness was not in the habit of reading scripts that came "over the transom," especially a bizarre science-fiction tale with "ropey" dialogue, but he soon was caught up in the story. A lunch was arranged with the bold young man who had sent the script. When Guinness met Lucas, he was surprised by his youth and impressed with his quiet self-assurance.

Lucas described Obi-Wan as a thoughtful, intelligent man of noble bearing, kind and powerful—a cross between Gandalf the Wizard in J. R. R. Tolkien's *Lord of the Rings* and the samurai swordsman often played by Toshiro Mifune. Ben also was a sort of otherworldly Dr. Doolittle, able to talk to robots and Wookiees, capable of influencing thought and speech patterns, and willing to spout aphorisms at the flash of a light saber. Guinness had no intention of playing a dotty old goat hiding in the sand dunes. He wanted Ben to have dignity and insisted on toning down his metaphysical clichés. Guinness helped Lucas focus on the conflict between Ben and Darth Vader: they discussed ways to make the characters both symbolic and real. Ladd was finally able to give his board of directors a name. "Guinness didn't sell tickets on his own, but it was nice that he was in the picture," he recalls.

Following the success of *Graffiti,* George asked Gary Kurtz to produce *Star Wars.* Lucas never saw himself and Kurtz as a team, although Kurtz was instrumental in running Lucasfilm. Bunny Alsup thinks the company just as easily could have been called Kurtzfilm, but this ignores the fact that George was writing and directing the films, and had hired Kurtz, of course. "Gary, along with producing the films, helped George with every aspect of the company," Alsup insists.

It was Kurtz's idea to shoot *Star Wars* in England. The production required at least five and possibly seven sound stages, far more than were available in Hollywood. After looking at studios in Paris, Rome, and London, Kurtz found what he needed at Elstree Studios, a thirty-minute drive from London. Ladd, who had produced films in England and knew the potential cost savings, gave his approval.

Lucas and Kurtz flew to England in May 1975 at their own expense. *Star Wars* hadn't received any money from Fox other than Lucas's writing fee. (The payments for directing and producing didn't begin until filming commenced.) Luckily, Lucas had received his first profit checks from *American Graffiti,* enabling him to push on without Fox's money. He and Kurtz hired Colin Cantwell, who had worked on *2001,* to design the spaceship models. Alex Tavoularis started preliminary storyboard sketches (designs for the special effects sequences) from McQuarrie's paintings, while McQuarrie busied himself turning out more illustrations.

There were few specialists left to turn to for the special effects in *Star*

Wars—it had become a lost art in Hollywood. Kurtz had supervised the cheap effects in Roger Corman's movies and quickly grasped what Lucas was after. "George wanted spaceships that were operated like cars," he remembers. "People turned them on, drove them somewhere, and didn't talk about what an unusual thing they were doing." Fox's production department didn't believe that the effects could be done within the time and budget allotted. Lucas didn't care if he used models on sticks—he wanted to see a different kind of space travel on screen.

Computer-controlled cameras had revolutionized the filming of TV commercials in the 1970s, but no one had used them extensively in a feature film. Kurtz hired John Dykstra, a special effects assistant on *2001* familiar with the new cameras. A strapping bear of a man in his early thirties, Dykstra wanted to put together a team of young effects wizards who would devise their own equipment and new ways to use it. Kurtz found an abandoned warehouse in an industrial park in Van Nuys, a suburb of Los Angeles, and in July 1975, Industrial Light & Magic (ILM) was created as a subsidiary of Lucasfilm Ltd.

Making movies is like the construction business. You are fighting all possible odds and everyone is seemingly against you.

—George Lucas

By the time *Star Wars* won the approval of the Fox board as a "go" picture in December 1975, Lucas had invested almost a million dollars of his own money in the film. Marcia gave her blessing, although if Fox pulled out, she and George would be left with nothing. "George takes enormous risks," she says. "He's very determined. He invested that money because he knew he was going to make that movie. He knows what he wants, and he knows how to get it. He's gambling, but he's gambling on himself and his own ability to come through."

Fox was less willing to gamble. When Lucas first brought *Star Wars* to Ladd, he promised to try to make the film for $3.5 million. George and Gary then drew up a real budget, which was closer to $12 million. After the deal was made, they showed the new budget to Ladd, who took a deep breath and sent them to Ray Gosnell, the Fox executive in charge of supervising the studio's movies. Gosnell wanted the budget cut to $5.5 million, although everyone knew that figure was no more realistic than the original estimate. Lucas countered with $10 million, but Fox insisted that another 10 percent be trimmed; finally, they settled on $8.5 million. Lucas could feel the tension beginning: "We knew we were right on the edge and that if just one tiny thing went wrong, it was going to go over budget."

Lucas resented Fox's attempts to nickel-and-dime him; he couldn't figure out if the studio was abandoning the project or just squeezing him in traditional Hollywood fashion. "They just assumed that everybody was cheating them and padding their budgets, but we weren't," Lucas explains. "Our budget was the actual budget."

The inevitable confrontation came in November 1975, when Ladd met with Lucas and Kurtz. Fox wanted to stop all work on *Star Wars* until a detailed budget was finalized, including the special effects. Lucas had learned from Coppola and *The Rain People* that if he went ahead, the studio eventually would pay him back. Lucas's money from *American Graffiti* took away Fox's most powerful negotiating tool, its ability to stop the flow of dollars. "We decided to go ahead with the picture whether they financed it or not," says Kurtz. "It forced them to make some quick decisions."

His independence guaranteed, Lucas went to England to hire his crew, complete the casting, and finish the final draft of his screenplay. Robert Watts was the film's production manager. The sandy-haired Welshman was another *2001* veteran and had extensive contacts throughout the British film industry. He was joined by production designer John Barry and his assistant, art director Norman Reynolds, whom Lucas had met in 1974 on the set of *Lucky Lady*. The initial production team was now set.

Casting the robots was crucial—Lucas loved his metallic creations. He makes little beeping noises like R2-D2, according to Jane Bay, and his attention to detail is reflected in C-3PO's fussiness. The latter role required someone good at mime who was willing to perform almost anonymously. Anthony Daniels, a twenty-nine-year-old English stage actor, was suggested to Lucas. They met at Fox's London offices while Lucas was finishing an audition of another actor, who was doing an impression of an automaton, twitching and winding down like a spent toy. Daniels spotted McQuarrie's painting of C-3PO and R2-D2 on a desert landscape with two moons in the background, and he was hooked. "I really related to that image," Daniels recalls. "I thought it was a beautiful picture and a beautiful character."

Noticing the actor's interest, Lucas explained that C-3PO was just like a person and described how the robot would walk, talk, and behave. Lucas's enthusiasm was contagious, and Daniels felt an immediate rapport with the young American. At the conclusion of their second meeting, Lucas grew quiet. Daniels looked at him with a concerned expression. "Well, can I play it?" he asked. Lucas grinned, answering, "Sure." He had made up his mind when he first saw Daniels next to the painting—he recognized the guileless gentleman he wanted for C-3PO.

The major requirement for R2-D2 was that the actor be small. (Many of the scenes called for the use of the mechanical R2-D2s.) John Barry knew Kenny Baker, an English music-hall performer, who was perfect for the part. Baker turned down the role at first; he thought he'd be uncomfortable inside a metal vacuum cleaner. The character had no lines, but Lucas knew it was essential to bring a human dimension to R2. Baker finally agreed to take the job.

Darth Vader and Chewbacca required bigger performers. Lucas anticipated the popularity of Vader. "People always love a good bad guy, and that kind of power is especially attractive to little kids. They've got their own friend Vader, and if their father gives them a hard time, watch out!" The prime candidate was David Prowse, a weightlifter who stood six feet, seven inches tall, and had played Frankenstein in low-budget British horror movies. He was offered his choice of Chewbacca or Vader and heeded the advice that everyone remembers the villain, although Lucas told him that his Welsh-accented voice was not suitable for Vader's dialogue. "He took the whole thing very seriously—he began to believe he really was Darth Vader," Lucas remembers.

Lucas envisioned Chewbacca as a cross between a large bear, a monkey, and Indiana, Marcia's female Alaskan malamute. (Indiana was also the inspiration for the name, if not the looks, of the lead character in *Raiders of the Lost Ark*.) Chewbacca leaped out of Lucas's imagination one day as Marcia and Indiana drove away from the house. Sitting next to Marcia in the front seat, the dog looked like a giant, shaggy creature. The name Wookiee had a stranger origin. During the sound editing of the chase scene in *THX*, San Francisco disc jockey Terry McGovern supplied off-screen voices. While improvising background dialogue, McGovern blurted out, "I think I ran over a Wookiee back there." Laughing, Lucas asked what a Wookiee was. "I don't know, I just made it up," answered McGovern. Lucas never forgot the name, waiting seven years to use it in *Star Wars*.

It was not easy finding someone to spend twelve hours a day in a body suit made of angora wool and yak hair. Ralph McQuarrie gave Chewbacca enormous feet to support his seven-foot height, and the possessor of some of the biggest feet in England (size 16) was a London hospital porter, Peter Mayhew. At seven feet, two inches, Mayhew fit the physical requirements, and he had acting experience as a giant in *Sinbad and the Eye of the Tiger*. Lucas told him that Chewbacca was lovable, if fierce, and had a heart of gold. That pleased the actor; this was an animal he wanted to play. Mayhew liked Lucas, too: "My first impression was that he was an average sort of guy," Mayhew recalls. "He didn't look like the image of a Hollywood director."

Lucas made little progress on his screenplay while in London. He wrote Marcia numerous letters to avoid working on the script. The heater in his apartment was faulty, the stove didn't work, and he was lonely. A letter in mid-November complained, "I can't see how we're going to get the movie started on time! There is just sooo much to get done. . . . I get a headache just thinking about it."

By the end of the year, Fox still had not given the official green light to *Star Wars*. Lucas could carry his economic bluff only so far; he didn't have enough money to finance the movie. He certainly wasn't going to turn to Francis Coppola again for assistance. Lucas was trapped in a peculiar Hollywood limbo: his movie wasn't really a movie until the studio said it was, in spite of a script, a cast, and a crew.

Ladd still had concerns about *Star Wars*. He seriously doubted that it could be finished in time for a projected Christmas 1976 release. And the budget was growing. Lucas insisted that he simply could not make the movie for $8.5 million. He needed at least $10 million, and Ladd needed special board approval to give it to him. When Lucas turned in a 160-page final screenplay, Ladd was even more worried, since the average length of a screenplay for a two-hour movie is 118 pages. Ladd later discovered that Lucas had *Star Wars* planned right down to the second—even the newsreel footage of the aerial battles was carefully timed for the script.

At the last minute, Lucas asked Bill Huyck and Gloria Katz to sharpen the dialogue in *Star Wars*. The Huycks added humor and bounce to the story, particularly the repartee between Han and Leia. Lucas kept only 15 percent of what they wrote, but the new dialogue gave him the confidence to move forward. A grateful Lucas promised the Huycks profit points in *Star Wars*.

Ladd had difficulty getting final approval from the Fox board of directors, conservative businessmen who had made their fortunes outside of the movie business. Some board members hated *Star Wars* so much that they refused to refer to it by name; they called it "that science movie." Despite heated opposition, Ladd finally triumphed. *Star Wars* was a go.

Star Wars came at a turning point for Fox. The company, although healthy by Hollywood standards, had only $150 million in assets, and annual sales of $300 million. On the Fortune 500 list of top corporations, Fox was 492nd, and seemed ripe for a takeover by a conglomerate. To forestall that possibility, Chairman Dennis Stanfill diversified Fox's assets with a ski resort in Colorado, the famous Pebble Beach golf course in

Northern California, and a soft-drink bottling plant in the Midwest. Ladd had assumed control of the film division, and his first three productions, including *Star Wars,* were coming to the marketplace in the summer of 1976. The future of Fox hinged on their fate.

Chris Kalabokes was a financial analyst at Fox in late 1975, responsible for evaluating the cost of the studio's movies against their potential earnings. When the folder marked *Star Wars* reached his desk in early December, Kalabokes was preparing his 1977 budget and recognized the project. This was the movie that had grown from $3.5 million to $10 million without a foot of film being shot.

He read the folder's contents, which included a brief synopsis of Lucas's original treatment, not his final screenplay. This *Star Wars* had Luke trying to save his brother; a two hundred-year-old Wookiee piloting a spaceship; and a twelve-year-old princess named Leia. "My Lord, we are now going to spend ten million dollars on a film that features something that looks like a giant stuffed animal?" Kalabokes wondered aloud. "We're basing our profits on this kind of story?" He questioned how the company could justify the expenditure.

There were things Kalabokes liked about *Star Wars,* too: "Good won out, and in the end, everyone was saved who had to be saved, and everyone bad was dealt with." When he made his presentation to the Fox board, Kalabokes recommended approval for *Star Wars,* saying, in effect: "Look, guys, there is a [financial] bite here, but there is no gross [profit] participant. Lucas is not taking money from the first dollar. He's getting paid a fee, and a very small fee. Everything looks proper. It's not crazy." Kalabokes remembers estimating that *Star Wars* might make as much as $35 million for Fox. "At the time," he says, "that looked like a lot of money."

7

THE AGONY AND THE ECSTASY OF *STAR WARS*

When you're directing, you have to get up at four thirty [A.M.], have breakfast at five, leave the hotel at six, drive an hour to location, start shooting at eight, and finish shooting around six. Then you wrap, go to your office, and set up the next day's work. You get back to the hotel about eight or nine, hopefully get a bite to eat, then you go to your room and figure out your homework, how you're going to shoot the next day's scenes, and then you go to sleep. The next morning it starts all over again.

—George Lucas on the making of *Star Wars*

George Lucas lived like this for seventy days between March and July 1976, in a country he disliked, surrounded by people who thought he was crazy, consumed with premonitions of disaster. Out of this personal hell came *Star Wars,* one of the most successful movies ever made, and possibly the last movie George Lucas will direct.

Elstree Studios was one of Britain's oldest film studios.[1] Alfred Hitchcock directed his early movies at the sprawling complex, located fifteen miles outside of London on twenty-eight acres in the suburb of Borehamwood. It had been almost deserted for two years when Gary Kurtz first saw it in 1975. "Drab, ugly, cold, depressing" is how Bunny Alsup remembers Elstree. "But they couldn't have found a better location for privacy. *No one* walked in off the street."

While Kurtz was scouting a *Star Wars* studio, Lucas was struggling with his screenplay, unable to resolve the fate of Obi-Wan Kenobi. Ben had nothing to do for the last half of the movie but was too important a character to fade into the metalwork. "The character stood around with his thumb in his ear," Lucas says. Marcia came up with a solution: Why not kill him off? Ben could continue to advise Luke in spirit, if not in body, by becoming part of the Force.

Returning to England, Lucas took Alec Guinness aside and broke the news that halfway through the picture, he was to become a disembodied voice. It's a shock to any actor to learn that his role is being eliminated; Lucas had convinced Guinness that he was the key to the film's believability. Guinness was angry. He called his agent and threatened to walk off the picture. "I'm not going to do this movie," he said to Lucas, barely suppressing his rage. Delicate negotiations ensued via transatlantic telephone before Guinness agreed to stay. He eventually forgave Lucas, and when filming was over, sent him a gift of Victorian tumblers. The accompanying note read, "This is just a small token of esteem to say how much I have liked working with you."

Other problems confronted Lucas at Elstree. He had nine sound stages filled with sets including a mammoth full-scale model of Han Solo's spaceship the *Millennium Falcon.* It was constructed by maritime engineers at docks two hundred sixty miles southwest of London and shipped in sections. Lucas walked through miles of John Barry's gleaming sets and then ordered every one to be made dirty and grimy. Art director Norman Reynolds remembers how depressed his crew was when the bright blue-and-white R2-D2 they had lovingly constructed was rolled in the dirt, kicked, and nicked with a saw. Lucas wanted an "organic" atmosphere— "not futuristic, not designy, and not noticeable." The actors had to dominate *Star Wars,* not the sets.

To supplement Ralph McQuarrie's production paintings, costume designer John Mollo gathered books about World War II battle gear and Japanese armor. Lucas wanted the costumes in *Star Wars* to be functional, not flashy. Luke wore a homespun shirt made from curtain-lining material, while Han Solo's clothes were fancier, in keeping with his roguish image. Darth Vader's original outfit consisted of a black motorcycle suit, a Nazi-style helmet, a gas mask, and a monk's cloak Mollo found in the studio's Middle Ages department. Princess Leia's clothes were vaguely medieval and enabled her to move easily in action sequences.

The robots and Chewbacca required the assistance of Elstree's makeup departments. Before going to Tunisia, Anthony Daniels spent a day standing naked in a cold room while two men covered him with Vaseline and wet plaster. The first body cast was imperfect, and Daniels had to undergo what he calls "the disgusting experience" a second time. The body cast became the model for C-3PO's metal shell. George and Gary spent hours kneeling before Daniels, trying to get C-3PO's knees to work.

Lucas's British crew didn't know what to make of a movie that starred two hunks of metal and a walking red rug. "This was a whole new ball game," explains production manager Robert Watts. "None of us knew what we were getting into. It built up an esprit de corps, although not across the entire crew." Lucas got along with most of the workers, but his relations became strained with his cameraman, assistant director, wardrobe designer, and editor—key members of his movie-making team.

Lucas didn't exactly inspire confidence when he ambled onto the set in scuffed-up sneakers, jeans, and a baggy Shetland sweater with a few holes in it. He was quiet and unassuming, unlike the loud and expansive Hollywood directors who usually worked in England. George's aloofness offended the *Star Wars* crew: the Brits didn't like being ignored. Lucas says, "The crew didn't know what I was doing; they thought I was nuts." The *Star Wars* crew didn't realize that their cheeky self-confidence intimidated Lucas. British film workers are convinced they are the best in the world. *Star Wars* marked the first time George worked with such strong, high-powered, and experienced people. The British crew members took pride in their craftsmanship and resented a young hotshot telling them how to do their work.

The inevitable confrontation came with Gil Taylor, a veteran cameraman who had filmed two movies Lucas greatly admired, *A Hard Day's Night* and *Dr. Strangelove*. The use of existing light gave both films a realism that Lucas wanted for *Star Wars*. George had developed a complex color scheme for his film: the Tatooine sequences had organic colors, warm shades of gold and brown like C-3PO's burnished parts; as the battle with the Empire neared, the colors changed to black, white, and gray, the shades of evil technology.

Along with natural lighting, Lucas wanted *Star Wars* to have the gauzelike look of a fairy tale. Taylor hated the bulky Vistavision cameras Lucas had ordered and refused to use soft-focus lenses or gauze. Lucas discovered that Fox executives had complained about the soft-focus footage and told Taylor to change it. Lucas was furious, not only with the studio but with his cameraman, who he felt had betrayed him. "Gil was a crotchety old man who didn't understand George's way," says Kurtz with typical understatement. Taylor refused to be browbeaten by Lucas and openly complained when Lucas physically moved the lights and cameras himself, an affront to any self-respecting cinematographer.

Lucas wanted to fire Taylor, but he left the actual decision up to Gary Kurtz. Although he thought of himself as Lucas's interpreter to the outside world, Kurtz was just as uncommunicative with strangers. Both men volunteered little information, offered terse answers to questions, and rarely socialized with their coworkers. "The crew got upset with both of us," Lucas now admits. "I ended up having to be nice to everybody, which is hard when you don't like a lot of the people."

Maybe Gil Taylor should have been fired, but neither Lucas nor Kurtz was willing to do it. Gary disliked confrontations, too, and was convinced that if Taylor was let go, the entire crew might walk off the set. The tense status quo continued throughout the production.

The actors also sensed the unspoken hostility on the other side of the camera. Hamill, Ford, and Fisher spent hours in the hallways of the Death Star, and their forced isolation eventually got to them. Carrie Fisher, who is part-Jewish, invented a game in which the word "Jew" was substituted for the word "you" in song titles and lyrics: "Jew Light Up My Life," "Jew Made Me Love You," and so on. Hamill explains, "If you do it once or twice, it's either in bad taste or not funny, but if you do thirty-five of them, you're rolling on the ground." An assistant director complained that the American actors were making anti-Semitic jokes and not behaving professionally. Harrison Ford says, "The only damper on the pure fun of that set was the almost-unanimous attitude of the English crew that we were totally out of our minds, especially George."

After two days of filming in England, Lucas was told that he could not work past 5:30 P.M., the traditional quitting time for stage crews. The question of working overtime was put to a vote by the crew (an English industry custom), and Lucas lost in a landslide. If he was setting up a shot at 4:30 and didn't finish in time, he had to return to that set the next day. The delays quickly threw him behind schedule. "I would lose half a day because they wouldn't let me go for another forty-five minutes. That made me very angry," Lucas says, still smoldering.

Lucas adapted—he saved the easiest shots for the end of the day. If he couldn't make the deadline, he sent over a second-unit cameraman to film the scenes, usually quick "insert" shots. Lucas tried directing both units simultaneously: Watts remembers him pedaling madly on a small bicycle as he raced to beat the deadline.

Lucas liked making movies on the run; it reminded him of USC, when time was of the essence and everything was sacrificed for the right shot.

The loose atmosphere on the second unit sometimes paid off. One of *Star Wars'* best moments (and Marcia's favorite example of George's "silly" side) comes when Chewbacca rounds a corner and encounters a tiny mouse robot. The Wookiee bellows, and the robot turns on its wheels and scampers away. "We were just standing around and got the idea to do that," Lucas remembers. "It wasn't in the script, it was an ad-lib."

I have a sneaking suspicion that if there were a way to make movies without actors, George would do it.

—Mark Hamill

For all his problems on *Star Wars,* Lucas never worried about his cast. He had chosen his actors carefully, and he had complete faith in their ability. In turn, his cast trusted him, even if it didn't understand him. Lucas usually filmed four or five "takes" of a scene (some directors go as high as twenty or thirty, and seventy takes are not unknown), but they were long ones. It was his way of giving the actors room to grow into a scene. The fluidity of *Star Wars* results from Lucas's seamless shooting style and his instinctive knowledge of when to move on to the next scene.

Lucas didn't enjoy dealing with actors and the inevitable jealousies that arise on a movie set. George's strategy was to remain low-key. His direction largely consisted of the oft-heard phrase "Faster and more intense." Hamill remembers a scene in the *Millennium Falcon* with Luke, Ben, Han, and the robots. "Everybody got all their lines right, which is hard, and then the scene's over and we look out. George was on a crane and said, 'Uh . . . let's do it again, only this time . . . do it better.'"

Lucas wouldn't even play the role of director. His assistant director usually yelled "Action!" If the cast and crew listened closely, they heard George mutter, "All right, cut." A moment later, the assistant yelled out the same instruction. "Most directors are insecure and I'm no exception to that," Lucas admits.

But Lucas is proud of the results. "Everybody says, 'Oh, the acting in George's films is terrible,' but I don't believe that," he says. "I think it's very good, and one of the reasons for my films' success. I haven't done anything to make the actors wonderful, but they make the story work, they make the film popular." Lucas thinks *Star Wars* is about *people,* not spaceships, and he is right. The special effects help only to create a new universe in which the story takes place and the characters interact.

Lucas needed the confidence of his cast to make his film work: "The scenes were extremely silly and stupid. If they don't trust you, it all falls apart." Lucas let his actors play a scene their way; he was happy to substitute their inspiration for his. But if he totally disagreed with their approach, he wouldn't bother to film it. "Very little time was wasted," says Ford. "George didn't have an authoritarian attitude like many directors: 'Kid, I've been in this business twenty-five years, trust me.' He was different. He knew the movie was based so strongly on the relationship among the three of us that he encouraged our contributions."

Ford became famous for saying to Lucas about the dialogue: "You can type this shit, George, but you sure can't say it." Lucas insisted that his cast never play a scene for its camp humor, even if the script seemed to call for it. *Star Wars* was not a camp movie and there would be no double-takes or sly grins.

The cast became a small family: Carrie and Mark were the little brother and sister, Harrison was the older sibling. All had problems with their written dialogue; Fisher gagged on lines such as "I thought I recognized your foul stench when I was brought aboard, Governor Tarkin." Hamill smiles. "It was not Noel Coward, let's face it," he recalls. Each actor knew what Lucas had invested in the characters and felt a responsibility to live up to his expectations.

Hamill quickly recognized that Luke Skywalker was modeled on Lucas himself, in name and spirit. (The character was named Luke Starkiller until the first day of shooting.) *Star Wars* was Hamill's first feature, but Lucas held no rehearsals, not even a read-through of the script. Hamill went to Tunisia, then England, hurried through costume fittings, watched test film of the robots, and toured the skeletal sets without benefit of a single lengthy conversation with Lucas about his character. "It made no sense at all," Hamill recalls. Just before shooting commenced at Elstree, Lucas took his cast to lunch at a Chinese restaurant. "There was this embarrassing silence when nobody said anything," Hamill says. Not unusual for an encounter with their director, the actors soon learned.

Lucas liked Hamill's ingenuity and eagerness; he brought a bold innocence to Luke, a fresh outlook toward the incredible events that befall him. Luke is a sounding board for the other characters: the loyal robots who regard him as their master, and Han Solo, to whom Luke is like a pesky little brother. Hamill soon realized that Lucas expected him to merge his own personality with Luke's—that's why he was cast. George took to calling Mark "the Kid," the same nickname Francis Coppola had bestowed on him eight years earlier.

Hamill wasn't the only performer confused by *Star Wars*. Carrie Fisher's only movie experience had consisted of one day's work on *Shampoo*, in which she seduces Warren Beatty. Fisher was nineteen when she arrived in England, frightened and nervous beneath her tough demeanor. She was sure she had been miscast: "I kept reading the script, and it was saying how incredibly beautiful Leia was," she remembers. "I didn't think I was pretty. I was a little Pillsbury doughgirl." Compounding Fisher's anxieties was Lucas's admonition to lose ten pounds before she arrived in England—she had lost only five. "I thought I was gonna arrive on the set and they'd say, 'Well, you didn't lose the other five, so we have this other actress waiting here.'" (Hamill once dreamt that he and Fisher slammed into the wall practicing their rope swing and were replaced immediately by Robbie Benson and Jodie Foster.)

Fisher had other problems—she was the only woman on the set. (Shelagh Fraser, who played Aunt Beru, finished in Tunisia.) The only nearby females were Fisher's hairdresser, makeup artist, and stand-in. "I wasn't bothered by being surrounded by men, no! God, I had no competition!" she says with a laugh. Routinely referred to as "the Girl," Fisher sometimes felt like a real-life version of the dolls that bear her likeness. Her character had no fun. She was pleased that Lucas gave Leia the opportunity to act decisively and talk tough, but she never got to talk about boys. Leia comes on screen firing her blaster, hardly the traditional damsel in distress.

Lucas imagined that Leia had been raised as a soldier, trained in the martial and political arts by the finest minds in the Alderaan system. "She is extremely bright and well educated and used to taking charge of situations," he explained in a publicity interview on the background of the *Star Wars* characters. "She is a natural-born leader." Leia was a space tomboy, sister Wendy grown up. Lucas thinks that young children can recognize Princess Leia. "She's sort of a drag and she's a nuisance," just like most little sisters.

Lucas did all he could to quash Fisher's femininity. A long white dress covered her from throat to ankle. Michael Ritchie had attempted to cast Fisher in his film *Smile* (about a bevy of beauty queens) because of "her tremendous body." When Ritchie saw *Star Wars,* he was shocked: "George had completely covered her up! I thought for sure that was his one commercial mistake. Even Dale Arden (from *Flash Gordon*) had cleavage!" Lucas went so far as to order Fisher's breasts taped to her chest with thick gaffer's electrical tape. "No breasts bounce in space, there's no jiggling in the Empire," Fisher jokes, adding, "Gary Kurtz had to tell me that. George didn't have the nerve." Lucas simply didn't want sexuality in his fairy tale—no mushy stuff.

Harrison Ford had the easiest job. He *was* Han Solo, the most contemporary and realistic character in the story; the audience could easily identify with him. George had given considerable thought to Solo and constructed a personal history for the character: abandoned by space gypsies, raised by Wookiees from age seven to twelve, a cadet at the Space Academy, and expelled for selling exam answers and drag-racing spaceships, he finally becomes a spice smuggler and enemy of the Empire. Han really wasn't a bad guy, even if he did smuggle. "In reality, he's just sort of a free-enterprise small businessman," Lucas says. George respects Han the same way he respects his father: for their belief in the virtue of private enterprise.

Resigned to his character's fate, Alec Guinness fine-tuned his performance, giving depth and dimension to Obi-Wan Kenobi. While the British crew openly mocked their young director, Guinness quietly supported George. He never lost faith in *Star Wars,* even when puzzled or unclear about how a scene would look on screen.

David Prowse became too involved in his role—he would stride around in his Darth Vader costume, casting a baleful eye on hapless production assistants. Prowse's costume was uncomfortable: quilted leather trousers, covered by four layers of canvas and leather, a breastplate, and two cloaks. He could barely breathe through the vent in his cowcatcher mask and couldn't see more than ten feet in any direction.

Lucas had great affection for Chewbacca and constructed a detailed culture for the Wookiees. Amalgams of cat, dog, and gorilla, Wookiees dwell in tribes on a damp jungle planet, occupying inflatable houses set atop giant trees. They live to be three hundred fifty years old, eat meat and vegetables, and are mammals. The six-breasted females deliver their offspring in litters; baby Wookiees are four feet tall at birth, with wide, adult-size eyes.

The Wookiees are George's own little anthropological case study, a primitive patriarchy with a complicated lineage structure, initiation rites, and a religion that rejects materialism. Wookiees have their own version of the Force, a natural empathy with plant life and their planet's ecology. After an Imperial invasion, the Wookiees are rounded up by slave traders and sold throughout the Empire. Han Solo rescues a group of prisoners that includes Chewbacca, who becomes his lifelong bodyguard and companion.

Peter Mayhew wasn't told any of this when cast as Chewbacca, but he instinctively studied animal reactions. The tall, slow-speaking actor saw

Chewbacca as an intelligent yet emotional creature who gets violently upset when his life is disrupted. Mayhew had no dialogue and was limited in his movements by his costume, but audiences seem not to be conscious of the person inside the furry suit. "When I haven't got the mask on, I'm sort of a normal person," Mayhew says. "But as soon as that mask goes on, the whole character comes alive and I can't do anything about it. It's just amazing."

Lucas had a mental dossier on C-3PO, too: The robot is 112 years old and Luke is his forty-third master (most of his previous employers were diplomats like Princess Leia). His logic system is located in his head, and his storage systems are in his heart and chest area. As a protocol robot, C-3PO is programmed not to reveal classified information, which explains his apparent ignorance of Princess Leia's hologram message.

C-3PO is devoid of irony and therefore the perfect foil for outrageous situations. His primary emotion seems to be exasperation with R2-D2. C-3PO reveals a side of Lucas when he says, "Actually, Artoo-Detoo was a nuisance. I couldn't say that we were close. I certainly don't have any feeling for him. I mean, it's nice to have him around. He has his place. But I wouldn't go so far as to say I'm fond of him. Under times of stress, some of my circuitry has a tendency to go a little overly emotional."

The man inside C-3PO also was emotional. Once filming started, Anthony Daniels feared he had made a terrible mistake. Lucas seemed to forget about Tony Daniels the actor, caring only for C-3PO the robot. Daniels was hurt and angry. "After the first few days, people forgot I was a person in there, and we're not just talking about George here, it was everybody. I was a *thing*. Everyone was irritated by me and I, of course, was irritated on the inside. It was all very unpleasant." But the mask was useful when he had to deliver lines like "Listen to them, Artoo! They're dying, and it's all my fault!" Daniels could at least cringe in private.

A performer working behind a mask is completely on his own. Daniels had no eye contact with the other actors or the director; he was robbed of his peripheral vision and constantly bumped into people and props. Mayhew, Prowse, and Baker had similar problems, but Daniels was the only professional actor of the group, and he took his work seriously. He learned his dialogue faithfully and delivered it forcefully, although it was muffled to the point of unintelligibility by his face mask. Daniels was shocked to discover that Lucas had originally intended to use someone else's voice for his character, even though Daniels' voice was largely responsible for C-3PO's popularity—it gave the robot the perfect tone of concerned prissiness. Daniels was wounded, however; he too was seduced by Lucas's enthusiasm, only to discover that the relationship was strictly professional. "I wanted him to like me as a performer *and* a person," Daniels says. "George makes me nervous, that's for sure. I mean, having lunch with George is no fun if you're by yourself."

I forget how impossible making movies really is. I get so depressed, but I guess I'll get through it somehow. . . . [2]

—George Lucas in a letter to Marcia Lucas
during the filming of *Star Wars*

Bad luck followed Lucas to England. Makeup expert Stuart Freeborn went into the hospital two weeks after production started, leaving most of the masks for the cantina aliens unfinished. The remote-controlled version of R2-D2 was walking into walls. The special effects crew was overzealous with its explosions and destroyed entire sets. Several stuntmen in stormtrooper outfits suffered concussions, and one had to be hospitalized.

Lucas had planned an elaborate monster for the garbage-compactor scene, in which Han, Luke, Leia, and Chewie are almost crushed to death.[3] The Dia-Noga was a sort of alien jellyfish with massive tentacles; the special effects people came up with what Lucas called "a big, wide, brown turd." He had to settle for a single cellophane tentacle, a compromise that irritates him to this day.

"Everything was going wrong," George says, a weary look returning to his face. "It was very trying. I'd never done a picture that went on for sixteen weeks. I cared about *every* single detail." Control is vital to Lucas while making a movie, and *Star Wars* was the first time he felt a production slipping away from him. He regularly got up at 5:30 in the morning, sat on the edge of his bed, and moaned. His friends were alarmed when they saw him—George was pasty-faced and tense, stricken by frequent headaches and stomachaches. "It wasn't funny; he was wrecked," remembers Bill Huyck. "People have gallows humor about films, but George had jumped off the gallows."

George and Marcia stayed in "Lost Cottage" in Hampstead, which seemed appropriate. Their house was burglarized during the filming and Marcia's jewelry and George's television set were stolen. George did not feel comfortable in England—he couldn't get a decent hamburger, the cars drove on the wrong side of the road, and Marcia couldn't find anything good to watch on TV. Lucas was homesick: he missed his house and his dog and his friends. Marcia wasn't having the time of her life, either. Their attempts to have a baby were unsuccessful. She became ill with the flu and had to be hospitalized. George suffered from his usual debilitating "director's" cough.

At Elstree, Lucas was falling further behind schedule; the sets were just completed as he began shooting on them. The painters worked frantically while George filmed in the opposite direction. When they were done, he'd swing around and shoot where they had just painted. "He's very perceptive about what's needed for the final film," Norman Reynolds observes. "The great thing about George is that he knows what's important and what isn't. Lots of directors don't understand that."

Lucas refused to rush the production. That required great self-control, given the deteriorating situation at ILM. John Dykstra was still experimenting with new camera techniques, and the background footage needed for rear projection filming in England had not arrived. When it did, Lucas was aghast: "It was terrible. I knew it wasn't going to work. The ships looked like little cardboard cutouts, and the lasers were big and fat and looked awful. We couldn't use any of it."

The only alternative was blue screen, a special process that makes the background disappear under special lighting, and matte paintings of the scene are substituted. Blue screen requires giant arc lights, making the sets very hot. It was the warmest English summer in years—electricians fainted in the rafters, and Peter Mayhew collapsed from heat exhaustion and dehydration.

Back in Hollywood, Ladd was concerned about the delays in filming and the lack of progress with the special effects. *Star Wars* was already over its allotted budget, but the devaluation of the British pound gave Lucas an extra $500,000 on paper. The planned Christmas release was abandoned and summer 1977 became the new target date. Ladd wanted a rough version of the movie completed by Christmas, and the music, dialogue, and sound effects to be recorded in January 1977.

Ladd visited Elstree in May and saw forty minutes of footage that was so bad it almost scuttled the movie. Dailies were not shipped back to the studio (*Star Wars* was an independent production), so Ladd had seen nothing. The poorly stitched assemblage of scenes without music or special effects unnerved him. The dialogue was laughable, the lighting was inconsistent, and the shots often didn't match. Ladd had a soul-searching talk with Lucas before being reassured that George indeed knew what he was doing.

Lucas was even more upset—"I just wish you had never seen this stuff," he told Ladd of the sloppily edited footage. Privately, he said to himself, "Oh, my God, I'm doing a terrible job here. It must be me." He showed Marcia the footage, and she agreed to take apart the movie and begin reediting from scratch. Lucas's confidence was shaken by the incident. What if the movie really was bad and Fox tried to take it away from him?

His paranoia seemed justified just a few weeks later. Still to be filmed was the assault on Leia's ship by the stormtroopers, the first dramatic sequence in *Star Wars*. John Barry had scavenged pieces of various sets to give the illusion of the blockade runner's interior, but Lucas quickly saw that the set wouldn't be convincing on film. There was no money for a new one but Lucas would not be deterred. "We're going to go over budget and build this other set," he ordered. Kurtz had to tell Fox; as expected, the studio was furious.

Barry built a new set in two weeks; by now, Lucas was five weeks over schedule and had two weeks of filming left. Fox gave him one week and then pulled the plug—Lucas had three days before *Star Wars* was shut down. He had yet to film Leia loading the hologram message into R2-D2, Vader's strangling of a rival general, and most of the opening battle. In desperation, he hired two more camera crews and had three units filming simultaneously on the same set.

Robert Watts photographed the stormtroopers rushing to battle, Kurtz shot the robots on another part of the stage, and Lucas directed Darth Vader. If he didn't get the footage, he didn't have a movie. Lucas felt betrayed by Ladd. "They came in and cut off my water on *Star Wars* and I was very upset over it," recalls George. At least *Star Wars* was over now. . . sort of.

In the end, it was a film that was entirely George's.
                              —Robert Watts about *Star Wars*

The sprawling San Fernando Valley where Industrial Light & Magic was located, depressed George. It reminded him of everything he hated about Southern California: the smog, the sleaze, and the phonies. He would have moved ILM to Marin County, but San Francisco lacked Hollywood's film labs. So Lucas had to fly to Burbank once a week, rent a car, and drive through the choking air on the Ventura freeway to ILM.

Lucas had instructed ILM to avoid the high-technology, high-cost effects that took so long to complete on *2001*. "I don't want to build a lot of expensive equipment and not get any shots," he told Dykstra. "It's not important how you do the shots. It's important what they look like." Dykstra wanted a special computer-controlled camera to give the illusion of "real" screen movement. No one had successfully used one in a feature film, and Lucas realized it had to be designed from scratch.

"There was some distance between George's understanding of what he wanted, and how to get it," says Dykstra, whose own special effects company now occupies the original ILM warehouse. "Like anyone with the guts to become a director and tackle something like *Star Wars*, his tendency was to want to do everything himself." Lucas's training as a self-sufficient filmmaker both helped and hindered him. He picked people to work for him who were innovative and skilled (and who added little to his budget), but he was unwilling to let them take charge.

Dykstra gathered an extraordinary group of sci-fi freaks, computer nerds, and technobrats from Hollywood and the Silicon Valley. ILM became their family and *Star Wars* was their labor of love, fueled by communal energy, creative electricity, and Lucas's money. ILM's staff worked long, if erratic, hours; they showed up at 10:00 P.M. or 3:00 A.M. in shorts, T-shirts, and floppy beach thongs. "It was like a whole class of people who were lost in a 1967 time warp," remembers Carol Titelman. The facility soon acquired the nickname of the "Country Club" because there was no dress code, no time clock, and virtually no organization. It was Dykstra's show—the crew's loyalty was largely to him, not Lucas.

Some of the specialists, like production illustrator Joe Johnston, came to ILM right out of college. Others, like cameraman Dennis Muren, were weaned on special effects classics like *The Beast at 20,000 Fathoms* and *The Seven Voyages of Sinbad*. Richard Edlund, who was responsible for shooting the miniature sets and models, explains, "We had a great crew of young unknowns, who had good ideas and hadn't had the opportunity to put them into practice." The staff grew to almost a hundred, but the average age was only twenty-seven.

The rest of the special effects industry thought ILM was crazy to try 365 effects shots in less than two years. ILM finally spent twenty-two months on the special effects, including the six months needed to design the equipment. The total bill came to about $2.5 million, 25 percent over budget. Each effect cost almost $7,000, or $150 per frame.

ILM used Ralph McQuarrie's production paintings and Colin Cantwell's prototype spaceship models for inspiration while Lucas was away. Joe Johnston began what would become more than 1,000 storyboards for the effects sequences, using illustrations, models, and the script itself. Cantwell's spaceships had to be redesigned because they were too sleek and NASA-like—Lucas wanted them to have a romantic, quasi-military feel.

Lucas also left Johnston with a ten-minute black-and-white sequence of aerial battles, which he had constructed from war movies like *Battle of Britain* and *The Bridges of Toko-Ri*. Each shot had to be duplicated by X-wing and T.I.E. fighter spaceships; Lucas essentially preshot and edited the climactic sequence of *Star Wars* months before he began filming the movie.

After six months of around-the-clock work, ILM had its first Dykstraflex camera, a system controlled by the cameraman that allowed him to pan, tilt, and track around a model, always keeping it in focus. The breakthrough was the camera's ability to repeat the identical movements from shot to shot; the effects sequences could be built like a music track, layer upon layer. The illusion was complete: none of the spaceships in *Star Wars* ever moved—only the camera did.

The star-field backdrop in space was made by punching holes in black plexiglass. More than seventy-five models were constructed, with astonishing detail work: on the rebel blockade runner, ILM artists built a tiny cockpit complete with *Playboy* pinups, all done to scale. The miniaturized laser cannons were fully motorized to swivel and tilt by remote control. The light sabers were four-sided blades coated with reflective aluminum, attached to a small motor. When rotated, they created a flashing light later enhanced by animation.

Fox's Gosnell periodically checked on ILM's progress while Lucas was still in England. "He'd come back and pull his hair out," remembers Ladd. "Ray would get red in the face when he'd start talking about ILM." The *Animal House* atmosphere at ILM didn't help to reassure the studio. One day Dykstra mounted a forklift, drove it over to an old refrigerator, and in front of the entire ILM crew, lifted and smashed the machine onto the cement floor again and again. "Everybody was just howling and laughing," remembers Rose Duignan, Lucas's assistant. Just then, in walked Gosnell. "It really looked bad, all these madmen in long hair, no shirts, and nobody was working," Duignan says. Lucas struggled to get ILM's staff into the film technicians' local, but union leaders had no use for ILM's resident weirdos. The decision saved Lucas thousands of dollars in overtime and benefits at the time. Later, he made it up to the ILM crew by paying them well above union scale.

The strain on Lucas was immediately apparent upon his return from England. "He was real tired, you could tell, and very pale," Duignan remembers. It shouldn't have come as a surprise—Lucas had just realized that *Star Wars* was going to have to be completely taken apart and reassembled, throwing him several months behind schedule. He would have to spend three days a week at ILM and four days editing at Parkhouse—there was no time for a day off.

To compound his miseries, Lucas discovered that ILM had almost no tangible accomplishments to show for more than a year's work. "They had three shots," Lucas says, the wonderment still in his voice. "They'd spent more than one million dollars of their two-million-dollar budget, and all they had was *three shots.*" For the first time during the making of *Star Wars* Lucas lost control, lashing out verbally at Dykstra. The burly special effects designer wasn't afraid to scream back. The argument quickly turned bitter and emotional.

Flying back to San Francisco that night, Lucas felt sharp chest pains. Marcia met him at the airport and as they drove home, the pains worsened. "It was terrible," remembers Marcia. "I was really sure he must be having a heart attack or something, because illness does not get George down. His way of getting rid of being sick is just to work harder." They sped to Marin General Hospital, where Lucas was diagnosed as suffering from hypertension and exhaustion. He stayed overnight and was advised to reduce the stress in his life. Lucas thought about his vow to retire after *Graffiti*, about the pressures to finish *Star Wars,* about his plans to make two sequels. He stared at the ghostlike countenance in the mirror across from his hospital bed: "That's when I really confirmed to myself I was going to change, that I wasn't going to make more films, I wasn't going to direct anymore. I was going to get my life a little bit more under control."

But relations between Dykstra and Lucas continued to deteriorate. Dykstra felt George didn't understand the technical work involved. "I was defensive as hell, too, because I was scared shitless," John admits. But he made the fatal mistake of telling Lucas what *couldn't* be done. "One of the first things I learned," says longtime Lucas associate Jim Bloom, "is you give George your opinion, but you don't tell him, 'No.'" Dykstra's reign over ILM ended when Lucas emerged from the hospital, determined to take control of the situation. George Mather became the new production supervisor and set up a timetable for the completion of all the effects sequences. Dykstra felt Lucas had lost faith with him just as *Star Wars* was beginning to come together.

Lucas also personally supervised the special effects photography. Dennis Muren led a second camera unit that worked from 3:00 P.M. to midnight; Richard Edlund's crew worked from 8:00 A.M. to 6:00 P.M. The sixteen-hour combined schedule lasted for almost six months. Lucas isolated Dykstra from most of the creative work and issued his instructions directly to the cameramen.

Lucas spent two full weeks at ILM, but if a visitor didn't know him by sight, he was easy to miss. Rose Duignan arrived for her job interview and sat next to a young guy in little tennis shoes, slumped in an office chair. "I immediately thought he was an equipment driver," she remembers. Rose worked closely with Lucas for several months, taking down his every word and distributing memos of his instructions to the ILM staff.

For all his complaining, Lucas enjoyed the camaraderie at ILM; it reminded him of the communal feeling at USC's patio. He stayed late each night, reluctant to go back to his lonely hotel room. Dennis Muren sat outside the warehouse one evening with Lucas, looking at the real stars. "It was the first time I had talked to him for any length of time, and I felt a real closeness to him," remembers Muren. "He was candid about the problems of making the film, what it was like in England, and how it had almost killed him."

I've seen a lot of people with problems and pressures, but never as bad as George's. How it all came together is mind-boggling—it came from the force of George's conviction and his vision.

—Carroll Ballard

If *Star Wars* was to be salvaged, Lucas knew it had to be in the editing. As he and Marcia reviewed the footage, George grew depressed; this was not the movie he had seen in his mind's eye for the past seven years. Even Marcia was nervous, although she tried to reassure Ladd that *Star Wars* was in fine shape.

There was too much work for Marcia alone, and George hired a second editor, Richard Chew, who had worked with Walter Murch on Coppola's *The Conversation*. The workload was still too burdensome, so Lucas hired Paul Hirsch, who had just finished cutting *Carrie* for Brian De Palma. The three editors spent weeks cataloging massive amounts of footage. George spent his mornings going from Moviola to Moviola, giving Marcia, Richard, and Paul notes of what he wanted done.

Carroll Ballard walked into Parkhouse at 6:00 A.M. one morning to find Marcia still cutting *Star Wars*—she had been there all night, with Lucas, looking wan and exhausted, at her side. "Making that movie was like backing up fifty feet from a rock wall, running at it at full speed, bashing your head, and falling flat on the ground—and doing it again until you busted that bloody wall down," Ballard says.

Slowly, *Star Wars* began to take shape. A subplot involving Luke and Biggs, his former older brother turned role model, was cut, as was Jabba the Hutt's confrontation with Han Solo—Lucas was disgusted at how crude the creature looked. There were some positive discoveries: Lucas realized that his color scheme had worked, giving sections of the movie a subconscious visual consistency.

Lucas had to refilm several sequences he had hurried through, or was unable to get, in Tunisia and England. Foremost among these was the space cantina scene. Stuart Freeborn's hospitalization had left Lucas with a collection of background monsters that looked as if they had stepped off the pages of Beatrix Potter: a walrus man, a mouse lady, and a pig-faced man—not exactly the galactic horror show Lucas had in mind. George pleaded with Ladd for another $100,000, but the Fox board of directors, heeding Gosnell's bleak reports about ILM, was in no mood to give any more money to *Star Wars*. Lucas wanted fifty monsters, but Ladd talked him down to twenty and a budget of $20,000 for all the remaining sequences. When Ladd saw the completed film, he realized Lucas's instinct had been right. "The cantina is a classic scene now," he says. "When I first saw it, it didn't bother me that much. I wondered how it could be made much better, but George really was able to enhance it."

Ladd had to make a formal presentation to the Fox board to get approval for the extra money. By this time, the budget was over $9 million and still rising. Ladd walked into the Fox boardroom, only to have one member angrily demand, "Would you please give us an explanation of why the budget has gone up on this picture?" Ladd quietly answered, "Because it's possibly the greatest picture ever made. That's my absolute statement." Then he got up and walked out. The board sat in stunned silence—Ladd was not one for overstating his case. Word of the confrontation spread like wildfire at Fox, and Lucas got his $20,000. Chris Kalabokes remembers thinking at the time, "Ladd would have backed that movie to twenty million dollars, he had so much faith in George Lucas."

Still to be filmed, besides the cantina scene, were several desert shots of R2-D2, the landspeeder, and the banthas. Lucas asked Carroll Ballard to photograph the scenes in Death Valley. The locale perfectly duplicated Tunisia, and Lucas now had a landspeeder that worked and a robot that walked.

At 5:00 A.M. on the day filming was to begin, Lucas's phone in Death Valley rang—it was Gary Kurtz from Los Angeles. Mark Hamill, who was needed for the desert shots, had been in an early morning car accident on the Pacific Coast Highway north of Los Angeles. "How bad is it?" groaned George. "We don't know, it doesn't look good for shooting," Kurtz answered. Lucas couldn't delay shooting—Fox would cut him off. Art director Leon Erickson had created a bantha suit for a Marine World elephant, and Lucas filmed the bantha scenes first. Elephants are not accustomed to the intense heat of Death Valley, and filming went slowly, as the beast kept shrugging off its heavy costume.

At the end of the first day's shooting, Lucas learned of the seriousness of Hamill's injuries. Mark had gone through the windshield of his sports car and undergone extensive plastic surgery on his face. Lucas used a double for Hamill's long shots and scrapped the closeups. "I was in terrible shape at that point," George recalls. "I really just wanted to get done with the damn movie and I didn't care what it turned out to be."

Lucas did care, of course. The construction of twenty completely new creatures for the cantina took almost six weeks. The job was so rushed that no one remembered to put air vents in the masks. Gary Kurtz had to slit them under the chin with a razor blade to allow the actors to breathe. Lucas added a jazz combo of alien musicians, with seven monsters tootling away on mock instruments to the strains of Glenn Miller.

The final special effects sequences were filmed in the Mayan ruins of Tikal National Park in Guatemala. Ladd had begged George to pick a nice local park for the jungle setting of the rebel base, but Lucas was satisfied only with the real thing: off went Richard Edlund and a second-unit crew to the Central American rain forests.

As the effects footage improved, the atmosphere at ILM lightened. "Some guy across the stage would say, 'Oh, another first!'" remembers Richard Edlund. "Some other new thing had been done that we knew hadn't been done before. This was going on every day and was very exciting." The most important shot in *Star Wars* was the opening one—the looming Star Destroyer would either make or break the movie's credibility. "If somebody sat down in a theater and saw this monstrous thing come over the screen and keep coming and coming, and they were awed by that, then we had our audience just where we wanted 'em," says Edlund. "But if they laughed, we were dead." Edlund shot the opening sequence five times until he was sure nobody would laugh.

Despite Lucas's worries, ILM achieved wonders: an entire new camera system was designed, manufactured, and implemented in four months. It needed only two weeks of debugging to straighten out the kinks, and then worked for the next eight months, eighteen hours a day, with only three days of down time. "It was totally a gamble," Dykstra says, "and it paid off." *Star Wars* revolutionized the look of contemporary movies, but Dykstra regrets that Lucas feels he didn't get his money's worth. "I respect his right to that opinion," says Dykstra, "but there's something in me that says, 'Goddammit, how would you have done it differently? Or better?'"

The special effects cost close to $3 million—they went over budget more than any other aspect of the picture and caused Lucas innumerable headaches. With hindsight, he does appreciate ILM's contributions: "You couldn't do that film today for less than eight million dollars for the special effects. I think *Star Wars* would probably cost between twenty-two million and twenty-five million dollars now." But when the opportunity came to show his appreciation, Lucas remained bitter. No one in the special effects company, including Dykstra, was given profit percentages in *Star Wars,* although some people received cash bonuses.

Lucas was totally exhausted by the end of 1976. He got a lift just before Christmas when he first saw the *Star Wars* trailer of coming attractions. "I was sort of proud of it," he remembers. "I said, 'You know, for better or worse, that's the movie I wanted to make. Whether people like it or don't like it, that's what I tried to do—there it is.'"

By January, Lucas had a first cut of the whole film. Marty Scorsese was begging Marcia to edit *New York, New York* in Los Angeles, and although George hated to see her go, she took the job. Marcia, too, was fed up with *Star Wars.* Paul Hirsch finished up while George began the complicated recording and dubbing work.

Lucas wanted the sound and music recorded in Dolby Stereo, an innovation in the mid-1970s. Fox opposed the idea, arguing that the equipment was not reliable and theater owners were reluctant to invest in it. Lucas had hired John Williams to write the *Star Wars* score, which was now completed. Williams had been nominated for ten Academy Awards, winning an Oscar for his music for *Jaws* in 1976. The Juilliard-trained composer had been working on *Star Wars* since March 1976.

Lucas still had to find the right voices for Darth Vader and C-3PO and the proper sounds for Chewbacca and R2-D2. George planned to rerecord Anthony Daniels' British-accented dialogue because he had always imagined C-3PO talking like a used-car dealer from Brooklyn. (A similar character was cut from *American Graffiti*—Lucas has trouble discarding what he considers an amusing idea.) But no one else's voice fit Daniels' precise body movements. "Tony was the only one who really believed in See-Threepio," Lucas says. "He gave the best performance, so I made See-Threepio an English butler." It took Lucas almost a year to realize what everybody on the set knew from the first day of filming—Anthony Daniels *was* C-3PO.

Darth Vader required a deep, commanding voice to communicate the menace of his character. James Earl Jones, the black actor whose roles have ranged from Othello to a garbage collector, has a resonant baritone that, when electronically modulated, was truly intimidating. Lucas considered testing Orson Welles for the part, but his voice seemed too recognizable. Jones was paid $10,000 and refused screen credit, not realizing that Darth Vader would become one of his most famous parts.

Before production began, Gary Kurtz had called Ken Mura, Lucas's former sound instructor at USC. He asked if there were any sound geniuses at USC, and it turned out one was just graduating. Ben Burtt was hired sight unseen and instructed to begin creating sounds for *Star Wars*. Burtt didn't meet Lucas until six months after he was put on the payroll, and they had only one conversation about the concept behind the sound of *Star Wars*. As with *THX* and *Graffiti*, Lucas did not want the movie's background noises to sound as if they had been manufactured in a recording studio. Lucas and Burtt felt the electronic, synthesized sound track had become a sci-fi cliché. "The sounds of the real world are complicated and kind of dirty," Burtt says. "They simply cannot be reproduced on a synthesizer."

Lucas had found the ideal person to create a new aural universe: Burtt had a tremendous interest in fantasy and adventure films and had collected sounds for years. Armed with a Nagra tape recorder, he constructed a sound fabric for *Star Wars* that encompassed all but the dialogue. (Even the footsteps had to be recorded because the sets were made of wood, not metal.)

Burtt broke down *Star Wars* into different categories: voices, weapons, vehicles, doors, even screams. He walked around his apartment, recording his blender, refrigerator, and stereo turntable. At USC he recorded movie projectors—their hum, mixed with static from the picture tube of his TV set, supplied the sound of the laser swords. He recorded jet engines at Northrup Aircraft and weapons and jet strafing runs at military bases. Burtt spent one day at Los Angeles International Airport recording jets taking off and, the next day, jets landing. Every few weeks he sent Lucas a tape with five or six sounds suitable for robots, spaceships, or weapons.

Burtt tried for an emotional impact with his sounds, especially when Chewbacca and R2-D2 "talked." He visited the Los Angeles zoo, game farms, and animal trainers in search of a Wookiee voice. Most captive animals don't vocalize; Burtt's results came from trained bears. He spent a day recording a four-month-old cinnamon bear, mixing its voice with those of three other bears, and a walrus, seal, and badger. He changed their pitch, slowed them down, and matched the results to slides Lucas had sent him of Peter Mayhew in costume. Bears vocalize from the back of their throats, so the sounds matched the Wookiee's mask movements.

R2-D2 was more of a challenge. "He needed more than cold, machine-like electronic sounds," Burtt decided. He recorded his own voice and spliced in the sounds of a flexible pipe being squeezed and metal scraps rustling around in dry ice. Burtt knew that alien speech needed to mimic a known language to succeed on screen—the Jawas spoke a speeded-up Zulu and Swahili dialect.

One of Burtt's best effects was Greedo, the alien killed by Han Solo in the cantina. A linguistics student who could imitate obscure dialects in a Danny Kaye-style pattern, was hired to speak the classic Inca dialect of Quechua. Burtt modulated it electronically to produce a strange, alien tongue. Lucas wanted subtitles for Greedo's dialogue, a move resisted by Kurtz and Fox. As usual, Lucas had a reason. "It teaches kids to read," he says, in all seriousness, of the twelve subtitled lines. "Kids don't want to read books or newspapers, but this was something I knew they would want to read." (Luckily for Lucas, kids wanted to read the novelization of his script—there are 5 million copies of *Star Wars*[4] in print.)

Lucas took Burtt's sounds, threw together a score from recordings of *Ben-Hur* and Holtz's *The Planets,* and was ready to screen *Star Wars*. The first audience consisted of Marcia, Alan Ladd, Jr., and his wife, Patty. They watched a very rough cut, with blank film in place of many of the special effects, but at its conclusion Ladd was greatly relieved. The picture ran a little over two hours and while incomplete, it was not the disaster that everyone in the audience had, at one time or another, secretly feared.

A month later, Ladd brought several members of his advertising, marketing, and distribution staff to San Francisco to see *Star Wars* in the Parkhouse screening room. It was a weeknight and the bus got lost on its way to San Anselmo, arriving almost two hours late. The screening room was outfitted with couches and easy chairs. Marketing chief Ashley Boone remembers thinking, "Someone has got more courage than they are entitled to, because this group is just liable to sit down and fall asleep."

No one fell asleep. The Fox executives watched in silence, but when the lights came on there was sustained applause. Production Vice-President Gareth Wigan said to Lucas, "That's the most moving picture I've seen in a long time." Lucas thought Wigan was trying to make him feel good; he smiled bravely and said, "Great." It wasn't until everyone adjourned to a nearby Italian restaurant that Lucas realized how much of an impact *Star Wars* had made. Ashley Boone sat slumped in his chair, looking flabbergasted. John Korty was at the screening and remembers Ladd questioning him closely about his reactions. "He was concerned whether kids would like it," says Korty. "But he was obviously caught up in it."

The Fox group boarded the plane back to Los Angeles. Alan Livingston, president of Fox's entertainment division with responsibility for the sound track album to *Star Wars,* sidled up to Boone during the flight and asked him if there was some way to persuade Lucas to release a disco version of the score. "I don't think I even answered him," Boone says, shaking his head in disbelief. Livingston wasn't the only executive to doubt the commercial appeal of *Star Wars.* Fox's marketing research had shown that women did not want to see a film with "wars" in the title. The robots didn't test well, nor did the science-fiction label Fox had stuck on the movie.

Lucas also showed *Star Wars* to his friends: Bill Huyck and Gloria Katz, John Milius, Matthew Robbins and Hal Barwood, *Time* magazine film critic Jay Cocks, Steven Spielberg, and Brian De Palma. "They all thought it was a disaster."

A rough cut was something this audience was accustomed to but "the opening crawl looked like somebody had written on a driveway, with the camera on a trash barrel," remembers Huyck. No one said anything at the movie's conclusion. Lucas admitted the film needed work, but he was unprepared for the merciless assault that followed. Brian De Palma was especially sarcastic in a good-natured way, teasing Lucas about the "almighty Force" and indicating that the rough cut version of the film was one of the worst things he had ever seen. Gloria Katz remembers, "Brian has a very wicked sense of humor and oh, he was so cruel." It was not one of Lucas's happier evenings.

Those who didn't criticize *Star Wars* expressed sympathy. "They were all my real close friends and they felt sorry for me more than anything else. There were a lot of condolences, which is even worse than saying you don't like the movie," Lucas recalls. Only Spielberg and Cocks reacted with enthusiasm—at dinner, they sat on one side of the table praising *Star Wars,* while De Palma faced them and made snide suggestions. "George didn't lose his appetite, that's the one thing I remember," Spielberg says. "He kept eating his dinner, nodding his head, taking it all in. But I don't believe he made many changes." Lucas let De Palma and Cocks rewrite the opening crawl, which he then modified. Other than that, he was resigned to the failure of *Star Wars:* "I figured, well, it's just a silly movie. It ain't going to work."

Lucas felt better when he arrived in England to supervise the recording of John Williams's score by the London Symphony Orchestra. He gave Williams great autonomy in writing the music, because he felt out of his element with anything except rock 'n' roll of the 1950s. Williams dissuaded Lucas from his original plan to use music by Dvorak and Liszt—it was better to have something original that would evoke a heroic era, said Williams. Williams visited Elstree only once and was shown a rough cut of the movie in late 1976. "George made it clear to me that things like direction, speed, and pace were very important and I took it from there," Williams says.

Lucas wanted the music to be like the classic Max Steiner scores for films like *Charge of the Light Brigade.* Williams leaned toward a romantic, orchestral sound that would act as an anchor for an audience transported to an unfamiliar universe. Lucas wanted 90 minutes of music in the 110-minute film, so Williams gave each character his or her own theme, repeating them with variations throughout *Star Wars.*

The music's impact was immediate and dramatic when incorporated into the film. "It was a mind-boggling difference," remembers Carroll Ballard, who saw *Star Wars* before and after Williams's score was added. "It gave the hokey characters a certain dimension. When you saw the film without the score, you couldn't take it seriously. But the music gave it the style of an old-time serial, and it was great fun." The London recording session was the most enjoyable experience for Lucas while making the film: "It was the one thing on the picture that was better than I had ever imagined. For once, I wasn't saying, 'Oh my God, what's happened?' Working with John was wonderful. It was just the way life should be."

Because of a shortage of studio space, Lucas had to mix *Star Wars* at night at the Goldwyn Studios in Los Angeles. He shared the studio Scorsese used during the day for *New York, New York,* which Marcia was still editing. To Lucas, this was *American Graffiti* all over again: "It's even worse when you're mixing at night, because you're in a dark room with no windows watching a movie go back and forth, back and forth. It's very hard not to fall asleep."

Lucas and Burtt mixed from 8:00 P.M. to 8:00 A.M. six nights a week in Goldwyn's Dolby Stereo room. Lucas was buoyed by frequent visits from his friends, who sat for hours watching footage and debating the artistic merit of his shots. Although they worked at the same studio, George and Marcia rarely saw each other.

The May 25 release date drew ever nearer. It was time to screen *Star Wars* for a real audience. As he had with *Graffiti,* Lucas scheduled a Sunday morning screening at San Francisco's Northpoint Theater on May 1, inviting a carefully selected cross-section of the movie audience—a small delegation from Fox, including Ladd and his wife, and Lucas's family and closest friends. George and Gary had their tape recorders to gauge the audience reaction. They didn't have long to wait: as soon as the opening crawl ended and the Star Destroyer appeared on the screen, the audience went crazy. "I was relieved more than anything else," Lucas remembers. "It was a very high moment—I knew the film worked." Privately, he and Kurtz were disappointed that the reaction wasn't quite as enthusiastic as it had been for *American Graffiti* in the same theater five years earlier. Lucas now felt secure, however, that *Star Wars* at least would make back Fox's investment. "But I had no idea of what was going to happen," he insists. "I mean, I had *no idea.*"

The Fox board of directors still had to see *Star Wars,* too. As expected, the screening was a disaster: several members fell asleep and most of them hated the movie. One admitted, after several drinks, that *Star Wars* might be all right, but he added that he didn't know anything about movies. One board member's wife marched up to Ladd and told him that someone should animate C-3PO's mouth, because nobody would understand how he talked when his lips didn't move.

The screening of *Star Wars* for cast and crew came three weeks later, on May 21 at the Beverly Hills headquarters of the Academy of Motion Picture Arts and Sciences. It, too, was at 10:00 A.M. on a weekend, with a luncheon that followed at Dr. Munchie's, a local restaurant. Lucas first showed a classic Chuck Jones cartoon, *Duck Dodger in the 21st Century,* and the laughter quickly cut through the tension in the audience. As *Star Wars* began, the laughter abruptly ceased. "We all sat with our mouths open, and all you could hear throughout the audience was '*Wowww!*'" remembers Richard Edlund.

The fruits of success were there for all to see, and those who had devoted part of their lives to *Star Wars* felt a surge of pride. "You put in about a total of two man-months on one shot, the shot lasts twenty-six frames on the screen, just over a second or two, and you wonder about it," says Edlund. "But the illusion was there. We didn't have to build a spaceship, we didn't have to send a guy out in space, and we gave the audience the impression that 'Oh, I'm back out in space again.'"

Even Tom Pollock, the prototype of the cynical Hollywood attorney, was touched. "The experience is not like any movie experience I have had since I was a child. It's reliving the first time you see a certain kind of movie when you're eight or nine years old. You feel you can never get it back again but seeing *Star Wars* is getting it back, and that's why it's successful. I know in my heart that George is totally in touch with his adolescent self—that's the secret of his success."

It just has to do with people happening to like dumb movies.
—George Lucas

Twentieth Century-Fox had a lot riding on *Star Wars* and its other two big summer pictures: a glossy soap opera called *The Other Side of Midnight* and a futuristic war movie, *Damnation Alley*. "We were very concerned that we might not have a successful year. And that would mean a wipeout for the corporation. It would be gone, easily acquired," Chris Kalabokes remembers. At the time *Star Wars* was released, Fox's stock was selling at about $12 a share. An unsuccessful year would drag down the price to $4 or $5 a share, and the company's fortunes would go with it. Four years later, Fox was sold to Denver oil millionaire Marvin Davis, who paid $70 a share. The principal reason for the high price was the success of *Star Wars*.

After the favorable screenings, Ladd was convinced that *Star Wars* was going to be a hit. "We felt it was going to be the biggest picture ever made," Ladd says now. Although he frequently expressed his opinion at Fox, it's clear that no one, Ladd included, anticipated just how big *Star Wars* would be. There were worries about the film being completed in time. To get any theaters in the hotly competitive summer marketplace *Star Wars* had to open in the usually lean box office period of May. If the film didn't perform immediately, it would be gone in two weeks.

Lucas had to ardently woo the science-fiction crowd—it was his hard-core audience. He personally paid for Kurtz and publicity supervisor Charles Lippincott to travel the circuit of sci-fi conventions, passing out thousands of buttons and bumper stickers and showing a carefully selected group of slides. Lucas remembers, "It had an effect, because there was a whole world of fanatics out there who were crazy to see this movie six months before it came out." Fox gave Kurtz expensive-looking posters with black lettering on a silver background that read: *"Star Wars,* coming to your galaxy soon."

The trailer had played in one thousand theaters since Christmas, but not everyone shared Lucas's enthusiasm for it. Ashley Boone remembers seeing it at a Westwood theater: "When Artoo-Detoo fell over, there were giggles and laughter. At the end, when it said, 'Coming to your galaxy this summer,' the audience groaned." The word quickly spread through Hollywood: *Star Wars* was a disaster. Even Ladd panicked and ordered the trailers off the screen. Boone yanked the one in Westwood and never heard another complaint.

Fox's advertising staff was unable to come up with an effective copy line for the *Star Wars* campaign. Some of the failures were embarrassing: "We have seen the epic adventure of the past. We are about to see the epic adventure of the future"; "Where your imagination ends, *Star Wars* begins"; "It is an adventure that is not only more than you can imagine, *it is more than you can imagine!*"

None of these pleased Lucas, nor did the graphics: crossed light sabers in the hands of Ben and Vader, with the logo "Imagine *Star Wars.*" He had in mind a more romantic poster of Luke and Leia swinging across on their rope, swashbuckler-style. Lucas also wanted the robots featured prominently, a demand that contradicted Fox's research. David Weitzner, in charge of Fox's advertising, eventually took the slogan right from the film itself: "A long time ago in a galaxy far, far away. . . ."

Lucas thought *Star Wars* would do as well as most Disney movies, which meant rentals of about $16 million. Science-fiction movies open strongly because of the eagerness of devotees; *Star Wars* had to survive for at least four weeks to be a real success. The film had to sell $32 million worth of tickets before Fox broke even. Ned Tanen saw Lucas two days before *Star Wars* opened and remembers George was concerned about its fate. Tanen told him, "You're drunk and crazy—this picture's going to be the biggest hit ever made." Lucas stared back at him—"Oh, no," he said. "It won't make more than fifteen million."

Star Wars was not an easy sell. Theater owners were leery of science-fiction films, and several made bids on *Star Wars* based on the business done by the last big sci-fi movie, *Silent Running*. Unfortunately for Fox, *Silent Running* didn't do much business. The film industry's confidence in a movie is gauged by the amount of money exhibitors will guarantee for the right to play it. *Star Wars* secured only $1.5 million in guarantees, rather than the $10 million expected of big movies. "It was embarrassing," says Ashley Boone.

Unable to get enough good theaters, Boone decided to open *Star Wars* on just one or two screens in each key major city or rural area. If the film did well initially, other theater owners might take it seriously. Lucas insisted upon some top-quality theaters capable of showing *Star Wars* in 70-millimeter widescreen and Dolby Stereo. Rather than spend $5 million on a national advertising campaign, Boone bought time on local TV stations, college newspapers, even the cable TV systems in college dormitories. "By the time this film opened, six million kids knew where it was playing," Boone says.

Star Wars opened in thirty-two theaters across the country on May 25, 1977. Boone gambled by opening it on a Wednesday, rather than the weekend, and began shows at 10:00 A.M. in New York and Los Angeles.

By 8:00 A.M., when the theater doors opened, there were long lines in both cities. Audiences were ready for *Star Wars*. Lucas had finished just in time: at Mann's Chinese Theater in Hollywood, the movie was already on the screen when the last reel arrived fresh from the lab.

Not far from the Chinese Theater, Lucas sat in a dark room, mixing the French-, German-, and Spanish-language versions of *Star Wars*. He had been doing this eighteen hours a day for the past two weeks. "I was really in a daze, shocked and beaten. I could hardly think straight," Lucas says. He claims he didn't remember which night *Star Wars* opened, or in what theater. Apparently Marcia didn't remember, either—they met as she was leaving work and he was arriving to work on *Star Wars*. They decided to have dinner together.

Marcia and George drove to a Hamburger Hamlet that just happened to be across the street from the Chinese Theater, where there was an immense traffic jam and crowds of people. "Jesus Christ, what's going on here?" Lucas wondered. As they rounded the corner, he and Marcia saw *Star Wars* in giant block letters on the theater marquee. "We just fell on the floor," Lucas remembers. "I said, 'I don't believe this.' So we sat in Hamburger Hamlet and watched the giant crowd out there, and then I went back and mixed all night. It wasn't excitement, it was amazement. I felt it was some kind of aberration."

Long lines or not, George and Marcia were on their way to Hawaii the next day, their first vacation since 1969. Bill Huyck and Gloria Katz joined them on the secluded island of Maui for ten days, as Lucas finally began to unwind. "George was just happy to be finished," says Bill. "He wasn't thinking about success at all." But Ashley Boone called Lucas almost nightly with the high grosses from *Star Wars*—the movie was making more money per theater than any film in history. Lucas's response was usually, "Wow. . . gee . . . that's amazing."

Ladd and his wife were also vacationing in Hawaii; when George and Marcia joined them in Honolulu, they shared a feeling of triumphant vindication. Steven Spielberg soon joined the Lucases, and he and George constructed an elaborate sand castle on the beach to celebrate the success of *Star Wars*. Spielberg wanted to make a James Bond-type movie, and Lucas suggested reworking one from the movie serials of the thirties and forties. Five years earlier, he had come up with an idea about a playboy adventurer who rescues girls and solves mysteries and "does all kinds of neat stuff." Spielberg reacted with enthusiasm and they vowed to make the picture together. George's retirement was proving short-lived.

His isolation from the success of *Star Wars* was brief, too. Accompanying

Spielberg was agent Guy McElwaine, who reported the movie had become a national phenomenon. There were nightly reports on the network news programs, and newspapers and magazines were filled with stories: *Star Wars* was part of the cultural vocabulary. If Lucas was surprised, Marcia was astonished; the movie she had once feared might be a turkey now looked to be the most successful film made to date. Lucas is glad he missed all the hoopla—it might have affected him. "I still don't take the whole thing very seriously," he says.

When Lucas arrived back home, letters and telegrams poured in from producers, movie executives, fellow directors, and thousands of newly anointed *Star Wars* disciples. There was even a telegram from Francis Coppola, offering congratulations and proffering a request: "Send money. Love, Francis." Coppola wasn't joking. *Star Wars* made almost $3 million in its first week at only thirty-two theaters. By July 4, it had sold almost $30 million worth of tickets. Two weeks after that, the total stood at $68 million. By the end of August, *Star Wars* had grossed $100 million faster than any film in Hollywood's eighty-year history.

Kurtz and Lippincott's efforts had paid off—by the time *Star Wars* opened, the movie sold itself. Fox's research showed that *Star Wars* had the largest number of word-of-mouth recommendations ever recorded. Lucas was surprised to see so many adults attend the movie. "I thought it was primarily for kids and families," he says. The appeal of *Star Wars* knew no ethnic or economic barriers: it did business in the South and in the black ghettos of Chicago. *Star Wars* offended almost no one and pleased almost everyone, the perfect movie for an audience in search of escape.

Time magazine called *Star Wars* "a grand and glorious film that may well be the smash hit of 1977 . . . a subliminal history of movies, wrapped in a riveting tale of suspense and adventure, ornamented with some of the most ingenious special effects ever contrived for film."[5] That was the general tone of the praise showered on *Star Wars,* but the film's appeal did not depend on favorable reviews. *Star Wars* touched audiences because George Lucas cared about his story and the people in it. He wasn't ashamed to express emotions like fear and bravery, love and sadness. "He showed people it was all right to become totally involved in a movie again; to yell and scream and applaud and really roll with it," Ladd says. Audiences could hiss at Darth Vader and cheer Luke and Leia as they swung across the Imperial hangar. *Star Wars* was an experience, not just a movie, one that people repeated again and again. More than one in twenty filmgoers in 1977 saw *Star Wars* more than once.

Unsure of the film's potential, Fox had delayed the overseas release until the end of 1977. Like Lucas's other films, *Star Wars* was so American in style and content that its appeal elsewhere was questionable. Its success abroad surprised Fox and Lucas alike. *Star Wars* was a smash hit in France, where Lucas had a cult following from *THX* and *Graffiti,* and was an enormous success throughout the rest of Europe, especially Germany and Italy. It didn't do as well in the Far East and Latin America, but the big question mark remained Japan, where *Star Wars* was delayed until summer 1978.

Ladd attended the Toyko premiere and was mortified when the audience sat in frozen silence, never applauding, laughing, or cheering. Convinced the picture was dead, Ladd went to dinner with Fox's Japanese distributor after the screening. The Japanese were jubilant, certain they had a huge hit. "You have no idea how great that picture played," one executive told Ladd, explaining that the highest compliment a Japanese audience paid a film was respectful silence. "I tell you, had that been the first preview, I think I would have said, 'Wait a minute. Sell it to television, do anything,'" Ladd says with a laugh.

The massive exposure *Star Wars* brought to Lucas far exceeded the publicity surrounding *Graffiti.* George asked John Korty to lunch a few weeks after the film opened, and as they sat in a Mill Valley coffeeshop, Lucas poured out everything he wanted to say about *Star Wars,* but couldn't. Korty recalls, "I realized that this was the interview one thousand journalists would slit their throats for. I did nothing but listen for two and a half hours. He had all his ideas and feelings about why it was a success, and he was working it out in his own mind, talking a lot about what America and the audience needed. It was not something to him that was just, 'Yippee, I'm going to make a million dollars!'"

Lucas had mixed feelings when *Star Wars* was nominated for ten Academy Awards (including Best Direction, Best Screenplay, and Best Picture) and the major awards from the Directors and Writers Guilds. Lucas considered the Academy Awards to be a sales tool for the studios, not a recognition of merit from his peers. "He never felt it was important to have an Oscar to be happy or successful or fulfilled or anything," says Marcia, who was nominated for best editing along with Richard Chew and Paul Hirsch. When George didn't win either of the Guild awards for writing or directing, he secretly was relieved; he knew his chances of winning an Oscar now were remote.

Lucas didn't even want to attend the awards ceremony in Los Angeles in April 1978. He agreed to accompany Marcia as her husband, not as the nominated director and writer. George knew how much the award meant to his wife—it was the culmination of an American fantasy nurtured by years of watching the annual Oscars telecast.

Sure enough, Marcia won, her face radiant as she cradled the gold-plated statuette and beamed at the TV cameras. For a poor little girl from North Hollywood, this was bliss. *Star Wars* won four other Oscars: John Barry for his art direction, John Mollo for his costume design, John Williams for his musical score, and John Dykstra, Richard Edlund, Grant McCune, John Stears, and Robert Blalack for their special effects. A special award was given to Ben Burtt for his imaginative sound effects. All his protestations to the contrary, Lucas was disappointed to lose the writing and directing awards; he had invested too much of himself in *Star Wars* not to be hurt. Kurtz was crushed because the movie did not win the Best-Picture Oscar—it went to *Annie Hall*, as did all the other major awards. Whatever regrets Lucas had, he didn't show them. As he and Marcia exited the Dorothy Chandler Pavilion in downtown Los Angeles, Marcia said, "You know, George, I think if this award was important to you, you might have won. I wanted it, and I did win. And you just didn't want it."

Even without the Best-Picture Oscar, *Star Wars* was very successful. Fox reissued the movie in the summer of 1978, although it had been continuously playing in theaters for more than a year. *Star Wars* sold another $46 million in tickets in five weeks. In 1979, another reissue was launched and another $23 million in tickets was sold in three weeks. In all, *Star Wars* has sold more than $524 million worth of tickets worldwide.[6]

Twentieth Century-Fox became very rich. In the world of Hollywood bookkeeping, $524 million in ticket sales yields only $262 million in film rentals, the share returned to the distributing studio. By the time Fox deducted its many fees and expenses, Lucas's share of the profits comes to about $40 million, which taxes have reduced to about $20 million. "It *was* half a billion dollars, and everyone thought I had forty percent of that," Lucas says. "Where did all the other money go?" Lucas understood the studio system and accepted its rules, for now. He couldn't have financed and distributed *Star Wars* himself, even with his *Graffiti* profits. But if and when there was another film, Lucas would do it his way. *Star Wars* would see to that.

Movies are more than they are just by virtue of being on film. I think a film can easily be more than the people who made it.[7]

Mike Nichols

Shortly after Lucas returned from Hawaii, Francis Coppola invited him to watch *Star Wars* with a paying audience. Lucas had been complaining about his movie for the past two years, and as the audience went wild, Coppola kept nudging him in the ribs. "I think after he saw it that time, he realized what it really was," Francis says. So did Coppola. When Lucas showed it to him in rough-cut form, Francis had said it seemed repetitious because there were too many gunfights.

Lucas still bum-raps *Star Wars* at the same time he proudly defends it. "I don't think, as a craftsman, that my films are extremely well made—they're kind of crude. I've always had an excuse that I haven't had unlimited resources, so I did the best with what I had. Ultimately, they are kind of dumb—it's the only way to put it. It's always amazing to me when people take them so seriously." *Star Wars* was made because George Lucas wanted to see it; he didn't realize that 100 million other people would want to see it, too.

Star Wars rediscovered the appeal of the classic American movie, the basic theme of good guy versus bad guy that had been tapped by every film star from Charlie Chaplin to John Wayne. "George simply went back to fundamentals," says John Korty. "In story, he's an American primitive; in technology, he's an American sophisticate." Lucas displayed in *Star Wars* a wholesome, naive faith in the essential goodness of people—something that had been missing in American movies for decades. Luke Skywalker triumphed in the end, Darth Vader was foiled, and audiences felt good. It was the same brand of optimism that Frank Capra captured in *Mr. Smith Goes to Washington* and *It's a Wonderful Life*. Lucas made a movie about winners, not losers, a prescription that brought great relief to movie audiences.

Star Wars was effective because, for all its fantastic elements, it had the ring of truth. George Lucas was the farm kid on Tatooine, hungering to escape a safe existence. He was the young initiate confronted with a difficult calling and finding the strength within himself to meet it. He was the brave warrior fighting an Empire (Hollywood) that threatened to stifle his vision and his soul. *THX 1138* ended when Lucas made his first escape; *Star Wars* marked the beginning of his new life. Like Luke, he had embarked on a dangerous mission to guarantee his independence; he also fell in love with a beautiful girl and like Han Solo, he gets her in the end; finally, he triumphs over the Empire with a carefully aimed missile that gives him his freedom.

George Lucas, Sr., was speechless at the success of *Star Wars*. He couldn't grasp that something so universally popular had come from his shy, rebellious son. The most impressive thing about *Star Wars* is that it is an original. Most of the other top-grossing films are adaptations of popular books: *Jaws, Gone With the Wind,* even Francis Coppola's *The Godfather.*

Walter Murch says, "*Star Wars* came out of nowhere—worse than nowhere, because the people who worked on the film had no idea what they were working on. They thought it was laughable because they couldn't see the vision behind it. It was in pieces. It's just that once you see the vision, then it all makes sense. George never lost sight of the vision."

8
HOW I SPENT MY RETIREMENT

Good, now George will be back with another picture. He won't retire
into moguldom, he likes to win too much.[1]
—Francis Coppola, the morning after *Star Wars* failed to win the
Academy Award for Best Picture

George Lucas was thirty-three years old at the end of 1977. His beard
was showing its first signs of gray. His jeans were well worn, his shoes
were scuffed, and he still drove a 1967 Camaro. But now Lucas was one of
the richest young men in the country with all the perquisites of stardom:
money, fame, power, influence. What was he going to do for an encore?

Quit, he thought. George hated working with actors and film crews. He
was ready to return to movies that required almost no one's participation
but his own. But first he felt he had to complete the trilogy he had begun,
although he would not direct the remaining two films. "As a director, I
wanted to do everything," explains Lucas. "It's very hard for me to
delegate things to other people. Well, the best way to do that is to take one
more step back and be forced to delegate everything. And see if I could
stand it."

There were other things to keep working on. Lazing in the Hawaiian
sun, Lucas dreamed of a new USC patio, a ranch in Marin County to
accommodate the growing number of friends working at Parkhouse.
Along with offices there would be editing and postproduction facilities, a
research library, and most important, the companionship and support of
other filmmakers. With the proceeds from two more *Star Wars* movies,
Lucas could have financial security *and* Skywalker Ranch.

191

The idea of retiring at the height of his fame, confounding Hollywood tradition, also appealed to a perverse streak in Lucas's personality. He once told Mark Hamill that the movie industry is fascinated by the rejection of success: "If you retire and don't do anything, you'll be sticking to your guns. And if you do something, you can say, 'Well, this project was so extraordinary that it brought me out of retirement.'"

Lucas had first to accept that he was a success before he could stop being one. His low opinion of *Star Wars* didn't make the adjustment easier. Jane Bay says, "If you have created something that you only hope will not be an embarrassment, and instead it is received with such overwhelming attention, that's something you have to come to grips with. I personally think George had difficulty accepting that."

Lucas had always thought *Graffiti* would be his biggest hit; he now thinks that of *Star Wars*. But his first success did not really prepare him for what followed *Star Wars:* "It was a terribly wrenching emotional experience, filled with anxiety and confusion," Lucas says. He wasn't accustomed to reading about himself in tabloids at supermarket counters: *The Star* reported in July 1977 that Lucas had purchased a $500,000 Lear jet with an interior design like that of the *Millennium Falcon.*[2] "If I hadn't had *Graffiti* first," Lucas says convincingly, "I would have gone nuts."

Star Wars added $20 million to Lucas's net worth and with the additional merchandising income, turned Lucasfilm into a $30 million corporation. Lucas told accountant Richard Tong, "I don't mind paying taxes, but I don't want to pay more than fifty percent." George and Marcia are the sole shareholders of Lucasfilm and all its subsidiaries, and there was a fear the IRS would view the *Star Wars* profits (paid to Lucas as salary) as unreasonable compensation, putting him in a higher tax bracket and costing him an additional $6 million in taxes. Lucas was not interested in tax dodges or shelters, however. "George is a very moral person, very highly principled," says Tong. "There was no question of fudging on taxes."

Lucas preferred not to worry about money. "You think, 'Oh wow, a whole lot of money,' but after they take out the taxes and the agents' fees and the lawyers' fees, and everything comes off the top, it isn't like there's a whole lot left," relates George. There was enough to make a noticeable change in George and Marcia's lifestyle, but Lucas tried to minimize it. He put all his *Star Wars* profits in investments like municipal tax-free bonds as collateral for *The Empire Strikes Back,* which he planned to finance himself. He kept out $50,000 a year to live on, certainly not an extravagant allowance. Lucas allowed himself a few guilty pleasures: he invested in Supersnipe, a Manhattan gallery that specialized in original comic-strip art, and bought a Ferrari sports car. It was, of course, a *used* Ferrari.

Given his traditional upbringing, Lucas's reluctance to flaunt his wealth came as no surprise. Lucy Wilson was disappointed, however, at his outright dismissal of the many charity solicitations that followed *Star Wars*. "I got a lot of phone calls from people wanting money and he'd just say no," remembers Wilson. Lucas and his wife do contribute to charities, although he's reluctant to say which ones for fear of being dunned again. The contributions are usually made anonymously, although Lucasfilm doesn't hide its donations to children's disease research. George's low profile is in keeping with the philosophy drummed into him by his father: you work hard to improve your own lot, not that of others. Giving money away rather than rewarding someone for a contribution or effort goes against George's grain.

Francis Coppola, who had been there with *The Godfather,* warned Lucas that the shock of sudden and unexpected success "is no different from the shock of death—you're in a transition period and when you come out of it, you're a different person." George was better equipped to deal with fame than Coppola because he had never sought it. He hated being recognized in local restaurants or having a group of adoring youngsters waiting outside to ask him for his autograph. "It made him feel that he was under a microscope." Says Jane Bay, "Prior to *Star Wars,* most people didn't know what George looked like."

I took over control of the merchandising not because I thought it was going to make me rich, but because I wanted to control it. I wanted to make a stand for social, safety, and quality reasons. I didn't want someone using the name *Star Wars* on a piece of junk.

—George Lucas

The best evidence that Lucas didn't anticipate the success of *Star Wars* comes from the sorry state of his business affairs at the time of the film's release. "It was chaos, that's the only way to describe it," says Bay, who joined Lucasfilm in August 1977. There were only ten people in the company. Publicity mastermind Charles Lippincott was in charge of merchandising, but no one expected the deluge of licensing offers.

Carol Titelman, hired to answer the incessantly ringing telephones at the Lucasfilm offices at Universal Studios, remembers, "At the end of the day the desk was literally covered with pink phone-message slips. I'd divide them into three piles: those to be answered right away, those who were sure to call back, and a third pile which we called 'Why bother?' No time for them. If you took all the calls that came in, you'd get no other work done."

Lucas was determined to control the follow-through on *Star Wars* as thoroughly as he had the making of the film. But he was saddled with a partner, 20th Century-Fox, that was his complete opposite in business philosophy and practices. When Lucas renegotiated his *Star Wars* contract at the time of *Graffiti's* success, he sought complete control of the merchandising. While writing *Star Wars,* Lucas fantasized about R2-D2 cookie jars, Wookiee mugs, and wind-up robots. "Gee, it would be nice if we could do it," he remembers thinking. "And if we do it, I want to make sure it's done right."

Fox saw merchandising only as a promotional tool for *Star Wars;* an effort was made to set as many deals as possible prior to the film's release. Fox subtracted a 15 percent fee for administering the legal contracts, with all subsequent revenues split 50/50 with Lucas. The studio demonstrated its lack of faith in *Star Wars* by giving away the merchandising rights in exchange for advertising. Marc Pevers, head of Fox's licensing division, also sold the rights to all *Star Wars* toys *in perpetuity* to Kenner Toys, an Ohio-based subsidiary of General Foods. The deal was made over Lucas's strenuous objections and it still nettles him. "We've lost tens of millions of dollars because of that stupid decision," he fumes.

Lucas realized that he and Gary Kurtz were incapable of supervising the merchandising bonanza. The services of a businessman, not a producer or director, were clearly required. Lucas interviewed several corporate executives before hiring Charles Weber, an investment banker with a solid financial background. Weber found Lucasfilm a company in disarray, with the undermanned staff working from 9:30 A.M. to 8:30 P.M. Lucas was initially involved in all of the day-to-day business decisions, but running Lucasfilm wasn't any different from working summers at L. M. Morris in Modesto—George could do it, but it wasn't any fun.

Lucasfilm began to grow under Weber's guidance. Sidney Ganis and Susan Trembly were hired from Warner Brothers as the company's new marketing and publicity department. It was weeks before the new employees met Lucas, and Trembly, Ganis's assistant, remained unimpressed: "Here was this slight, short man and I thought, That's George Lucas? Well, he doesn't look so powerful." Lucas also bolstered his Northern California staff. Duwayne Dunham was hired as an in-house editor to prepare a new version of *American Graffiti,* containing the footage cut in 1973. Universal wanted to rerelease the movie (now bolstered by stereo music) to capitalize on Lucas's popularity from *Star Wars.*

A young science-fiction writer, Alan Dean Foster, was hired to ghost-write a novelization of the *Star Wars* screenplay. (The book carries Lucas's name as its author.) Within three months of its release, the novelization was the number one paperback best-seller; Lucasfilm owned all the profits. The sound-track album, featuring John Williams's Oscar-winning score, was also a moneymaker. Fox was initially reluctant to release the two-record album, but it became the largest-selling film score from a nonmusical in Hollywood history. Fox made almost $16 million from the album, paying a 5 percent royalty to Lucas.

There were also millions of *Star Wars* action figures sold. There were C-3PO masks and R2-D2 thermoses. *Star Wars* posters were outselling sex symbol Farrah Fawcett-Majors' bathing suit pose by a five-to-one margin. Lucas had only one criterion for approving a license: quality. If a product wasn't up to George's standards, it was turned down. "We turned down some *big* licenses," he remembers.

There was still a tremendous bootleg market in *Star Wars* memorabilia, including posters, stills, poor-quality videocassette copies, and pirated spaceship models. Unable to stop it, Lucas began to supply legitimate merchandise at reasonable prices to members of the Official *Star Wars* Fan Club. The motive wasn't profit, because Lucasfilm barely broke even on the mailing costs. In the first six months after *Star Wars* came out, Lucas got more than six thousand letters, asking for everything from autographs to detailed histories of the characters. Lucas realized that if he didn't control this market, some enterprising businessperson would.

For $5, a fan club member gets four issues of a special newsletter, a four-color poster, six 8x10 color photos of the *Star Wars* characters, a jacket patch, and a pencil. Lucas feels a responsibility to the fans, but his gratitude goes only so far. "I don't want to turn my life over to them," he says, "because to me, it's only a movie. A lot of fans whose lives are consumed by *Star Wars* think my life must also be that way, and it's not."

Some *Star Wars* aficionados take the movie *very* seriously. Maureen Garrett, president of the fan club, says of those who eat from *Star Wars* utensils, dress in *Star Wars* accessories, and sleep in *Star Wars*-decorated bedrooms, "It's unhealthy to take it to that extreme. But maybe it's better than some other obsession, alcoholism or drug addiction. Some people are so lonely—it's just a great way to fill a very lonely life."

Star Wars also attracted more than the usual number of sci-fi and religious weirdos. One day a knife-wielding fan walked into Lucas's Los Angeles office, claiming he cowrote *Star Wars* and demanding a share of the profits. If the secretaries didn't believe him, the man said, they should look in the parking lot, where he had left the *Millennium Falcon*. Burglar alarms were installed at Parkhouse after disturbing collages were left on the front porch, and Lucy Wilson had a panic button put on her desk. Even George, Sr., and Dorothy were accosted by fans who had walked across the country to find their son, claiming to be sent from God. George, Sr., couldn't believe that one.

Since the *Star Wars* characters were licensed trademarks of Lucasfilm, no one was allowed to wear the costumes and masks for profit. Public appearances were sanctioned only by Lucas himself and limited to TV and award shows and parades. George refused to allow the characters to sell anything but the movie itself. (He relented only for public service commercials about heart disease, and appearances on "Sesame Street.") Anthony Daniels, Kenny Baker, David Prowse, and Peter Mayhew were brought to the United States and toured the country under the supervision of Miki Herman. The tour culminated in front of Hollywood's Chinese Theater, where the four nonhuman characters had their footprints immortalized in cement.

Not everyone was thrilled, especially the actors whose identities were kept secret. Lucas wanted to preserve the illusion of the characters off the screen as well as on, a requirement that particularly irritated Daniels. Few of the glowing reviews for *Star Wars* mentioned Daniels' name—instead, critics praised Mark Hamill and C-3P0. The other disguised actors shared similar frustrations, although Mayhew was more understanding: "I realized it would spoil the illusion if you did appearances or sold photographs as you really looked."

Lucas was generous to key members of his cast and crew to the tune of more than $2 million. There were eleven "gift" profit points handed out on *Star Wars*—each net profit point was worth about $300,000. Lucas got *only* $30 million himself. Gary Kurtz got 5 percent of the net profits, as specified in his contract. Alec Guinness contractually had two profit points. In exchange for their work on the screenplay, Bill Huyck and Gloria Katz were also given two points. Lucas gave individual single percentage points to composer John Williams, ILM supervisor Jim Nelson, and attorney Tom Pollock.

Above all, Lucas wanted to reward his lead actors. "I gave them points because they make the biggest contribution to a hit film after the writer and director," Lucas explains. Mark Hamill, Carrie Fisher, and Harrison Ford divided 2 percent of the *Star Wars* profits among themselves. Lucas also distributed cash bonuses that totaled almost $100,000 to eighteen people who worked on the production—the checks ranged from $2,000 to $10,000, all of it money out of Lucas's own share of the profits. Along with cash bonuses, Lucas gave Ralph McQuarrie and Joe Johnston percentages of the *Star Wars* merchandising profits, in recognition of their contribution to the film's design. Each of these points was eventually worth $50,000.

Not everyone was satisfied. Dykstra and most ILM workers were given neither cash nor points. Anthony Daniels, miffed about not getting a percentage like Hamill, Fisher, Ford, and Guinness, spurned his cash bonus. McQuarrie still isn't sure if he was adequately compensated for the contribution he made. "I wonder if I haven't been ripped off," he says quietly. "But then, why should George pay me any more than he had to? He's a pretty cool businessman." These complaints almost seem petty. No filmmaker had ever shared the wealth of a successful picture with so many of the people who contributed to its success. Even those who didn't labor on *Star Wars* were included in the bequest. Steven Spielberg had suggested that Lucas and his closest friends exchange profit percentages in their films, and George, with some misgivings, agreed. He gave Spielberg one point in *Star Wars* in exchange for one in *Close Encounters of the Third Kind*, a fair enough trade. Lucas made a similar deal with John Milius for a point in *Big Wednesday*, a movie glorifying Milius's surfer days that was one of 1978's biggest bombs. Lucas is now sorry he traded points with Milius: "I simply made a bad investment." He was a good enough friend to trade points; he was a good enough businessman to regret it later.

Still, the profit-sharing gesture was considered revolutionary in Hollywood, where money is hoarded. "It was a wonderful thing that inspired the rest of us," says Milius. To Lucas, it was simply a matter of friendship, a commitment made before anyone could imagine the size of the payoff. There was one person who had no piece of the *Star Wars* booty: Francis Coppola. "Why should he?" says Lucas. "He had no connection to the movie."

After *Star Wars*, Lucas decided to move ILM to Marin County. John Dykstra took over the Van Nuys building for his own company, but Lucas didn't realize Dykstra planned to use the crew and equipment from *Star Wars* on a new TV series from Universal. "Battlestar Galactica" was a blatant attempt to capitalize on the *Star Wars* space craze. With the ILM crew supplying the special effects it was little wonder that "Galactica" closely resembled Lucas's movie.

Dykstra remains defensive about "Galactica": "There was no profit participation from *Star Wars*, so we were really out to lunch. It was George's money and George's movie, but none of us got any points. "Battlestar" was the first project that came through the door that promised to pay the bills to keep my buddies and me employed." Dykstra contends that "Galactica" was not a ripoff of *Star Wars,* but he does acknowledge, "The effects were the same, and maybe I feel guilty about that."

Lucas didn't mind imitation, but he thought "Galactica" was trying to re-create *Star Wars.* At his urging, Fox sued Universal for copyright infringement, an action unusual in Hollywood, where the major studios try to avoid litigation with one another. Universal, a studio Lucas enriched by $50 million with *American Graffiti,* countersued Fox, claiming *Star Wars* was a ripoff of its 1972 release *Silent Running,* which featured three small robots names Huey, Dewey, and Louie. Lucas has pursued the matter—both suits are now on appeal—only because of the confusion the TV series caused in the public's mind. "People thought *I* did it," Lucas says. "I got hundreds of letters from people saying, 'I think your TV show is terrible.' It was very upsetting."

Lucas was also upset at the indiscriminate licensing of "Galactica" products, which were not up to *Star Wars* standards. When a child died from injuries suffered while playing with a "Galactica" toy, the judge singled out generic *Star Wars* toys as the culprit. Not only had Lucas been ripped off, he was being blamed for a TV series and shoddy toys he had not sanctioned. "He took moral offense at what producer Glenn Larson and Universal were doing," says Hal Barwood. "He believes that there's a right and wrong and you just don't behave the wrong way."

The object is to try and make the system work for you, instead of against you. And the only way you can do that is through success, I'm afraid.

—George Lucas

There was never any question in Lucas's mind that there would be a sequel to *Star Wars.*[3] In thinking of the best way to invest his newfound wealth, Lucas didn't have far to look: he was his own best risk. He lent $20 million to Lucasfilm as collateral for the bank credit needed to finance *The Empire Strikes Back.* Lucas had always made a distinction between his company's money and his own funds, but he knew that if *Empire* failed, he and Marcia were in just as much financial trouble as Lucasfilm.

The real purpose of *Empire,* as Lucas saw it, was to help finance Skywalker Ranch. If Lucas didn't make a sequel within two years, however, his rights reverted back to Fox, along with the rights to all future *Star Wars* pictures. Retirement-minded as he was, Lucas wasn't about to give Fox a movie he had fought to take away from them. *Empire* would be made with his money, his way, or it wouldn't be made at all.

Fox never expected Lucas to finance *Empire* by himself. This was George's triumph—he had played by Fox's rules, gambled on the long-term payoff rather than upfront cash, and he had won. Now it was time to play by his rules. Fox had loaned Lucas $10 million to make *Star Wars* and kept 60 percent of the profits. "Which I thought was a little steep," Lucas says. "But I said, 'Okay, you took that risk. I'm willing to take the risk on the next one. I'm willing to put up my own money.'" Lucas told Fox, "You don't get the sixty percent anymore. Now we can start negotiating." The studio's reaction was predictable. "They were absolutely outraged," Lucas remembers. "When the tables got turned and the same system worked against them, they felt betrayed and cheated."

The *Empire* deal worked out by Tom Pollock was unusual by Hollywood standards. Lucasfilm started with 50 percent of the gross profits, a share that eventually rose to 77 percent. Fox had to pay all the distribution costs (such as prints of the movie and advertising) and only had the right to release the film to theaters for seven years—after that, all rights reverted to Lucas. He also owned all TV and merchandising rights. Fox had to put up a $10 million advance payment, which it recovered from guarantees paid by theater owners.

Fox was in an uproar over Lucas's demands, but they had to acquiesce. The studio only had first refusal on *Empire,* and Lucas made it clear he would gladly take the film elsewhere if Fox rejected his terms. That he could do so was debatable, but no one at Fox wanted to spend four years in a legal battle when there was money to be made. The contract was drawn up and presented to Alan Ladd, Jr., on the Jewish holiday Yom Kippur, a day of repentance. Tom Pollock told Ladd, "This is your day of atonement."

Chairman Dennis Stanfill publicly criticized the terms of the *Empire* agreement, capping a long-standing power struggle between him and Ladd for control of Fox. Over the July Fourth weekend in 1979, Ladd and his executive team deserted Fox and set up their own mini-studio across town at Warner Bros. The only studio executive George Lucas had ever trusted was no longer involved with *Empire.*

That gave Lucas all the more reason to demand a revised merchandising agreement giving Lucasfilm the 15 percent administration fee and, ultimately, 90 percent of the profits. A potential dispute was shaping over Fox's rights to the characters in *Empire* in addition to those in *Star Wars.* Lucas solved it by giving Fox 10 percent of the merchandising profits from all the *Star Wars* movies, including future ones. It was another provision that stuck in Fox's craw, but one they had to accept to get *The Empire Strikes Back*.

Fox's questions about who was going to write, direct, and star in *Empire* were met by Lucas's curt reply, "None of your business." His only assurance to the studio was that *Empire* would be delivered in time for a summer 1980 release.

Lucas now had another battle to wage. International Creative Management, the talent agency that represented Lucas through Jeff Berg, was another beneficiary of the success of *Star Wars*. By collecting 10 percent of Lucas's *gross* earnings, the agency received almost $4.5 million. But Lucas had dissolved his association with Berg after *Star Wars* concluded production. He had been unhappy with the agent's reluctance to press Fox for control of the sequel rights, a concession Lucas won himself by going directly to Ladd.

Now Lucas didn't need an agent. He made his own deals, negotiated by Tom Pollock and his other lawyers. He had no objections to ICM continuing to collect from *Star Wars,* but he saw no reason for the agency to have a piece of *Empire.* Berg was disappointed and upset. "Agents take it very personally when you leave," Lucas says. "I thought Jeff was a good agent and had done a great job for me. I just didn't need him anymore."

ICM thought otherwise. Its position was that Berg had made the deal for the original film, so the agency automatically had the right to make the deals for any subsequent films. Lucas's response was succinct: "We don't need your help, we don't want you to negotiate, buzz off." Settlement talks failed and the matter was submitted to binding arbitration. In summer 1980, the decision was delivered. Lucas won—ICM had no rights to the sequels. The ruling set a precedent in Hollywood that cost ICM and other talent agencies considerable potential revenue. To Lucas, it was simply a question of fairness. ICM didn't deserve the money from *Empire* because it didn't do anything to earn it.

I wanted to try it, I did, and I failed.
        —George Lucas on the making of *More American Graffiti*

Before Lucas could begin work on *Empire,* he had unfinished business with *American Graffiti,* which did well when Universal reissued it in 1977. Universal owned *Graffiti* and its characters, and Lucas owed the studio one more picture, because they had passed on *Star Wars.* Hollywood studios are never too proud to make money; Ned Tanen wanted Universal to make a *Graffiti* sequel and suggested Lucas might want to be involved.

Lucas didn't want to write or direct the sequel—he was done with the story. But he didn't want characters who had been carefully molded from his own life ripped off or mutilated. Lucas asked Howard Kazanjian, another USCinema graduate, to produce the film Lucas tentatively titled *Purple Haze,* after the famous Jimi Hendrix song.

Lucas saw the opportunity this time to experiment with Universal's money. He was also goaded by the example of Francis Coppola's *Godfather II,* which was considered deeper and more significant than its predecessor. Bill Huyck believes that Lucas was determined to make *Graffiti II* more serious, too, providing that he could do whatever Francis did, only better. Whatever his motivation, Lucas could not re-create the energy in *More American Graffiti* (as the sequel came to be called) that infused the first film.

A major problem facing *More* was the audience's knowledge of the fate of the major characters, detailed in the final titles of *American Graffiti.* Where to go from there? Bill Huyck and Gloria Katz, who cowrote the original screenplay, foresaw the problems in the *Graffiti* sequel. "The story, when continued, is sort of sad and awful, and very painful. Not only that, the period is more serious. No way I wanted to get involved with it," Huyck said.

When Lucas went to reassemble the original cast, Richard Dreyfuss was the only holdout. The actor refuses to discuss the reason, but it's clear that Dreyfuss considered himself a star—he had won a Best-Actor Oscar in 1977 for his role in *The Goodbye Girl*—and he wanted a salary commensurate with his new status. "George had a strict code of you take it or leave it," says Cindy Williams, who tried unsuccessfully to persuade Dreyfuss to reconsider. "He didn't want to putter around with what he considered star treatment. I think Ricky's refusal took some of the wind out of his sails on the movie."

Without Dreyfuss, Lucas had a serious problem. His two basic stories involved Curt and Laurie (the Dreyfuss and Williams characters) and the changes they underwent in the sixties, and the saga of Debbie (Candy Clark's platinum blonde), now a topless dancer who has an affair with a local politician. The other two stories had Milner (Paul LeMat) trying to beat the factory racing team at a local drag strip, and the adventures of Terry the Toad (Charles Martin Smith) in Vietnam. With Dreyfuss gone, Lucas had to invent a new character, Andy (played by *Star Wars* reject Will Seltzer), who was a campus radical and Laurie's younger brother. Carol, Mackenzie Phillips' preteen character, appeared as both a flower child and a bewigged country-western singer. Even Harrison Ford was tapped to play a cameo role as Officer Falfa, a narcotics cop who loves to bust hippies.

At Lucas's request, Kazanjian came up with a list of young California screenwriters. Lucas chose B. W. Norton, Jr., son of a respected screenwriter, and a UCLA film school graduate friendly with the Huycks. Norton had several screenplays to his credit, including *Cisco Pike* and *Convoy,* both counterculture movies. It was Lucas's philosophy that writers should always try to direct their films, so he told Bill Norton that if he did a good job on the script, he could direct the movie.

Norton was thrilled, but he was wary, too. Lucas's insistence on control was legendary. "I assumed he would have a lot to say," Norton says with a smile. But Lucas removed himself, both physically and spiritually, from *More American Graffiti.* He did few revisions on Norton's screenplay and promised him complete freedom in directing the film, a promise he kept. Lucas now admits, "I didn't have much of an emotional investment in the project."

Still, Lucas was responsible for the content and style of *More.* When Norton arrived in San Anselmo in mid-1978 for a weeklong script conference with Lucas and Kazanjian, he found that the film was already outlined in broad strokes: instead of the long night during which *American Graffiti* took place, the sequel reintroduced its characters on the same night (New Year's Eve) in four successive years, 1965 through 1968.

Lucas wanted to shoot each of the four stories in a different film format and screen size. Milner's race was in 1950s exploitation style, using a wide-angle, stationary camera. The Vietnam sequences were on 16-millimeter film, like TV reports on the war. Laurie and Steve's campus riot resembled a Hollywood version of student rebellions like *The Strawberry Statement* and *Getting Straight.* Debbie's Haight-Ashbury trips were in multiple-image split-screen, a technique used in *Woodstock.*

Norton didn't like Lucas's decision to cut from one story to another in mathematical fashion. "I felt it was a very dangerous thing to do because if you became emotionally involved in one story, you'd be wrenched out of that and introduced to a new story." It was Universal's money and Lucas's production, so Norton did as he was told. Lucas now agrees Norton was right: "If anything brings the film down, that's it," he concurs.

More American Graffiti can be seen as Lucas's revenge against Universal, although he genuinely wanted the movie to succeed. Norton brought the film in within its $6 million budget and forty-five-day schedule—Lucas saw to that. But Lucas had no qualms about spending the $6 million on a cinematic experiment that didn't work. For the first time in his professional career he was not directly on the line, and he felt little pressure to live up to his own standards. He did succeed in keeping Universal virtually isolated from the production—Norton never had a meeting with anyone from the studio until *More American Graffiti* had finished shooting.

The sequel cost eight times as much as *American Graffiti* but was made at the same breakneck speed. Norton had to film four mini-movies, filled with riot scenes, college campuses, drag-strip crowds, and hundreds of period cars. The climactic race scene needed four thousand people in the grandstand—Lucas attracted them by promising free *Star Wars* toys. The Vietnam sequences were filmed in the Sacramento Delta, midway between Stockton and Modesto, a locale that duplicates Southeast Asia with surprising realism.

Lucas showed up on the set for the first day of filming *More American Graffiti*, mostly to luxuriate in the pleasure of having someone else direct. He only wanted to film second-unit Vietnam action scenes, using a long camera lens for the rough-and-ready look of combat footage, thereby providing the film's most dramatic moments. The Vietnam scenes became Lucas's own little *Apocalypse Now* (which Coppola was still filming in the Philippines). With the aid of cinematographer Caleb Deschanel, the medical evacuation scenes in *More American Graffiti* are brutally realistic, punctuated by the victims' screams, the chatter of machine-gun fire, and the smoke from burning villages.

With Lucas on and off the set, there was initial confusion at first as to who was in charge. Cindy Williams needed a rewrite for one of her lines and called Lucas. "Ask your director," he said. "I'm just the producer." When Lucas looked at *More American Graffiti* in the editing room two months later, he may have wished otherwise. The film had serious problems. Tina Hirsch, a relative of *Star Wars* editor Paul Hirsch, was the editor on *More*, but Lucas took over as soon as she handed in her first cut. This has become his practice with the films he produces rather than directs—he gives editors the freedom to do their job, but if he thinks he can make a film better, he won't hesitate to jump in.

More American Graffiti was a challenge. Debbie's story, in which she was a groupie to a rock band, didn't work at all. Lucas used split-screen images to cover up the story defects, hoping to remind audiences of late 1960s' "acid" movies like *The Trip*.

Marcia edited the split-screen scenes, which used as many as eighteen separate images. Norton had never enjoyed editing and spent most of his time reading magazines while Lucas and Duwayne Dunham huddled over their machines. He didn't like the split-screen approach, however, and said so. George listened carefully, and then did what he wanted. As with the split-screen footage, Lucas tends to "try things out" and then leave them in. "There were a lot of givens in that movie that Bill couldn't really get behind," Lucas acknowledges. "But I've got the film in my hands, and I'm the one making it happen. And I am the boss."

The Vietnam sequences in *More American Graffiti* are a showpiece of Lucas's editing skills. Only two helicopters were filmed, landing troops on a riverbank amid vicious crossfire. When Lucas was done cutting the scene, there seemed to be a dozen choppers landing. Dunham looked for transition shots as Lucas slapped the film together. Both men felt jazzed as the scene took shape. "We started going and it was like there was no stopping," Dunham recalls. "It was like we suddenly struck a nerve. This was real editing. This was creating something that didn't exist, material that when it was put together was something new. It was as excited as I've ever seen George get."

Lucas didn't care if *More American Graffiti* was successful as long as he could savor moments like those. Universal had made an advance TV sale of almost $3 million; at worst, the studio would earn back its investment. *More American Graffiti* barely fulfilled even those modest goals—it broke even only after sales to pay TV, two years after its release. It was a commercial failure, even though Universal lavished time and money on its release. Lucas was concerned—*More American Graffiti* was a gamble, and he had lost badly. He was about to take an even greater risk with *The Empire Strikes Back*, a sequel to one of the most successful films ever made. And he was going to use his own money—if he failed again, he could lose everything. Now *that* was a scary thought.

Perhaps *More*'s failure stemmed from the incongruity of the creator of *Star Wars* producing a movie about drugs, death, war, and promiscuous sex. Maybe audiences weren't ready to laugh at LSD and the Vietnam War and the liberation of housewives. The title may have led them to believe this was the original *American Graffiti* with added footage. And "Happy Days" was offering for free on TV what Universal had once sold to theaters. Whatever the explanation, as Ned Tanen puts it, "The picture never opened. It wasn't a case of opening strong and then falling off, or not getting word of mouth, or opening small and staying small. It just didn't open at all."

Lucas knew it after the first preview at the Northpoint Theater. Tanen was there as Dorothy Lucas came striding up the aisle to the back of the theater, where George was waiting. "She walked right by him and said, 'It's supposed to be funny, George. Not very funny.' She kept right on walking," says Tanen. "His sister [Wendy] also said, 'It should have been a lot funnier, George. Not very funny.' They just left him standing in the lobby, leveled." He tells this story with a certain glee, a residue of his dispute with Lucas over the cutting of *American Graffiti*. But Lucas knew something was awry without his mother telling him. "There was something about the feel of the picture that people didn't want to go see. You would expect with a sequel that the first week would be sensational, but nobody came."

The Universal distribution executives, in their unerring wisdom, thought *More American Graffiti* would be more successful than the original film. Tanen isn't sorry they made it. "I thought it was a very good movie and a very noble attempt," he says. Bill Norton is proud, too—if nothing else, Toad was the first deserter to be a hero in a major studio movie, and it was radical for movies in 1978 to examine the Vietnam War at all.

Lucas could tell himself this wasn't the film he would have made, but it *was* the film he produced. He had a new level of responsibility, but the film essentially remained out of his control. He still isn't eager to discuss *More American Graffiti*, although he is candid about its drawbacks: "I was disappointed in *More*, and there's a lot of things I don't like about the film. But there are things I *do* like. I'm not ashamed I made it." Lucas says he doesn't worry about failing—enormous success resigned him to its inevitability. Yet *More American Graffiti* is deemphasized in Lucasfilm's publicity handouts on George's career. Reminded of this, Howard Kazanjian lets out a heavy sigh. "Well," he says, "I like not to mention it, either."

George didn't think directing was that much fun. He didn't want to be the general of the army anymore. He wanted the sergeants to take over.

—Miki Herman on the making of *The Empire Strikes Back*

George Lucas had his work cut out for him on *Empire*—a hundred million people expected it to be *better*. *Star Wars* had tapped Lucas's childhood psyche for inspiration—did he have enough left for *Empire*? The movie had to stand on its own as an original work, while keeping the energy and freshness of its predecessor. The general consensus in Hollywood was "Good luck, George."

"I was very nervous when I started the second film," Lucas admits, an unease heightened by the negative reaction to *More American Graffiti*. Lucas knew that compared to *Star Wars*, *Empire* was going to be more downbeat, and he was afraid he'd alienate his audience. But sequels to successful movies have their advantages: a built-in audience and quick name recognition. Lucas had already made the prototype—everyone now knew what a Wookiee looked like. The sequel had to explore the relationships and emotions that Lucas had glossed over in *Star Wars*. This time audiences would have the chance to examine the content more closely.

Lucas needed a writer and director who understood the essence of *Star Wars,* but who weren't afraid to bring a new perspective to the material. It was still Lucas's private universe. "I feel Chewbacca is still my Wookiee and R2-D2 is still my little robot,"[4] he sheepishly told *Rolling Stone* magazine after *Empire* was finished. Lucas also cared about *Empire* because his money was at stake—this wasn't *More American Graffiti.* If his new film bombed, he went down with it. "At the same time, I said to hell with it," Lucas recalls. "I figured I could always make documentaries."

Lucas hired Leigh Brackett to write the screenplay for *Empire.* Brackett was a veteran screenwriter in her sixties who cowrote *The Big Sleep* and other movies for director Howard Hawks and had penned a brace of science-fiction novels. She had perfected the quick repartee that Lucas was incapable of writing—her screenplays were among the models for Bill Huyck and Gloria Katz's spunky dialogue in *Graffiti* and *Star Wars.* Lucas had one lengthy meeting with Brackett to outline the story and turn his notes over to her, and by March 1978 Brackett's first draft was done. It was also her last—she died of cancer two weeks later.

Lucas reexperienced the sinking feeling he associated with *Star Wars.* He had a very rough script that needed work and no ready replacement for Brackett. *Empire* would soon begin preproduction, which meant getting a screenplay done immediately. There was nothing to do but write it himself. George and Marcia had planned a vacation in Mexico over the Easter holiday with Michael Ritchie and his wife; while everyone else sunned themselves on the beach, Lucas sat in a hotel room, writing the movie he had vowed he would never write.

Lucas shelved Brackett's script and started anew. If he could get a first draft done, he could turn it over to a new writer, and they could pass versions back and forth until Lucas was satisfied. "That way he can't lose control of it," Huyck points out. Lucas spent the rest of the spring and most of the summer of 1978 finishing a first draft, and he still didn't have a writer until one suddenly dropped into his lap.

Steven Spielberg held Lucas to his word about going ahead with their 1930s action-adventure movie, *Raiders of the Lost Ark.* Spielberg had been impressed with a screenplay he read by a young Chicago advertising copywriter, Lawrence Kasdan. Spielberg sent *Continental Divide* to Lucas in late 1977, and George immediately saw the kind of crisp writing *Raiders* needed. Kasdan was hired to write *Raiders,* although he barely knew director Spielberg or producer Lucas.

By August 1978 Kasdan had finished his screenplay and hand-delivered it to Lucas in San Anselmo. George took the script and laid it aside, telling Kasdan he would read it that night. They went to lunch, and Lucas abruptly launched into the story of Leigh Brackett's untimely death, his problems with *Empire,* and his need for a writer to polish the new draft. He'd be happy to give Kasdan screenplay credit on *Empire* (Lucas planned to take none himself), but asked whether Kasdan would mind sharing it with Brackett. He wanted her estate to benefit from a profit percentage of the film.

Kasdan sat opposite Lucas, a look of shock on his face. "Don't you think you should read *Raiders* first?" he gulped—he had handed it to Lucas not ten minutes earlier. "Well, if I hate *Raiders,* I'll call you up and cancel this," Lucas said with a smile—he knew that wouldn't be necessary. George considers himself a quick and accurate judge of people; Kasdan's questions and enthusiasm during the *Raiders* story conferences had displayed a keen sense of story and dialogue. "Also, I was desperate," Lucas admits. "I didn't have anybody else."

The idea of writing a sequel to Hollywood's most successful film intimidated Kasdan, but he felt he understood *Star Wars,* which he describes as "jaunty, wise-ass, fast, very modern—sort of a teen-aged thing, a polished chrome kind of feel." Spielberg was about to begin his big-budget extravaganza, *1941,* so *Raiders* was at least two years away. Lucas sensed Kasdan's dilemma and resolved it for him. "Let *Raiders* go until Steven can work on it," George said. "You work on *Empire.*"

Finding the right director was a thornier task. Lucas had to prove that he could pull away from *Empire* and let someone else make it. George wanted to look at the entire cycle of films one day and see how each director had added to the story and characters. Gary Kurtz compiled a list of more than one hundred directors, and Lucas narrowed the field to twenty before he began screening their movies. He was looking for a consistent visual tone in a director's work, as well as how he handled dramatic scenes and developed characters. Above all, Lucas needed a collaborator who wasn't cynical about the material.

Irvin Kershner fit the criteria. Lean and balding, in his late forties, Kershner was a veteran filmmaker who somehow had remained apart from the Hollywood system. A former classical musician who played violin and viola, Kershner had studied and taught film at USC. Kershner's films, such as *Loving,* showed an insight into human relationships, a sense of humor and timing, and an accomplished visual technique. He also worked fast, a requirement on *Empire.*

Lucas warned Kershner that *Empire* would be the most difficult project he had ever undertaken. The film was to be made in three farflung locales: a Norwegian glacier that would duplicate an ice planet, Elstree Studios in England, and ILM in Marin, where Lucas planned to spend most of his time. Kershner had his own reservations. Lucas's strong-willed reputation was common knowledge in the movie industry and Kersh, as he was called, made it clear he couldn't function without creative freedom. "I also wondered if I wanted to do a second film based on somebody else's primary dream," he recalls.

Kershner knew he would be the conductor, not the composer. But Lucas promised him, "It'll be your film," and added an extra responsibility by telling Kersh, "You know, the second part of this series is the most important one. If it works, then we'll make a third and maybe a fourth. If it doesn't work, it'll be old hat and it'll destroy the real bloom on the project. So it's all up to you!"

As a final inducement, Lucas took Kershner to his Parkhouse office, where the walls were filled with the architectural plans for Skywalker Ranch. Kershner was impressed: "It was really an extraordinary dream. All the billions of dollars ever made in the film business, and *no one* has ever plowed it back into a library, research, bringing directors together, creating an environment where the love of films could create new dimensions." Kershner was sold on *Empire* from that moment. "I trusted George," he says simply.

Lucas easily reassembled the rest of his creative team: associate producer Robert Watts, production designer Norman Reynolds (John Barry had taken a directing assignment of his own), makeup expert Stuart Freeborn, illustrator Ralph McQuarrie, costume designer John Mollo, editor Paul Hirsch, and composer John Williams. The only question was whether to rehire Gary Kurtz as producer. Lucas had not forgotten the tensions on *Star Wars,* which he felt were exacerbated by Kurtz's indecisiveness, particularly his handling of Gil Taylor. But Kurtz wanted to produce *Empire* and in spite of his own reservations and the advice of those closest to him, Lucas relented. "I suspected there would be problems and I knew I was asking for trouble," Lucas now says. But he felt he owed Kurtz a second chance.

There were some new faces on the production team: cinematographer Peter Suschitzky, son of a noted British cameraman; assistant director

The Wookie looks like the director, but the real version is the little fellow beside Chewbacca. Lucas is next to the camera crew he battled with during the making of Star Wars.

Twentieth Century-Fox President Alan Ladd, Jr., and George Lucas try to reassure each other that Star Wars *is going to work out on the Elstree set in April 1976.*

A dream realized: Richard Chew, Marcia Lucas, and Paul Hirsch after winning their Oscars for editing Star Wars *at the Academy Award ceremonies in Los Angeles on April 3, 1978. George walked away empty-handed.*

The retired director: Executive Producer Lucas visits the Elstree set of The Empire Strikes Back *in April 1979 and reminisces with* (from left) *Mark Hamill, Carrie Fisher, and Harrison Ford. Lucas didn't even have a director's chair with his name on the back.*

Meeting with a master: Japanese Director Akira Kurasawa (far left) *talks through a translator to Francis Coppola and George and Marcia Lucas on a beach at Hokkaido, Japan, during the making of* Kagemusha, *November 1979.*

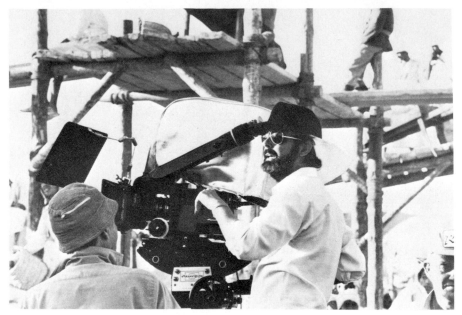

George filming second-unit footage in Tunisia for Raiders of the Lost Ark, *August 1980. Despite his vow never to direct a big movie again, Lucas can't resist getting behind the B or secondary camera.*

Neither Lucas nor Harrison Ford (Indiana Jones) seems to be enjoying himself in the sweltering heat of the Tunisian summer. Despite his French Foreign Legion headdress, scarf, and gloves, Lucas became badly sunburned.

Lucas fulfills his fantasy of being an anthropologist as he and Director Steven Spielberg pose in front of their "savages" during the final filming days of Raiders *in Hawaii, October 1980.*

The men responsible for three different visions of Star Wars: *(from left)* Empire Strikes Back *Director Irvin Kershner, Lucas, and* Return of the Jedi *Director Richard Marquand.*

The chairman of the board of Lucasfilm Ltd. Originally taken for a profile on Lucas in
Fortune *magazine.*

Artoo-Detoo and See-Threepio from Return of the Jedi. *Photo credit: Albert Clarke*

The Lucas few people see: proud father George with daughter Amanda at Parkhouse, 1982.

David Tomblin, who had previously worked with Kershner; and associate producer Jim Bloom, who had started his career in 1972 as a gofer on *American Graffiti*. In September 1978 Bloom supervised the move of ILM to San Rafael, where the operation was started anew. Richard Edlund and Dennis Muren, *Star Wars* veterans who made the move north, were put in charge of all special effects for *Empire*. The sequel to *Star Wars* was becoming a reality.

I trust your instincts as to what is satisfying to an audience. I think you have a pretty good fix on that.[5]

—Lawrence Kasdan to George Lucas

When Lucas sent Alan Ladd, Jr., his first draft of *Empire*, he added a handwritten note on the front page: "Here's a rough idea of the film. May the Force be with us!" A *P.S.* added, "Best read listening to the *Star Wars* album." It was November 1978 and filming was to begin in five months. Lucas gathered Kershner, Kasdan, and Kurtz in his Parkhouse office, turned on a tape recorder, and set to work. Over the next two weeks each page of Lucas's script was dissected; George explained the purpose of each scene, what he wanted to achieve dramatically, and how Kasdan could improve it.

Empire had three acts, each about thirty-five minutes long by Lucas's estimate. The script was to be no more than 105 pages: "short and tight," he told Kasdan. All agreed *Empire* had to grapple with the philosophical issues raised by *Star Wars*, but Lucas wanted them disposed of quickly. *Empire* had to be fast-moving, not complex. Lucas emphasized two rules over and over: speed and clarity. "The trick is to know what you can leave to the audience's imagination," he said. "If they start getting lost, you're in trouble. Sometimes you have to be crude and just say what's going on, because if you don't, people get puzzled."

Empire had the classic revenge story: the basic plot concerns Luke's attempts to save his friends from the clutches of Darth Vader, who uses Han, Leia, and Chewie as bait in his trap for Luke. Vader's goal was to turn Luke to the dark side of the Force. Lucas told his collaborators that they had to explain clearly who the major characters were and what was about to happen to them, so the audience could anticipate what was to come. George wasted no time in reintroducing key elements from *Star Wars*: the rebellion against the Empire, the love/hate relationship between Princess Leia and Han Solo, the rivalry/loyalty between Han and Luke, and the platonic affection between Luke and Leia. "It was the classic triangle plot," explains Lucas. "One good guy, one bad guy. Who is the girl attracted to?"

Lucas also wanted to delve further into implications of the Force. Obi-Wan Kenobi was back as a shadowy apparition, so Lucas gave the Emperor a physical presence, making him a hooded figure with burning yellow eyes and an unnerving evil aura—even Vader was afraid of him. Lucas also gave Ben an ally, the Jedi master-teacher Yoda, a strange creature eighteen inches tall, with a wizened face, gray hair, and an inverted style of speech: "Harm I mean you not. Away put your weapon." In Lucas's Jedi cosmology, Yoda had been a teacher for eight hundred years, picking only those students "with the deepest commitment and the most serious minds." Yoda combined the old eccentric Lucas had originally designed for Ben with the disarming simplicity of a child; he explained the Force and acted as occasional comic relief.

The other new character introduced in *Empire* was Lando Calrissian, a slick, riverboat-gambler type, who was more elegant and charming than his friend Han Solo. Lando was also a schemer and con artist, capable of betraying his friends to save his planet from the Empire. Lando lived in the planet Bespin's Cloud City, one of several new locales Lucas introduced. Others included the snow planet Hoth, which serves as the rebels' army base until they are attacked by Imperial troops, and Dagobah, Yoda's Bog Planet. There were also new creatures: Wampas, huge snow beasts, and Tauntauns, camel-like mounts. Lucas made sure the new animals and settings were introduced at the outset of *Empire,* so audiences would immediately recognize that this was a new movie.

In rewriting Brackett's *Empire* script, Lucas used an editor's perspective to crosscut between scenes, jumping from Luke's training with Yoda on Dagobah to Han and Leia's capture by Vader. He added physical humor, such as the *Millennium Falcon* rushing to light speed only to have nothing happen. And who else would refer to the *Falcon* as "a hamburger-shaped spaceship"? Lucas also enlarged the role of Han Solo and decided to leave his fate unresolved. The freezing of Han in a carbon chamber added tension to his love scenes with Leia, a relationship that initially worried George. "Nothing is more boring than two people acting lovey-dovey all the time," Lucas complained. "There's no conflict." (This presumably was no reflection on his long-standing relationship with Marcia.) But Lucas still had trouble writing dialogue for his characters, as this assurance by Han to Leia demonstrates: "Don't worry, I'm not going to kiss you here. You see, I'm quite selfish about my pleasure, and it wouldn't be much fun for me now." Snappy, it's not.

Lucas's biggest problem was the revelation that Darth Vader is Luke's father. After *Star Wars,* audiences knew Luke was the hero and couldn't be killed. "The way you can get an audience going is to make them believe that you as a filmmaker are going to do some really rotten thing," Lucas told his collaborators. George wanted the audience to think that Luke *would* kill Vader, with all the horrible implications of patricide. He was also thinking about part three of *Star Wars,* when "we bring everybody together for the final confrontation."

Lucas also wanted his version of the Christ story in *Empire.* Luke beheads Vader in an underground cave, only to find his own head inside Vader's black helmet—it is the equivalent of Jesus' temptation in the desert. In their final battle, Vader tempts Luke with the dark side of the Force, but fails—or does he? The final shot of Luke and his new mechanical arm is designed to suggest that Luke might *become* Vader—like father, like son.

Kershner and Kasdan were astonished by Lucas's incisive story sense— he went right to the key scenes, laid them out and justified them. "George writes in very broad strokes," explains John Korty, who has seen Lucas evolve as a screenwriter. "He breaks everything down into elements of entertainment. Is this an action picture? Do we care about this character? How does he get from *A* to *B,* and what does he say along the way?" Lucas was also emphatic about being faithful to the *Star Wars* legacy; he knew his fans were fanatics. "Every little sentence has been gone over and specu- lated upon and looked at sixteen different ways," Lucas told Kasdan.

Kasdan took copious notes at the story conference, went back to Los Angeles, and returned with his first twenty-five pages of *Empire,* which Lucas and Kershner promptly tore apart. Lucas has the disconcerting habit of ignoring good work and criticizing what he doesn't like. Kasdan's writing got progressively better, but he never lost his initial feeling of powerlessness: "I always feel I'm serving George—this is his stuff. I'm not there to tell him what it should be, but how it can be better, and to constantly force my point. Until he just says, 'No, that's not what I want it to be.'"

Kasdan's main criticism was that Lucas glossed over the emotional content of a scene in his hurry to get to the next one. Gary Kurtz agreed and left the story conferences feeling troubled about *Empire.* He thought the ending failed to resolve the characters' conflicts and that Lucas was relying too much on the revelations contained in part three of *Star Wars.* Lucas's response to these criticisms was typical: "Well, if we have enough action, nobody will notice." If Lucas has a weakness as a filmmaker, it comes in sacrificing thematic and character development for action. Kurtz says, "He's afraid of going too slow."

As *Empire* began to take shape on paper, Lucas was reassembling the original cast. If even one actor defected the continuity between the first film and *Empire* would be shattered. At the same time, Lucas was prepared to write anybody out of the story who wouldn't continue—no one was indispensable. Lucas offered higher salaries than he paid on *Star Wars* and guaranteed the three principal actors profit participation. (Lucasfilm offered to buy back their points, making them seem even more valuable to their owners.) Lucas didn't have to be so accommodating—Mark Hamill and Carrie Fisher, unlike Harrison Ford, had agreed to do two sequels in their original contracts.

Ford was in a good position to renegotiate and he did, asking for several times the money he made on *Star Wars*. He was ultimately paid no more than his costars, however. Like the rest of the principal cast, Ford had become a star, able to work when he pleased. He had made a career decision to stop being Han Solo, but none of his post-*Star Wars* films were successful. If Ford were to play Han again, the character had to have more dimension, he told Lucas. He wanted to be a handsome, dashing rogue, which fit Lucas's plan to duplicate the love triangle in *Gone With the Wind:* Han as Rhett Butler, Leia as Scarlett O'Hara, and Luke as Ashley Wilkes. "It has to be a real triangle with real emotions and at the same time, it has to end up with goodwill," Lucas said.

Fisher had also grown since *Star Wars*. She was now confident, relaxed, and radiant. Lucas still couldn't decide whether to make her a Barbie doll or an Amazon, but Fisher received tons of mail from girls and their mothers expressing admiration for Princess Leia's independence and fearlessness. As she told Lucas, "I'd like to have a door open and you'd catch me with one of my buns off. And I'd say, 'Look, my planet's been blown up, my boyfriend's been frozen, I've been tortured, I've been chased around in space for years now, I'm just gonna take so much.'" Fisher never got her wish—instead, she was given a new braided hairstyle called "1930s Nordic" and still had to deliver lines like "The ion cannon will fire several blasts which should destroy any enemy ships in your flight path."

The role of Ben Kenobi brought Sir Alec Guinness more acclaim and money than any other performance in his distinguished career. Eight months before *Empire* was to begin production, he developed an eye infection that threatened to blind him. He was prohibited from working under bright lights, but Guinness was determined to do the brief scenes with Yoda and Luke that required his presence. Mark Hamill, too, was recovering from his injuries. Lucas wrote a scene early in the film in which Luke is mauled by a Wampa, then healed in a futuristic medical lab. When Luke recovers, his face looks different; audiences never realized the scene carefully disguises Hamill's plastic surgery. Luke was still an ugly duckling, just now coming into his own as a man and a Jedi. Lucas wanted him to be less clumsy in *Empire* and made Luke an expert swordsman. But his true coming of age had to await *Return of the Jedi*.

The most recalcitrant returnee was Anthony Daniels, who felt like smashing C-3PO's metal body with a sledgehammer by the end of *Star Wars*. "I had an awful lot of frustration and hostility towards that costume," says Daniels; but not towards the character—he had become very fond of C-3PO. Still incensed at what he considered to be Lucasfilm's decision to downplay his contribution, Daniels gave thought to refusing to appear in the sequel. But financial considerations (including a small profit percentage) won out, as did his concern about his character. "I actually like See-Threepio enough to want to look after him, and that is where insanity starts to come in," Daniels says.

The most sensitive part to cast in *Empire* was Lando. Still smarting from criticism that *Star Wars* was racist, George conceived of Lando as "a suave, dashing black man in his thirties" and specified in his script that half of the Cloud City residents and troops were to be black (in the actual film, only a few blacks are visible). Lucas sought Billy Dee Williams for the role from the outset, after seeing him in *Lady Sings the Blues*. Williams was reluctant to play what he thought was a token black, but soon realized that Lando could be portrayed by a black or white actor. "The part requires a universal, international quality, which I have," Williams says. "Lando is an alternative to the usual WASP hero."

Lucas says he uses aliens and robots to make (however subtly) a point about discrimination—at one point, R2-D2 and C-3PO are barred from entering the space cantina. "Chewbacca's nonhuman and nonwhite," Lucas says. "I realize it seems rather obscure and abstract, but it was intended to be a statement." Lucas claims to be a fervent believer in equality. "I get upset over injustice and inequality," he says. The robots and Chewbacca were there to demonstrate that no matter how odd or different people seem, they can still be true and faithful friends. This is an unusual form of humanism, to be sure, but Lucas says he was trying to make a point. "A lot of problems could diminish if we realized we're all the same underneath our costumes," he says.

Lucas also insists that he didn't cast James Earl Jones as Darth Vader because he saw the character as a black villain—he simply thought Jones had the best voice for the role. "We got attacked in *Star Wars* because there were no Puerto Ricans in it," Lucas complains. "I mean, come on—you can't win." Lucas is now more sensitive to these complaints. In *Empire* and *Return of the Jedi,* he was careful to cast several black actors as background players.

I thought I'd stand back and see how everything falls apart because I'm not there. And it didn't.
     —George Lucas on the making of *The Empire Strikes Back*

Empire started filming March 5, 1979, almost three years after *Star Wars* began production. Lucas was nowhere in sight. The terrain had shifted from the sandy deserts of Tunisia to the frozen expanses of Norway. The tiny town of Finse, population seventy-five, huddled below a giant, brittle blue glacier which served as the setting for the ice planet Hoth. For seven weeks a skeleton crew of technicians and one actor, Mark Hamill, braved blinding blizzards, suffered painful whiteouts, and shivered through *average* temperatures of ten degrees below zero.

The winter of 1978–79 was the worst to hit northern Europe in years. For several days the crew of seventy was stranded in the Finse ski lodge, cut off from the rest of the world by avalanches that blocked the railroad tracks. By the time they left, the *Empire* crew had shot only thirty-three thousand feet of film, instead of the expected seventy-five thousand feet. Like Lucas's other productions, *Empire* was not off to a good start.

Filming began at Elstree a week after the crew left for Norway. It was a reunion of sorts for most of the *Star Wars* company, and Lucas attended to help launch his new enterprise. He planned to stay for two weeks, return for another two weeks in the middle of production, and then spend two weeks at the conclusion of filming. It was a typically frenzied shooting schedule: 64 sets, 250 scenes, a 4-month schedule, and an $18.5 million budget. Lucasfilm even built a new stage at Elstree to accommodate the *Millennium Falcon*—it measured 250 feet by 122 feet and was 45 feet high.

For all Lucas's attention to detail, the production was a shambles before shooting commenced. When Kershner returned from Norway, he had no idea of what was usable footage or what would have to be duplicated on the set. The cost of labor and materials had skyrocketed since 1976, and everyone was aware of just how successful *Star Wars* had been. Despite a work force of eight new electronically operated R2-D2s and more sophisticated mechanical effects, Kersh found that many of the "gadgets" didn't work. "The problems just accelerated as we shot," he remembers.

Kershner was determined that *Empire* be a significant film in its own right, not just a pallid continuation of *Star Wars*. (He looked at the original film only once, a year before he began the sequel.) The former musician saw *Empire* as the middle movement of a symphony, a contrast to the fast pace of the opening allegro: "It has to be slower and more lyrical," he explains. "The themes have to be more interior, and you don't have a grand climax. That became the challenge."

Kershner is a vegetarian and a student of Zen Buddhism; he was very taken with the philosophical implications of the Force. He studied fairy tales and mythology and saw *Empire* as a way to reach the subconscious fantasy life of children. "I wanted them to see the expression of a lot of their anxieties, fears, and nightmares and offer a way to deal with them," Kersh explains. Lucas was concerned with introducing the characters in a new environment, but Kershner wanted to explore their relationships. Working with actors delighted him; he would act out their scenes, whip up their enthusiasm, and worry about their health.

But Kershner was less decisive than Lucas about what he wanted on film. Every scene in *Empire,* not just the special effects, had been carefully storyboarded. Kershner would often come up with a better idea at the last minute and redo the scene, wasting the valuable time spent on rehearsals and lighting the set. "That was both his strength and his weakness," says Gary Kurtz. "George would never do that—he'd stick to the storyboard and fix it in the editing room. It worked to our advantage because Kersh's scenes were often better than planned, but they also took a lot more time."

Lucas, in daily telephone contact with Kurtz and Kershner, urged them to scale down and speed up. The scenes with Yoda were particularly time-consuming. Muppet cocreator Frank Oz operated and vocalized Yoda, but no one knew whether the creature would work in the cramped and humid confines of the Dagobah set, filled with mud and tangled underbrush. Stuart Freeborn had constructed a bizarre green-skinned creature from a cast of Oz's puppet hand. His eyes blinked and rolled, his nose twitched, and his head could be cocked at expressive angles. Yoda sounded like Grover, one of Oz's "Sesame Street" characters, but he had his own distinctive personality.

Kershner didn't share Lucas's fascination with the troublesome creature: "Everything about Yoda was a fraud," he grumps. "Every angle, every movement—we did it all with video cameras and monitors, microphones, four Muppet operators—it was a mess." Guinness was more fond of Yoda—if he didn't want to deliver one of his philosophical speeches, he'd say to Kershner, "Why doesn't the little green thing do this one?"

For everyone concerned, *Empire* became a grind. "It was the most wearing film I've ever done," says Robert Watts, who supervised the filming. "It went on and on and on. We had fun, but not as much as on *Star Wars.*" The most difficult sequence was the freezing of Han Solo in a large block of carbonite. Kershner wanted the set to recall the mad-scientist movies of the 1930s: a forty-foot-high cylinder of spiraling metal was constructed with elaborate electrical equipment and high-contrast lighting. Steam filled the air, plastic materials melted and emitted danger-ous fumes, and plaster periodically toppled off the set. "Physically, it was a much more demanding picture than *Star Wars,*" remembers Kurtz. "This one would have laid George out."

Lucas wasn't exactly having the time of his life in San Rafael. Moving ILM from Van Nuys to Marin was expensive and chaotic; only six people who worked on the *Star Wars* special effects returned for *Empire.* By February, when the first shots were supposed to be delivered to England, ILM was still settling in, a beehive of construction workers, electricians, and matte artists.

Lucas was determined not to leave ILM unsupervised this time. He directed the special effects while Kershner directed the live action. As Lucas watched hours of spaceships gliding silently through space, he gave Miki Herman specific instructions and inspirational clichés, all of which she dutifully wrote down. "One bad idea can wipe out a hundred good ideas," Lucas intoned—the wisdom according to Chairman George.

Lucas had a lot on his mind. His ideas were transferred into story-boards so everyone could understand what he was thinking, another improvement over *Star Wars.* Joe Johnston drew the storyboards, but Lucas designed the shots, giving *Empire* his visual imprint as well as Kershner's.

Lucas was more open to suggestions on *Empire.* There were 605 special effects shots, twice as many as in *Star Wars.* ILM had to construct a mythical Cloud City designed by Ralph McQuarrie with elaborate art deco stylings; white snowspeeders that would stand out against the glacial backgrounds; and the latest additions to Lucas's bestiary. Phil Tippett, who created the hologram chess game in *Star Wars,* designed a miniature Tauntaun whose joints moved autonomously, although the creature still looks phony on screen. More successful was the AT-AT, a spindly-legged armored engine of destruction that made a tremendous impression on audiences.

After working two shifts a day for five months, the ILM crew was exhausted. "This place was burn-out town," remembers Tom Smith, who became the manager of ILM near the end of *Empire.*

Lucas spent all day and most of the evening at ILM, not getting home until 9:00. He walked with what his friends call his "editing slump," and the bags under his eyes were pronounced. George had only the strength to eat and turn on the TV before falling asleep. Yet he found time to detail his plans for Skywalker Ranch, and his lawyers began purchasing land off aptly named Lucas Valley Road in northern Marin County. George also began revising Kasdan's script for *Raiders*. Miki Herman saw Lucas almost daily and marvels at his fortitude: "I don't know how one person has that much energy."

Ideally, George would like to come up with an idea for a film, have somebody go out and shoot it, and then get all the footage in a room so he could finish the movie all by himself, without anyone else imposing their ideas on him.

—Gary Kurtz

Lucas made a conscious effort to keep his distance during the filming of *Empire*. He was hoping for the same kind of collaborative harmony with Kershner that he had with Bill Huyck and Gloria Katz, but this was his director, not his friend. Disagreements between George and Kershner were inevitable, even if Lucas hesitated to express his objections. He resented the actors changing their dialogue—with Kershner's approval—because they also changed his story.

Lawrence Kasdan was in England in March 1979 and joined Lucas on the set one day. They both stood well in back of the cameras during filming and exchanged quizzical looks. "Is that the way you heard it?" Kasdan asked after one scene. Lucas shook his head. "George was very worried about seeming intrusive," Kasdan recalls. "So I said nothing and George said nothing, and the scenes that have bothered me the most were shot while George and I stood on the stage."

Lucas became alarmed as *Empire*'s budget and schedule ballooned. What he saw in the editing room disturbed him, too, although he said nothing at first. "When I looked at it creatively in the beginning, I was very upset," Lucas admits. "But I appreciated what Kersh was trying to do and I sympathized with his problems. The film was well directed, it was just differently directed." Lucas's approach was more pragmatic—get the footage and worry later about how it fits together.

Lucas admits that *Empire* is a beautifully photographed film, better looking than *Star Wars*. But he doesn't think many of the artistic touches were necessary. "It looks pretty because Kersh took a lot of time to do it,"

217

Lucas says. "It's a great luxury that we really couldn't afford. And ultimately it doesn't make that much difference." Lucas was irritated more at Kurtz for not restraining Kershner—that was the producer's job. Kurtz thought it was more important to make Kershner feel comfortable. "The director needs to do what he needs to do, that's all," Kurtz says with a shrug. Lucas saw it another way: "Gary never said no to anything."

Filming Yoda stretched Lucas's final two weeks into six, although he cut out many of "the little green thing's" scenes. Lucas finally leveled with Kershner about the growing financial pressures: "I really needed his help to get the damn movie done." Lucas appeared on the set more frequently, trying to apply "the right kind of pressure at the right moment," as he puts it. "It was a soft hand I used," Lucas says in his Yoda voice.

Former art director John Barry supervised the second unit on *Empire* after he lost his own directing job, but after only two weeks he died of a brain hemorrhage. It was a personal and professional loss for Lucas—not only was Barry a good friend, his skills were desperately needed.

Paul Hirsch assembled the scenes as they were filmed, wading through more than sixty hours of film. Lucas decreed that the final film could be no longer than two hours, so considerable cutting was required. When George arrived in England in June 1979 he looked at a rough cut of *Empire* and experienced the same sense of vertigo he felt at the first screening of *Star Wars:* "I was extremely upset, because I felt it wasn't working at all. Here I was, way over budget, running out of money, and I had a movie I thought was not good," he remembers. Lucas took the first eighty minutes and cut out half the footage. He knew that Kershner was trying to make a good movie—"It was just a lot better than I wanted to make it," Lucas says. "And I was paying for it."

Lucas's revised version was heavily criticized by Kershner, Hirsch, and Kurtz. "A lot of it didn't work and some of it was cut too fast," Kershner says. Lucas finally lost his temper. Duwayne Dunham, who accompanied George, sat in amazement as his boss exploded: "You guys are ruining my picture! You are here messing around and we're trying to save this thing!" Kersh calmly pointed out what he thought Lucas had done wrong, but George became even more upset. "It's my money, it's my film, and I'm going to do it the way I want to do it," he declared.

At that point, Paul Hirsch spoke up. "George," he said, "it's not 'you guys' against 'us guys.' We're all working on this thing together. You help us and we help you and we're all a team." The real issue was whether the picture was good or not. Lucas had pulled a classic Hollywood power play, but it was done in desperation. He panicked at the thought that Supereditor (as he calls himself) couldn't save this movie. "I had struggled to get this thing in shape," Lucas acknowledges. "But they were right. It didn't really work very well. *That* was what made me angry—I couldn't make it work." Kershner suggested some new changes and the next day Lucas went back and recut the film, following the director's advice. "It came together beautifully," he says.

Lucas was embarrassed about losing control, but the incident proved therapeutic—it let out emotions he had been keeping bottled up. "I never got on Kersh about the fact that he was over schedule and putting a great burden on me and my life. Everything I owned was wrapped up in that damn movie. If he blew it, I lost everything. He would go on and do another movie, but I was really under the gun at that point." Lucas had worried much the same way about *Star Wars,* but that was *his* movie.

Empire wasn't the only drain on Lucas's capital. Lucasfilm had grown tremendously, and by the time *Empire* began production, the company (including ILM) had a weekly payroll of almost $1 million. Lucas's first production loan for *Empire* was from the Bank of America in Los Angeles, which lent money to most of the major movie studios. The original budget was $15 million, but it rose to $18.5 million before any film was shot. A few weeks into production, Kurtz told Lucas that the film would cost $22 million because of the delays in Norway and at Elstree. At this point, *Empire* was costing Lucas nearly $100,000 a day. Once again, the specter of Francis Coppola dogged Lucas; Bank of America had seen its $12 million loan to Coppola for *Apocalypse Now* grow to $32 million, a situation the bank was determined to avoid. When Lucas went back for an additional $6 million, he was told, "We're not going to give you another dime." Lucas protested that *Empire* wasn't even half done. "We don't care," Lucas heard back from the bank.

A desperate Lucas flew to England and begged Kershner and Kurtz to speed up the production. The script was pared, sets were eliminated, and Kersh and the cast rehearsed on their days off. "A film like this is like a series of compromises," Kershner says. "I did not try for the kind of perfection that destroys films. I took terrible gambles with the cameras and with the performances, and I did the best I could."

It was not good enough. Lucas was literally out of money. Lucasfilm president Charles Weber got a call from the Bank of America on a Monday afternoon in mid-July. After Wednesday, Weber was told, the bank would no longer advance Lucas any funds until his loan was repaid in full. "I had a million-dollar payroll due on Friday and another million-dollar week after that. I didn't know what we were going to do," Weber recalls.

Weber persuaded another movie banker, First National Bank of Boston, to take over Bank of America's commitments and guarantee a new loan of $25 million (plus prime interest, at that time around 20 percent). The payroll was met and everyone breathed a bit easier. Soon Lucas found out even *more* money was needed, at least $3 million. The nightmare would not end. The Boston bank officer told Weber, "You swore to us you could do this for twenty-five million dollars. You swore to the Bank of America you could do it for eighteen and a half million. You started at fifteen million. Where is this going to end? We're not going to loan you any more money."

Someone was eager to lend Lucas money. But 20th Century-Fox wanted a complete restructuring of the *Empire* deal in exchange. Lucas decided to go down fighting before he'd crawl back to Fox. Weber flew to Boston to personally request the final $3 million. He brought a promise from Lucas to the bankers: "I will guarantee you that if this picture does not break even, I will eventually pay you back out of my own pocket, if it takes me the rest of my life." The bank wasn't moved—it would agree to the loan only if Fox guaranteed it.

"So I had to go to Fox to get a guarantee for the loan," Lucas says gloomily. "It was humiliating." Fox wanted 15 percent of the profits from *Empire,* a demand that took two years to negotiate. (Lucas still ended up keeping all the profits, giving Fox only a better distribution arrrange- ment.) "We were in a very bad bargaining position, because we really needed that three million dollars," Lucas remembers. The deal with Fox took so long to work out that First National Bank of Boston advanced Lucasfilm the money without the guarantee. But Fox walked away with a vastly improved deal on *Empire* and *Jedi.* "We're still suffering from it," Lucas complains.

Lucas takes responsibility for the near fiscal disaster on *Empire,* al- though at the time he blamed Kurtz and Kershner for going $10 million over budget. A lack of communication was the real villain—Lucas couldn't be in two places at once, and wherever he wasn't, problems invariably arose. "Gary did the best job he could, he made enormous contributions, but he was in over his head," Lucas says. "If anybody is to blame, it's me. Because I was the one who knew and I stayed over here [in Marin] until it was too late."

By the time *Empire* was completed it cost Lucas $33 million, including interest. It was the biggest expenditure ever made by an independent filmmaker. Lucas, ever the pessimist, thought *Empire* would do only 30 percent of the business of *Star Wars,* still making it a top-grossing movie. If it didn't do that well, Lucas faced a lifetime of loan payments.

Fox scheduled a May 21 release of *Empire* in the United States and

Canada. Lucas made one last trip to England to help John Williams and the London Symphony Orchestra record the sound track; Lucasfilm made its own record deal this time. Fox wasn't enthusiastic when it received the finished film, because Lucas owned too much of it. Studio executives believed that he would make all the money and Fox would look stupid in the eyes of Hollywood. When Lucas's marketing chief Sidney Ganis went to Los Angeles for a meeting at the studio, he could sense the tension in the room. Ganis waited until the middle of the meeting before sending a group of mechanical R2-D2s skittering across the table; everyone in the room broke up laughing.

This time Lucas had complete control of his film's advertising. He wanted to emphasize *Empire*'s romantic aspects: "We had a hard time getting girls to see *Star Wars*. I wanted to say that this one was more female-oriented and had a love story. I wanted a broader base." It's difficult to imagine a film with broader appeal than *Star Wars,* but Lucas seemed to want to prove that *Empire* was for adults as well as kids.

On the strength of *Star Wars'* success, Fox collected $26 million from theater owners two weeks before *Empire* even opened. (Merchandisers paid Lucasfilm $15 million in license prepayments of which Fox got 10 percent.) Ashley Boone, now Lucas's marketing consultant, suggested that *Empire* play continuously for twenty-four hours at the Egyptian Theater in Hollywood. *Star Wars* fans started lining up on May 18, three days before the opening, and fan club president Maureen Garrett was among them. As the clock neared the first show on May 21, the audience screamed the countdown. When the Fox logo appeared on the screen, Garrett remembers, "The whole place was shaking like an eight point five earthquake. It was an awesome, incredible experience."

Within three months Lucas had recovered his $33 million investment. *Empire* sold more than $300 million worth of tickets across the world in its initial release, producing film rentals of $165 million for Fox—it is the third most successful film in Hollywood history, trailing only *Star Wars* and *E.T.* with worldwide ticket sales of $365 million. *Empire* made an additional $51 million in operating profits for Lucasfilm after recovering its initial investment. Fox earned almost $40 million in distribution fees, not bad for a deal that "hurt" the studio.

Lucas made another radical decision by Hollywood standards: he shared more than $5 million from the profits of *Empire* with not only cast and crew members, but with every one of his employees, from ILM stagehands to the nighttime janitorial staff. Each Lucasfilm worker got a bonus check calculated on the length of employment, rather than specific contributions made to *Empire*. Lucas also gave profit percentages to twenty-five other people, including Anthony Daniels, Peter Mayhew, and Kenny Baker, and handed out more than $100,000 in cash bonuses to twenty-nine others.

For all the agony it caused him, *Empire* demonstrated that Lucas could produce a film that still reflected his vision, while enjoying a creative relationship with a director. Lucas learned from Kershner that pace wasn't everything and that more attention should be paid to character and idea development. Lucas also earned the respect of his crew as a producer, not just as the owner of the company. Assistant director David Tomblin calls him the best producer he's ever worked with "because his all-around knowledge, approach, and attitude are absolutely remarkable." The only casualty was Gary Kurtz, who left Lucasfilm after the release of *Empire*. Kurtz had hoped to direct a film for Lucas, but after *Empire,* he set up his own company, Kinematographics, and launched his own projects. He produced *Dark Crystal* for Muppet creators Jim Henson and Frank "Yoda" Oz.

Joe Johnston thinks that when people look back on *Empire,* they won't think of it as an Irvin Kershner or a Gary Kurtz film, "they'll think of it as a George Lucas picture. It's not that Kersh was a puppet director, it's just that George has such a good influence over people that they're willing to accept his ideas. They know his way is the right way to do it."

Either he's chasing them, or they're chasing him.[6]
—George Lucas on the plot of *Raiders of the Lost Ark*

In January 1979 George Lucas, Steven Spielberg, and Lawrence Kasdan met at Jane Bay's house in Los Angeles to hash out the story for *Raiders of the Lost Ark.*[7] Lucas had three synopses of adventures for Indiana Smith, but had put them on the shelf when he decided to make *Star Wars*. In 1975, as he struggled to complete the *Star Wars* script, he met with director Phil Kaufman, another San Francisco-based filmmaker. Lucas told him the story of a 1930s-era college professor/playboy hero, a cross between Clark Gable and Dick Powell, who battled the Nazis by day and squired beautiful women in diaphanous gowns to fancy nightclubs in the evening.

Kaufman saw a way to combine the idea with the legend of the Lost Ark of the Covenant, detailed in *Spear of Destiny,* a book about Adolf Hitler's fascination with religious artifacts. The two filmmakers met frequently over a three-week period, filling yellow tablets with story ideas. But

Kaufman was offered another picture to direct and dropped the project. No big deal, Lucas thought. Indiana Smith and his Lost Ark of the Covenant went back on the shelf.

That was not the last of Phil Kaufman. When *Raiders* was made, Lucas offered him a profit percentage for his contribution to the story. Kaufman initially accepted, but his lawyers demanded a story credit, too. Lucas was reluctant to give it because he had written two story outlines before bringing in Kaufman. If Kaufman got a story credit on the first *Raiders* movie, the Writers Guild would give him credit on the sequels, too. After sometimes-bitter negotiations, Kaufman got his credit and his profit percentage, but the incident strained the friendship between the two filmmakers.

Lucas didn't think about *Raiders* again until June 1977, when he and Spielberg decided to combine their prodigious talents. Spielberg's career had begun when he got off a tour bus at Universal Studios in 1968; he stayed there for the next two years, directing TV episodes and movies, and finally feature films. He had started making movies when he was only eight, using his sisters as the cast and his backyard as a set. Eventually Spielberg fashioned his own film program at Long Beach State, well outside the snobby USC–UCLA film school axis. Universal President Sidney Sheinberg saw *Amblin'*, a short, professional-looking film Spielberg made at Long Beach, and signed him to a seven-year contract. The rest is box office history: *Jaws, Close Encounters,* and most recently *E.T.* and *Poltergeist.* Spielberg has the only track record that rivals Lucas's. When Spielberg and Lucas came together on *Raiders,* the Hollywood establishment quaked.

Yet the two crown princes have totally different approaches to movie making. Spielberg moves his camera instinctively, designing elaborate shots and angles and filming the action as it happens. Lucas makes his films in the editing room and imagines his cuts even as he shoots. Spielberg likes to film numerous takes of a scene, spending whatever is required—*1941* cost $34 million in 1979, and Universal barely got its money back. Lucas's penny-pinching on the set is legendary.

Spielberg wanted *Raiders* to be the movie equivalent of a ride at Disneyland, inexpensive but believable. Lucas wanted it to remain true to the 1930s serials, with gruff dialogue, plenty of action, and cheap sets. As with *Star Wars,* Lucas insisted that *Raiders* be played straight—the characters and situations were not to be mocked. The audience had to laugh with the picture, not at it.

Lucas divided the screenplay into sixty scenes, each two pages long, and outlined six cliffhanger situations, from a truck chase to the hero being sealed alive in a tomb. A thrill turned up every twenty pages or so. "It's a serialesque movie," Lucas says. "It's also basically an action piece. We want to keep things interspaced and at the same time build tension."

The success of *Raiders* depended on the opening sequence. "It has to seem to go on for one-third of the movie, then give the audience a chance to rest before we hit them with the next cliffhanger," Lucas said. Spielberg thought up the giant rock that pursues Indiana from the Mayan treasure cave, but it was Lucas who re-created moments from the "Adventure Theater" TV shows he had watched as a child: the sun hitting the staff and illuminating the X-marked spot, and the snakes in the Pharaoh's tomb. The ending, when the Ark disappears into the bowels of Washington's bureaucracy, is reminiscent of *Citizen Kane,* and was devised by Phil Kaufman.

Lucas envisioned Indiana Jones (the name was changed because Spielberg thought Smith was too common!) as a scruffy playboy. He dressed like Humphrey Bogart in *Treasure of the Sierra Madre,* with leather jacket, peaked-brim hat, khaki pants, and a bullwhip. Lucas again incorporated his personal fantasies into his lead character: Indiana was an outlaw archeologist, a bounty hunter of antiquities, rebellious and amoral in the tradition of Han Solo. But Lucas insisted Indiana have some moral scruples. "He has to be a person we can look up to. We're doing a role model for little kids, so we have to be careful. We need someone who's honest and true and trusting."

Lucas gave Indiana two enemies, the equivalents of Darth Vader and the Emperor. One was a rival French archeologist, the corrupt version of the hero. The other heavy was a Nazi, "a real slimy villain," as Lucas described him. Completing the equation was the girl, a female version of Rick, Humphrey Bogart's café owner in *Casablanca.* Marion Ravenwood was a typical Lucas heroine, a damsel in distress who is cocky, competent, and cold-blooded.

Lucas spent most of his time at the story conference talking Spielberg and Kasdan out of their more elaborate ideas. "George's biggest thing with movies is logic," Spielberg says. "He would say, 'That's going to be hard to swallow.' And he was right." Lucas's gift as a producer is his ability to simplify a story, then a screenplay, and finally the movie. Films grow complicated and filmmakers forget why they're making them, George was fond of saying. Lucas's movies seem complex, but are actually simple, which is why *Star Wars* and *Raiders* can easily be understood by seven-year-olds.

Kasdan didn't like Lucas's simplistic approach any more than Kershner and Norton had. But collaborating with Lucas was a pleasant experience, nevertheless. "It's almost entirely without ego. There's a lot of pride and a lot of strutting our stuff. But it's very, very affectionate," Kasdan says. Kasdan wrote *Raiders* in six months, reshaping the story, fleshing out the characters, and giving them snappy dialogue. Lucas acknowledges that *Raiders* is one-third his movie, one-third Spielberg's, and one-third Kasdan's.

Lucas's original budget for *Raiders* was only $7 million—it ended up costing $22 million. He wanted a small second-unit crew to film stock footage, which he could edit into the movie so it looked as if it had been shot around the globe. In fact, *Raiders was* filmed all over the world—in Tunisia, France, Hawaii, England, and San Francisco. Lucas also wanted it made quickly in eighty-five days. Spielberg finished in seventy-three days.

Spielberg and Lucas had long been friends, but now they had to establish a professional relationship. Spielberg wanted Frank Marshall, who had worked with director Peter Bogdanovich on several movies, as his producer. Lucas wanted his own man on *Raiders,* too, principally to keep down the costs. Howard Kazanjian, whom *More American Graffiti* director Bill Norton affectionately describes as "the squarest human being I've ever met," was his choice. "We really needed somebody who would not be a nice guy," Lucas explains. "It's hard to be a tough guy in that situation. Howard can do it." There was some tension between Marshall and Kazanjian, but Lucas thought it helped keep costs down.

The production was scheduled so tightly, remembers associate producer Robert Watts, "that one had no time to think." Kasdan had written scenes located in Nepal, Cairo, and the Mediterranean—Lucas decided to show a map of the world with little animated travel routes instead. Filming took place in Tunisia, this time during the 130-degree heat of summer, and La Rochelle, France, where there were limestone submarine pens with a duplicate World War II German U-boat. Lucas wanted *Raiders* filmed at a breakneck pace: "By the end of it, we should all be panting, saying, 'We just made it!'" he told his crew.

Spielberg envisioned Indiana Jones as more of a sleazy alcoholic, not the playboy in black tie and tails that Lucas had invented. The compromise was someone "like Harrison Ford," as Lucas described him. gruffly romantic and ruggedly handsome. George wanted an unknown for the role, someone he could inexpensively sign to a three-picture contract, to cover the planned sequels. The first choice was Tom Selleck, a young actor about to star in the CBS TV series "Magnum, P.I." Lucas tried to negotiate Selleck's release, but CBS thought that anyone Lucas wanted was too valuable to let go.

Spielberg next suggested Ford himself—Lucas sighed when he heard the name. He wanted to use different actors in each of his films, and Ford was about to appear in his fifth consecutive Lucasfilm production. Ford had read the script shortly after Kasdan finished it, but his attitude was the same as it had been on *Star Wars*. "They could find me if they wanted me," he says dryly. Secretly, he hungered for the part—it was a chance to make audiences forget Han Solo. Ford remembers, "It was clearly the most dominant single character in any of George's films, quite in variance with his theories about movie stars and what they mean."

Steven was so conscientious with this movie, it was amazing.
—Frank Marshall on the making of *Raiders of the Lost Ark*

George Lucas's primary contribution to *Raiders* ended once the film began shooting: he had structured the story, supplied the characters and climaxes, and set the tone. Now it was Spielberg's turn. Lucas didn't even have an office at Elstree, where much of the movie was filmed, and he showed up for only five weeks on location. Yet he managed to communicate to Spielberg the movie he wanted to see. "They made *Raiders* together, absolutely," says·associate producer Kathy Kennedy.

Lucas principally acted as a brake on Spielberg's vivid imagination. When Steven wanted two thousand Arab extras, George talked him down to six hundred. When Spielberg wanted a 1930s flying wing bomber for a key scene, Lucas lopped off two of the four engines, saving $200,000. Lucas was a perfectionist to a degree that Spielberg was not, but he saw *Raiders* as a B production, not a glossy Hollywood A movie.

Lucas resisted the occasional impulse to show Spielberg how to film a scene. Instead, he'd quietly murmur, "Well, it's your movie. If the audience doesn't like it, they're going to blame you." Spielberg wasn't deterred—he still did things his way. The warning became a joke—when Lucas won a point, Spielberg said, "Okay, but I'm going to tell them that *you* made me do it."

The only time Lucas regretted making *Raiders* was in Tunisia, where he was badly sunburned on the first day of location shooting in the desert. George's complexion was permanently damaged; even now when his face is exposed to the sun, it turns beet red. The crew nicknamed him Howard Hughes because of the tissues around his burned ears. Despite his discomfort, Lucas filmed some second-unit scenes, getting a key shot of a treacherous monkey giving a Nazi salute that Frank Marshall had spent days trying to photograph.

Lucas went on location mostly to keep Spielberg company, he claims, but being together heightened the chance of conflict. "You never know in a situation like that," Lucas admits. "But I figured we could survive it." The two men could not have been more dissimilar on the set: Spielberg, yelling excitedly, dressed in a gaudy Hawaiian shirt; Lucas, sitting quietly in the background, chin in hand, rarely saying a word. Yet the friendship did survive.

In Lucas's mind, Spielberg is the better filmmaker: "He's unique, the most naturally talented director I've ever met. I had to learn everything I know. Whatever talent I have is in a whole different area, being in tune with a mass sensibility. My talent is not particularly in making films." Lucas finally had learned how to delegate responsibility, to give someone a job and let him live with the results. It helped that the results were excellent.

Lucas was a firm believer in the autonomy of the director as the major creative force on a film, but he wasn't averse to fiddling around with *Raiders* in the editing room—it became his movie, if only for a short time. Spielberg had been guaranteed final cut by Lucas, but after completing his first version, he willingly turned it over to George. This was a first for Spielberg and his editor Michael Kahn—he had asked friends for suggestions but always made his own changes. George filled the screening room at Parkhouse the first time he and Marcia watched Spielberg's cut, because he didn't want to see *Raiders* without an audience. He called Spielberg the next morning. "I've got to tell you, you're *really* a good director," Lucas said admiringly. Kathy Kennedy remembers Spielberg's elation. "There aren't a lot of people around who can say that to Steven. Who's going to tell the president of the United States that he's doing a good job? But when George tells you, that's it," confirms Kathy.

George thought a little fine-tuning wouldn't hurt *Raiders*. Michael Kahn joined him at Parkhouse and together they cut seven minutes out of the first half of the movie, making it tighter, slicker, and more fun. Spielberg questioned some changes, but on the whole he was pleased and impressed. "I would trust George with any movie I ever direct to reedit in any way he sees fit," Spielberg promises. "He knows the secret of what an editor can do to a movie, how he can enhance a film. I think he was born with it. If he wasn't a moviemaker, he'd run a newspaper—he'd be Charles Foster Kane."

George had a secret weapon in Marcia. Like every director who has worked with her, Spielberg thinks she has an excellent eye. Marcia is indispensable to Lucas because she compensates for his deficiencies. Where George is not unduly concerned with character and lacks faith in the audience's patience, Marcia figures out how a movie can be made warmer, how the characters can be given depth and resonance. She was instrumental in changing the ending of *Raiders,* in which Indiana delivers the Ark to Washington. Marion is nowhere to be seen, presumably stranded on an island with a submarine and a lot of melted Nazis. Marcia watched the rough cut in silence and then leveled the boom. She said there was no emotional resolution to the ending, because the girl disappears. "Everyone was feeling real good until she said that," Dunham recalls. "It was one of those, 'Oh, no, we lost sight of that.'" Spielberg reshot the scene in downtown San Francisco, having Marion wait for Indiana on the steps of the government building. Marcia, once again, had come to the rescue.

The battle wasn't over when *Raiders* was completed. Paramount Pictures was the only studio willing to accept what became known as Lucas's "killer deal." He originally wanted to finance *Raiders* himself, but he was still embroiled in the fiscal muck of the *Empire* loans. Tom Pollock and Charles Weber offered *Raiders* to every major studio, while Lucas and Spielberg drew up a one-page contract between themselves. Steven got a $1 million directing fee, Lucas eventually received a $1 million producer's fee, and Lucasfilm received another $1 million as the production company. Spielberg also was guaranteed a percentage of the gross profits, the money Paramount received from theater owners; Lucas had to wait for net profits.

Hollywood was dumbfounded by the audacity of the terms and the knowledge that someone was bound to agree to them. Ladd was still at Fox when the deal was first discussed, but by the time Kasdan finished the screenplay, Ladd was gone and Fox was off the list. That left Universal, Warner Bros., Paramount, Columbia, and Disney. Weber sent out a form letter with the script. "We wanted the studio to put up all the money, take all the risk, and give us the best terms anyone ever got," Weber recalls with a smile. Studio chiefs were outraged, but Weber is still smiling. "Everybody called up within an hour and said, 'We want to talk with you.'"

Paramount President Michael Eisner's reaction was typical. "It was an unmakable deal," he recalls. "You put in all the dollars and he gets all the profits." But *Raiders* was the best script Eisner had ever read, and the idea of turning down a movie directed by Steven Spielberg and produced by George Lucas was unnerving. Eisner never spoke to Lucas during the negotiations, only with Weber and Pollock. Eisner wanted the sequel rights to *Raiders,* not just an option on them, and he wanted strong financial penalties against Lucas if *Raiders* went over budget and schedule. He got the penalties, but Paramount can't make a *Raiders* sequel without Lucas.

The deal was made, but Lucas refused to honor anything other than a signed contract—he didn't trust the studio. Most movie contracts aren't drawn up until films are well into production—Hollywood operates on its own form of the honor system, the deal memo. "Nobody else could get away with asking for a signed contract up front in a million years," Eisner says. The only sticking point was Lucas's refusal to guarantee Paramount that he would be executive producer on *Raiders*—Lucas was enjoying this. Eisner recalls, "All he said was 'Trust me.' So now we had Steven, who had just spent a lot of money [*1941*], George saying trust me, and us having to guarantee completion money for a film that might cost fifty million dollars. It was not a standard deal, to say the least."

Eisner accepted everything except the "Trust me." That was the deal-breaker. Desperate for a solution, Eisner called Bill Huyck and Gloria Katz, whose movie *French Postcards* had been financed and released by Paramount. The Huycks were blunt: "You blew it," they told Eisner. "George wants to be trusted." After a sleepless night, Eisner called Weber and accepted the terms. "I just decided to go the whole way," he explains. "And once I said, 'I trust you,' it was the most professionally produced film I've ever seen. Not a dime over budget, handled totally smoothly, and never a fight. When he said it, I believed it."

The *Raiders* deal turned out to be profitable for all concerned because of the movie's incredible success. *Raiders* has sold almost $335 million worth of tickets worldwide. Paramount Pictures has made $49 million in film rentals, recovering its $22 million production investment in the process.[8] Spielberg has made in excess of $22 million, more than he had earned from all his previous hit movies combined. (His personal profits from *E. T.* may exceed $75 million.) Lucasfilm made $21 million from *Raiders,* but Lucas personally earned only $2.5 million as producer. The other profit participants, including actors and crew members, have divided more than $7 million in profit percentages. Lucasfilm now gets 50 percent of everything *Raiders* earns after Spielberg's share is deducted. But Paramount has the right to distribute *Raiders* forever.

Making *Raiders* strengthened the friendship between Lucas and

Spielberg, who will also direct the next Indiana Jones movie, which Bill Huyck and Gloria Katz have written. "It deepened our ideas about a combined future," Spielberg agrees. Lucas was reassured that he could collaborate with a close friend and have neither the movie nor the friendship suffer as a result. Skywalker Ranch was predicated on the success of such relationships.

Most of all, Lucas enjoyed producing *Raiders;* pleasure was a sensation he had almost forgotten in film making. "I probably had more fun on that picture than any other," Lucas says. "I didn't have to do anything but hang out. I had all the confidence in the world in Steve and I was not at risk financially. I was hoping it would come in on budget, but if it didn't . . . well, for once, I wasn't at risk."

9
RULING
THE EMPIRE

Let's face it, ruling the Empire is a boring job. I am not kidding. It's not dramatic, it's boring.[1]

—George Lucas

The day starts early for George Lucas—he crawls out of bed at 6:00, as the morning sun makes its first assault on the fog that blankets San Francisco Bay and San Anselmo.[2] He has lived in Parkhouse since 1980, but it still seems strange—the rooms are too big, the furniture too luxurious. It feels like the house of a wealthy corporate executive, with a household staff, an elaborate security system, and three cars in the garage: a Ferrari, a Mercedes Benz, and a BMW sedan.

But Marcia, sleeping beside him; Indiana awaiting him; and daughter Amanda, stirring in her crib, remind Lucas that *he* is the successful executive. Time for another day at the office.

If Lucas is writing a new film, he'll lock himself in his green-accented writing room, in back of the house. He'll light a fire and stay in his little alcove where his pad and pencils are for as long as it takes to finish the number of pages he sets as his goal. Writing is Lucas's least favorite activity; when he is creatively blocked, his body becomes tight and rigid, his face drawn.

George would rather be editing, molding sequences out of the material someone else had to go to the trouble to shoot. Running the film through the KEM machine in his editing room, he is blissful. He is also compulsive. Lucas won't leave until he is satisfied with a sequence, even if it means staying until 2:00 A.M.

The routine goes on for twelve hours a day, six days a week. He only takes Sunday off at Marcia's insistence. People who are worth more than $60 million don't have to work so hard. Lucas could kick back, watch TV, travel, dabble in real estate, live the good life, San Anselmo-style. Yet he drives himself so relentlessly that his friends are concerned about his health. There is less tension than existed earlier in his career, but new pressures test his stamina. Marcia worries: "He's doing a thousand things all the time."

Lucas doesn't look like he's responsible for a multimillion-dollar corporation. There is a bounce to his gait as he walks down a winding path from the back of his house to his office. He is fresh-faced and well rested; dressed in his standard uniform: plaid shirt over an undershirt, worn blue jeans, sneakers.

His large, comfortable office is furnished with oak antiques; he has framed comic strips of Prince Valiant, Krazy Kat, and Little Nemo on the walls. Pictures of Marcia and Amanda sit atop the bookcase behind his desk, and across the room another bookcase contains Britannica's *Great Books* and various graphics magazines. Also on the shelves are symbols of Lucas's adolescence: plastic re-creations of a cheeseburger, a Coke, and a strawberry milk shake. Toys are scattered throughout the room: a rocket ship, a large model car, an intimidating Boba Fett (the bounty hunter in *Empire*) doll. Lucas's office looks more like a playroom.

But this is business. His office is used sparingly—he opens his mail there and returns the phone calls that have been carefully screened by Jane Bay. Most of them concern the movie he's making, the one he's about to make, or the one he just finished. Lucas shakes a paperweight as he speaks, swirling snow around a miniature AT-AT. His voice has lost its flat Modesto nasality, but he still talks in a monotone, his voice rising and falling in inflection as he gets excited or bored. The calls are rarely personal—George doesn't like talking on the phone, although it relieves him of personally confronting problems. "Either I can solve it over the phone or it can't be solved," he tells an associate in England.

George also talks to friends, like Hal Barwood and Matthew Robbins, who are having trouble deciding what project they should do next. He tells them to cut down their options and go with the one they believe in. The conversation is punctuated by George's nervous laughter, which sounds forced on the telephone. He is never still while talking, rearranging the tiny wooden *Star Wars* figurines on his desk.

Lucas relaxes only when business is done. He sits at his drafting table, facing pictures and maps of Skywalker Ranch. He is the primary designer of his utopian community; he sketches the size and shape of the buildings and lays out rough designs, although professional architects complete the plans. Skywalker duplicates the California Victorian style of Parkhouse, maintaining the continuity from his first shabby office in 1974, to the ranch, which may cost $50 million by its completion.

"I just wanted to take the fun and camaraderie we had and move it to a slightly larger environment that is also comfortable, relaxing, and warm," George says of Skywalker. The creative atmosphere influences the creative product, he believes. Steel and glass make movies cold and impersonal— just look at Hollywood.

Some days, Lucas drives up Highway 101 to Lucas Valley Road, where the ranch occupies almost three thousand acres. He watches his tiny drawings come to life: buildings being framed, roofs put up, stained-glass windows mounted. Lucas loves seeing his ideas realized—he can spend all day at his drafting table. "I used to do it with cars, then I did it with film, and now I do it with the ranch," he says, pleased by this obsessive trait.

Lucas no longer has the excuse that he *has* to do something. "The future and past will all be finished," he reflects. "Then I have to sit down and start doing something different." He fantasizes about lying around the house, playing with his daughter in the swimming pool. But he also remembers the message of *American Graffiti:* "You can't stay seventeen forever. Life is a changing process. You have to sort of go with the flow."

The flow takes Lucas to an anonymous business district in nearby San Rafael, site of the nerve center of Lucasfilm. The casual passerby has no inkling that five white stucco buildings, marked with orange trim and pseudo-Mediterranean tile roofs, and inconspicuously lettered *A, B, C, D,* and *E,* are a magician's lair. They include the Kerner Company Optical Research Lab, better known as Industrial Light & Magic, and, in an adjoining building, is the computer division. Cheerful greenery surrounds the buildings; inside, the walls feature original production sketches, paintings, and posters from Lucasfilm productions. There are also displays of bizarre offerings from *Star Wars* fans, the people who make this all possible.

These buildings, Skywalker Ranch, and Parkhouse comprise "Lucasland," a term that makes Lucas bristle, although his friends and employees often use it. Lucasland is a self-contained community, a new version of the nineteenth-century company town. Last Thanksgiving, the paternal owner gave away turkeys to his employees, 431 ten-pound birds in all. In 1979 the number of employees and family members attending the annual July Fourth picnic at the ranch was less than fifty; by 1980 it had grown to three hundred, and then to *nine hundred* in 1981.

On July 4, 1982, more than one thousand people showed up for an all-day-and-night celebration featuring barbecued hot dogs and hamburgers, beer and wine, organized softball, volleyball, and croquet games, plus boccie ball and horseshoes. There was swimming at the lake (lifeguards present), followed by a dance featuring a rockabilly band. Horse-drawn surries and haywagons shuttled Lucaslandians to and from the parking lots, and a brass band played in the meadow. Walt Disney couldn't have done it any better.

Disney's dreams came true because his brother Roy ran the business and paid the bills. Lucas has no sibling to turn to, although Marcia acts as his counselor and confidante. George sets the direction for Lucasfilm and makes everyone believe that he knows what he's doing. Richard Edlund likens it to working on a special effects sequence with Lucas: "You may not understand the sequence yet, but you know that *he* does. By talking with you, he's building his understanding and yours at the same time."

Lucas reluctantly accepts his role as chairman of the board of Lucasfilm Ltd. He started paying himself a salary only at the end of 1981. Lucasfilm has average annual revenues of more than $26 million, a number that can multiply quickly when a hit movie is released. Lucas keeps his company private so that he doesn't have to tell anyone how much he makes (except the government). But being a successful executive is not his idea of fun.

"Running the company to me is like mowing the lawn," Lucas says, coming full circle from age eight to thirty-eight. "It has to be done. I semi-enjoy it, once in a while." As a child, Lucas found a way out of his dilemma; he saved his money and bought a power mower. He'd love to make Lucasfilm a self-propelled machine—but for now, he must push it.

Pushing it means showing up at President Bob Greber's office for his twice-weekly meetings. He speaks and meets with Greber and his executives at other times, but this ritual might be called "George Needs to Know." Present are Greber, vice-president and chief operating officer Roger Faxon, finance vice-president Chris Kalabokes, vice-president and general counsel Kay Dryden. They have a direct line to Lucas. They are his extensions, doing what he can't do. Lucas is pulled in so many different directions that he has little time to spend with his employees. "They're just going to have to do it on their own," he says. "Everybody can't have me."

For four hours each week, Lucasfilm has Lucas. The meeting is informal; George leans back on the couch, his arms outstretched. Greber, serious but relaxed, sits on his desk—in his mid-forties, he is the oldest person in the company. Faxon, a former congressional budget analyst, has his glasses perched on his nose and a yellow legal pad on his lap. Dryden also has a legal pad, on which she takes copious notes. There is no formal agenda, but Greber keeps things moving. Items are discussed briefly with occasional humorous asides; the atmosphere is relaxed and open.

The renovation of a Lucasfilm-owned office building is brought up, and George looks around the room. "What do you recommend?" he asks. When everyone agrees on a decision, he nods his head: "That's my mind on it, too." Imperceptibly, Lucas is in charge—he rattles off questions about earthquake liability and insurance like a seasoned corporate analyst. When he's made his decision, he invariably says, "My feeling is . . ." Told that someone needs to fly to Japan on business, Lucas jokes: "This is how deals are made—all to get a free airline ticket." Then the smile disappears. "Get the specifics of exactly why this trip is necessary," he instructs Greber.

Those close to Lucas agree that he has gradually become a happier, more relaxed person; he is less shy, if still not outgoing. In Greber's office he is open and communicative, expressing his thoughts without hesitation or reserve. Lucas still shuns the limelight—a request that he autograph one hundred *Raiders* story records elicits a look of wide-eyed disbelief. "What?" he exclaims, amazed that Faxon would dare make the request. Ascertaining that it was not for charity, he dismisses the idea with a wave of his hand. These are the times, Greber says later, that Lucas would rather be somewhere else. "He would prefer never to speak to people like me if he could get away with it," Greber states.

Lucas possesses the instincts of the natural businessman, a trait rare in filmmakers. He has the ability to make decisions and to anticipate their consequences. "Most people pass the buck," says Michael Levett, head of Lucasfilm merchandising. "George makes decisions and lives with them." Lucas hates indecisiveness—he is not a person who floats through life. He lays a foundation for his thoughts and then methodically builds on it. "His business acumen astounds me," Greber attests.

Lucas smiles when he hears these compliments—he almost flunked math in eighth grade. He may not understand tax shelters or oil depreciations, but as he says, "We can manage very well with things I *can* understand. If it makes sense to me, then it's okay." Lucas's business philosophy is dollar-in, dollar-out, the legacy of George, Sr. "Survival of the fittest," Lucas is fond of saying. "I'm glad I have this simpleminded, small-town, conservative business attitude. I'm just like a small shopkeeper." Minding a $26 million candy store, he might add.

Lucas has mixed feelings about the rest of his patrimony. It wasn't fun having to buy clothes out of an allowance, or having the cost of undone chores deducted each week. "It straightened me out, so I've sort of done all right in my life," he says of his practical upbringing. "But sometimes I wonder if it was really worth it—if I've turned out that much better as a result." Lucas is tired of the hard work, perseverance, and patience that have made him a success.

Surprisingly, his father has the same doubts. "I'm kind of a perfectionist, I guess," says George, Sr., echoing his son. "To some extent I neglected my family. For years, I was at work at seven A.M., six days a week. I wouldn't quit until I had done something to *my* satisfaction, and I never wanted to lose. I was a loner—I didn't want to take anyone else on, because if I got into trouble I'd bring them down with me." Lucas worries about the same things, an inheritance he'd rather do without.

It's 6:00 P.M. when George goes next door to the offices of Industrial Light & Magic. The company's identity is revealed by an elaborate circular logo above the receptionist's desk: a magician in full tuxedo and tails, black top hat and white gloves, a red rose in his lapel, a wand in one hand, surrounded by a machine gear and the curved letters *ILM*. Security is tight. There are two receptionists in the foyer and foreboding signs warning visitors to check in. The precautions are necessary: ILM is where Lucas's imagination becomes real. Spaceships dangle from the ceiling, rock music blares in a room lined with hundreds of model airplane and tank kits. A poster on the wall shows Sinbad flying on a celluloid carpet. In four sealed vaults lie the crown treasures: models and miniatures of the *Millennium Falcon,* the Death Star, the Snow Walkers, even Luke, Han, and Leia. "This is where the future is made," says ILM manager Tom Smith.

Lucas comes to ILM every evening when a film is in or nearing production. Walt Disney strolled down Dopey Drive and Goofy Lane to visit with his animators; Lucas spreads his pollen from department to department at ILM. The illustrators, monster-makers, and costume designers would like to see him more often but, as Lucas says, "There aren't enough hours in the day for me to do everything I have to do."

Joe Johnston and George Jensen are working diligently at drafting boards as George enters the storyboard room and takes off his leather jacket. He picks up a red marking pen and both illustrators groan. The walls are lined with thumbtacked drawings of each shot in the climactic battle sequence in *Return of the Jedi;* Lucas immediately sees that one shot is missing. He unpins the illustrations and moves them around, projecting the movie in his head. The storyboards not only give him a sense of how a scene fits together but enable him to reject specific shots before they are filmed.

When the red marker comes out, there's no doubt whose point of view will prevail. Lucas has the last say on everything. He is brutal about what he doesn't like: large red marks obliterate several carefully rendered drawings. Lucas grunts, "Let's eighty-six this one." The goal is a smooth flow of images. "I want it all to be *action!* No waiting time!" If Lucas criticizes, he also exhorts. "This is it, come on guys, we've got to get serious about this. The time is now!" The pep talk always works—Lucas drums up as much enthusiasm as a revival preacher. "Great," he says with satisfaction as he surveys a wall blotchy with red *X*'s.

As Lucas picks up his jacket and heads for the door, Johnston jokingly calls after him, "If you need us around midnight, we'll still be here." Lucas laughs, but the comment disturbs him. He is halfway down the stairs when he turns and goes back, sticking his head into the room. "Will you really be here that late?" he asks—his concern for their welfare seems genuine.

As Lucas proceeds through ILM, his invariable greeting is "How's everything goin'?" said in a toneless murmur. "The fact that I don't say hello and smile and be friendly doesn't mean I don't care," Lucas says in his own defense. "If anything, I care too much." But he seems uneasy around his employees, and they are unsure of how to approach him. Distance, not intimidation, defines the relationship, and both sides maintain it. Lucas's inability to accept his position is evident when he enters a recently completed dubbing stage and a carpenter approaches him for an autograph. Lucas is taken aback but reluctantly complies. "I didn't ask to be famous," he says later, standing in the parking lot. He looks at his feet and mutters, "But I guess that's all part of it."

George Lucas has coped with whatever "it" is, changing little in dress, attitude, or philosophy. But when he walks through an office, an imperceptible wave goes through the room, and a small entourage amorphously accumulates around him, as if he were too special to be related to on a normal level. "I know a lot of people who are afraid to talk to him. They just don't know what to say," Joe Johnston states with a shrug. Lucas can be intimidating to those who don't know him. Jane Bay once hired a receptionist and Lucas didn't speak to her for three months, not even to ask her name.

His demeanor has improved since then. "I think he's just more comfy on the planet now," says Bill Neil, who has known Lucas since *The Rain People* in 1968. George thanks people for their contributions and occasionally chats with them on his rounds. He is sparing in his compliments—marketing chief Sidney Ganis remembers receiving only two in three years. "I think George would like to freeze a lot of people and bring them out only occasionally," observes a bitter Anthony Daniels. Lucas is sensitive to people's emotions—anyone who could create a Wookiee and R2-D2 can't be all bad. "George isn't a person who physically expresses his affection for people, but he definitely feels it," insists Jane Bay.

Sometimes Lucas's uncommunicativeness confuses his associates. When the computer building was under construction, Lucas questioned the placement of a door. The next day the door was moved to the other side of the room. Lucas was bewildered. "I didn't ask for this door to be over here," he said. The next day the door was moved back to its original location. Ed Catmull, head of the computer division, says, "People take him very literally."

I'm most envious about George on one major topic: he has been able to separate the life and times of motion pictures from the life and times of George and Marcia Lucas.

—Steven Spielberg

The real George Lucas, if one exists, returns to Parkhouse at 7:00 P.M. The private time of an intensely private man begins. Lucas becomes just another guy who likes to lie in bed, watch TV, and read a magazine. The compulsive Lucas is now the slothful Lucas, shedding all his obligations and responsibilities. It wasn't always this easy. Lucas's vow to work a forty-hour week and to take two vacations a year lasted for one year after the release of *Star Wars*. "Then I was right back where I started. Work is when you aren't in command of your own time," he says with a frown.

When Dan Rather announces, "Good evening, this is the western edition of the 'CBS Evening News,'" Lucas is finally in command of his own time. Marcia makes dinner—she still does most of the cooking—while George takes his daughter Amanda into the TV room and gives her a bottle. The room is equipped with a large-screen TV, video tape recorder, and video disk player. Lucas is a news glutton—it's the only TV he watches, other than an occasional movie or documentary—and the network news is his nightly ritual.

He reads a variety of publications, from the *New York Times* and *Los Angeles Times* to *Time* magazine and *Cinefex,* a special effects journal. "It's important for him to know what is going on in the world," notes Jane Bay. "He has definite opinions about the direction of the planet." The news helps Lucas unwind: there are bigger problems than the ones he faces.

The resiliency of George and Marcia Lucas's relationship is impressive.

Ten years ago they were so broke they had to borrow money to take a vacation. Now they spend their evenings flipping through real estate catalogs of exotic residences for millionaires: villas in Spain, islands in the South Pacific, ski lodges in Switzerland, although they have no intention of buying. "Each of them has had to deal with it in their own way," Bay says of the Lucases' evolution. "The impression that I get is that they just keep getting stronger as a couple."

Marcia admits it has been a struggle. She was never pleased that George's hobby was also his work. She nags him to read books for recreation, not research. Almost grudgingly, he now reads contemporary novels by James Michener and James Clavell and classics by Robert Louis Stevenson and O. Henry. They line the shelves of the family library, a warm room with a cozy fireplace and Eskimo artifacts. Marcia also gets George to play tennis with her, his sole form of exercise, as a small paunch testifies.

Marcia can still make George laugh—"She's a funny lady," Bill Neil says approvingly. "She's loosened him up considerably." She also serves as the butt of her husband's dry, sardonic humor. At the *Raiders* wrap party in Hawaii in 1980, George persuaded producer Frank Marshall to tumble into Marcia's birthday cake and was ecstatic when the stunt came off flawlessly. Marcia's off-color remarks still make Lucas blush, but he's more affectionate now than in the past—he'll even put his arm around her in public. Marcia once told Neil, "People think George is a very unloving guy. But when we're alone, he's tender and cuddly with me."

Parkhouse is the fulcrum of the Lucases' life. "We're basically homebodies," George says; he and Marcia avoid parties, restaurants, and travel. They go to New York twice a year. After *Empire* was a solid hit, they went on an infrequent spending spree, buying art, clothes, and furnishings.

Yet New York, Los Angeles, and London are alien territory to Lucas, who prefers Marin County's blend of wealthy bankers and hippie dropouts. San Francisco is half an hour's drive, offering ballet, opera, and theater. Since the arrival of Amanda, they leave the house only to see movies. "I don't like the city," Lucas says with finality; "I like the country." San Anselmo is hardly rural America, but it has the same lazy quietude Modesto possessed in the 1950s. In his own way, Lucas has gone home again.

Careful informality is Lucas's way of dealing with his financial and creative success. "I'm sort of amazed all the time," Marcia says, looking around Parkhouse. Despite their millions from *Graffiti* and *Star Wars,* it wasn't until late 1980 that they felt comfortable enough to renovate the house. Marcia's biggest transition was leaving their Medway home, where she and George had lived for nine years; it was so small she could clean it herself. Now she lives in a mansion, dependent on a household staff.

"Once in a while, it's a little uncomfortable feeling you really can't do it all by yourself," she says.

When Marcia Griffin married George Lucas in 1969, she thought he would never be more than a director of weird movies. So when he became the most successful filmmaker in Hollywood history, Marcia didn't know how to react. She felt guilty about her sudden prosperity; both she and George feel they don't deserve it. Marcia resented her rich friends when she was young; now she wears a large diamond ring and does her errands in a Mercedes Benz. "I think some of the striving has been taken out of my life," Marcia says quietly. "I was a great achiever, a self-made girl who started from nothing and worked hard and got rewarded. In a way, I regret having all the obstacles removed."

To keep thoughts like these at a distance, Marcia throws herself into Lucas's new enterprises. She has humanized Lucasfilm, organizing a fourteen-team softball league and a company sailing club. Bob Greber calls her Lucasfilm's cheerleader, adding, "I think people sometimes forget that Marcia Lucas owns half of this company and is a very important part of it." Marcia transformed Lucasfilm's Los Angeles headquarters from an egg warehouse into a model office building. She has a design staff of twenty-five at Skywalker Ranch.

Marcia misses the gratification that editing brought her, however. Her friends regret that she has retired, much as they are sorry George quit directing. Marcia was ready to become a mother and since adopting Amanda, the idea of cutting film all night seems unappealing. Yet her ambitions have not disappeared. She will receive a credit as editor of *Return of the Jedi,* along with Sean Barton and Duwayne Dunham. She and George discuss the possibility of her directing, a step Marcia has avoided—how can you compete with George Lucas? She has been offered pictures to direct, and George has urged her to try. "You know as much as anybody about what one goes through directing," he tells her. But the scripts haven't been good, and Lucas warns her that if she doesn't like the script, the movie won't be good. He could hire Marcia to direct one of his own projects, a prospect that makes them both uncomfortable. "I prefer her to work for other people because then she's on her own and nobody's going to say, 'Oh, she got that job because of George,'" he remarks.

Marcia won't have to worry about directing in the near future—Lucas has her programmed for domesticity. He has always wanted a big family, and although it hasn't worked out that way, he still wants as many as six children. George has fond memories of his own childhood, especially his close relationship with his sister Wendy: "You have something else other than the outside world," he says. Their first "child" was Indiana, whom George and Marcia have spoiled since 1971. The arrival of Amanda has filled a great void in their lives. It was difficult for George to accept the idea of infertility; once he overcame that barrier, he threw himself into fatherhood with the same dedication he brings to his movies. The corporation was never a substitute for a family.

"George is a very controlled person, but there's no way he hides what he feels about that child," Alan Ladd, Jr., says. "Amanda is the biggest personal change I've seen in him in the last ten years. He's got this internal glow." Marcia thinks George's openness with his family has seeped into the rest of his life. "He has less opportunity to shut down," she observes.

By becoming a parent, will Lucas find it difficult to think like a child? "The key moment in every person's life is not marriage but parenthood," says Tom Pollock. "You grow old then. It may bring a maturity to his films that he hasn't had, and that may not be good for them commercially." The possibility does not distress Lucas: "Sometimes I get the feeling that if I have any more success, it's going to be obscene. I'm embarrassed by it. I'm beginning to impress even myself, and I don't like that."

Lucas is aware of the hazards of being a celebrity, but he refuses to live his life in fear. He accepts his responsibilities, although he would like nothing better than to be left alone. Lucas brightens at the mention of *E.T.*, which has replaced *Star Wars* as the most successful film to date. Now it's Steven Spielberg's turn in the spotlight, an opportunity Lucas hopes to use to fade from sight.

Success is difficult to evade. Carol Titelman, who worked at Lucasfilm when *Star Wars* was released, remembers thinking, "My God, George is going to be a very rich man." Even Lucas was curious about his wealth— he asked accountant Richard Tong to find out how much he had made, how much he had spent, and what was left over. "I have a feeling that perhaps as much as half a million dollars went through the cracks," he told Marcia. Lucas was worried that *he* had lost the money through corporate carelessness. Tong went back to his ledgers from the time George and Marcia had a joint income of $25,000, and added up nine years' worth of profits and expenditures. The total sum left unaccounted for was $15,000. "That really delighted him," Tong remembers.

I don't make pictures just to make money. I make money to make more pictures.[3]

—Walt Disney

After *Empire*, Lucas had to decide what to do with all the money he hadn't lost. In May 1978 George and Marcia formed a company that purchased the one hundred-year-old Bulltail Ranch in Nicasio, just north of San Anselmo.[4] Set on 1,882 acres of rugged brown hills and deep valleys, Bulltail was once a thriving cattle and dairy ranch. Within two years, Parkway Properties bought thirteen parcels adjacent to Bulltail, including Big Rock Ranch, which climbed the nearby hills. The total spread came to 2,949 acres and cost Lucas almost $3 million. (The price was cheap because of county requirements that the land be kept agricultural, which scared off condominium developers.)

Skywalker Ranch promised to fulfill many of Lucas's long-standing goals: it would give him a headquarters unlike that of any other movie company. It would be a motion picture think tank, where movies would be conceptualized, rather than physically made. It would be neither a film studio nor a film campus, but something in between—exactly what, Lucas still doesn't know. Even the huge profits of *Star Wars* and *Empire* weren't sufficient to build and operate the ranch. But using merchandising as its base, Lucasfilm could expand into nonfilm investments that would guarantee Skywalker's completion whatever Lucas's future success in the movie business. Lucas liked the idea of confounding Hollywood again—his films would subsidize the ranch, not its owner.

Chris Kalabokes, the financial analyst who had reluctantly approved *Star Wars* at Fox, joined the company when he heard Lucas describe Skywalker. "That was a vision I could trust," he recalls. Other business associates thought the decision was alarmingly irrational. Where would the money come from? Was George serious?

Lucas listened to his inner voice again. "I don't know why I'm building the ranch," he admits. "It's coming up with an idea and being committed to it without any logical point of view, I know. But it's just a feeling I have."

To realize his dream, Lucas knew that somebody had to take charge of his company, and he didn't want the job. "I needed a businessman," Lucas says. Charles Weber, the slim, soft-spoken corporate executive who had specialized in high-finance real estate ventures, was his choice. Weber's professional confidence impressed Lucas and soothed his worries about money matters. He gave Weber a simple directive—Charlie could run Lucasfilm and if he made money, he could run it as he saw fit. If he didn't make money, he was out of a job. "Leave me out of it," he told Weber, who was skeptical that Lucas could remove himself from his own company.

Lucasfilm found a home in the shadow of Universal Studios, an old brick-faced egg and dairy warehouse next to the Hollywood Freeway. When the purchase was finalized, Lucas confided to Richard Tong, "One of these days, Universal is going to really want this piece of property and I'm really going to make them pay for it."

Lucas was reluctant to set up corporate headquarters so close to Hollywood. It meant flying regularly between San Francisco and Burbank, a trip he loathed. He wanted to base Lucasfilm in Marin. But Weber, permanently settled in L.A., persuaded him that it was best to stay near Fox, which still controlled the only income-producing activity for the company, the merchandising. An ambitious remodeling program was begun on the old warehouse, renamed the Egg Company; the cost quickly went from $200,000 to $2 million.

George felt his by-now familiar premonitions of doom, as the Los Angeles staff expanded from five employees to fifteen, then fifty, then almost one hundred. "I wasn't happy with it ever," Lucas now says. But he rarely expressed his displeasure to Weber, other than to remind him that Lucasfilm should be kept small and intimate. Weber patiently explained that if the company was going to pay for the ranch, he needed to expand.

Lucas wanted the Egg Company to be an ideal environment for creative and business people. The original skylight was buttressed with giant oak rafters; beneath it, an indoor courtyard was filled with tables, director's chairs, and hanging plants. George laid out the large, roomy offices, and Marcia designed the stunning interiors: dark green walls with burnished wood trim, antique desks and tables, a polished oak balcony overlooking the courtyard. "I remember working at Sandler Films, sitting in a dark cubicle," Marcia says. "I want every employee to have a decent place to work."

The inspiration for Lucasfilm may have been Zoetrope, but Lucas was determined that the end product be different. Coppola feels he paved the way for Lucas, although he admits George never could stand the "disheveled" way he ran his company. Coppola lacks a sophisticated business aptitude, but Lucas is shrewd and parsimonious. Coppola staffs his company with old friends, while Lucas hires professional money managers. Francis lives on the edge; George hugs the cliffs. "I react to the way Francis does business by going overboard in the other direction," Lucas acknowledges. "He wanted to be a mogul, but not me. I want to make more movies and help young filmmakers develop. But first I'll build a solid base for financial security."

Still the grasshopper and the ant, after all these years. Lucas and Coppola rarely speak now, but their influence on each other's life is still strong. During a giddy period after the success of *Star Wars,* they schemed to take over the movie business by buying theaters and setting up their own distribution company. "All the things you wished you could do if you had the money," remembers Coppola, a bit wistfully. Lucas remembers Coppola even suggesting that they start their own religion, using the Force as the scripture; George thought Francis had gone off the deep end.

Coppola's and Lucas's dream still coincided. Francis was an early convert to electronic cinema while making *Apocalypse Now,* laying images atop one another. While Coppola gave interviews about the marvels of video editing, however, Lucas was putting together a $5 million computer company. "It's just a different philosophy about the way movies should be made," Lucas says.

In 1980 Coppola purchased a dilapidated Hollywood studio for $6 million. It was a vain atttempt to reproduce a hip version of the old studio complexes, complete with actors, writers, and technicians signed to long-term contracts. Francis had become the establishment he once decried, while conservative George, of all people, remained a rebel. Lucas didn't want a studio, only its creative spirit.

Coppola has never been concerned about his lack of money. "I always operate as if I'll be rich, because if I'm broke, that will take care of itself," he says with a shrug, a philosophy that makes Lucas cringe. Coppola asked Lucas to lend him $1 million when he bought Zoetrope Studios; to his amazement, Lucas didn't have it. George was scrambling to come up with $3 million to finish *Empire.* Lucas never approved of Coppola's move to Hollywood: "I thought Francis was betraying all of us in San Francisco who had been struggling to make this community a viable film alternative," Lucas says. Even so, he told Coppola, "If I had the million, I'd give it to you. But I don't have it."

Coppola, like most of Hollywood, was unaware of Lucas's fiscal plight, a closely guarded secret. He was hurt and vowed never to go to George for help again. Less than two years later, Coppola was in trouble once more, having spent $23 million on *One From the Heart,* his electronic showpiece. Coppola held press conferences bemoaning his fate but never asked Lucas to aid him. "I don't think George is wired that way," Francis says, speaking softly. "Part of friendship is understanding what the limitations are. Some people have that kind of generosity in their nature, it's easy for them. For other people, it's just not."

Lucas told Coppola's associates that if Francis needed help, he only had to ask for it. "He never did," George says, not a bit ruefully. Lucas had previously offered to buy Coppola's houses and office building and sell them back to him as a form of interest-free loan, but Coppola never took him up on the offer.

Ron Colby and Mona Skager, who have known Lucas since 1968, were furious that George did not step forward in Francis's time of need. Skager says, "If you put yourself in the same situation, how would you feel? Just hurt. Hurt that you wouldn't come through for your friend. It's like your brother wouldn't help you out." Were it not for Coppola, Colby says, Lucas would be making industrial films. Lucas reacts sharply to these criticisms: "Does that mean for the rest of my life I have to give and give to Francis just because he was the first one to exploit me?"

Lucas and Coppola now maintain the semblance of a friendship. They cosponsored a film by one of their mutual heroes, director Akira Kurosawa; without their help, *Kagemusha* would not have been finished or released outside of Japan. Coppola still daydreams about Lucas producing a film for him, returning the favor of *Graffiti:* "We cooked up a lot of good stuff together and on a certain kind of movie, it would be great." The onetime teacher and his too-successful pupil still exchange Christmas presents and invite each other to their respective company parties, but they have drifted apart and the separation is deep and probably permanent—they inhabit different worlds. "We're all products of our background," Coppola says, a simple explanation for the most complex relationship in George Lucas's life.

The future is going to be with independent filmmakers. It's a whole new kind of business. We're all forging ahead on the rubble of the old industry.

—George Lucas, in a speech to the Modesto Rotary,
May 29, 1973

George Lucas may have brought Hollywood to its knees, but he has also kept it alive.[5] *Star Wars, Empire,* and *Raiders* have removed more than $150 million in profits from the coffers of two major studios that have had to content themselves with distribution fees. Tom Pollock says, "George has siphoned money out of the system that cannot be used again to make movies, other than his own." Lucas is the biggest profit participant in the history of the film business. Hollywood has benefited from his success, however. Many movies rode the profitable coattails of Lucas's string of blockbusters. Without Lucas, the movie business might have fallen on even harder times. The success of *Raiders* allowed Paramount to make twelve less successful films.

"George Lucas is *not* what the rest of the business is about," says Ned Tanen. "Nobody has ever done what he has done. Nobody. George Lucas is over there, and the rest of the business is over here." Lucas is the man who got away, who beat the system by building his own system. "The studio system is dead," Lucas insists. "It died fifteen years ago when the corporations took over and the studio heads suddenly became agents and lawyers and accountants. The power is with the people now. The workers have the means of production."

Can that be George Lucas, the conservative businessman from Modesto, spouting socialist Hollywood rhetoric? Of course not. Lucas is talking about the *creative* power of the independent writer, director, and producer, a goal to which he has dedicated his career. With power comes the envy of those who do not possess it. Lucas and Hollywood have taunted each other for more than a decade; he finds Hollywood crooked and sleazy, while the film industry resents his success and arrogance. "They don't care about movies," George says. "The advantage I've also had over the studios is that I do care."

For all his distrust of Hollywood, Lucas understands how the movie business works. As far back as film school, Lucas came to the realization that he didn't need development deals, agents, or executive producers. *He could make movies.* Agents, lawyers, and studio executives don't know how to light, shoot, or cut film. They live off people who know how to do these things—they are parasites.

Yet Hollywood is not without its temptations. "There are lots of lures," Lucas admits (flattery, money, sex, drugs). "I mean, I'm as seduceable as the next guy," he says. "I figured that if I did stay there, I'd become part of it. I didn't want to be that kind of person. I've never had the confidence that I was strong enough to resist all the temptations." Lucas's personality and upbringing made it next to impossible for him to accept Hollywood on its terms.

Lucas turned what could have been a career liability into an asset. "They can't understand someone who doesn't want to be part of the action," Lucas once said of the studios. "It makes me a total enigma, the most effective presence I could have." Hollywood is the Death Star, and Lucas is the eternal rebel. He still bears the psychic scars of having *Graffiti* and *THX* taken from him and remembers Fox hounding him at every step of making *Star Wars*. Alan Ladd, Jr., observes, "I think George feels, with reason, that he was deceived, cheated, and lied to." These bitter memories propelled Lucas toward independence. Artistic freedom became not only a goal, but a form of revenge.

Did Lucas really suffer? The cuts in *Graffiti* and *THX* were not major, and he ultimately restored the material to both films. Ned Tanen, who took *Graffiti* away from Lucas in spite of overwhelming evidence that the film was popular, thinks not: "Good God, George, what did anybody do to you? Did you have nine pictures canceled? Were you physically abused by people? Were you thrown out of offices bodily? What happened to you that was so terrible?" It is all Lucas can do to contain himself when he is presented with these arguments. He has a moral disdain for Hollywood that goes beyond his own complaints. "Anybody with any moral convictions hates the way the studios do business," he argues. But Lucas is in a position to do something about it. He can twist the screws, verbally and financially. "I enjoy it only because I got screwed in the beginning and now I'm able to do it to them."

Lucas subscribes to an Old Testament code of justice. He is tolerant and peace-loving until wronged. Then in his fury he is righteous: "I do not forgive. And I do not forget. It's part of my makeup. I've always been that way." Success has tempered Lucas's thirst for retribution. The incredible power he wields has made him more discriminating in its application. "But I can still hold a grudge," he warns.

There are exceptions, of course. Alan Ladd, Jr., is one of the few Hollywood studio executives whom Lucas considers decent, in spite of their clash over last-minute filming on *Star Wars*. Ladd is proud of his status and has used it to set up an arrangement in which Lucas brings projects to his attention and consults on their progress.

On the other end of the spectrum is Marvin Davis, the Colorado oil baron who bought 20th Century-Fox for $680 million in 1981. Lucas is friendly with Davis, inviting him to Parkhouse and attending the millionaire's annual charity ball in Denver. They have one thing in common— lots of money. The aggressive 350-pound entrepreneur and the small, reserved filmmaker share little else. "He's a shark," Lucas says of Davis, who recently sold the TV rights to *Star Wars* for an estimated $60 million, over Lucas's objections. "But there's a difference between being a shark and being sleazy. Most people are cowardly, but Marvin is not a coward. He's tough, but you know that going in." Davis might become the latest in a series of big-brother figures to Lucas, beginning with Alan Grant and continuing to Francis Coppola. Marvin is the tough businessman that George, in some ways, would like to be. Davis is one of the few people in Hollywood who can make a decision stick, a quality Lucas greatly admires.

Yet Lucas can't wholeheartedly embrace business practices that he considers unfair and unscrupulous. Those who violate the basic tenets of morality (honesty, fairness, generosity) are eventually undone, Lucas believes. He is so honest that during the ICM arbitration over *Empire,* his staff was instructed to tell ICM's lawyers *everything,* even if it was harmful to his case.

Lucas wants the kind of ethical company that does not exist in Hollywood. His father's employees stayed with L. M. Morris for as long as twenty years and George wants to develop that same loyalty in Lucasfilm. He tries to set a moral example. When you have someone over a barrel, don't push your advantage. When you negotiate a deal, be tough and demanding, but never unreasonable or unfair. When you have a success, share the profits. "It's just a matter of doing what's right," Lucas says.

Lucas refuses to do what he thinks is wrong, which explains his bitter dispute with the Writers and Directors Guilds. Lucas has never been fond of the Hollywood unions—he applied for membership in them fresh out of film school and was summarily rejected. He saw them as barriers to making movies, reinforcing Hollywood's image as an exclusive club.

Star Wars and *Empire* were made in England, and Lucas had little contact with the Directors Guild after he joined for *American Graffiti.* Shortly after *Empire* was released, the guild notified Lucas that he was being fined $250,000 for putting director Irving Kershner's name at the end of the movie rather than the beginning. It was the same place Lucas's directing credit had been on *Star Wars,* but the guild hadn't complained then. If Lucas had put the director's name at the beginning, the union rules would then require that all the major credits go there, destroying the impact of the opening shot.

Kershner didn't care where his credit appeared, but the guild did. Lucasfilm was a personal credit, not a corporate name, it said. If Lucasfilm's credit followed Fox's logo, Kershner's credit had to be there, too. Lucas thought credits were typical examples of Hollywood ego posturing. They had nothing to do with making movies, although he made sure that the Lucasfilm credit was prominently displayed.

Lucas's request for an exemption (usually granted if the director agrees) was turned down. The Directors Guild insisted that he withdraw the movie from theaters (at an estimated cost of $500,000), change the titles, and *still* pay the fine. Lucas was incensed that he and Kershner were being harassed by their own union. Lucas didn't think it was fair to the profit participants to charge the fines to *Empire*. If he was going to make a stand, the costs would come out of his own pocket.

Lucas sued the Directors Guild, insisting on a court trial rather than arbitration. The guild announced that if it lost in court, it would fine Kershner for working for a company that had never signed a guild contract. (Because *Empire* was made in England, Lucasfilm didn't have to.) Reluctant to involve Kersh in the dispute, Lucas settled with the guild, paying a $25,000 fine. He didn't change the credits on *Empire*. The Directors Guild then informed the Writers Guild of its victory, and the Writers Guild fined Lucas $50,000. Again Lucas settled, this time for $15,000. The experience upset him deeply. He felt he had been made into a whipping boy for no reason other than his success.

Lucas quit both unions, over not the fines, but the rationale behind them. "I feel the unions tried to extort money from me for their own coffers. They used a thin technicality, but the only reason they were doing it was to get money," Lucas says. He was especially outraged that the Directors Guild did not share the $25,000 fine with Kershner—at least the Writers Guild sent Kasdan and Leigh Brackett's estate $5,000 each. Lucas has since re-signed with the Writers Guild, forcing it to recognize Lucasfilm as a corporate entity, but he is adamant about never personally joining the writers or directors unions. He doesn't have to belong to write or direct films, but he knows his absence is noticed. Like his decision to drop out of the Academy of Motion Picture Arts and Sciences, it symbolizes how unneccessary Hollywood has become to him.

Lucas's remaining link to Hollywood is the distribution of his films. The studios control the system by which movies are booked, shipped to theaters, and advertised. Lucas can finance and make his own films, but he can't get them to the audience. He needs a movie studio for that.

"As long as the studios control theatrical distribution, you can never be your own master," says Tom Pollock. Steven Spielberg has suggested starting a distribution company with Lucas to free them from studio bondage, but George is reluctant. He doesn't make enough movies to supply a distribution operation and pay for its overhead. Instead, he's waiting for satellite and video technology to overtake the movie business. The time is not far off when movies will be beamed to theaters (and home TV sets) by satellites, eliminating the studios' cumbersome distribution system. Anyone who can get a signal up to the sky will have access to theaters. Technology will democratize film, and Lucas wants to be a signer of that declaration of independence.

In some ways, Lucasfilm has become a colonial power itself by virtue of its size and impact. Lucas says he mistrusts accountants, bureaucrats, and administrators, but he employs forty-three of them. He champions the cause of the filmmaker, not the studio, but he has fashioned his own ministudio. *Star Wars* also helped breed a slavish devotion to the block-buster movie in Hollywood, making it more difficult to produce smaller, less commercial films. The idea with which Lucas began his own career, low-cost movies with unknown actors, somehow got lost along the way. Now he wants to find it again.

HAN SOLO: I never would have guessed that underneath the person I knew was a responsible leader and businessman. But you wear it well.

LANDO CALRISSIAN: Yeah, I'm *responsible* these days. It's the price of success. And you know what, Han? You were right all along. It's overrated.

—From *The Empire Strikes Back*

Lucas's worst fears about what could happen to Lucasfilm came true after *Empire* was released in 1980. The *Star Wars* profits had been invested and the dividends were not only paying for the company's overhead, but also freeing George from having to make movies and providing the financial base for Skywalker Ranch. Charles Weber had turned Lucasfilm into a thriving, successful miniconglomerate—*too* successful, as far as its chairman was concerned.

When Lucas extricated himself from the financial mess of *Empire,* his small, familial company of twelve people had become a well-heeled corporation with an annual overhead of $5 million, and 280 employees spread across California. His plans to consolidate the company in Marin seemed to have been forgotten. Most of Lucasfilm was already in Northern California, but the headquarters remained in Los Angeles, a community George despised.

Lucas always came back from Los Angeles feeling angry and frustrated.

The Egg Company had originally had ten offices to house executives, secretaries, and receptionists. Now the building was enlarged, middle-management executives were driving Mercedes-Benzes and Porsches leased by Lucasfilm (annual cost, $300,000), and the Los Angeles staff was requesting its own cook. "It got totally out of hand," Lucas complains. "We were one step away from the delivery boy having a company Porsche. We were up here living in poverty row and they had a palatial estate."

Lucas saw the corrupting influences of Hollywood at work: his executives joined civic organizations, went to cocktail parties, and became what George had always vowed never to become—part of the industry. "I always felt a little uncomfortable being in the Hollywood community as a representative of Lucasfilm," says Weber. "I was constantly being told by George that nobody should be in Hollywood." Lucasfilm was a Marin County operation as far as Lucas was concerned. He had to get his people out of L.A.

Chronically unable to confront difficult problems, Lucas searched for a way out. He had never taken Lucasfilm seriously, allowing executives to tell him what they thought he wanted to hear. Remembers Weber, "From the day he hired me, I was a foreign entity. He was the filmmaker, and we were the business people." Lucas's daily contact with his Los Angeles office consisted of a forty-five-minute phone conversation with Weber; he usually contributed a "Yeah" or "No" to the list of questions and issues Weber had prepared. What Lucas never said was "Stop it right now. This company is getting out of hand," which is what he was thinking.

As always, it was a question of control. "While I'd been saying, 'Charlie, this is your company,' when it came down to it I realized it was my money and I cared a lot more about how it was spent than I had in the beginning," Lucas admits. The matter came to a head when Weber wanted to borrow $50 million to turn Lucasfilm's passive investments into majority ownership in a variety of companies, from DeLorean automobiles to communications satellites.

Weber also wanted Lucas to bring other movie and TV producers into Lucasfilm, lending them his name and expertise. "Charlie is a businessman, and he doesn't realize how hard it is to come up with a creative thing, not to mention *consistently* creative things," Lucas says. Like Walt Disney, Lucas didn't want his name on anything he couldn't personally supervise. When Weber suggested that the ranch represented too much of a cash drain, Lucas had enough. "The ranch is the only thing that counts," he told Weber. "That's what everybody is working for. And if that is getting lost in the shuffle, then something's terribly wrong here."

George suffered sleepless nights, chronic headaches, and bouts of dizziness throughout the fall of 1980. "I'm not very brave about these situations," he says. "I'm somewhat insecure and slightly a coward." When he came back from Los Angeles just before Thanksgiving, he was stricken with stomach pains. Medical tests showed he had an incipient ulcer, which disappeared when medicated. Lucas internalized himself right into the hospital.

There was no one to turn to other than Marcia. It was a painful process for both of them as Lucas grappled with his dilemma. The conclusion was unavoidable: he was going to have to let half of the Los Angeles staff go, move everybody else up north, and pare Lucasfilm to a manageable size. Weber was called up to San Francisco and Lucas, sweating profusely, his voice hoarse and hollow, told him of the decision. Weber, usually impassive in business situations, was shocked. He had hoped to renegotiate an already generous salary package, and now he was told that Lucasfilm was being snatched from him.

George wanted Weber to stay with the company—he still admired Charlie and he felt guilty as hell. Weber agreed to moderate his demands and drove to the airport. Half an hour later he was summoned back to Parkhouse. Lucas had decided that Lucasfilm couldn't be his and Weber's company at the same time. Accountant Richard Tong called George just after Weber left and recalls, "He sounded like he'd been through the wringer. Talk about ill, he sounded like he was dying." Lucas's sole comment on the firing of Weber is "The one thing I regret is I didn't do it earlier."

When the Los Angeles staff returned to the Egg Company following the Christmas holidays, they were given the bad news. Only thirty-four of the eighty employees were asked to make the move north. There were bruised egos and bitter recriminations, mostly directed at Lucas. George felt terrible about disrupting people's lives and went to great lengths to ease his conscience. Laid-off employees were given six months to find new jobs and generous cash settlements. Lucas even hired a vocational counselor to help them.

In a strange way, the experience was cathartic for Lucas. Marcia thought George learned one of life's valuable lessons: "When a situation is not working out, you confront that situation and you fix it. This was an uncomfortable situation for George, and he didn't confront it. In his reluctance to confront it, it just got worse and worse." By regaining control of Lucasfilm, George was again the center of his universe.

On May 28, 1981, Lucasfilm Ltd. officially relocated its corporate headquarters from Los Angeles to Marin County, completing what a press release called "the long-planned consolidation of the company." Mistakes had been made, money had been lost, dues had been paid. Changes of direction are expensive, but Lucas knew where he wanted to go.

Bob Greber, who had been chief financial officer, was made executive vice-president and chief operating officer. Lucas initially kept Weber's title of president and chief executive officer (he has since given it to Greber) as well as retaining his own position as chairman. Greber's background was similar to Weber's—he had managed $60 million worth of Merrill Lynch's investments. But Greber accepted a condition that was unacceptable to Weber: "Basically, I implement those things George wants done."

Greber had some conditions of his own. Lucas had to openly and directly express his feelings about Lucasfilm. Greber told him, "You've got to tell me whether you like something or not. You just can't sit there and take it." Greber prepared a report that explained just how much money Lucasfilm had, how much it was spending, and how much was left over. Lucas was pleased: "Before, I'd gotten a seventy-five-page report that didn't say anything." He wanted to know the bottom line: cash-in, cash-out. Greber told him and won Lucas's trust.

Greber is accommodating, but he isn't a yes-man. Lucasfilm is not a company where orders are issued and the troops snap to attention. At times the atmosphere seems unnaturally idyllic: bright, motivated people all roughly the same age, with many of the same interests. The top executives are men with the exception of Kay Dryden and Merchandising Vice-President Maggie Young, but many of the middle-management jobs (publishing, merchandising, fan club) are held by women. These employees share Lucas's parsimonious philosophy: "'They're looking to save every dime they can," says Charles Weber.

Lucas's belief in corporate ethics, group decisions, and a family atmosphere filters down from the top. He has instilled a sense of pride in his employees through his own example. "The best boss and fellow workers a person can have," fan club president Maureen Garrett says in earnest. "I can't put it any other way." Secretaries and stage technicians are made to feel as if *they* are the artists. Because they share George's dream, they want to help him make it come true. Lucasfilm attracts the best people because of this reputation. What other filmmaker shares the wealth of his films with *all* his employees? "One act of kindness can carry you through a year of hell on a production," says librarian Debbie Fine. "The loyalty that man engenders is incredible."

As Lucas increasingly becomes a corporate overseer, his personal contact with his employees diminishes. At the 1981 Christmas party he had no idea who most of the one thousand guests were. His friends worry that he has been consumed by the corporation, which is fast becoming a new sea of faceless workers. Lawrence Kasdan senses an "IBM military" feel to Lucasfilm's corporate offices, nicknamed The Tower, after the evil-looking black administration building at Universal Studios. If a filmmaker screens a movie at Lucasfilm, he gets a computerized bill charging him for the projection room and any telephone calls he made, just like at Universal.

As the company grows, so does the internal bickering and division between the "haves" and the "have-nots." The production staff feels bullied and slighted; once again, they see executives driving around in company-leased Mercedes. And although ILM is completely unionized, as are the construction crews at Skywalker and Sprocket Systems, Charles Weber is among those who foresee problems: "People are going to think since they work for George Lucas, why is there any limitation to what they can make?" Lucas bristles at such criticism—Lucasfilm's annual overhead is $9 million, most of it in salaries. He calls the average wage scale at his company "awesome," the result of periodic surveys that ascertain the going rate in Hollywood. But three years between movies is a long time and Lucasfilm has had to diversify to pay for all this. The company has invested $10 million in oil and natural gas wells, and owns $5 million worth of real estate in Marin County alone. Other properties include office buildings in San Francisco and the Egg Company in Los Angeles, now leased as office space to filmmakers like Randal Kleiser. There are plans for a new commercial development in the Bay area that will combine a marina with a shopping center, a first-class restaurant, and condominiums. Greber expects Lucasfilm's passive investments to grow and speaks of profit centers and the prospect of creating TV programs. "If we can take care of that dream that George and Marcia have, it would be wonderful—as long as it's sensible," Greber says. That kind of talk was one reason Charles Weber lost his job.

Outside of passive investments and the movies themselves, Lucasfilm's only consistent source of profit is merchandising.[6] There are literally hundreds of licenses for toys, decorator telephones, talking clocks, bicycles, lunchboxes, letter openers, children's and adult's underwear, pinball machines, video games, bumper stickers, candy, and ice cream and the bowls to eat it from. Lucasfilm also supervises the publication of novelizations, children's books, souvenir books, and comic books based on the *Star*

Wars and Indiana Jones films. The record group oversees sound-track albums, story records, and jazz and disco spinoff albums. The in-house art department designs some of the merchandise and creates stationery and company logos. No ad is done without Lucasfilm's approval, no license granted before careful scrutiny of the manufacturer and distributor. Lucas's philosophy of responsibility and control has become corporate policy.

From May 1977, when *Star Wars* was released, through May 1983, merchandising of Lucasfilm products approached $2 billion in retail sales, *before* the release of *Return of the Jedi*. The company gets a royalty of between 1 and 7 percent on most items, although on products like T-shirts, Lucasfilm's share is closer to 50 percent. Lucas always recognized the potential in merchandising but even he never imagined that a *Star Wars* label could mean a 20 percent increase in sales.

Lucas's personal beliefs suffuse the merchandising. Exploitative items are not sold, whether vitamins (he doesn't want to encourage kids to pop pills) or Princess Leia cosmetic kits (makeup can be harmful to children's skin). South Africa is boycotted in every respect but film sales, which are under Fox's control, because Lucas disagrees with the country's apartheid racial policies. He reviews every prototype toy (if Kenner Toys sold nothing but *Star Wars* merchandise, it would be the fifth largest toy company in the world) and maintains a veto power on all food tie-ins. Sugar cereals are verboten, but Hershey bars, Cokes, and milkshakes are okay. That was the stuff Lucas lived on as a kid—it's part of the American way of life.

There will be no one to stop us this time.

—Darth Vader in *Star Wars*

When the term "software" came to mean everything from movies and TV programs to floppy computer disks and video games, Lucas hated it. But he soon realized that he could become one of its premier suppliers. A new era was dawning and, ever the pragmatist, Lucas planned to take advantage of it.

He had enjoyed video games since they made their first appearance in the mid-1960s with "Pong," although he never became an addict like Spielberg, who has arcade games in his home and office. Lucas wanted more elaborate video games with sophisticated computer memories and player participation. Interactive games bring the player *into* the process, rather than simply allowing him to manipulate it. But in 1977 it seemed self-indulgent to start a computer company to develop games. That decision may have cost Lucas at least $1.8 billion, which were the revenues Atari, Inc. brought to Warner Communications in 1982. Atari profits to date easily dwarf the combined film rentals of *Star Wars*, *Empire*, and *Raiders*.

Lucas also wanted to develop a complete computerized postproduction system: editing, sound editing, sound mixing, and film printing. It let him rationalize developing computer games, computer animation, and computer simulation (re-creating images) at the same time. An outside firm constructed a computer-simulated spaceship battle, and the results looked as good as anything ILM had photographed. The process was costly and not yet economically feasible, but it *could* be done.

Starting a computer company from scratch is expensive and time-consuming. Lucas has already spent $8 million and still hasn't completed his postproduction system, which will revolutionize the mechanics of making movies. The drudge work will be done by the computer, leaving the filmmaker to think about how the movie fits together. Lucas wants to be on the cutting edge of film technology. People expect the creator of *Star Wars* to be ten steps ahead of the next guy.

Ed Catmull, the young director of the computer graphics department at the New York Institute of Technology, became Lucasfilm's resident electronic genius. Catmull resembles the traditional technofreak: long hair, thick glasses, and a Ph.D. in computer science. Lucas told him to spend a year studying how to marry film to computers and how much it would cost. "Trust me," Lucas said. "We'll have our computer division."

In one of Lucasfilm's nondescript buildings, Lucas's promise is coming true. Bicycles line the building's hallway; the rooms are cooled by special air conditioners that maintain the optimum temperature for computers. At the end of one hall is a room filled with twenty-five minicomputers, equipped with $1,100 circuit boards that do the work $250,000 computers used to perform. In an adjoining laboratory red, green, and blue laser beams zip around a $100,000 laser table, a prototype system built at Lucasfilm with the help of outside consultants. In the graphics room, computers generate "calculated synthetic images": a landscape of tall mountains topped by fluffy clouds is invitingly realistic; close examination reveals it consists of millions of tiny computer dots. No one wears white lab coats—the usual outfit is jeans, sneakers, and work shirts. The staff is uniformly young, white, and intense-looking. These people *are* creating the future.

The year Catmull spent analyzing Hollywood taught him that the movie industry was fifteen years away from the dimmest comprehension of computer science. In 1980 he compiled a three-year budget for developing electronic editing, sound mixing, and computer graphic systems. If time and money allowed, he would also work on a digital film printer for special effects shots and on computer-generated images as well. Swallowing hard, Catmull told Lucas the cost: $10 million. He ended up with $6 million for equipment, research, and staff and went after the top people in the computer business. Most of them were excited to work for George Lucas.

The computers didn't arrive until early 1981, but the computer development group was soon animating some scenes in *Return of the Jedi.* Eventually, computers may supply most of the exotic locales and devices in *Star Wars,* but not until computer time is cheaper than real time.

Lucas thinks that movies soon will be made and distributed on high-resolution video systems, with a picture quality superior to that of film. The advantages are numerous: video can be seen immediately, doesn't have to be lugged to and from a lab, and can be easily duplicated. Lucas also likes the flashing lights on a video control board, and the headphones. "I can pretend I'm a space pilot," he says jokingly.

When Lucas's postproduction system is perfected, a director will be able to take his movie home with him in a briefcase. He can watch the dailies or versions of different cuts on cassettes and disks. Unlike other computerized movie systems, Lucas designed his with the filmmaker in mind. Sound effects and music can be added as the film is edited, transferred from one taped version to another. The process saves hours of painstaking editing, the kind of work Lucas always hated.

Digital sound mixing saves time and money by allowing the director to alter dialogue without bringing actors in to rerecord it. The digital printer produces more sophisticated special effects than film labs can create—if there is a scratch down the middle of a frame of film, the computer can fill it in. Video images are less sharp than film, but the computer can double the number of scan lines, thus doubling the clarity of the image. The graphics simulator can create opening titles and duplicate exotic planets and strange creatures. "We're not going to simulate complete reality. You don't synthesize people," Ed Catmull says reassuringly. "Filmmaking is still telling stories with live actors."

Actors aren't required in video games, however. The *Star Wars, Empire,* and *Raiders* game cartridges are designed to make money and to reinforce Lucasfilm's reputation for distinctive, high-quality fun—they were best-sellers when introduced by Parker Brothers, a subsidiary of Kenner Toys. In June 1982 Lucas also joined forces with industry giant Atari to create computer software.

Lucas waxes eloquent on the subject of his simulation games, which he plans to make through his own company. A *Star Wars* game disk will come with a computerized control board that lets the pilot fire lasers, fly an X-wing fighter, and see a realistic point-of-view film shot on a TV screen. Suddenly a tie-fighter attacks. The player fires and either gets blown up himself (at which point the game ends) or blows up his attacker and proceeds toward the Death Star.

Other disks will place the player in the middle of a soap opera, a football game, a jungle adventure, or a slapstick comedy. "It's a movie, only you end up shooting ten different movies," Lucas says, bubbling with enthusiasm. "You'll have all these options and every time you play with the show, it can be a whole different movie."

Lucas always liked the fairy tale in which the anxious suitor has to guess which door conceals the princess—each door leads to a new adventure. His computer games trade on the same element of surprise, becoming dramatic experiences. George says, "It's melding games and psychology, and it's the most exciting thing I've found since I first got into film. It combines all the things I care about a lot: games (which are really toys), education, and storytelling. And you can do them all at once."

It is sort of a cinematic yacht club.

—George Lucas on Skywalker Ranch

Lucas Valley Road winds gently through the rolling hills of Marin County. Towering California redwoods suddenly block out the light, and the fog swirls around the large, unmarked gate. Down the recently paved road is a lake bordered by oaks, bays, and alders. There are bobcats and mountain lions in the hills; birds chatter and quail dart by. Almost three hundred head of cattle roam the meadows, looking for greenery that has survived the brutal sun. Vegetable gardens have just been planted, and the horse stable is almost finished. Skywalker Ranch is taking shape.

When Lucas saw Bulltail and Big Rock ranches for the first time, he wanted the view from each building to be unimpeded by any other structure. Each area was to give the illusion of total privacy. Lucas wanted to preserve the natural harmony of the land wherever possible; Marin County officials say he's one of the few developers to exceed the aesthetic requirements imposed on him.

Skywalker's buildings are surrounded by rock walls, made from stone quarried on the property. A mill shop makes double-hung Victorian windows, and a stained-glass studio fills the frames. The Skywalker Fire Department has two 1950 fire engines, fully restored and painted a bright burgundy, the Skywalker color featured on jackets and the ranch logo. The old cookhouse is now the accounting office; the bunkhouse is the headquarters for the ranch hands, who mend fences and check power lines. Hal Barwood and Matthew Robbins were the first tenants in the guesthouse, where visiting filmmakers will work. The back of the house has been divided into four hotel-size units with bathrooms and dining areas. The only kitchen is the communal one, where everyone takes meals.

Down a winding road, dominating Bulltail's central valley, is the mainhouse group, where Lucas will work and where the administrative and production offices will be relocated. There will be a recreation hall and a sophisticated computerized security system that electronically senses intruders and forest fires. An unarmed patrol service watches the ranch twenty-four hours a day; they are benign cops, Lucasland's equivalent of the polite Disneyland police. A second security gate bars access to the main house to anyone not in possession of a computer card. Beneath the shaggy meadows is an elaborate power distribution system, masses of telephone and computer cables, and a self-sufficient irrigation and water distribution system.

Lucas designed all this, in concept if not in detail. The ranch is the latest and greatest of his homemade environments. Marcia Lucas thinks that George deserves it. "The ranch is his reward for working hard," she says. "It's almost like he gets to treat himself." Skywalker Ranch may be Lucas's only concession to the pressures of success. "He's just a simple human being no longer leading a simple life," observes Bill Neil. "I think his not knowing how to really use money may be out of hand with the ranch."

Lucas's legal and business advisers agree. Bob Greber considers the ranch to be the real owner of the company—it gets all the dividends of Lucas's success. If Lucas sold it upon completion, it's doubtful he could get more than $7 million. If Skywalker fails, his only option may be to donate it to a local college and take a tax write-off. Greber hopes it will create income for Lucasfilm, but as he notes, "I *have* to look at it that way." If the ranch keeps Lucas and his friends happy, well then some good should come of it.

Lucas wants to keep Skywalker small, intimate, and noncommercial. He doesn't want half of Hollywood migrating to Lucas Valley Road. "It's extremely exclusive," he says of his "club's" membership. "It's limited to Marin County filmmakers who in most cases are my friends. We've all grown up together." There are no vacancies—and no desire for more friends. Lucas says he isn't being elitist, just realistic: "I'm trying to create an environment where we are free to exchange ideas, where someone isn't going to say, 'I gave you that idea and I want five points in your picture or I'll sue you.'"

Can the past be recaptured in an idyllic setting where good friends leave their egos at the front gate? It's possible, but not everyone believes in Camelot. To some friends, Skywalker Ranch is like George Lucas's Xanadu, the immense mansion built as a monument to Charles Foster Kane's accomplishments, which ends up becoming his tomb in *Citizen Kane*. Making films just isn't as much fun as it used to be. "Now it's a job," John Milius complains. "It's just work. It's not the same thing as it was then."

Instead of passion, people now have ulterior motives, ones they may not even recognize. Carroll Ballard foresees problems. "The people George wants out there are all independent types who want to do their own thing, which is why we're all friends to begin with." Ballard pauses and his face brightens. "But without utopian visions, where are we?"

I need talented young filmmakers to work for me. I know from experience that they don't grow on trees.

—George Lucas

If Lucas paid a spiritual debt to USC by creating Skywalker Ranch, he has also assumed a financial obligation to the private university. He has donated almost $5 million for a new USC cinema-TV center and inspired several million more in contributions from Steven Spielberg and Johnny Carson. It is Lucas's way of putting something back into the system that helped create him. His talent may have been natural, but USC drew it out of him. "I knew nothing about making films before I got to that school. It made me what I am today," he says.

Lucas lectured at the downtown campus for a few years after he graduated, but he quit after *Star Wars* when he was mobbed by students. He'd always planned to give USC a lump sum at the end of his career— who ever heard of a thirty-four-year-old alumnus contributing millions of dollars? But when there was difficulty raising the $13 million necessary for the new film school, he decided to act sooner. In November 1980, after seeing plans for new sound stages, a recording studio, a TV theater, and state-of-the-art editing rooms, Lucas pledged $3.6 million; the next day, he raised it to $4.7 million.

"The temptation for anybody might have been to take that five million dollars and start his own film school, on his own terms," says USCinema chairman Russ McGregor. Lucas didn't even want his name on a building. When asked by young people how to get into the movie business, Lucas tells them to go to film school—any film school, not just USC. He is embarrassed to be the ultimate film-student success—at USC they call it the Lucas syndrome, class after class who see film school as the pathway to riches and fame. "The only example I think I set is you don't have to put up with a lot of bullshit," Lucas says.

But he admits to less than altruistic motives in supporting USC—he needs young talent as much as anyone else. "What we're really talking about is ensuring the future of the industry," he says. Former students have directed the top five grossing films of all time and are responsible for more than $2 billion at the box office, but Lucas's generation is approaching middle age. The secret to success in Hollywood is new talent, and film schools breed talent. "Somehow in Hollywood there's no awareness of that," George complains. "The feeling is anyone can get off the bus and direct films."

The villains of the piece, of course, are the movie studios, which raid the film schools for talent while refusing to repay them. Lucas once suggested that the five major studios give back to USC just 1 percent of the profits they earned from the work of USCinema graduates. The suggestion went unheeded. "I've told George that all his negative comments about Hollywood would come back to haunt him," Tom Pollock says.

When USC gets its high-tech cinema center, the old army barracks will be torn down; the patio will be filled with rubble. Lucas is helping the old become the new, but there is something unique about grubby buildings with no windows, something that can't be duplicated in the new film complex. Dave Johnson, who taught Lucas at USC, looks around his cluttered office and reflects, "The atmosphere was and still is something special. You learned more out there in the patio from your fellow students than you'll ever learn in the classroom. This building's made out of wood, which is warm; there's grass growing, the banana tree, the bougainvillea bush that blooms every year. This is a warm, friendly place, not cold steel and cement. It's reality, it's grubby, it's conducive to what we're trying to do. If we lose that, we're gonna lose an awful lot."

George is the best kind of producer in the sense that he gives you the clout when you need it and he stays away otherwise.

—John Korty

Lucas is in an enviable position: he doesn't have to make movies. But he loves them too much not to. He may not direct films again, and writing them is too painful, but he can always be a producer. Lucas brings three special gifts to a movie he produces: his storytelling and editing talents, and his credibility.

It seems ironic that Lucas, the rabid independent who resented Warner Bros. assigning him an executive producer on *THX,* has taken on that role himself. It gives him all the benefits of movie making and none of the headaches. He can find flaws in a story line and not have to rewrite the script. He can offer editing hints, but he doesn't have to recut the film. Lucas is an ideal producer *because* he was a director—he understands the importance of freedom.

Coppola may have been the Godfather to one generation of filmmakers, but Lucas is Godfather II. Since *Star Wars,* he has helped Lawrence Kasdan, Willard Huyck and Gloria Katz, Akira Kurosawa, John Korty, Haskell Wexler, and Walter Murch place films at major studios. He has even repeated what Coppola did for him, using his presence to reassure a nervous studio about a young director's talent, as he did with Kasdan on *Body Heat.* The Ladd Company was ready to finance the movie, but Kasdan had never directed before. Lucas went over the script, watched screen tests, advised on the casting, saw the daily footage, and helped with the editing. Essentially, he was the studio executive on the project. "If everything goes wrong, they can yell at me," Lucas says with a laugh. "I'm just there to add a little confidence to the situation so they don't think the filmmaker's going crazy."

But Lucas didn't put his name on *Body Heat,* despite Ladd's urging and the fact that he was paid $250,000 and 5 percent of the film's profits to act as unofficial executive producer. Lucas explains, "When I put my name on something, I have to get paid for it, otherwise it just becomes a charity thing. People in Hollywood say, 'Well, if you can get hold of one of George's friends, you can get George for nothing.' I can't do that." There were other reasons for Lucas's reluctance to be publicly associated with *Body Heat,* a steamy R-rated film about a sexual triangle, featuring nudity and profanity. Lucas told Kasdan how the media would react: "The people who made *Star Wars* are now making porno films!" Lucas knows his name represents a certain kind of picture, and *Body Heat* wasn't it. He did agree to be named as executive producer on John Korty's animated film for Ladd, *Twice Upon a Time,* but it had a G rating.

Lucas says that he doesn't have to endorse a movie's morality to support it. Friendship is the sole reason he becomes involved: "I don't start out thinking, 'Well, gee, if I help them now, I can sign them to a contract or I can get them to do another movie for me.' My feeling is you give something to somebody because you like them and you believe in what they're doing. You don't do it with any thought of repayment or return."

Lucas talks of creating his own small production unit with staff writers, Monday morning story conferences, and a slate of four or five movies a year, but he doesn't seem too serious. Still, it's the closest he's come to moving Hollywood to San Anselmo. There will be another Indiana Jones film released in 1984 and an occasional abandoned project might be revived, such as *Radioland Murders,* an elaborate murder mystery written by the Huycks and set in a 1930s radio station. The options are numerous and Lucas has the time and money to pick and choose exactly what he wants.

"He has found his new calling," Tom Pollock says of his longtime client. "George can make wonderful movies by hiring the right people and not having to direct himself. I hope he continues to do it, without the pressure of *having* to do it. Making movies is fun when you don't have to do all the hard work."

10
A TIME NOT SO FAR AWAY

It's not what you say, or what people think of you, it's what you *do* that counts.

—George Lucas

It was a June Saturday night in Modesto and the teenagers were cruising McHenry Avenue, leaning out the windows of their souped-up custom cars, yelling to their friends. The traffic was so thick that George and Marcia Lucas had difficulty getting to the Modesto Elks Lodge. Lucas smiled at the familiar scene—he was an original cruiser from 1962. But instead of wearing a white T-shirt and sitting behind the wheel of his Fiat Bianchina, Lucas had on a coat and tie and was driving his $35,000 BMW. You can't stay seventeen forever.[1]

The Lucases were on their way to Thomas Downey High School's twentieth class reunion. George hadn't existed for most of the three hundred attendees when they were in school together—if they remembered him at all, it was as a shy, skinny kid with big ears who got into a terrible car accident just before graduation. But he was the one who had immortalized his classmates in *American Graffiti*. The only other '62 Downey graduate with a claim to fame was Dan Archer, who played a few seasons for the Oakland Raiders. Nobody asked for his autograph.

Lucas had been looking forward to the reunion, until stories about it began appearing in the newspapers, like the one in the *Los Angeles Times* headlined "Lucas Recalled as a 'Wimp.'" Most of the disparaging remarks were made by people who barely knew Lucas, like Dennis Kamstra, a salesman of animal pharmaceuticals—he told a reporter that Lucas was his locker partner, "the kind of wimp you used to slap around

265

with a towel." Lucas was quiet and small, but he insists he was no wimp. "I never got beaten up in school, that's for sure. I had my friends," Lucas says.

The negative comments, whether said in ignorance or envy, should have warned Lucas of what was to come. As soon as he put on the name tag bearing his high school picture, heads turned and voices whispered. Soon George was besieged by autograph-seekers thrusting programs, cocktail napkins, placemats, and business cards at him. Lucas spent much of the evening patiently signing his name for people he didn't even know, the first time so many adults had asked for his autograph. He had naïvely assumed that the luster of his *Star Wars* fame had worn off.

In a class whose graduates had become teachers and doctors, account-ants and pharmacists, real estate and water bed salesmen, George Lucas was a star. "People came up whom I'd gone to school with since I was in kindergarten and said, 'Gee, I don't know whether you'll remember me . . .' Why wouldn't I remember them? You know somebody for fifteen years, you're not going to forget them," he says. Other friends like John Plummer, who have kept in touch with Lucas, were distressed to see the toll success had taken on him: the gray hairs in his beard, the lines on his forehead, the bags under his eyes. Plummer says, "It's a sad commentary when your career begins to consume you."

George had looked through his high school yearbook before going to the reunion and was surprised to see how many classmates had written encouraging messages about his artistic ability. Lucas told one matronly woman he saw for the first time in twenty years, "You told me in my yearbook that I'd be where I am today." Lucas grins, then adds, "Gave her a big thrill." If anything distinguished Lucas from his 584 Downey High classmates, it was that he had been lucky enough to find something he was good at, then busted his ass to become better.

At the Elks Lodge on this Saturday night, however, everyone thought Lucas had hidden talents that had gone unperceived, that he had been lucky beyond imagination, that he was a genius who had flowered late in life. Lucas did little to dispel that image—he joshed with classmates, patiently put up with questions from reporters, and got to enjoy some time with old friends.

The unreality of the event was highlighted near its conclusion. A TV camera crew entered the hall to tape a segment for a local news show. Lucas grabbed his friend Bruce Valentine, who also wears glasses and has a gray-flecked beard, and switched nametags. The TV reporter began an earnest interview with Valentine, only realizing her mistake when the crowd could no longer contain its laughter.

Lucas had made his point. It didn't matter *who* was George Lucas—it was a name and a reputation, not a person. For the first time, Lucas truly perceived the gulf between his past and his present life. It was as if Luke had returned to Tatooine and been given a hero's welcome. "I'm in such a different world," Lucas says, shaking his head at the memory of the reunion. "In that situation it was literally like I was from another planet."

Getting here was a lot more fun than being here.

—Marcia Lucas

What do you do if you're thirty-nine, worth more than $60 million, and you feel like you're from another planet? George Lucas is stopping to look around. It's time he changed directions, and his problem is that he has too many options. He could run Skywalker Ranch, direct the course of Lucasfilm Ltd., make more *Star Wars* and *Raiders* movies, design interactive computer games, go back to college, or bring college to himself—the possibilities seem endless. If this is a midlife crisis, it could be a lot worse.

For a variety of reasons, the bits and pieces of Lucas's life are coalescing, depositing him at a crossroads. "It's a great opportunity a lot of people don't ever get," Lucas says. "I may be making a big mistake, I'll maybe lose two or three years of my life screwing around, but I feel it's something I have to do." Destiny is again knocking on Lucas's door; his inner voice, which has never failed him, has a one-word message: "Stop." Lucas now spends more time with his family, has started jogging at the ranch (he *hates* jogging), and plays with his daughter. He and Marcia plan to adopt more children and they have become his new motivation. If Marcia has failed to temper Lucas's obsession with work, Amanda and her siblings-to-be will probably succeed.

Dropping out of sight isn't easy when you're George Lucas. Like it or not, he is under a magnifying glass, scrutinized by *Star Wars* fans, Hollywood columnists, and film lovers everywhere. Lucas, whose naïveté would be tiresome if it weren't genuine, summarizes his career by saying, "I just sort of started off in one direction and found myself going in another, despite my best interests." The other direction led to *American Graffiti, Star Wars, Empire, Raiders,* and *Jedi,* four (and presumably five) of the most successful movies ever made.

Yet the next few years are crucial to Lucas. He has a good idea of what he'll be doing, but it's fun to pretend otherwise. The release of *Jedi* completes the first *Star Wars* trilogy. The ranch will be finished. He may start a production company. He'll be actively involved in his computer company, developing educational video games. And he'll probably make small esoteric movies, on film or high-resolution videotape. Lucas wants to learn more about anthropology and social science and expects to import private tutors to Skywalker. There are too many choices—Lucas doesn't know where to turn first.

At the July 4, 1981, Lucasfilm picnic a time capsule filled with personal, corporate, and movie memorabilia was placed in the cornerstone of the main house at Skywalker Ranch. The black cylinder (designed at ILM) contained *Star Wars* action figures, books of artwork from *Star Wars* and *Empire,* a Snow Walker paperweight, the original Lucasfilm contract with Universal for *American Graffiti* and an "unnamed science-fiction adventure," copies of most of Lucas's screenplays, and a small button that contained two words crucial to the success of George Lucas: "Question Authority."

It's hard for Lucas to question authority when he's the chairman of a multimillion-dollar corporation. Yet he won't let go of Lucasfilm until he's sure it can support him and his wildest dreams. Those who have heard George vow to remove himself from films or the company have never seen him leave anything alone. There are serious doubts whether Lucasfilm can survive without Lucas, although his goal is to become dispensable. He wants to find a few talented people who will find more talented people, who can run Lucasfilm without him. Time to switch, Lucas says, "from a real high-intensity menu to a low-intensity one."

The one division of Lucasfilm that will continue to get the boss's attention is the computer development group. Lucas's next major goal is to revamp the educational system in America, augmenting teachers, textbooks, and lectures with interactive video disks. Lucas doesn't believe he'll come close to this goal, but then Skywalker Ranch once seemed an impossibility. He is spurred by his conviction that computer games might as well be put to good use: "I don't care how wrong they are, they aren't going to stop. The best thing to do is make the programming more humane."

Lucas thinks he's the right man for the job. He has a company attuned to the sensibilities, desires, and gratifications of young people all over the world. Lucas's films duplicate adolescence. They're roller-coaster rides that supply the emotional highs and lows that children and teenagers experience. With his own computers and programmers, Lucas can make education entertaining.

The only thing Lucas looked forward to in high school was educational movies. Wouldn't it be great if all of school was like this? he thought at the time. "We'd just see movies all the time and not have to listen to these boring lectures or read these terrible assignments." Well, why *not* make school into movies on TV? Why not get the best material and the best teachers and make tapes and disks part of the school curriculum? Kids won't realize how much they're learning because they'll think they're playing games. Many classes will require only teaching assistants and video machines, vastly reducing the cost of public education. Lucas calls this "subversive education," the logical extension of the daydreams he had while watching movies in high school. He never was interested in math or literature because those subjects were bludgeoned into his head, and he resisted mightily. Lucas wants to change the methodology of teaching, but he doesn't seem to care that he's fashioning an educational system in his own image. He's not just another voice in the educational marketplace— he's the creator of *Star Wars* and has a tremendous influence on people under the age of eighteen. There are times when he says to himself, "Gee, do I have a right to do this?" But he also has an answer ready: "Somebody's going to do it, and the worst thing is for it to happen randomly."

Lucas has a *plan*, which puts him ahead of 99 percent of the rest of the people on this planet. He thinks his methods are better because he teaches the right things: respect for family, the virtues of being fair, honest, and generous. He knows he'll never replace the current educational system; it's far too entrenched: "But I may possibly, if fate allows, point to a new direction. And maybe more capable individuals with infinitely more resources could come up with a better system and actually do it."

He's following his own path. No one can choose it for him.
  —Obi-Wan Kenobi speaking to Luke Skywalker in *Star Wars*

Lucas has never kept his beliefs to himself. *THX* was an intellectual debate between reality and illusion that had always intrigued him. *Graffiti* was a celebration of his own adolescence. It wasn't until *Star Wars*, however, that he applied a layer of morality to his message. He has occasionally questioned the consequences of his actions, but he plows ahead anyway. Lucas admits that he offers simpleminded solutions to complex problems, "but if someone would just take one of those simple-minded solutions, the world might be a better place to live."

Lucas is a strange blend of naïve openness and cyncial skepticism, and defining right and wrong is easy for him. Freedom, liberty, and justice are the virtues celebrated in *Star Wars*—Lucas can't see anything wrong with that. "George is very worldly," says Matthew Robbins. "He just thinks the world should be a certain way."

Lucas is adept at punching the right buttons to evoke his world. The basic principles of child psychology underlie all three *Star Wars* movies, coated with the gloss of fantasy and disguised with fast editing. "All you have to do is give the audience an emotion," Lucas says. "It's so simple. You either make them laugh, you make them cry, or you scare them, and you've got yourself a hit. If you can do two of those things in a picture, you've got a mega-hit. I can make 'em laugh and I can get 'em excited. I can give 'em a thrill and make 'em laugh at the same time, but I can't make 'em cry."

Lucas is ready and willing to manipulate his audience. *Star Wars* is filled with fighting, yet no blood is visible. *Empire* was considered too violent to be seen by children in Sweden. *Raiders* evoked protests over its violence and intensity and was censored in many countries.

Lucas tries to make a distinction between violence and intensity in his films. "All good movies should be exciting and scary. Intense just means it works." He says he took great pains to deemphasize the killings in *Star Wars* and still professes concern over two Imperial guards who are shot on camera. But the sight of the blackened, smoking remains of Uncle Owen and Aunt Beru is more upsetting than most of the laser battles, as is the torture robot seen approaching Princess Leia as her cell door discreetly closes. Lucas relies on implicit violence, whose effects may be just as damaging to children. *The Empire Strikes Back* escalated the level and intensity of the fight scenes, with a closeup of Luke's hand being sliced off. By *Raiders*, Lucas seemed inured to random violence in movies he produces. Yet on a personal level, he is still offended by it. When Lawrence Kasdan toyed with killing one of the major characters in *Jedi*, Lucas lectured him, "You are a product of the nineteen eighties. You don't go around killing people—it's not nice."

Lucas is a firm believer in dramatic conflict. He remembers his own feelings of anger and frustration as a child, knowing that children subconsciously respond to the expression of those emotions on a large screen. While the amputation of Luke's hand in *Empire* has a psychological justification (a clear expression of boys' castration fears), justifying the random violence in *Raiders* is more difficult. Lucas uses terms like "therapeutic" and "nondestructive," but few nine-year-olds can erase from their memories the image of the Nazis' faces melting at the film's conclusion.

Lucas tries harder than most filmmakers to avoid being violent, racist, sexist, or fascist, although he's accused of all these sins by some critics. He says the criticism doesn't bother him, first, because he doesn't think it's true, and second, because he makes his movies ultimately for himself. "I make movies that I enjoy. And I know how to make movies that are entertaining because I love movies myself," Lucas says.

That sounds dangerously simplistic, but it's true. Lucas also believes that movies are good for people. During a story conference on *Jedi*, Lucas told Kasdan, "The whole emotion I am trying to get at the end of this film is for you to be emotionally and spiritually uplifted and to feel absolutely good about life. That is the greatest thing that we could ever possibly do." And Lucas has done it. Movie audiences are made up of individual people with common needs, which Lucas satisfies in the same way he satisfies his own.

His films tell us more about ourselves than we may wish to know. We cheer Luke Skywalker because we know most of us will never do what he's doing (and what Lucas did): beat the system. We cheer Indiana Jones because it was so much easier in 1936 to tell whom the bad guys were— they wore Nazi uniforms. Lucas offers more than just escapist entertainment; he gives us a vision of what could be and what should be, but not in our world. His films are set in the past or the future, but never the present.

The major criticism of Lucas is that he's incapable of making a movie about *today*, concerning contemporary adults who live and work and love and die. He seems permanently stuck in adolescence. Lucas thinks there's room for all kinds of movies; the fact that *Star Wars* was designed for young people does not automatically make it bubble gum for the mind. He simply targeted an audience that had not yet formed its prejudices. Movie critics are adults, however, and Lucas is critically perceived as a purveyor of popular pap. Pauline Kael accused *Star Wars* of turning movies into toys. Critic David Thomson once wrote, "I have never felt in a Lucas film that if I went out for a pee or a hot dog, I would miss anything. It is not in the nature of the films that there is anything so important there."[2]

Lucas thinks most critics are unfit to pass judgment on any director's work. It's easy to be glib about *Star Wars*, he says—there are things he'll criticize himself. "But if it was nothing," he muses, "why did everyone like it so much? What we're talking about here is effectiveness—the more people who see it, the more effective the film is." Lucas wasn't subtle about the message in *Star Wars:* there comes a time when you can't hide from problems and you have to take responsibility for your actions. "But because I don't come out and say MESSAGE in big red letters, it goes right past everybody," Lucas says. The first *Star Wars* trilogy is a complex series of films, the product of considerable research and thought. At the same time, Lucas sees them as "dumb" entertainments. He has no use for the

Star Wars devotees who treat them as scripture. "Come on," Lucas says, "they're only *movies*."

They're very influential movies, however. By aiming them at a particularly impressionable audience, Lucas is inviting close scrutiny. The effect of *Star Wars* on several generations of young filmgoers may not be apparent for years, but it is clearly a powerful one. Lucas is dealing with the big issues here, God and the Devil, good and evil, and the ways he illustrates them resonate in moviegoers' minds. Film is a perishable medium, but the images stay with us, becoming part of the way we define ourselves. *Star Wars* has become a culture unto itself.

The technical criticisms of Lucas are not as widespread, but there are flaws in his movie making. He sacrifices story development for action and has little respect for the intelligence of the audience. He is afraid they'll get bored because he's bored. Carl Foreman, who gave Lucas his first scholarship, admires Lucas's technical skills. "But when it comes to characters, he's shit," Foreman says. "He knows the medium, he knows celluloid. But he has no time for characters." One of the most telling comments came from a crew member on *Return of the Jedi,* who leaned back after hours spent setting up a special effects shot and muttered, "Someday I want to work on a movie that makes you think."

But critics are foolish to write off Lucas as dumb or insensitive. No one else has been able to duplicate the innocence and uninhibited creative energy in his films. Even Hollywood respects those qualities. "He's unique unto himself," says Paramount's Michael Eisner. "There's no question that he'll have a place as a great American artist." Being recognized as an artist holds no more allure for Lucas than being called a genius. Marcia used to get angry when critics put down George as a commercial moviemaker, not a serious director, because his films made lots of money. She would complain, but Lucas didn't care.

George thinks artists are created by the media, not by their work. He explains, "I could be a great artist if I wanted to be, just by saying the right things to the press and the critics and by making the right kind of movies that are obviously art with a capital A." He's never had time for such foolishness. Yet he cares about his reputation; he wants to be taken as seriously as Francis Coppola, who *is* considered an artist. Failure sharpens the aura of the artist, while success obliterates it. As long as Lucas's films are popular, they won't be taken seriously, not even by the movie industry, which has yet to give him a Best-Picture or Best-Director Oscar.

To Lucas, *Star Wars* is popular art, "the stuff that becomes the significant residue of a civilization." Lucas's home and offices are filled with art that was never taken seriously but is now worth a fortune. He collects Norman Rockwell paintings and original comic strips, not because of their monetary value or because they justify his own work. "As dumb as it seems, they say something about the nineteen thirties and forties in this country, about a certain idealism that people believed in then, that is never going to happen again," he says. Lucas thinks of *American Graffiti* like that, as a living piece of history. One hundred years from now, an anthropologist can screen *Graffiti* and learn a great deal of what it was like to be a teenager in America just before the world turned upside down. Now *that*, Lucas thinks, is valuable.

Maybe someday I'll be able to shoot a film I'm proud of.

—George Lucas

Lucas wants to rediscover the virtues of being an amateur. He has wanted to make esoteric movies like *THX* since he left USC; now he has the time and money and equipment to do it. A thirteen-year-old dream may not turn out at all as Lucas imagined. But he's determined to make films that are abstract and emotional, without plot or characters. He won't talk about specific ideas—he seems unsure exactly what he wants to do—but it's clear that these impressionistic works are the complete opposite of his professional films.

"I've been warped by storytelling," Lucas says. He used to hate conventional drama, but he's become alarmingly proficient at it. Now he wants to go in the other direction, toward films that are "nonlinear, noncharacter, and nonstory, but still evoke emotions." Lucas wonders if he can still make people laugh and cry with an abstract movie. He wants to see how many of the familiar signposts in a film can be ignored before the moviegoer gets lost.

Contemporary American culture fascinates Lucas—it's the stuff of his dreams and movies. He wants to record other aspects of society the way he did teenage cruising in *Graffiti*. He sees himself as a camera-laden Indiana Jones, in search of celluloid artifacts. "I'm interested in how and why a society works and how the people in it think," Lucas explains. He created his own society in *Star Wars*. Now he wants to document the real world.

Whatever Lucas finds with his experimental films he'll probably keep to himself: "If they don't work, I'm certainly not going to show them to anybody. If they do work, they'll probably get a very limited release." There is no sizable audience for avant-garde movies, but if one comes out bearing Lucas's name, audiences probably will line up. Then again,

Lucas may not like his "crazy movies" and will stop doing them altogether. "It's not the end of the world if I decide I don't like it," he says. "But at least I'll get to try it."

Those most intrigued by Lucas's plans are his friends, most of whom regretted his decision to stop directing. Steven Spielberg and John Milius want to see Lucas make the "George film," the one that pulls the best stuff out of him. Lucas has recycled his past in his previous movies. "He has a lot to say *now*," Milius notes. "It could be very interesting to see what he comes up with."

Lucas's retreat to experimental films may be a way of hiding from the next logical film in his limited body of work. Maybe he's afraid of what he'll find out about himself; it's safer to play with images that aren't so specific. Lucas says he'll return to directing, but only if he can control the situation. "I'm tired of painting Sistine Chapels," he says. "I'd rather go back to little four-by-five canvases." He'll shoot them himself, cut them himself, and spend a long time on them. He wants to be self-indulgent for a change. "I've earned it." But Lucas won't be able to escape himself. Walter Murch says, "You are what you make, and the films make you. You put so much of yourself into your films. There's no way around it. You can only make what you are."

I've got to find a clone of myself. I'm getting too old for this.
　　　　　　　　—George Lucas on the set of *Return of the Jedi*

The most logical thing for George Lucas to direct is more *Star Wars* movies, which is precisely what he won't do. He only completed the first trilogy, he says, because "I had a slight compulsion to finish the story." *Jedi* may be the last film George Lucas really cares about. He has little emotional investment in future Indiana Jones movies, or even in the next *Star Wars* trilogy, should it ever be made. Nothing will match the all-consuming sense of mission that he brought to the first three films.

Many people associated with *Star Wars* will be relieved if the saga doesn't continue. "Massa George says ah kin go, at the end of 'eighty-five—a freed man!" jokes Harrison Ford, who still has a *Raiders* sequel to complete before his emancipation. If Lucas made all six of the remaining *Star Wars* movies at three-year intervals, the story wouldn't conclude until the year 2001 (someone's idea of a sci-fi in-joke).

There are times when Lucas is ready to chuck the whole thing. Walking across Elstree Studios during the filming of *Jedi*, he fantasizes selling *Star*

Wars—the concept, the characters, and the plots for all six films.

What if the inheritor of the *Star Wars* legacy screwed up and made a lousy movie? Wouldn't that be painful? Not at all, Lucas says. "I've always thought I did a bad job. This might make me feel better." To some people, the idea of Lucas selling *Star Wars* is like Moses auctioning off the Ten Commandments. It may not be prudent from a business point of view, either: six *Star Wars* movies could easily sell a billion dollars' worth of tickets. Lucas is just perverse enough to do it, however. There are other things in life.

Later, he admits that the fantasy of dumping *Star Wars* is an escape valve, giving him the illusion he can always back out. "Emotionally, it would be very hard to do," he admits. Lucas is aware that *Star Wars* and its sequels are bankable investments. His battles with 20th Century-Fox taught him that films are products to be exploited to their fullest value. "They're not sacred, as far as I'm concerned," Lucas says. "They're ultimately tools." Lucas the businessman intends to wring every possible dollar out of his prize property.

Lucas says he can separate this mercenary instinct from the artistic side of making movies, in which the filmmaker tries never to compromise his values for money. His hard-nosed business attitude is a recent development, but not an unexpected one. He has specific goals and he needs money to achieve them. He has a company and people who depend on him for their livelihood. If it was just he, Marcia, Amanda, and Indiana, he might pack up and quit, but he can't. The films are only a means to an end, says Lucas: "This company isn't designed to go on for the next thousand years. It's designed to service me while I'm alive and to give me the things that I want to do. All I have to do is cash in my chips and say, 'I'm through.'"

The chips are riding on *Return of the Jedi*—the degree of its success will define how much free time and money Lucas has to pursue his dreams. The end of the *Star Wars* trilogy is the pivotal point in Lucas's life so far. *Jedi* is a movie he first wanted to make as *Apocalypse Now:* the story of the little guys fighting the technological superpowers and winning because they *believe* in themselves. By finally expressing this theme in *Jedi*, George is also summarizing his own career.

Lucas has learned something since 1977—the pace of *Jedi* is closer to that of *Raiders* than to either of the previous *Star Wars* movies. There are elements from swashbucklers, biker films, and adventure stories. It's his favorite script, although he worries that the more he likes a script, the less popular the film is. He is so fond of *Jedi* that he even flirted with the idea of directing it. Sanity quickly returned: "I took one look at the amount of work and thought, Oh my God, my life is complicated enough.'"

There is a special satisfaction for Lucas in seeing his little saga neatly wrap itself up, like the fairy tale it really is. Lucas worried that audiences would expect something more spectacular than the obvious resolution. But he had to be true to the story, which literally poured out of him—he wrote the first draft of *Jedi* in four weeks, a far cry from the two years it took him to write *Star Wars*. Everything had to be just right—Lucas knows how much his fans care. Although *Revenge of the Jedi* was the first title announced, Lucas always intended for the film to be called *Return of the Jedi*. He just didn't want to give away the plot. The switch came less than six months before *Jedi*'s release and cost several thousand dollars.

Lucas thought it would cost too much money to top *Empire,* and *Jedi* is really less expensive, given inflation. All of it was George's own money, a fact impressed upon everyone associated with the production. The schedule was shorter than *Empire*'s, too, although ninety-two days is not short to anyone working on a movie. Lucas wanted to disguise *Jedi* when it filmed in Arizona and California so that the company would not be besieged by *Star Wars* fans. Lucas picked the title *Blue Harvest,* pretending it was a horror film. He even had T-shirts printed up bearing the title and another phrase, "Horror Beyond Imagination." Someone asked if that was what *Blue Harvest* was about. "No," said Lucas, "that's the making of the movie."

Lucas didn't want to repeat the financial crisis on *Empire* and was more visible on the set of *Jedi*. He calls it "hanging around" and "watching out," but insists he was not directing: "No matter what people think, you can't direct over somebody's shoulder. It's too subtle an art." Richard Marquand seemed not to resent his presence, and Lucas had fun operating the fourth or fifth camera on second-unit shots. "I'm more of a security net than anything else," Lucas says.

The movie Marquand was making was not the movie Lucas would have made, however. There are times when he stifled a thought like "Shit, if I could just get in there and clean it up. . . ." There were scenes he watched in the editing room that made his teeth grind. "I find I'm more intolerant now than I've been in the past," Lucas admits. But he also knows that the movie may be different, but not necessarily better or worse. "If I wanted it the way *I* wanted it, I'd direct it myself," he says. "But since I've given that up, I have to accept the way somebody else directs it."

It has been a long day at Elstree. As usual, Lucas has to solve everyone's problems, from deciding how to dispose of the *Millennium*

Falcon when *Jedi* is finished to checking the waggling tongue of Jabba the Hutt. Lucas climbs into his Mercedes limousine, which is awaiting him at the studio gate; his body literally sags. He leans his head back against the seat in exhaustion.

"Marcia complains that I either live in the past or in the future, but never in the present," George says, his voice slipping an octave lower as the limo silently glides back to London and Claridge's, the posh hotel where his family is staying. "In a way, she's right. I'm always thinking about what's going to happen or what has happened. I think when I finish this film I'll be able to live in the present—maybe." Lucas looks out the window as the car pulls up to Claridge's, and a stiffly dressed doorman materializes at the door. Lucas grabs his thin briefcase, bids his visitor good-bye, and exits the car, heading for the ornate gold doors to the hotel's lobby. He looks strangely out of place, this small, bearded American in blue jeans and sneakers, rubbing shoulders with visiting Arab sheiks, European businessmen, and the elite of London society. Even the doorman, towering over Lucas, regards him with a slight air of disdain, not realizing that the object of his scorn could afford to *buy* Claridge's. Lucas looks back at the car, the streetlights glinting off his glasses, and then he is gone, lost among the rich and famous.

The door to your cage is open. All you have to do is walk out, if you dare.

—George Lucas

Lucas thinks he was put here for a purpose, but he's not sure he has fulfilled it. Maybe it was *Star Wars,* or maybe Skywalker Ranch. Maybe it still lies ahead in his educational computer games. Marcia Lucas looks back on her life with George and says, "It's like reading a good book. You never want to finish it, because you will have read it and you won't ever be able to read it that way again."

Lucas sees his life as a camera winding down. As it runs out of power, the camera's image speeds up. Now he's trying to slow down the images of his life, but time is growing ever more scarce, even as his aspirations grow bigger and bigger. Lucas has been so successful because of his ability to transfer his vision onto the screen. Now his visions are too big for a screen—they may even be too big for him. Lucas has lived his life with his destiny extended before him like a carrot on a stick. One of his least favorite fantasies is about when he dies. He thinks God will look at him and say, "You've had your chance and you blew it. Get out."

Hardly likely. The door to George's cage opened when he regained consciousness in a Modesto hospital on June 12, 1962. He saw his path to the sky and he's been walking up it ever since. "There is no try," Yoda lectured Luke. "There is only do or do not." When it came down to that choice, Lucas did.

FILMOGRAPHY

Student and Short Films

LOOK AT LIFE (1965)

Directed by George Lucas for a University of Southern California Cinema School class in film animation.

HERBIE (1966)

Directed by George Lucas and Paul Golding for a USC lighting class; features a jazz score by Herbie Hancock.

1:42:08 (1966)

Written and directed by George Lucas; stars race car driver Pete Brock; made on location in the Mojave Desert.

THE EMPEROR (1967)

Directed by George Lucas; edited by Paul Golding; stars Bob Hudson, disc jockey at KBLA Radio, Burbank, California.

THX 1138:4EB (ELECTRONIC LABYRINTH) (1967)

Written and directed by George Lucas; cast and crew supplied by United States Navy; winner of first prize at Third National Student Film Festival.

ANYONE LIVED IN A PRETTY HOW TOWN (1967)

Directed by George Lucas; written by Lucas and Paul Golding, based on a poem by E. E. Cummings; photographs by Rick Robertson.

6-18-67 (1967)

Directed by George Lucas; filmed in Page, Arizona, during the filming of *McKenna's Gold;* financed by a scholarship from Producer Carl Foreman and Columbia Pictures.

FILMMAKER (1968)

Written, directed, photographed, and edited by George Lucas; documentary of the making of *The Rain People,* a 1968 film directed by Francis Coppola; stars Coppola, Shirley Knight, James Caan, and crew members of Zoetrope Productions; running time: original version, 64 minutes; revised version, 32 minutes.

Feature Films

THX 1138 (1971)

PRODUCTION INFORMATION AND PRINCIPAL CREDITS. Filmed in the San Francisco Bay Area for 40 days in 1969 on a budget of $777,000; filmed in Technicolor and Techniscope; released by Warner Bros. on March 11, 1971; original running time: 88 minutes; restored running time: 95 minutes; MPAA rating: PG; a Warner Bros. release of an American Zoetrope production; *executive producer:* Francis Coppola; *producer:* Lawrence Sturhahn; *director:* George Lucas; *screenplay:* Lucas and Walter Murch, from a story by Lucas; *directors of photography:* Dave Meyers, Albert Kihn; *editor:* George Lucas; *art direction:* Michael Haller; *music:* Lalo Schifrin; *sound montages:* Walter Murch.
CAST. *THX:* Robert Duvall; *SEN:* Donald Pleasance; *LUH:* Maggie McOmie; *SRT:* Don Pedro Colley; *PTO:* Ian Wolfe; *NCH:* Sid Haig; *TWA:* Marshall Efron; *DWY:* John Pearce; *Chrome Robots:* Johnny Weismuller, Jr., Robert Feero; *IMM:* Irene Forrest; *ELC:* Claudette Bessing.
TECHNICAL CREDITS. *Location sound:* Lou Yates, Jim Manson; *associate producer:* Ed Follger; *titles and animation:* Hal Barwood; *property master:* Ted Moehnke; *costumes:* Donald Longhurst; *production assistants:* Stan Scholl, Nick Saxton, George Burrafato; *continuity:* Lillian McNeill; *car stunts:* Jon Ward; *bike stunts:* Duffy Hamilton.

AMERICAN GRAFFITI (1973)

PRODUCTION INFORMATION AND PRINCIPAL CREDITS. Filmed in Marin and Sonoma counties, California, in 1972 for 28 days on a budget of $775,000; filmed in Technicolor; completed at American Zoetrope Studios, San Francisco; released by Universal Pictures August 1, 1973; rereleased May 26, 1978, in restored version; running time: 110 minutes; MPAA Rating: PG; nominated for five 1973 Academy Awards: Best Picture, Direction, Original Screenplay, Supporting Actress (Candy Clark); Film Editing; winner of 1973 Best Screenplay Awards from New York Film Critics and National Society of Film Critics; a Universal Pictures release of a Lucasfilm Ltd./Coppola Company production; *producer:* Francis Coppola; *coproducer:* Gary Kurtz; *director:* George Lucas; *screenplay:* George Lucas and Gloria Katz and Willard Huyck; *visual consultant (supervising cameraman):* Haskell Wexler; *operating cameramen:* Ron Eveslage, Jan D'Alquen; *editors:* Verna Fields, Marcia Lucas; *art direction:* Dennis Clark; *sound montage and rerecording:* Walter Murch; *casting:* Fred Roos, Mike Fenton; *design consultant:* Al Locatelli; *costume design:* Aggie Guerard Rodgers; *production manager:* James Hogan; *first assistant director:* Ned Kopp.
CAST. *Curt:* Richard Dreyfuss; *Steve:* Ron Howard; *John:* Paul LeMat; *Terry:* Charles Martin Smith; *Laurie:* Cindy Williams; *Debbie:* Candy Clark; *Carol:* Mackenzie Phillips; *Disc Jockey:* Wolfman Jack; *Bob Falfa:* Harrison Ford; *Joe:* Bo Hopkins; *Carlos:* Manuel Padilla, Jr.; *Ants:* Beau Gentry; *Peg:* Kathleen Quinlan; *Eddie:* Tim Crowley; *Mr. Wolfe:* Terry McGovern; *Budda:* Jana Bellan; *Blonde in T-Bird:* Suzanne Somers; *Falfa's girl:* Debralee Scott; *Herby and the Heartbeats:* Flash Cadillac and the Continental Kids.
SUPPORTING CAST. Kay Lenz, Jan Wilson, Kay Ann Kemper, Caprice Schmidt, Irving Israel, Joe Spano, Chris Pray, Susan Richardson, Donna Wehr, Jim Bohan, Ron Vincent, Fred Ross, Jody Carlson, Cam Whitman, John Bracci, Debbie Celiz, Lynne Marie Stewart, Ed Greenberg, Gordon Analla, Lisa Herman, Charles Dorsett, Stephen Knox, John Brent, Bob Pasaak, Joseph Miksak,

George Meyer, William Niven, James Cranna, Del Close, Charlie Murphy, Jan Dunn, Johnny Weismuller, Jr., Scott Beach, Al Nalbandian.

TECHNICAL CREDITS. *Second assistant director:* Charles Myers; *assistant to the producer:* Beverly Walker; *production associates:* Nancy Giebink, Jim Bloom; *choreographer:* Toni Basil; *dialogue coach:* Gino Havens; *production sound:* Arthur Rochester; *set decorator:* Douglas Freeman; *gaffer:* William Maley; *key grip:* Ken Phelps; *property master:* Douglas Von Koss; *key hair stylists:* Gerry Leetch, Betty Iverson; *script supervisor:* Christina Crowley; *transportation supervisor:* Henry Travers; *sound editing:* James Nelson; *music coordinator:* Karin Green; *titles and optical effects:* Universal Title.

STAR WARS (1977)

PRODUCTION INFORMATION AND PRINCIPAL CREDITS. Filmed in Tunisia and EMI-Elstree Studios, Borehamwood, England, for 82 days, from March to August 1976; special effects created at Industrial Light & Magic, Van Nuys, California, from 1976 through March 1977; total budget: $11.5 million; filmed in Panavision, color by Technicolor, prints by Deluxe; completed at Lucasfilm Ltd., San Anselmo, and Samuel Goldwyn Studios, Hollywood; recorded in Dolby Stereo; released by 20th Century-Fox on May 25, 1977; rereleased July 21, 1978, August 15, 1979, April 10, 1981, and August 13, 1982; running time: 121 minutes; MPAA Rating: PG; nominated for ten 1977 Academy Awards: Best Picture, Supporting Actor (Alec Guinness), Direction, Original Screenplay, Art Direction, Sound, Costume Design, Film Editing, Visual Effects, Original Score; won Academy Awards: Art Direction (John Barry, Norman Reynolds, Leslie Dilley, Roger Christian), Sound (Don MacDougall, Ray West, Bob Minkler, Derek Ball), Editing (Marcia Lucas, Richard Chew, Paul Hirsch), Visual Effects (John Stears, John Dykstra, Richard Edlund, Grant McCune, Robert Blalack), Original Score (John Williams); Ben Burtt received a Special Achievement Award for sound effects creation; *Star Wars* also won two awards from the Los Angeles Film Critics Association; John Williams won three Grammy Awards for *Star Wars* music; a 20th Century Fox release of a Lucasfilm Ltd. production; *producer:* Gary Kurtz; *written and directed by* George Lucas; *director of photography:* Gilbert Taylor; *production design:* John Barry; *music:* John Williams (performed by the London Symphony Orchestra); *editors:* Paul Hirsch, Marcia Lucas, Richard Chew; *special photographic effects supervisor:* John Dykstra; *special production and mechanical effects supervisor:* John Stears; *special dialogue and sound effects:* Ben Burtt; *production supervisor:* Robert Watts; *production illustration:* Ralph McQuarrie; *costume design:* John Mollo; *art direction:* Norman Reynolds, Leslie Dilley; *makeup supervisor:* Stuart Freeborn; *production sound mixer:* Derek Ball; *casting:* Irene Lamb, Diane Crittenden, Vic Ramos.

CAST. *Luke Skywalker:* Mark Hamill; *Han Solo:* Harrison Ford; *Princess Leia Organa:* Carrie Fisher; *Grand Moff Tarkin:* Peter Cushing; *Ben (Obi-Wan) Kenobi:* Alec Guinness; *See-Threepio (C-3PO):* Anthony Daniels; *Artoo-Detoo (R2-D2):* Kenny Baker; *Chewbacca:* Peter Mayhew; *Lord Darth Vader:* David Prowse; *Uncle Owen Lars:* Phil Brown; *Aunt Beru Lars:* Shelagh Fraser; *Chief Jawa:* Jack Purvis. REBEL FORCES. *General Dodonna:* Alex McCrindle; *General Willard:* Eddie Byrne; *Red Leader:* Drewe Henley; *Red Two (Wedge):* Dennis Lawson; *Red Three (Biggs):* Garrick Hagon; *Red Four (John "D"):* Jack Klaff; *Red Six (Porkins):* William Hootkins; *Gold Leader:* Angus McInnis; *Gold Two:* Jeremy Sinden; *Gold Five:* Graham Ashley. IMPERIAL FORCES. *General Taggi:* Don Henderson; *General Motti:* Richard Le Parmentier; *Commander #1:* Leslie Schofield.

TECHNICAL CREDITS. *Supervising sound editor:* Sam Shaw; *sound editors:* Robert R. Rutledge, Gordon Davidson, Gene Corso; *supervising music editor:* Kenneth Wannberg; *rerecording mixers:* Don MacDougall, Bob Minkler, Ray West, Mike Minkler, Lester Fresholtz, Richard Portman; *Dolby Sound consultant:* Stephen Katz; *orchestrations:* Herbert W. Spencer; *music scoring mixer:* Eric Tomlinson; *assistant film editors:* Todd Boekelheide, Jay Miracle, Colin Kitchens, Bonnie Koehler; *camera operators:* Ronnie Taylor, Geoff Glover; *set decorator:* Roger Christian; *production manager:* Bruce Sharman; *assistant directors:* Tony Waye, Gerry Gavigan, Terry Madden; *location manager:* Arnold Ross; *assistant to the producer:* Bunny Alsop; *assistant to the director:* Lucy Autrey Wilson; *production assistants:* Pat Carr, Miki Herman; *gaffer:* Ron Tabera; *property master:* Frank Bruton; *wardrobe supervisor:* Ron Beck; *stunt coordinator:* Peter Diamond; *continuity:* Ann Skinner; *titles:* Dan Perri; *second-unit photography:* Carroll

281

Ballard, Rick Clemente, Robert Dalva, Tak Fujimoto; *second-unit art direction:* Leon Erickson, Al Locatelli; *second-unit production managers:* David Lester, Peter Herald, Pepi Lenzi; *second-unit makeup:* Rick Baker, Douglas Beswick; *assistant sound editors:* Roxanne Jones, Karen Sharp; *production controller:* Brian Gibbs; *location auditor:* Ralph M. Leo; *assistant auditors:* Steve Cullip, Penny McCarthy, Kim Falkinburg; *advertising/publicity supervisor:* Charles Lippincott; *unit publicist:* Brian Doyle; *still photographer:* John Jay.

MINIATURE AND OPTICAL EFFECTS UNIT. *First cameraman:* Richard Edlund; *second cameraman:* Dennis Muren; *assistant cameraman:* Douglas Smith, Kenneth Ralston, David Robman; *second unit photography:* Bruce Logan; *composite optical photography:* Robert Blalack (Praxis); *optical photography coordinator:* Paul Roth; *optical printer operators:* David Berry, David McCue, Richard Pecorella, Eldon Rickman, James Van Trees, Jr.; *optical camera assistants:* Caleb Aschkynazo, John C. Moulds, Bruce Nicholson, Gary Smith, Bert Terreri, Donna Tracy, Jim Wells, Vicky Witt; *production supervisor:* George E. Mather; *matte artist:* P. S. Ellenshaw; *planet and satellite artist:* Ralph McQuarrie; *effects illustration and design:* Joseph Johnston; *additional spacecraft design:* Colin Cantwell; *chief model maker:* Grant McCune; *model builders:* David Beasley, Jon Erland, Lorne Peterson, Steve Gawley, Paul Huston, David Jones; *animation and rotoscope design:* Adam Beckett; *animators:* Michael Ross, Peter Kuran, Jonathan Seay, Chris Casady, Lyn Gerry, Diana Wilson; *stop-motion animation:* Jon Berg, Philip Tippet; *miniature explosions:* Joe Viskocil, Greg Auer; *computer animation and graphic displays:* Dan O'Bannon, Larry Cuba, John Wash, Jay Teitzell, Image West; *film control coordinator:* Mary M. Lind; *film librarians:* Cindy Isman, Connie McCrum, Pamela Malouf; *electronics design:* Alvah J. Miller; *special components:* James Shourt; *assistants:* Masaaki Norihoro, Eleanor Porter; *camera and mechanical design:* Don Trumbull, Richard Alexander, William Shourt; *special mechanical equipment:* Jerry Greenwood, Douglas Barnett, Stuart Ziff, David Scott; *production managers:* Bob Shepherd, Lon Tinney; *production staff:* Patricia Rose Duignan, 'Mark Kline, Rhonda Peck, Ron Nathan; *assistant editor (opticals):* Bruce Michael Green.

MORE AMERICAN GRAFFITI (1979)

PRODUCTION INFORMATION AND PRINCIPAL CREDITS. Filmed on location in Marin County and Stockton, California, from August through October 1978; total budget: $7.5 million; filmed in Panavision; recorded in Dolby Stereo; completed at Lucasfilm Ltd., San Anselmo; released by Universal Pictures on August 3, 1979; running time: 112 minutes; MPAA Rating: PG; a Universal Pictures release of a Lucasfilm Ltd. production; *executive producer:* George Lucas; *producer:* Howard Kazanjian; *director:* B. W. L. Norton; *screenplay:* Norton (based on characters created by George Lucas and Gloria Katz and Willard Huyck); *director of photography:* Caleb Deschanel; *editor:* Tina Hirsch; *art director:* Ray Storey; *supervising sound editor:* Ben Burtt; *sound:* David McMillan; *sound rerecording:* Bill Varney, Steve Maslow, Greg Landaker; *casting:* Terry Liebling, Gino Havens.

CAST. *Debbie Dunham:* Candy Clark; *Little Joe:* Bo Hopkins; *Steve Bolander:* Ron Howard; *John Milner:* Paul LeMat; *Carol/Rainbow:* Mackenzie Phillips; *Terry the Toad:* Charles Martin Smith; *Laurie Bolander:* Cindy Williams; *Eva:* Anna Bjorn; *Major Creech:* Richard Bradford; *Ralph:* John Brent; *Newt:* Scott Glenn; *Sinclair:* James Houghton; *Lance:* John Lansing; *Carlos:* Manuel Padilla; *Beckwith:* Ken Place; *Teensa:* Mary Kay Place; *Eric:* Tom Ruben; *Bobbie:* Doug Sahm; *Andy Henderson:* Will Seltzer; *Moonflower:* Monica Tenner; *Felix:* Ralph Wilcox; *Vikki:* Carol-Ann Williams; *Wolfman Jack:* Himself.

SUPPORTING CAST. Country Joe McDonald, Barry "the Fish" Melton, Robert Hogins, Robert Flurie, Peter Albin, Harold Aceves, Rosanna Arquette, Tom Baker, Eric Barnes, Becky Bedoy, Buzz Borelli, Ben Bottoms, Patrick Burns, Tim Burrus, George Cantero, Chet Carter, Dion Chesse, Gil Christner, Don Coughlin, Mark Courtney, Michael Courtney, Denny Delk, Frankie Di, Steve Evans, Nancy G. Fish, Rockey Flintermann, Michael Frost, Jonathan Gries, Paul Hensler, Julie Anna Hicks, Robert E. Hirschfeld, Erik Holland, Jay Jacobus, Naomi Judd, Leslie Gay Leace, Delroy Lindo, Dwight Reber, Sandra Rider, Kevin Sullivan, Morgan Upton, John Vella, Dan Woodworth, Clay Wright.

TECHNICAL CREDITS. *Sound effects editors:* Richard Anderson, Bonnie Koehler; *dialogue editor:*

Richard Burrow; *music editor:* Gene Finley; *unit production manager:* Tom Joyner; *first assistant director:* Thomas Lofaro; *second assistant director:* Steven Lofaro; *assistant film editors:* Duwayne Dunham, Gloria Gunn; *optical coordinators:* Peter Donen, Bill Lindemann; *camera operators:* Hiro Narita, Bryan Anderson; *technical assistants:* Andy Aaron, Howie, Laurel Ladevich; *makeup:* Don Le Page; *hair stylist:* Paul Le Blanc; *costume designer:* Agnes Rodgers; *costume supervisor:* Mary Still; *script supervisor:* Alice Tompkins: *research:* Deborah Fine; *Vietnam technical adviser:* Paul Hensler; *production assistants:* Louis G. Friedman, Colin M. Kitchens, Albert Corners, Ren Navez, Lewis Dean Jones; *production secretary:* Shelley Tharaud; *assistant to the producer:* Leah Schmidt; *set decorations:* Doug Von Koss; *property master:* Burt Wiley; *key grip:* Jonathan Guterres; *gaffer:* Michael Pantages; *special effects:* Don Courtney; *construction coordinator:* Dale Woodall; *unit publicist:* Joan Eisenberg; *still photographer:* Bruce Herman; *transportation supervisor:* Henry Travers; *location coordinator:* Lope Yap; *auditors:* William Rodenbaugh, Rick Frazier; *montage design:* Scott Bartlett; *opticals:* Cinema Research Corp.; *titles:* Universal Title; *helicopter camera pilot:* David Jones; helicopters furnished by Wright Airlift International, Inc.

THE EMPIRE STRIKES BACK (1980)

PRODUCTION INFORMATION AND PRINCIPAL CREDITS. Filmed on the Härdangerjøkulen Glacier, Finse, Norway, and at EMI-Elstree Studios, Borehamwood, England, for 175 days, from March 5, 1979, to September 24, 1979; special effects created at Industrial Light & Magic, San Rafael, California 1979–80; total cost: $32 million; filmed in Panavision, color by Rank Film Laboratories, prints by Deluxe; completed at Lucasfilm Ltd., San Anselmo, California; recorded in Dolby Stereo; music recorded at Anvil Studios, Denham, England; rerecording at Samuel Goldwyn Studios, Hollywood; visual effects filmed in VistaVision; released by 20th Century-Fox on May 21, 1980; rereleased July 31, 1981, and November 19, 1982; running time: 124 minutes; MPAA Rating: PG; nominated for three 1980 Academy Awards: Best Original Score, Art Direction, Sound; won Academy Awards: Best Sound (Bill Varney, Steve Maslow, Gregg Landaker, Peter Sutton); a Special Achievement Award for visual effects was given to Brian Johnson, Richard Edlund, Dennis Muren, and Bruce Nicholson; a 20th Century-Fox release of a Lucasfilm Ltd. production; *executive producer:* George Lucas; *producer:* Gary Kurtz; *director:* Irvin Kershner; *screenplay:* Leigh Brackett, Lawrence Kasdan (from a story by George Lucas); *director of photography:* Peter Suschitzky; *production design:* Norman Reynolds; *music:* John Williams (performed by the London Symphony Orchestra); *editor:* Paul Hirsch; *special visual effects:* Brian Johnson, Richard Edlund; *associate producers:* Robert Watts, James Bloom; *design consultant and conceptual artist:* Ralph McQuarrie; *art directors:* Leslie Dilley, Harry Lange, Alan Tomkins.

CAST. *Luke Skywalker:* Mark Hamill; *Han Solo:* Harrison Ford; *Princess Leia:* Carrie Fisher; *Lando Calrissian:* Billy Dee Williams; *See-Threepio (C-3PO):* Anthony Daniels; *Darth Vader:* David Prowse; *Chewbacca:* Peter Mayhew; *Artoo-Detoo (R2-D2):* Kenny Baker; *Yoda:* Frank Oz; *Ben (Obi-Wan) Kenobi:* Alec Guinness; *Boba Fett:* Jeremy Bulloch; *Lando's Aide:* John Hollis; *Chief Ugnaught:* Jack Purvis; *Snow Creature:* Des Webb; *performing assistant for Yoda:* Kathryn Mullen; *voice of emperor:* Clive Revill. IMPERIAL FORCES: *Admiral Piett:* Kenneth Colley; *General Veers:* Julian Glover; *Admiral Ozzel:* Michael Sheard; *Captain Needa:* Michael Culver; *other officers:* John Dicks, Milton Johns, Mark Jones, Oliver Maguire, Robin Scobey. REBEL FORCES: *General Rieekan:* Bruce Boa; *Zev (Rogue 2):* Christopher Malcom; *Wedge (Rogue 3):* Dennis Lawson; *Hobbie (Rogue 4):* Richard Oldfield; *Dak (Luke's gunner):* John Morton; *Janson (Wedge's gunner):* Ian Liston; *Major Derlin:* John Ratzenberger; *Deck Lieutenant:* Jack McKenzie; *Head Controller:* Jerry Harte; *other officers:* Norman Chancer, Norwich Duff, Ray Hassett, Brigitte Kahn, Burnell Tucker.

TECHNICAL CREDITS. *Set decorator:* Michael Ford; *construction manager:* Bill Welch; *assistant art directors:* Michael Lamont, Fred Hole; *sketch artist:* Ivor Beddoes; *draftsmen:* Ted Ambrose, Michael Boone, Reg Bream, Steve Cooper, Richard Dawking; *modelers:* Fred Evans, Allan Moss, Jan Stevens; *chief buyer:* Edward Rodrigo; *construction storeman:* Dave Middleton; *operating cameramen:* Kelvin Pike, David Garfath; *assistant cameramen:* Maurice Arnold, Chris Tanner; *second assistant cameramen:* Peter Robinson, Madelyn Most; *dolly grips:* Dennis Lewis, Brian Osborn; *matte photography consultant:* Stanley

Sayer; *gaffer:* Laurie Shane; *rigging gaffer:* John Clark; *makeup and special creature design:* Stuart Freeborn; *chief makeup artist:* Graham Freeborn; *makeup artists:* Kay Freeborn, Nick Maley; *chief hairdresser:* Barbara Ritchie; *Yoda fabrication:* Wendy Midener; *costume designer:* John Mollo; *wardrobe supervisor:* Tiny Nicholls; *wardrobe mistress:* Eileen Sullivan; *property master:* Frank Bruton; *property supervisor:* Charles Torbett; *property dressing supervisor:* Joe Dipple; *head carpenter:* George Gunning; *head plasterer:* Bert Rodwell; *head rigger:* Red Lawrence; *sound design and supervising effects editor:* Ben Burtt; *sound editors:* Richard Burrow, Teresa Eckton, Bonnie Koehler; *production sound:* Peter Sutton; *sound boom operator:* Don Wortham; *production maintenance:*Ron Butcher; *rerecording:* Bill Varney, Steve Maslow, Gregg Landaker; *music recording:* Eric Tomlinson; *orchestrations:* Herbert W. Spencer; *supervising music editor:* Kenneth Wannberg; *assistant film editors:* Duwayne Dunham, Phil Sanderson, Barbara Ellis, Steve Starkey, Paul Tomlinson; *dialogue editors:* Curt Schulkey, Leslie Shatz, Joanne D'Antonio; *optical coordinator:* Roberta Friedman; *assistant sound editors:* John Benson, Joanna Cappuccilli, Ken Fischer, Craig Jaeger, Nancy Jencks, Laurel Ladevich; *foley editors:* Robert Rutledge, Scott Hecker; *foley assistants:* Edward M. Steidele, John Roesh; *sound effects recording:* Randy Thom; *recording technicians:* Gary Summers, Howie, Kevin O'Connell; *production supervisor:* Bruce Sharman; *assistant production manager:* Patricia Carr; *production coordinator:* Miki Herman; *first assistant director:* David Tomblin; *second assistant directors:* Steve Lanning, Roy Button; *location manager:* Philip Kohler; *continuity:* Kay Rawlings, Pamela Mann; *casting:* Irene Lamb, Terry Liebling; Bob Edmiston; *assistant to producer:* Bunny Alsop; *assistant to director:* Debbie Shaw; *assistant to executive producer:* Jane Bay; *production assistants:* Barbara Harley, Nick Laws, Charles Wessler; *stunt coordinator:* Peter Diamond; *stunt doubles:* Bob Anderson, Colin Skeaping; *production accountant:* Ron Phipps; *assistant accountant:* Michael Larkins; *set cost controller:* Ken Gordon; *location accountant:* Ron Cook; *still photographer:* George Whitear; *unit publicist:* Alan Arnold; *assistant publicist:* Kirsten Wing; STUDIO SECOND UNIT. *directors:* Harley Cokliss, John Barry; *director of photography:* Chris Menges; *assistant director:* Dominic Fulford; *second assistant director:* Andrew Montgomery. LOCATION SECOND UNIT. *director:* Peter MacDonald; *director of photography:* Geoff Glover; *operating cameraman:* Bob Smith; *assistant cameramen:* John Campbell, Mike Brewster; *second assistant cameramen:* John Keen, Greg Dupre; *dolly grip:* Frank Batt; *production manager:* Svein Johansen; *assistant directors:* Bill Westley, Ola Solum.

PRODUCTION AND MECHANICAL EFFECTS UNIT. *Mechanical effects supervision:* Nick Allder; *location unit supervisor:* Allan Bryce; *senior effects technicians:* Neil Swan, Dave Watkins; *robot fabrication and supervision:* Andrew Kelly, Ron Hone; *effects technicians:* Phil Knowles, Barry Whitrod, Martin Gant, Brian Eke, Guy Hudson, Dennis Lowe; *effects engineering:* Roger Nicholls, Steve Lloyd; *electrical engineer:* John Hatt; *electronics consultant:* Rob Dickinson; *model construction:* John Pakenham; *effects assistants:* Alan Poole, Digby Milner, Robert McLaren; *effects secretary:* Gill Case.

MINIATURE AND OPTICAL EFFECTS UNIT. *Effects director of photography:* Dennis Muren; *effects cameramen:* Ken Ralston, Jim Veilleux; *camera operators:* Don Dow, Bill Neil; *assistant cameramen:* Selwyn Eddy, Jody Westheimer, Rick Fichter, Clint Palmer, Michael McAlister, Paul Huston, Richard Fish, Chris Anderson; *optical photography supervisor:* Bruce Nicholson; *optical printer operators:* David Berry, Kenneth Smith, Donald Clark; *optical line-up:* Warren Franklin, Mark Vargo, Peter Amundson, Loring Doyle, Thomas Rosseter, Tam Pillsbury, James Lim; *optical coordinator:* Laurie Vermont; *laboratory technicians:* Tim Geideman, Duncan Myers, Ed Jones; *art director—visual effects:* Joe Johnston; *assistant art director:* Nilo Rodis-Jamero; *stop motion animation:* Jon Berg, Phil Tippett; *stop motion technicians:* Tom St. Amand, Doug Beswick; *matte painting supervisor:* Harrison Ellenshaw; *matte artists:*Ralph McQuarrie, Michael Pangrazio; *matte photography:* Neil Krepela; *additional matte photography:* Michael Lawler; *matte photography assistants:* Craig Barron, Robert Elswit; *chief model maker:* Lorne Peterson; *modelshop foreman:* Steve Gawley; *model makers:* Paul Huston, Tom Rudduck, Michael Fulmer, Samuel Zolltheis, Charles Bailey, Ease Owyeung, Scott Marshall, Marc Thorpe, Wesley Seeds, Dave Carson, Rob Gemmel, Pat McClung; *animation and rotoscope supervisor:* Peter Kuran; *animators:* Samuel Comstock, Garry Waller, John Van Vliet, Rick Taylor, Kim Knowlton, Chris Casady, Nina Saxon, Diana Wilson; *visual effects editorial supervisor:* Conrad Buff; *effects editor:* Michael Kelly; *assistant effects editors:* Arthur Repola, Howard Stein; *apprentice editor:* Jon Thaler; *production administrator:* Dick Gallegly; *production secretary:* Patricia Blau; *production associate:* Thomas Brown; *production accountant:* Ray

Scalice; *assistant accountants:* Glenn Phillips, Pam Traas, Laura Crockett; *production assistant:* Jenny Oznowicz; *transportation:* Robert Martin; *still photographer:* Terry Chostner; *lab assistant:* Roberto McGrath; *electronics systems designer:* Jerry Jeffress; *systems programming:* Kris Brown; *electronic engineers:* Lhary Meyer, Mike MacKenzie, Gary Leo; *special project coordinator:* Stuart Ziff; *equipment engineering supervisor:* Gene Whiteman; *design engineer:* Mike Bolles; *machinists:* Udo Pampel, Greg Beaumonte; *draftsman:* Ed Tennler; *special projects:* Gary Platek; *supervising stage technician:* Ted Moehnke; *stage technicians:* William Beck, Bobby Finley, Leo Loverro, Edward Hirsh, Dick Dova, Ed Breed; *miniature pyrotechnics:* Joseph Viskocil, Dave Pier, Thaine Morris; *optical printer component manufacturer:* George Randle Co.; *camera and movement design:* Jim Beaumonte; *special optics designer:* David Grafton; *special optics fabrication:* J. L. Wood Optical Systems; *optical printer component engineering:* Fries Engineering; *high-speed camera movements:* Mitchell Camera Corp.; *ultra-high-speed camera:* Bruce Hill Productions; *color timer:* Ed Lemke; *negative cutting:* Robert Hart, Darrell Hixson; *Dolby consultant:* Don Digirolamo; *additional optical effects:* Van Der Veer Photo Effects, Modern Film Effects, Ray Mercer & Company, Westheimer Company, Lookout Mountain Films; *aerial camera system:* Wesscam Camera Systems (Europe); *aerial cameraman:* Ron Goodman; *assistant:* Margaret Herron; *helicopter:* Dollar Air Services Limited; *helicopter pilot:* Mark Wolfe.

Cloud Plates photographed with Astrovision by Continental Camera Systems, Inc.; snow vehicles supplied by Aktiv Fischer; R2 bodies fabricated by White Horse Toy Company; special assistance from Giltspur Engineering and Compair.

RAIDERS OF THE LOST ARK (1981)

PRODUCTION INFORMATION AND PRINCIPAL CREDITS. Filmed in France, Tunisia, Hawaii, and at EMI-Elstree Studios, Borehamwood, England, for 73 days, from July through October 1980; special effects created at Industrial Light & Magic, San Rafael, California, 1980–81; total cost: $22.8 million; filmed in Panavision, color by Rank Film Laboratories, prints in Metrocolor; completed at Lucasfilm Ltd., San Anselmo, California; recorded in Dolby Stereo; released by Paramount Pictures on June 12, 1981; rereleased July 1982; running time: 115 minutes; MPAA Rating: PG; nominated for eight 1981 Academy Awards: Best Picture, Director, Cinematography, Original Score, Art Direction, Visual Effects, Sound Recording, and Editing; won for Art Direction (Norman Reynolds, Leslie Dilley, Michael Ford); Visual Effects (Richard Edlund, Kit West, Bruce Nicholson, Joe Johnston); Sound (Bill Varney, Steve Maslow, Gregg Landaker, Roy Charman); Editing (Michael Kahn); Special Achievement Award for effects editing to Ben Burtt and Richard L. Anderson; a Paramount Pictures release of a Lucasfilm Ltd. production; *executive producers:* George Lucas, Howard Kazanjian; *producer:* Frank Marshall; *director:* Steven Spielberg; *written by* Lawrence Kasdan (from a story by Lucas and Philip Kaufman); *director of photography:* Douglas Slocombe; *production design:* Norman Reynolds; *music:* John Williams (performed by the London Symphony Orchestra); *editor:* Michael Kahn; *visual effects supervisor:* Richard Edlund; *mechanical effects supervisor:* Kit West; *associate producer:* Robert Watts; *casting:* Mike Fenton and Jane Feinberg, Mary Selway; *second-unit director:* Michael Moore; *stunt coordinator:* Glenn Randall; *costume design:* Deborah Nadoolman; *first assistant director:* David Tomblin.

CAST. *Indiana Jones:* Harrison Ford; *Marion Ravenwood:* Karen Allen; *Belloq:* Paul Freeman; *Toht:* Ronald Lacey; *Sallah:* John Rhys-Davies; *Brody:* Denholm Elliot; *Dietrich:* Wolf Kahler; *Gobler:* Anthony Higgins; *Satipo:* Alfred Molina; *Barranca:* Vic Tablian; *Colonel Musgrove:* Don Fellows; *Major Eaton:* William Hootkins.

SUPPORTING CAST. Bill Reimbold, Fred Sorenson, Patrick Durkin, Matthew Scurfield, Malcom Weaver, Sonny Caldinez, Anthony Chinn, Pat Roach, Christopher Frederick, Tutte Lemkow, Ishaq Bux, Kiran Shah, Souad Messaoudi, Terry Richards, Steve Hanson, Frank Marshall, Martin Kreidt, George Harris, Eddie Tagoe, John Rees, Tony Vogel, Ted Grossman, Jack Dearlove.

STUNTS. Terry Leonard, Martin Grace, Vic Armstrong, Wendy Leach, Sergio Mione, Rocky Taylor, Chuck Waters, Bill Weston, Paul Weston, Reg Harding, Billy Horrigan, Peter Brace, Gerry Crampton, Romo Garrara.

TECHNICAL CREDITS. *Production supervisor:* Douglas Twiddy; *assistant production manager:* Patricia Carr; *second assistant directors:* Roy Button, Patrick Cadell; *location manager:* Bryan Coates; *continuity:* Pamela Mann; *associate to Mr. Spielberg:* Kathleen Kennedy; *additional photography:* Paul Beeson; *operating cameraman:* Chic Waterson; *assistant cameraman:* Robin Vidgeon; *second assistant cameraman:* Danny Shelmerdine; *dolly grip:* Colin Manning; *gaffer:* Martin Evans; *head rigger:* Red Lawrence; *art director:* Leslie Dilley; *set decorator:* Michael Ford; *construction manager:* Bill Welch; *property master:* Frank Bruton; *assistant construction manager:* George Gunning; *assistant art directors:* Fred Hole, Michael Lamont, John Fenner, Ken Court; *production illustrator:* Ed Verreaux; *production artists:* Michael Lloyd, Ron Cobb; *sketch artists:* Roy Carnon, David Negron; *decor and lettering artist:* Bob Walker; *draftsman:* George Djurkovic; *scenic artist:* Andrew Garnet-Lawson; *modeler:* Keith Short; *chief buyer:* David Lusby; *art department assistant:* Sharon Cartwright; *head plasterer:* Bert Rodwell; *supervising plasterer:* Kenneth Clark; *master painter:* Eric Shirtcliffe; *construction storeman:* Dave Middleton; *property master (Tunisia):* Peter Hancock; *property supervisor:* Charles Torbett; *armorer:* Simon Atherton; *wardrobe supervisor:* Rita Wakely; *wardrobe assistants:* Sue Wain, Ian Hickinbotham; *chief makeup artist:* Tom Smith; *makeup artist:* Dickie Mills; *chief hairdresser:* Patricia McDermott; *hairdresser:* Mike Lockey; *stunt arranger:* Peter Diamond; *senior effects technician:* Peter Dawson; *effects technicians:* Terry Schubert, Rodney Fuller, Trevor Neighbour; *effects engineering:* Terry Glass; *special effects equipment supervisor:* Bill Warrington; *special effects electrician:* Chris Condon; *special effects carpenter:* Roy Coombes; *special effects welder:* Yves De Bono; *effects assistants:* Ken Gittens, Ray Hanson; *animal handlers:* Michael Culling, Steve Edge, Jed Edge; *sound design:* Ben Burtt; *supervising sound effects editor:* Richard L. Anderson; *sound effects editors:* Steve H. Flick, Mark Mangini; *supervising dialogue editor:* Curt Schulkey; *dialogue editor:* Andy Patterson; *assistant dialogue editor:* Eric Whitfield; *production sound:* Roy Charman; *sound boom operator:* John Salter; *production maintenance:* George Rice; *rerecording:* Bill Varney, Steve Maslow, Gregg Landaker; *music recording:* Eric Tomlinson; *orchestrations:* Herbert W. Spencer; *supervising music editor:* Kenneth Wannberg; *assistant film editors:* Phil Sanderson, Bruce Green, Colin Wilson; *apprentice film editor:* Julie Kahn Zunder; *apprentice sound editor:* Peter Grives; *foley editor:* John Dunn; *sound effects recording:* Gary Summers; *recording technician:* Howie Hammerman; *research:* Deborah Fine; *assistants to Mr. Marshall:* Patty Rumph, Barbara Harley; *assistant to Mr. Spielberg:* Marty Casella; *assistant to Mr. Kazanjian:* Laura Kenmore; *assistant to Mr. Lucas:* Jane Bay; *production assistants:* Gill Case, Daniel Parker; *doctor:* Dr. Felicity Hodder; *production accountant:* Arthur Carroll; *assistant accountant:* Michael Larkins; *location accountant:* Stefano Priori; *still photographer:* Albert Clarke; *unit publicist:* Derek Robbins. SECOND UNIT. *operating cameramen:* Wally Byatt, Gerry Dunkley, David Worley; *assistant cameraman:* Chris Tanner; *second assistant cameraman:* Eamonn O'Keefe; *dolly grip:* Jim Kane; *first assistant director:* Carlos Gill; *second assistant director:* Michael Hook; *continuity:* Maggie Jones; *doctor:* Dr. Hassam Moossun. SPECIAL VISUAL EFFECTS. *optical photography supervisor:* Bruce Nicholson; *production supervisor:* Thomas Smith; *art director—visual effects:* Joe Johnston; *matte painting supervisor:* Alan Maley; *visual effects editorial supervisor:* Conrad Buff; *production coordinator:* Patricia Blau; *production associate:* Miki Herman; *animation supervisors:* Samuel Comstock, Deitrich Friesen; *effects cameraman:* Jim Veilleux; *camera operators:* Bill Neil, Don Dow; *assistant cameraman:* Clint Palmer; *optical printer operators:* David Berry, Kenneth Smith, John Ellis; *optical line-up:* Mark Vargo, Warren Franklin, Tom Rosseter; *assistant art director:* Nilo Rodis-Jamero; *illustrator:* Ralph McQuarrie; *matte artist:* Michael Pangrazio; *matte photography:* Neil Krepela; *matte photography assistant:* Craig Barron; *modelshop foreman:* Lorne Peterson; *model makers:* Steve Gawley, Mike Fulmer, Wesley Seeds, Paul Huston, Charlie Bailey, Sam Zolltheis, Marc Thorpe, Bruce Richardson, Ease Owyeung; *animators:* John Van Vliet, Kim Knowlton, Garry Waller, Loring Doyle, Scott Caple, Judy Elkins, Sylvia Keulen, Scott Marshall; *assistant effects editors:* Peter Amundson, Howard Stein; *assistant film editor:* Duwayne Dunham; *production coordinator:* Laurie Vermont; *cloud effects:* Gary Platek; *special makeup effects:* Christopher Walas; *laboratory technicians:* Tim Geideman, Duncan Myers, Ed Jones; *still photographer:* Terry Chostner; *administration assistant:* Chrissie England; *production accountants:* David Kakita, Shirley Lee, Laura Kaysen; *still lab technicians:* Roberto McGrath, Kerry Nordquist; *electronic systems designer:* Jerry Jeffress; *computer engineering:* Kris Brown; *design engineer:* Mike Bolles; *electronics engineers:* Mike MacKenzie, Marty Brenneis, Gary Leo; *electronic technicians:* Christi McCarthy, Bessie Wiley, Melissa

Cargill; *equipment engineering supervisor:* Gene Whiteman; *machinist:* Udo Pampel; *special projects:* Wade Childress; *supervising stage technician:* Ted Moehnke; *stage technicians:* William Beck, Dick Dova, Bobby Finley III, Edward Hirsh, Patrick Fitzsimmons, John McCleod, Peter Stolz; *pyrotechnics:* Thaine Morris; *ultra-high-speed camera:* Bruce Hill Productions: *color timer:* Robert McMillian; *negative cutter:* Brian Ralph; *additional optical effects:* MGM Optical, Modern Film Effects; *titles:* MGM Titles. TUNISIAN UNIT. *production coordinator:* Tarak Ben Ammar; *production supervisor:* Mohamed Ali Cherif; *production manager:* Hassine Soufi; *first assistant director:* Naceur Ktari; *location managers:* Habib Chaari, Abdelkrim Baccar; *assistant art director:* Hassen Soufi; *accountant:* Ridna Turki. FRENCH UNIT. *production manager:* Dorothy Marchini; *first assistant director:* Vincent Joliet; *production assistant:* Junior Charles; *accountant:* Stella Quef. PERUVIAN-HAWAIIAN UNIT. *production coordinator:* Dan Nichols; *second assistant director:* Louis G. Friedman; *location manager:* Maile Semitokol; *gaffer:* Alan Brady; *transportation captain:* Harry Ueshiro; *accountant.* Bonne Radford.

RETURN OF THE JEDI (1983)

PRODUCTION INFORMATION AND PRINCIPAL CREDITS. (Information on *Jedi* not complete at press time.) Filmed in Buttercup Valley, Death Valley, and Smith River, California; and at EMI-Elstree Studios, Borehamwood, England, beginning January 1982; special effects created at Industrial Light & Magic, San Rafael, California, 1981–1983; color by Rank Film Laboratories; prints by Deluxe; completed at Lucasfilm Ltd., San Anselmo, California; recorded in Dolby Stereo; rerecorded at Sprocket Systems, San Rafael, California; music recording at Anvil-Abbey Road Studios, London; additional sound recording at Mayflower Film Recording Ltd., London, and Goldwyn Sound Facility, Hollywood; a 20th Century-Fox release of a Lucasfilm Ltd. production; *executive producer:* George Lucas; *producer:* Howard Kazanjian; *coproducer:* Robert Watts, Jim Bloom; *director:* Richard Marquand; *screenplay:* Lawrence Kasdan and George Lucas (from a story by Lucas); *director of photography:* Alan Hume; *production design:* Norman Reynolds; *music:* John Williams (performed by the London Symphony Orchestra); *editors:* Sean Barton, Marcia Lucas, Duwayne Dunham; *special visual effects:* Dennis Muren, Ken Ralston, Richard Edlund; *mechanical effects:* Kit West; *costume designers:* Aggie Guerard Rodgers, Nilo Rodis Jamero; *makeup and creature design:* Phil Tippett, Stuart Freeborn; *sound design:* Ben Burtt.

CAST. *Luke Skywalker:* Mark Hamill; *Han Solo:* Harrison Ford; *Princess Leia:* Carrie Fisher; *Lando Calrissian:* Billy Dee Williams; *C-3PO:* Anthony Daniels; *Chewbacca:* Peter Mayhew; *Anakin Skywalker:* Sebastian Shaw; *the Emperor:* Ian McDiarmid; *Yoda:* Frank Oz; *the voice of Darth Vader:* James Earl Jones; *Ben (Obi-Wan) Kenobi:* Alec Guinness.

SUPPORTING CAST. *Darth Vader:* David Prowse; *R2-D2:* Kenny Baker; *Moff Jerjerrod:* Michael Pennington; *Admiral Piett:* Kenneth Colley; *Bib Fortuna:* Michael Carter; *Wedge:* Denis Lawson; *Admiral Ackbar:* Tim Rose; *General Madine:* Dermot Crowley; *Mon Mothma:* Caroline Blakiston; *Wicket:* Warwick Davis; *Mogaar:* Kenny Baker; *Boba Fett:* Jeremy Bulloch; *Oola:* Femi Taylor; *Fat Dancer:* Claire Davenport; *Teebo:* Jack Purvis; *Logray:* Mike Edmonds; *Chief Chirpa:* Jane Busby; *Ewok Warrior:* Malcom Dixon; *Ewok Warrior:* Mike Cottrell; *Nicki:* Nicki Reade; *Stardestroyer Controller #1:* Adam Bareham; *Stardestroyer Controller #2:* Jonathan Oliver; *Stardestroyer Captain #1:* Pip Miller; *Stardestroyer Captain #2:* Tom Mannion; *Jabba Puppeteers:* Toby Philpott, David Barclay, Mike Edmonds; *Puppeteers:* Michael McCormick, Deep Roy, Simon Williamson, Hugh Spirit, Swim Lee, Michael Quinn, Richard Robinson; *Ewoks:* Margo Apostocos, Ray Armstrong, Eileen Baker, Michael Henbury-Balham, Bobbie Bell, Patty Bell, Alan Bennett, Sarah Bennett, Pamela Betts, Dan Blackner, Linda Bowley, Peter Burroughs, Debbie Carrington, Maureen Charlton, William Coppen, Sadie Corrie, Tony Cox, John Cumming, Jean D'Agostino, Luis De Jesus, Debbie Dixon, Margarita Fernandez, Phil Fondacaro, Sal Fondacaro, Tony Friel, Dan Frishman, John Gavam, Michael Gilden, Paul Grant, Lydia Green, Lars Green, Pam Grizz, Andrew Herd, J. J. Jackson, Richard Jones, Trevor Jones, Glynn Jones, Karen Lay, John Lummiss, Nancy Maclean, Peter Mandell, Carole Morris, Stacy Nichols, Chris Nunn, Barbara O'Laughlin, Brian Orenstein, C. Harrell Parker, Jr., John Pedrick, April Perkins, Ronnie Phillips, Katie Purvis, Carol Read, Nicholas Read, Diana Reynolds,

Daniel Rodgers, Chris Romano, Dean Shackenford, Kiran Shah, Felix Silla, Linda Spriggs, Gerald Staddon, Josephine Staddon, Kevin Thompson, Kendra Wall, Brian Wheeler, Butch Wilhelm; *Mime Artists:* Franki Anderson, Ailsa Berk, Sean Crawford, Andy Cunningham, Tim Dry, Graeme Hattrick, Phil Herbert, Gerald Home, Paul Springer; *Stunt Performers:* Bob Anderson, Dirk Yohan Beer, Marc Boyle, Mike Cassidy, Tracy Eddon, Sandra Gross, Ted Grossman, Frank Henson, Larry Holt, Bill Horrigan, Alf Joint, Julius Leflore, Colin Skeaping, Malcom Weaver, Paul Weston, Bob Yerkes, Dan Zormeier.

TECHNICAL CREDITS. *First assistant director/second unit director:* David Tomblin; *casting:* Mary Selway Buckley; *location director of photography:* Jim Glennon; *additional photography:* Jack Lowin; *production sound:* Tony Dawe, Randy Thom; *supervising music editor:* Kenneth Wannberg; *music recording:* Eric Tomlinson; *orchestrations:* Herbert W. Spencer; *chief articulation engineer:* Stuart Ziff; *production supervisor:* Douglas Twiddy; *production executive:* Robert Latham Brown; *unit production manager:* Miki Herman; *assistant production manager:* Pat Carr; *associate to producer:* Louis G. Friedman; *conceptual artist:* Ralph McQuarrie; *art directors:* Fred Hole, James Schoppe; *set decorators:* Michael Ford, Harry Lange; *property master:* Peter Hancock; *chief hairdresser:* Patricia McDermott; *stunt coordinator:* Glenn Randall; *stunt arranger:* Peter Diamond; *production controller:* Arthur Carroll; *production accountant:* Margaret Mitchell; *second assistant directors:* Roy Button, Chris Newman, Michael Steele, Eric Jewett, Russell Lodge; *production assistant:* Ian Bryce; *production coordinator:* Lata Ryan; *coordination assistants:* Sunni Kerwin, Gail Samuelson; *script supervisor:* Pamela Mann Francis; *location script supervisor:* Bob Forest; *location casting:* Dave Eman, Bill Lytle; *assistant to Mr. Kazanjian:* Kathleen Hartney Ross; *assistant to Mr. Bloom:* John Syrjamaki; *assistant to Mr. Lucas:* Jane Bay; *assistant art directors:* Michael Lamont, John Fenner, Richard Dawking; *set dresser:* Doug Von Koss; *construction manager:* Bill Welch; *assistant construction manager:* Alan Booth; *construction supervisor:* Roger Irvin; *general foreman:* Bill Iiams; *construction foremen:* Greg Callas, Guy Clause, Doug Elliott, Stan Wakashige; *paint foreman:* Gary Clark; *sketch artist:* Roy Carnon; *scenic artist:* Ted Michell; *decor and lettering artists:* Bob Walker; *set draftsmen:* Reg Bream, Mark Billerman, Chris Campbell; *production buyers:* David Lusby; *construction storeman:* David Middleton; *operating cameramen:* Alec Mills, Tom Laughridge, Mike Benson; *focus puller:* Michael Frift, Chris Tanner; *assistant cameramen:* Leo Napolitano, Bob La Bonge; *second assistant cameramen:* Simon Hume, Steve Tate, Martin Kenzie, Michael Glennon; *gaffers:* Mike Pantages, Bob Bremner; *aerial photography:* Ron Goodman, Margaret Herron; *helicopter pilot:* Mark Wolfe; *key grip:* Dick Dova Spah; *best boy:* Joe Crowley; *dolly grip:* Chunky Huse, Reg Hall; *matte photography consultant:* Stanley Sayer; *chief makeup artists:* Tom Smith, Graham Freeborn; *makeup artists:* Peter Robb King, Dickie Mills, Kay Freeborn, Nick Dudman; *hairdressers:* Mike Lockey, Paul Le Blanc; *assistant articulation engineer:* Eben Stromquist; *armature designer:* Peter Ronzani; *plastic designer:* Richard Davis; *sculptural designers:* Chuck Wiley, James Howard; *key sculptors:* Dave Carson, Tony McVey, Judy Elkins, Derek Howarty; *chief moldmaker:* Wesley Seeds; *moldmakers:* Ron Young; *creature technicians:* Dan Howard, James Isaac, Brian Turner, Jeannie Lauren, Richard Spah, Jr., Ethan Wiley, Randy Dutra, Kirk Thatcher; *creature consultants:* Jon Berg, Chris Walas; *production creature coordinator:* Patty Blau; *latex foam lab supervisor:* Tom McLaughlin; *animatronics engineer:* John Coppinger; *wardrobe supervisor:* Ron Beck; *costume supervisor:* Mary Still; *wardrobe mistress:* Janet Tebrooke; *shop manager:* Jenny Green; *jeweler:* Richard Miller; *creature costumers:* Barbara Kassal, Edwina Pellikka, Anne Polland, Elvira Angelinetta; *assistant property master:* Charles Torbett; *property supervisors:* Dan Coangelo, Brian Lofthouse; *U.S. property:* Holly Walker; *propmakers:* Bill Hargreaves, Richard Peters; *property assistant:* Ivan Van Perre; *master carpenter:* Bert Long; *master plasterer:* Kenny Clarke; *master painter:* Eric Shirtcliffe; *supervising rigger:* Red Lawrence; *supervising stagehand:* Eddie Burke; *sail coordinators,* Bill Kreysler, Warwick Tompkins; *sails engineering:* Derrick Baylis, Peggy Kashuba; *assistant film editors:* Steve Starkey, Conrad Buff, Phil Sanderson, Nick Hosker; *sound effects editors:* Richard Burrow, Teresa Eckton, Ken Fischer; *assistant sound editors:* Chris Weir, Bill Mann, Gloria Borders, Suzanne Fox, Kathy Ryan, Nancy Jencks; *rerecording mixers:* Gary Summers, Ben Burtt, Roger Savage; *rerecording engineer:* Tomlinson Holman; *boom operators:* David Batchelor, David Parker; *sound assistants:* Shep Dawe, Jim Manson; *dialogue editors:* Curt Schulkey, Laurel Ladevich, Bonnie Koehler, Victoria Sansom; *choreographer:* Gillian Gregory; *location choreographer:* Wendy Rogers; *production accountant:* Colin

Hurren; *assistant accountants:* Sheala Daniell, Barbara Harley; *location accountants:* Diane Dankwardt, Dick Wright, Pinki Ragan; *transportation coordinator:* Gene Schwartz; *transportation captains:* John Feinblatt, H. Lee Noblitt; *studio transportation managers:* Vic Minay, Mark La Bonge; *location contact:* Lennie Fike; *still photographers:* Albert Clarke, Ralph Nelson, Jr.; *research:* Deborah Fine; *unit publicist:* Gordon Arnell; *assistant publicist:* June Broom.

PRODUCTION AND MECHANICAL EFFECTS UNIT. *Special effects supervisor:* Roy Arbogast; *special effects foreman:* William David Lee; *special effects floor controller:* Ian Wingrove; *senior effects technician:* Peter Dawson; *chief electronics technician:* Ron Hone; *location special effects:* David Simmons, Gary Zink, Eddie Surkin, John Stirber, Bruno Von Zeebroeck, John Chapot, William Klinger, Jr., Kevin Pike, Donald Chandler, Mike Wood; *wire specialist:* Bob Harman.

MINIATURE AND OPTICAL EFFECTS UNIT INDUSTRIAL LIGHT & MAGIC. *Art director-visual effects.* Joe Johnston; *optical photography supervisor:* Bruce Nicholson; *general manager, ILM:* Tom Smith; *production supervisor:* Rose Duignan; *matte painting supervisor:* Michael Pangrazio; *modelshop supervisors:* Lorne Peterson, Steve Gawley; *animation supervisor:* James Keefer; *visual effects editor:* Arthur Repola; *effects cameramen:* Don Dow, Selwyn Eddy III, Bob Elswit, Scott Farrar, Rick Fichter, Bill Neil, Mike McAlister; *assistant camera operators:* Peter Daulton, Maryan Evans, Kim Marks, Pat Sweeney, Randy Johnson, David Hardburger, Bob Hill, Ray Gilberti, Patrick McArdle, Toby Heindel, Bess Wiley, David Finder; *production coordinators:* Warren Franklin, Laurie Vermont; *optical printer operators:* Mark Vargo, John Ellis, David Berry, Ken Smith, Donald Clark; *lab technicians:* Tim Geideman, Duncan Myers; *optical line-up:* Tom Rosseter, Ed Jones, Ralph Gordon; *production illustrator:* George Jensen; *matte painting artists:* Chris Evans, Frank Ordaz; *matte photography supervisor:* Neil Krepela; *assistant matte cameraman:* Craig Barron; *chief model makers:* Paul Huston, Charlie Bailey, Michael Fulmer, Ease Owyeung; *model makers:* Chuck Wiley, Marghi McMahon, Marc Thorpe, Bill Buttfield, Bill George, Toby Heindel, Larry Tan, Barbara Gallucci, Sean Casey, Richard Davis, Randy Ottenberg, Jeff Mann, Scott Marshall, Ira Keeler; *head effects animator:* Kim Knowlton, Garry Waller; *effects animators:* Sam Comstock, Mike Lessa, Renee Holt, Terry Windell; *visual effects editors:* Peter Amundson, Bill Kimberlin, Howard Stein; *assistant visual effects:* Robert Chrisoulis; *administrative staff:* Chrissie England, Laura Kaysen, Pauls Katsh, Karen Ayers, Sonja Paulson, Karen Dube; *supervisor-still photography:* Terry Chostner; *still photographers:* Roberto McGrath, Kerry Nordquist; *electronic system design:* Jerry Jeffress, Kris Brown; *electronic engineer:* Mike MacKenzie, Marty Brenneis; *computer graphics:* William Reeves, Tom Duff; *equipment engineering supervisor:* Gene Whiteman; *machinists:* Udo Pampel, Conrad Bonderson; *apprentice machinists:* David Hanks, Chris Rand; *equipment maintenance:* Wade Childress, Michael Smith, Cristi McCarthy; *design engineer:* Mike Bolles, Ed Tennler; *supervising stage technician:* T. E. Moehnke; *stage foreman:* Patrick Fitzsimmons; *stage technicians:* Joe Fulmer, John McLeod, Dave Childers, Harold Cole, Bob Finley III; *pyrotechnician:* Thaine Morris, Peter Stolz; *steadicam plate photography:* Garrett Brown; *color timers:* Jim Schurmann, Bob Hagans; *negative cutter:* Bob Hart; *additional optical effects:* Lookout Mountain Films, Monaco Film Labs, Movie Magic, Pacific Title, Visual Concepts Engineering.

SOURCE NOTES

I conducted more than sixty hours of tape-recorded interviews with George Lucas, in addition to telephone calls, informal conversations, and queries, conducted over a period from November 1981 through February 1983. But Lucas's recollections did not tell the full story. They were supplemented by the reminiscences, opinions, and evaluations of eighty-four other individuals who consented to in-person tape-recorded interviews. More than twenty other interviews were conducted over the telephone, and numerous individuals were contacted to confirm or explain specific details of Lucas's career.

Information gleaned from the interviews with Lucas and those who know or work with him makes up 95 percent of the material in this book. All quotations are attributed to the speakers, and all are taken from transcripts of the tape-recorded interviews. The interviews were also used to cross-check different versions of the same event. Although Lucas often had the most detailed memories, his recollections were not accepted at face value and were compared to differing accounts of the same events.

Specific references to books and periodicals about Lucas and the film business are noted in the chapter summaries. There are few reliable reference works on Lucas and his contemporaries, the most thorough being *The Movie Brats* by Michael Pye and Lynda Myles (New York: Holt, Rinehart and Winston, 1979). Few other books discuss Lucas in depth. James Monaco's *American Film Now* (New York: Random House, 1979); David Thomson's *Overexposures: The Crisis in American Filmmaking* (New York: Morrow, 1981); and *Anatomy of the Movies,* edited by Davide Pirie (New York: Macmillan, 1981) provided an overview of today's Hollywood and Lucas's position in the industry.

When the Shooting Stops, by film editor Ralph Rosenblum and Robert Karen (New York: Viking, 1979), offered a valuable perspective on the editor's art. Charles Snow's reminiscences of Walt Disney, *Walt: Backstage Adventures With Walt Disney* (Los Angeles: Communication Creativity, 1979) provided several analogies between Lucas and one of his personal heroes. Insights into the mentality of a movie director were provided by

The Film Director as Superstar, a collection of sixteen interviews with filmmakers by Joseph Gelmis (New York: Doubleday, 1970).

Although personal interviews were conducted with everyone who had a long or meaningful relationship with Lucas, there were gaps in historical material and detail. Several books published under Lucasfilm's auspices were helpful in filling those gaps.

Once Upon a Galaxy: A Journal of the Making of "The Empire Strikes Back" by Alan Arnold (New York: Ballantine, 1980) featured in-depth interviews with many of those involved in *Empire* and other Lucas projects. *The Making of "Raiders of the Lost Ark"* by Derek Taylor (New York: Ballantine, 1981) was also valuable.

Lucas provided original screenplay drafts for each of his films, from *THX 1138* through *Return of the Jedi.* These were supplemented with information from the published versions of the final scripts: *American Graffiti* by George Lucas, Gloria Katz, Willard Huyck (New York: Ballantine, 1973); *The Art of "Star Wars,"* edited by Carol Titelman (New York: Ballantine, 1979); *"The Empire Strikes Back" Notebook,* edited by Diana Attias and Lindsay Smith (New York: Ballantine, 1980); and *"Raiders of the Lost Ark": The Illustrated Screenplay* by Lawrence Kasdan (New York: Ballantine, 1981).

The latter three volumes, along with *"The Empire Strikes Back" Sketchbook* by Joe Johnston and Nilo Rodis-Jamero (New York: Ballantine, 1980) supplied original production sketches and illustrations and showed the complex evolution of the special effects.

The 1976 Ballantine novelization of *Star Wars* by Lucas (actually written by Alan Dean Foster) was useful, as were three subsequent paperback novels of the *Star Wars* saga: *Splinter of the Mind's Eye* by Alan Dean Foster (New York: Ballantine, 1978), and *Han Solo's Revenge* (New York: Ballantine, 1979) and *Han Solo and the Lost Legacy* (New York: Ballantine, 1980), both by Brian Daley.

Lucas provided transcripts of tape-recorded story conferences in which he participated on *The Empire Strikes Back* with Leigh Brackett (November 28–December 2, 1977), *Raiders of the Lost Ark* (January 23–27, 1978) with Steven Spielberg and Lawrence Kasdan, and *Return of the Jedi* with Kasdan and Richard Marquand. These shed light on the specific films and on Lucas's philosophy of film making and methods of collaboration.

Also helpful were transcripts of interviews conducted by Carol Titelman in 1977, in which Lucas pretended to be the characters C-3PO, Chewbacca, Han Solo, and Princess Leia.

Bantha Tracks, the newsletter of the Official Star Wars Fan Club, provided useful details and perspectives on Lucas and his films.

Several periodicals supplemented the personal interviews. Most magazine articles were used as general background, and specific quotations are individually credited. Chronologically, they are "From *American Graffiti* to Outer Space" by Donald Goddard (*New York Times,* September 17, 1976); "George Lucas Goes Far Out" by Stephen Zito (*American Film,* April 1977); "*Star Wars:* The Year's Best Movie" (*Time,* May 30, 1977); "*Star Wars*" by Fred Herman (*Modesto Bee,* June 5, 1977); "George Lucas on Opening Night" by Gregg Kilday (*Los Angeles Times,* June 14, 1977); "*Star Wars*" (*People,* July 18, 1977); "The Force Behind George Lucas" by Paul Scanlon and "Grand Illusions" by Michael Rogers (*Rolling Stone,* August 25, 1977).

Also: "George Lucas" (*People,* January 2, 1978); *Current Biography* article on Lucas, January 1978; "Making *Star Wars*" by Paul Mandell (*Cinefantastique,* Spring 1978); "George Lucas's Galactic Empire" (*Time,* March 6, 1978); "The New Wave of Film Makers" by Robert Lindsey (*New York Times,* May 28, 1978); "George Lucas: An Interview" by Audie Bock (*Take One,* May 15, 1979); "George Lucas—Hell Raiser to Millionaire" by Alice Yarish (*San Francisco Examiner,* February 20, 1980); "*The Empire Strikes Back*" by Gene Siskel (*Chicago Tribune,* May 4, 1980); "The Empire Pays Off" by Stratford P. Sherman (*Fortune,* October 6, 1980); "The Saga Beyond 'Star Wars'" by Aljean Harmetz (*New York Times,* December 20, 1980); "Northern California Lures the Movie Maverick" by Aljean Harmetz (*New York Times,* March 1, 1981); "The Man Who Found the Ark" (*Newsweek,* June 15, 1981).

Three in-depth interviews with Lucas were particularly helpful: "*The Empire Strikes Back*" by Jean Vallely (*Rolling Stone,* June 12, 1980); "The George Lucas Saga," three parts, by Kerry O'Quinn (*Starlog,* July, August, September, 1981); "I'm the Boss" by Mitch Tuchman and Anne Thompson (*Film Comment,* September 1981). "The Art of Moving Pictures" by Bruno Bettelheim (*Harper's,* October 1981) was valuable in measuring the philosophical and cultural impact of Lucas's work.

Several television programs featuring Lucas and his films were viewed: "The Making of *Star Wars*," first aired on ABC in September 1977; "The *Star Wars* Holiday Special," aired November 17, 1978, on CBS; "SPFX: *The Empire Strikes Back*," aired September 1980 on CBS. Also examined were scripts from radio dramas based on *Star Wars* and *Empire* and a transcript of a 1969 Lucas interview with National Educational Television.

Specific references or quotations are explained in the notes that follow. Unless otherwise identified, all quotations are taken directly from my interviews.

Epigraph
(Page xi)

1. "Skywalker, Skywalker. And why do..." From the fifth draft of *The Empire Strikes Back* by Lawrence Kasdan.

The Crash
(Page xiii)

1. "All the ding-a-lings...." John Milner's observation is by George Lucas in the first draft of *American Graffiti* (August 4, 1971).

1 It Wasn't My Fault
(Pages 1–9)

1. Figures on ticket sales and revenues were supplied by Lucasfilm and confirmed by the studio releasing the movie.

2. "Failure has a thousand..." Sir Alec Guinness from an interview in *Once Upon a Galaxy: A Journal of the Making of "The Empire Strikes Back"* by Alan Arnold (New York: Ballantine, 1980).

3. Observations from the set of *Return of the Jedi* were made over ten days in January and February 1982.

2 When Things Were Simpler
(Pages 11–39)

1. The history of Modesto is based on pamphlets from the Modesto Chamber of Commerce and was supplemented by interviews with Carl Baggse, public information specialist for the Stanislaus County Board of Education, on a two-day trip to Modesto in November 1981.

2. The Lucas family genealogy is detailed in a letter to Lucas from his Aunt Eileen King (September 6, 1977).

3. Details of George Lucas's childhood came from inspection of family albums, home movies, Lucas's baby book, school records, and other personal memorabilia. Also helpful was "George Lucas: Mastermind of the *Star Wars* Family" by John Culhane in *Families* (March 1982): 71.

4. "What I enjoy most..." George Lucas from *Uncle Scrooge McDuck* by Carl Barks (Los Angeles: Celestial Arts, 1981).

5. "Sixteen long years..." from the May 10, 1977, version of the *American Graffiti* script by George Lucas, Gloria Katz, Willard Huyck.

6. "Radio creates a..." George Lucas from an interview in *Seventeen* entitled "On Location" by Edwin Miller (March 19, 1973): 53.

7. "He is his..." George Lucas from a story conference for *Return of the Jedi.*

8. "*Graffiti* Is the Story of His Life" by Judy Klemesrud (*New York Times*. October 7, 1973) was helpful in the writing of this section.

9. "Any vision about..." Bruno Bettelheim in "The Art of Moving Pictures" (*Harper's,* October 1981): 82.

3 **Reality Stops Here**
(Pages 41–72)

1. "Movie making is like . . ." Norman Mailer in *The Film Director as Superstar* by Joseph Gelmis (New York: Doubleday, 1970).

2. Charles Snow's observation is from *Walt: Backstage Adventures with Disney* (Los Angeles: Communication Creativity, 1979).

3. Some of Lucas's comments about USC were made during interviews for the *Los Angeles Times.*

4. "Just think what . . ." From John Milius's first draft screenplay of *Apocalypse Now,* dated October 11, 1969.

5. "Behind every successful . . ." Frank Capra's comment was related to Marcia Lucas by Lucille Capra, Capra's wife.

6. Background information for this section came from Charles Champlin's column, "A Critic at Large," in the *Los Angeles Times* (November 13, 1967). Walter Murch discussed this era in a *Los Angeles Times* interview by Betty Spence (August 30, 1981), entitled "Walter Murch: Virtuoso of Sound."

7. "This film is . . ." A letter to Marcia Griffin from George Lucas on the set of *McKenna's Gold* in Arizona (June 23, 1967).

4 **Coping with Coppola**
(Pages 73–98)

1. "There is disagreement . . ." Francis Coppola at a press conference held at Zoetrope Studios in Hollywood (February 4, 1981).

2. "It's sort of romantic . . ." Francis Coppola from *"Star Wars,"* in *Time* (May 30, 1977): 28.

3. "The essential objective . . ." From a publicity release issued by Zoetrope Studios upon its formation in 1969.

4. "Seems good old-fashioned . . ." From *Adam Film World* (Vol. ?, no. 6, 1979).

5 **Rocking Around the Clock**
(Pages 99–130)

1. "Making a film . . ." Norman Mailer in *The Film Director as Superstar* by Joseph Gelmis (New York: Doubleday, 1970).

2. "It's hard work. . . ." George Lucas quoted in "The George Lucas Saga," Part III, by Kerry O'Quinn in *Starlog* (September 1981): 54.

3. "It's like taking . . ." George Lucas in an interview in *Rolling Stone* by Jean Vallely (June 12, 1980): 32.

4. "I was really . . ." Ibid, p. 34.

5. The *San Francisco Actor,* a publication of the Screen Actors Guild (September 1973), was helpful for this chapter. So was Lucas's personal correspondence. All ticket sales and rental figures for *American Graffiti* are from Lucasfilm and Universal Pictures.

6 **The Vision of *Star Wars***
(Pages 131–158)

1. Background research for this chapter included personal correspondence between George and Marcia Lucas in November and October 1975, as well as Lucas's private notebooks. Background information on Marcia Lucas came from "The New Hollywood" by Daphne Davis in *Playgirl* (September 1975): 109. Books and movies that influenced Lucas during this period were examined and provided valuable insights into the evolution of *Star Wars*. They included "John Carter of Mars," the eleventh of Edgar Rice Burroughs's "Martian Tales" from *Amazing Stories* magazine in 1941 and 1943. *The Iron Men of Mongo*, a Flash Gordon novel by Alex Raymond, adapted by Con Steffanson (out of print), was also a strong influence on Lucas. The movie serial adventures of Flash Gordon were viewed; *Space Soldiers Conquer the Universe* (1934) was of particular interest. *The Uses of Enchantment: The Meaning and Importance of Fairy Tales* by Bruno Bettelheim (New York: Random House, 1975) was a strong influence on Lucas's thinking, as was *The Hero with a Thousand Faces* by Joseph Campbell (New York: Pantheon, 1949). Carlos Castaneda's adventures with a Yaqui Indian mystic in *Tales of Power* (New York: Simon & Schuster, 1974) was a major influence on the Force.

2. "*Star Wars* was . . ." from *Once Upon a Galaxy: A Journal of the Making of "The Empire Strikes Back"* by Alan Arnold (New York: Ballantine, 1980).

3. Financial figures are taken from Fox's annual reports and financial statements.

4. "The script is . . ." George Lucas in his speech to the Modesto Rotary (August 29, 1973).

5. "The true art . . ." Don Juan in *Tales of Power* by Carlos Castaneda (New York: Simon & Schuster, 1974).

7 **The Agony and the Ecstasy of *Star Wars***
(Pages 159–190)

1. Background information on EMI-Elstree Studios is from *The Elstree Story*, a promotional booklet put out by the studio in 1981.

2. "I forgot how . . ." George Lucas in a letter to Marcia Lucas (October 28, 1975), from Nefta, Tunisia.

3. *Cinefantastique* was helpful in describing the special effects for *Star Wars*, especially the Spring 1978 issue.

4. *Star Wars* by George Lucas (New York: Ballantine, 1976).

5. "A grand and glorious . . ." *Time* article on *Star Wars* (May 30, 1977): 41.

6. All *Star Wars*–related financial figures are from Lucasfilm and confirmed by 20th Century-Fox.

7. "Movies are more . . ." Mike Nichols in *The Film Director as Superstar* by Joseph Gelmis (New York: Doubleday, 1970).

8 **How I Spent My Retirement**
(Pages 191–230)

1. "Good, now George will . . ." Francis Coppola from a note sent by his wife, Eleanor, to the Lucases in April 1978.

2. The description of Lucas's "jet" was in *The Star* (July 1977).

3. Of particular value for background information on *The Empire Strikes Back* was "Behind the Scenes on *Empire*," an article in *American Cinematographer* (June 1980): 546–600. Also helpful was "Of Ice Planets, Bog Planets, and Cities in the Sky," an article by Don Shay in *Cinefex* (August 1980): 4–24.

4. "I feel Chewbacca..." George Lucas in an interview by Jean Vallely in *Rolling Stone* (June 12, 1980): 32.

5. "I trust your..." Lawrence Kasdan in a story conference for *Return of the Jedi*.

6. "Either he's chasing..." George Lucas in a story conference on *Raiders*.

7. Useful information on *Raiders of the Lost Ark* is contained in "*Raiders of the Lost Ark* and How It Was Filmed," *American Cinematographer* (November 1981): 1096–1106. Helpful on the *Raiders* deal with Paramount was "A Deal to Remember" by Ben Stein in *New West* (August 1981): 84. Also informative on *Raiders* is Janet Maslin's "How Old Movie Serials Inspired Lucas and Spielberg," in the *New York Times* (June 7, 1981).

8. All *Raiders* financial figures are from Lucasfilm and confirmed by Paramount Pictures.

9 Ruling the Empire
(Pages 231–263)

1. "Let's face it..." George Lucas in a story conference on *Return of the Jedi*.

2. Personal observations of Lucasfilm and Lucas were made during several visits to Marin County between November 1981 and November 1982.

3. "I don't make..." Walt Disney in *Walt: Backstage Adventures with Walt Disney* by Charles Snow (Los Angeles: Communications Creativity, 1979).

4. Information about Skywalker Ranch came from the "Environmental Assessment Report" prepared for Marin County by Susan D. Hilsinki (November 1978) and from "Lucas Skywalker Ranch Remains a Big Mystery," an article in *Daily Variety* by Herb Michelson (July 13, 1981). Background information was supplied by "How Lucas Got the OK to Build Big," in *Point Reyes Light* (June 11, 1981); "How Some Marin Moviemakers Got Their Jobs...and Lost Them," by Spencer Read in *Twin Cities Times* (October 15, 1982).

5. Information on George Lucas's withdrawal from Hollywood was supplemented by "Lucas Severs Last Hollywood Ties" by Jim Harwood in *Daily Variety* (April 6, 1981).

6. Merchandising information is from Lucasfilm licensee and product lists.

10 A Time Not So Far Away
(Pages 265–278)

1. Details of the Thomas Downey Class Reunion on June 27, 1982, came from the following newspaper accounts: "The *Graffiti* Generation" by Fred Herman in the *Modesto Bee* (June 6, 1982); "Lucas Recalled as a 'Wimp,'" Associated Press story in the *Los Angeles Time* (June 11, 1982); "Where Were They in '62?" by Ivan Sharpe in *San Francisco Examiner and Chronicle* (June 27, 1982); "*Graffiti* Revisited" by John Esparza in the *Modesto Bee* (June 28, 1982); "Classmates Put George Lucas in the Spotlight" by Mark A. Stein in the *Los Angeles Times* (June 28, 1982).

2. David Thomson's comments about Lucas are from *Overexposures, The Crisis in American Filmmaking* (New York: Morrow, 1981).

INDEX

Academy Awards. *See* Oscars
Adolescence of George Lucas. *See*
    Childhood and adolescence
Alice Doesn't Live Here Anymore, 138
Alsup, Bunny, 81, 126, 127, 147–48,
    153, 159
American Graffiti, 1, 21, 27, 34, 101–30,
    136–38, 140, 192, 269, 273
    awards received by, 124
    cars in, 31–32
    cast of, 109–11
    characters in, 30, 33–34, 105–6
    cruising in, 27, 28, 30
    earnings from, 125–28
    editing of, 116–17, 121–22
    financing of, 102–5, 107, 108, 111–16
    music in, 32–33, 105, 108–9, 117
    plot of, 29
    preview screenings of, 117–22
    reviews of, 124
American Zoetrope, 83–89, 97, 99–100
Annie Hall, 188
Anyone Lived in a Pretty How Town, 58
Apocalypse Now, 89, 129–30
Artoo-Detoo. *See* R2-D2
Ashley, Ted, 88, 96, 97, 99
Auteurism, 46

Baker, Kenny, 131–32, 156, 196, 222
Ballard, Carroll, 39, 78, 80, 174, 175,
    181
Bank of America, 219
Barry, John, 155, 160, 170, 188, 218

Barton, Sean, 8
Barwood, Hal, 48, 50, 51, 118, 125, 147,
    180, 198, 232, 259
Battlestar Galactica, 197–98
Bay, Jane, 54, 192, 193, 237, 238
Beach Boys, 108
Berg, Jeff, 101–3, 106, 107, 118, 120,
    134, 135, 137, 200
Bettelheim, Bruno, 39
Blalack, Robert, 188
Bloom, Jim, 91, 113, 173, 208
Body Heat, 262
Boone, Ashley, 179–80, 183–85, 211
Brackett, Leigh, 206, 207
Braverman, Chuck, 48, 69
Burtt, Ben, 178–79, 181, 188

Caan, James, 75
Cannes Film Festival, 102
Cantwell, Colin, 153, 171
Carpenter, John, 48
Cars, 24–27, 34, 45, 57
    in *American Graffiti*, 30–31
Castaneda, Carlos, 140
Catmull, Ed, 238, 256
Champlin, Charles, 68, 124
Chasman, David, 102
Chew, Richard, 174, 187
Childhood and adolescence of George
    Lucas, 12–28, 34–39
Clark, Candy, 201
Close Encounters of the Third Kind, 197
Coanagelo, Barney, 112

Cocks, Jay, 180
Colby, Ron, 74, 80, 85, 86, 92, 93, 245
Columbia Pictures, 69, 107
Comic books, 17–18
Coppola, Francis, 37, 39, 48, 71–82,
    83–90, 99–100, 116–21, 125, 164,
    193, 201, 243, 262, 272
    American Graffiti and, 107, 108, 112,
    115, 117–21, 122
    Apocalypse Now and, 129, 219
    relationship with Lucas, 78–82,
    128–30, 244, 245
    Star Wars and, 146, 147, 152, 186, 189
Corman, Roger, 79, 87–88
Coutourie, Bill, 48
Cruising, 27–30
C-3PO, 131, 132, 146, 155, 167–68,
    177, 213

Dalva, Robert, 48, 60–61
Daniels, Anthony, 131, 160–61, 167–68,
    177, 196, 197, 213, 222, 238
Davis, Marvin, 183, 247–48
Delta Kau Alpha (DKA), 51–52
Dementia 13, 79
De Palma, Brian, 48, 150–52, 180
Deschanel, Caleb, 48, 49, 203
Directors (directing), 46, 53, 54, 91–93
Directors Guild, 248–49
Disney, Walt, 54
Disneyland, 21
Dreyfuss, Richard, 110, 111, 114–15,
    123–24, 127, 201
Dryden, Kay, 234
Duignan, Rose, 172, 174
Dunham, Duwayne, 53, 54, 194, 203,
    204, 218, 228
Duvall, Robert, 92, 95
Dykstra, John, 154, 169–73, 176–77,
    188, 197–98
Dykstraflex camera, 172

Editing (editors), 53–54, 61, 62, 117
Edlund, Richard, 171, 173, 176, 182,
    188, 208–9, 234
Efron, Marshall, 92
Egg Company, 243, 251, 254
Eisner, Michael, 228–29, 272
Elstree Studios, 153, 159–60, 169, 214
Emperor, The, 58

Empire Strikes Back, The, 1, 3, 39, 204–22,
    257, 270
    cast of, 211–13
    characters of, 209–11
    contract with 20th Century-Fox,
    198–200
    earnings and profits of, 221
    editing of, 218–19
    filming of, 214–18
    financing of, 219–20
    plot of, 209–11
    profit points and bonuses for cast and
    crew of, 221–22
    screenplay for, 206–7, 209, 211
    special effects for, 209, 216–17
Erickson, Leon, 176
Ewoks, 6, 8

Faxon, Roger, 234
Fehr, Rudi, 96, 97
Ferguson, Doug, 125
Fields, Verna, 48, 61, 64, 116, 117, 120,
    124, 127, 138
Film Festival (1970), 102, 103
Filmmaker, 76–77
Fine, Deborah, 80, 100, 253
Finian's Rainbow, 71–74
First National Bank of Boston, 219–20
Fisher, Carrie, 7, 151, 152, 162, 164–65,
    196, 212
Flash Gordon serials, 142
Force, the, 139–41, 145–46, 148, 209–10
Ford, Harrison, 110, 114, 116, 121, 130,
    151, 152, 164, 166, 196, 201, 212,
    225, 226, 274
Foreman, Carl, 69–71, 74, 272
Foster, Alan Dean, 194–95
Frankenstein, George, 16, 19, 26, 28,
    36, 37
Freeborn, Stuart, 168, 175, 208, 215
Freiheit, 56–57

Gale, Bob, 48
Ganis, 194, 221, 237–38
Garrett, Maureen, 195, 221, 253
Godard, Jean-Luc, 46
Godfather, The, 100, 107, 115
Golding, Paul, 56, 58
Gone With the Wind, 212
Gosnell, Ray, 154, 172, 175
Grant, Alan, 25–26, 34, 35, 37

Greber, Bob, 234–35, 240, 253, 259
Guinness, Sir Alec, 133, 152–53, 160, 166, 196, 212, 215

Hailey, Oliver, 88
Hamill, Mark, 133, 151, 152, 162–65, 175–76, 191–92, 196, 212–13, 214
Hardin, Terri, 3
Health of George Lucas, 8, 47, 60, 168, 173, 226, 252
Herbie, 56
Herman, Miki, 50, 66, 196, 205, 216, 217
Hirsch, Paul, 174, 177, 187, 208, 218
Hirsch, Tina, 203
Hollywood, Lucas's relationship with and attitude toward, 245–51
Hopkins, Bo, 114
Hornbeck, Bill, 120
Hudson, Bob, 58
Huyck, Willard, 3–4, 30, 34, 48, 50, 78–79, 84, 102–3, 105–6, 124, 127, 157, 168, 180, 185, 196, 201, 206, 229, 230, 263

Immerman, Bill, 137
Industrial Light & Magic (ILM), 54, 154, 169, 197, 216, 236, 237
International Creative Management (ICM), 200
Irving, Amy, 152

Jabba the Hutt, 6, 7
Jensen, George, 236
Johnson, Dave, 53, 66, 67, 261
Johnston, Joe, 171–72, 196–97, 216, 222, 236, 237
Jones, James Earl, 178, 213

Kael, Pauline, 271
Kahn, Michael, 227
Kalabokes, Chris, 158, 175, 183, 234, 242
Kasdan, Lawrence, 8, 139, 206–7, 209, 211, 217, 222, 224, 225, 254, 262, 271
Katt, William, 152
Katz, Gloria, 30, 31, 34, 79, 84, 102–3, 105–6, 127, 157, 180, 185, 196, 201, 206, 229, 230

Kaufman, Phil, 222–23
Kazanjian, Howard, 9, 43, 48, 51, 201–2, 205, 225
Kennedy, Kathy, 226, 227
Kershner, Irvin, 55, 207–8, 209, 211, 214–19, 220, 222, 248–49
Kleiser, Randal, 45, 47, 48, 51, 52, 56–57
Knight, Shirley, 75–76
Korty, John, 85, 87, 100, 121, 126, 180, 187, 189, 211, 261, 262
Kubrick, Stanley, 142
Kurosawa, Akira, 46, 245
Kurtz, Gary, 101, 103, 107–10, 112, 114–16, 118, 122, 125–27, 182, 183, 186, 194, 196, 207
   The Empire Strikes Back and, 208, 209, 211, 215, 218–20, 222
   Star Wars and, 107, 129, 136, 153–55, 161, 162, 165, 170, 175, 176, 178

Ladd, Alan, Jr., 135–37, 148, 150, 153, 154, 155, 157, 169–70, 174–76, 179, 182, 183, 184–87, 199, 209, 228, 241, 247, 262
Lady Ice, 103
Lanterna Films, 85–86
Larson, Glenn, 198
LeMat, Paul, 110, 111, 114, 201
Lester, Richard, 46
Levett, Michael, 235
Lewis, Christopher, 52
Lippincott, Charles, 183, 186, 193
Livingston, Alan, 180
Look at Life, 56
Lucas, Amanda (daughter), 238, 240, 241
Lucas, Ann (sister), 13, 19
Lucas, Dorothy (mother), 12–15, 18, 19, 20, 27, 59, 65, 83–84, 89, 118, 196, 204
Lucas, George. *See specific movies and other topics*
Lucas, George Walton, Sr. (father), 12–17, 20, 23, 24, 26, 27, 35–37, 41–42, 53, 59, 61, 89, 118, 120, 126, 190, 196, 236
Lucas, Katherine (sister), 13, 39
Lucas, Marcia (née Griffin), 4, 50, 61–66, 69, 70, 77, 95–96, 97, 102, 103, 120, 124–26, 227, 228, 231, 243, 252, 259, 267, 272, 277

as editor, 82–84, 111, 116, 117, 138, 174, 177
first meeting and dating with George, 61–62
home life of, 238–41
marriage to George, 82–83
personal background of, 64–65
Star Wars and, 142, 147, 150, 168–70, 174, 181, 185, 187, 188
Lucas, Wendy (sister), 14, 16–18, 20, 38, 59, 204
Lucasfilm Ltd., 2, 5, 125, 126, 192–96, 198, 199, 219, 221, 229, 234–35, 240, 242–44, 249–56
computer division of, 256, 268
educational activities of, 268–69
investments of, 251, 254
merchandising activities of, 254–55
relocated in Marin County, 250–53

McCune, Grant, 188
MacDougal, David, 69, 70
McElwaine, Guy, 186
McGovern, Terry, 156
McGregor, Russ, 261
McKenna's Gold, 69–71
McOmie, Maggie, 92
McQuarrie, Ralph, 104, 149–50, 153, 155, 156, 171, 196–97, 208, 216
Mailer, Norman, 104
Malkin, Barry, 82
Marquand, Richard, 6–9, 276
Marshall, Frank, 225, 239
Mather, George, 173
Mayhew, Peter, 156–57, 167, 169, 196, 222
Medium Cool, 82, 83
Milius, John, 34, 39, 46, 48, 50–51, 65, 71, 78, 89, 125, 128–29, 180, 197, 260, 274
Modesto, California, 11–12, 21, 26–30, 33, 34
Moehnke, Ted, 92, 93
Mollo, John, 160, 188, 208
More American Graffiti, 1, 25, 200–206
Morris, L. M., 13
Mura, Ken, 44, 178
Murch, Walter, 4, 33, 48, 49–51, 67, 71–73, 77, 88–89, 91, 93, 95, 96, 117, 127, 141, 190, 274
Muren, Dennis, 171, 173, 174, 209

National Student Film Festival, 71
Neil, Bill, 95, 237, 239, 259
Nelson, Jim, 196
New York, New York, 177
Nichols, Mike, 189
1941, 223
Norton, B. W., Jr. 202–4, 225
Nyegaard, Roland, 60, 65

O'Bannon, Dan, 48
1:42:08, 57–58
Oscars, 5, 124–25, 187–88
Oz, Frank, 215

Paramount Pictures, 100, 122, 228–29
Parker Brothers, 5
Parkhouse, 126, 141, 231, 239
Personal characteristics of George Lucas, 2–3, 93
generosity, 127
Marcia Lucas on, 62, 63, 66
in relationships with Lucasfilm employees, 235–38, 254
at University of Southern California, 50–53
writing habits, 143, 231
Personal wealth of George Lucas, 1, 3, 192–93
Peters, Gene, 67
Pevers, Marc, 194
Phillips, Mackenzie, 110, 201
Picker, David, 102–4, 135
Pleasance, Donald, 92, 95
Plummer, John, 16, 18, 19, 23, 25, 27, 28, 35–37, 46, 47, 60, 65, 83, 266
Pollock, Tom, 38, 97, 101, 104, 108, 125, 127, 133, 135, 136, 138, 182–83, 196, 199, 200, 228, 229, 241, 246, 249, 261, 263
Postproduction system, computerized, 256, 257
Prowse, David, 156, 166, 196

Raiders of the Lost Ark, 1, 97, 133, 206, 207, 217, 222–30, 257, 270, 271
Rain People, The, 74–77, 81, 82, 85
Religion, 19–20
Star Wars and, 139–40. *See also* Force, the
Retirement, 191–92

Return of the Jedi, 1, 3, 5–9, 213–14, 257, 270–72, 274–76

Reynolds, Norman, 9, 155, 160, 169, 208

Ritchie, Michael, 5, 84, 103, 147, 165

Robbins, Matthew, 48–52, 55, 67, 90, 118, 125, 147, 180, 232, 259, 269

Roos, Fred, 52, 109–10, 127, 152

R2-D2, 131–32, 141–42, 146, 155, 156, 167, 168, 175, 177–79, 213

San Francisco Chronicle, 124

Scorsese, Martin, 39, 48, 84, 138, 177

See-Threepio. *See* C-3PO

Selleck, Tom, 225–26

Seltzer, Will, 201

Sheinberg, Sidney, 124, 223

Silent Running, 198

6-18-67, 70

Skager, Mona, 76, 81, 86, 87, 119, 245

Skywalker Ranch, 5, 198, 217, 232–33, 242, 251–52, 258–60, 268

Sloan, Mel, 57–59

Smith, Charles Martin, 110, 201

Smith, Tom, 216, 236

Snow, Charles, 54

Somers, Suzanne, 31, 110

Spielberg, Steven, 39, 48, 54, 55, 68, 119, 122, 180, 185–86, 197, 249, 274
    Raiders of the Lost Ark and, 206, 207, 222–30

Stanfill, Dennis, 157–58, 199

Star Wars, 1–3, 15, 39, 94, 102, 103, 107, 129, 131–200, 250, 269–75
    advertising and promotion of, 183–85
    appeal of, 189–90
    casting of, 150–53, 155–57
    characters of, 134–35, 139, 144–46, 196
    contract with 20th Century-Fox for, 137–38
    dialogue in, 148–49, 157, 164
    direction of, 163–64
    earnings and profits of, 184, 186, 188, 192, 196–97
    as fairy tale, 138–39
    fan club, 195
    financing of, 154–55, 175
    first screenings of, 179–83
    on location in Tunisia, 131–33
    making of, 159–79
    merchandising of products associated with, 137, 194, 195, 257

music for, 195
    novelization of, 194–95
    Oscars won by, 187–88
    overseas release of, 187
    plot of, 134–35, 144–49
    popular response to, 185–86
    profit points and bonuses given to cast and crew of, 196–97
    religious and moral message of, 139–40, 143, 271. *See also* Force, the
    sound of, 177–79, 181
    special effects in, 153–54, 169–77
    writing of, 134, 138, 141–49, 157, 160

Star Wars movies, 198–200, 269–71, 274–75

Stiers, David Ogden, 92

Sting, The, 125

Sturnham, Peter, 208

Tanen, Ned, 30, 68, 106, 107, 115, 116, 118–24, 136, 184, 200, 204–5, 247

Taylor, Gil, 161–62

Television, 16–17

Thomas Downey High School, twentieth class reunion at, 265–66

Thomson, David, 271

THX 1138, 1, 14, 39, 74, 75, 88–97, 101–3, 138, 140, 142, 269
    Coppola and, 88–90, 92, 93, 96, 97
    critical and popular response to, 96–97
    plot and characters of, 90–91
    political content of, 93–94
    sex scenes in, 92, 94–95

THX 1138:4EB, 68–69, 71

Tippett, Phil, 216

Titelman, Carol, 124, 171, 193, 241

Tomblin, David, 7, 208, 222

Tomorrow Entertainment, 103

Tong, Richard, 78, 125, 127, 192, 241–43, 252

Trembly, Susan, 194

Turman, Glynn, 151

20th Century-Fox, 122, 132, 136–38, 153–55, 157–58, 175, 177, 179–84

2001: A Space Odyssey, 142

2187, 47

United Artists, 102, 104, 135

United States Information Agency (USIA), 60–61

Universal Studios, 106–8, 117, 118, 120, 122, 135–36, 197, 200–202, 204, 205
University of Southern California (USC), 35, 41–42, 67, 68, 260–61
  film program at, 43–44
  films made by Lucas at, 55–59
  "mafia" (Dirty Dozen) at, 48–49

Video games, 5, 255–58

Walters, Richard, 103
Ward, David S., 48
Warner Bros., 71–73, 75, 88–90, 96, 97, 99, 102, 199
Watts, Robert, 155, 161, 162, 170, 208, 215–16
Wealth of George Lucas. *See* Personal wealth of George Lucas

Weber, Charles, 194, 219–20, 228, 229, 243, 250–54
Weitzner, David, 184
Welles, Orson, 178
Wexler, Haskell, 35, 81, 82, 112, 115, 124, 127
Wigan, Gareth, 179
Williams, Billy Dee, 213
Williams, Cindy, 110, 111, 114, 123, 151, 201, 203
Williams, John, 177, 181, 188, 195, 196, 208, 221
Wilson, Lucy, 4, 126, 143, 148, 193, 196
Wolfman Jack, 32, 58, 122
Writers Guild, 249
Wyles, David, 69

Zemeckis, Bob, 48
Zoetrope. *See* American Zoetrope
Zoetrope Studios, 81